THE GOTTI WARS

Taking Down America's Most Notorious Mobster

JOHN GLEESON

SCRIBNER

New York   London   Toronto   Sydney   New Delhi

Scribner
An Imprint of Simon & Schuster, Inc.
1230 Avenue of the Americas
New York, NY 10020

First Scribner hardcover edition May 2022

SCRIBNER and design are registered trademarks of The Gale Group, Inc., used under license by Simon & Schuster, Inc., the publisher of this work.

For information about special discounts for bulk purchases, please contact Simon & Schuster Special Sales at 1-866-506-1949 or business@simonandschuster.com.

The Simon & Schuster Speakers Bureau can bring authors to your live event. For more information or to book an event, contact the Simon & Schuster Speakers Bureau at 1-866-248-3049 or visit our website at www.simonspeakers.com.

Interior design by Wendy Blum

Manufactured in the United States of America

1 3 5 7 9 10 8 6 4 2

Library of Congress Cataloging-in-Publication Data has been applied for.

ISBN 978-1-9821-8692-0
ISBN 978-1-9821-8694-4 (ebook)

To Robin Wilcox, my wife and the best thing that has
ever happened to me, which is saying something,
because I have been very fortunate.

To Molly and Nora Gleeson, the best daughters in
the whole wide world and universe. Words cannot
express how much I love them and how proud I am of them.

To Paul and William Neira, my cool stepsons,
who welcomed us into their lives with grace,
good humor, and patience.

To my parents, Patrick and Kathleen Gleeson,
who would be so proud of all seven of their kids.

To those other Gleeson kids: Kathy Cosgriff, Winnie Keaney,
the late Eileen Hirce, Bubby Gleeson, Kevin Gleeson, and Mary Beth
Carvin, who loved and took such great care of their baby brother.

And to Susan Gleeson, my first wife, who lived
the events described in this book with me and
supported me throughout.

CONTENTS

CONTENTS

CAST OF CHARACTERS

Main Justice

* William Barr, Attorney General
* Robert Mueller, Assistant Attorney General, Criminal Division

U.S. Attorney's Office, Eastern District of New York

* Raymond Dearie, U.S. Attorney
* Andrew Maloney, U.S. Attorney
* Reena Raggi, U.S. Attorney
* Mary Jo White, Chief Assistant

AUSAs:

* Mike Considine
* Pat Cotter
* Jonny Frank
* Diane Giacalone
* John Gleeson
* Bob LaRusso
* Geoff Mearns
* Lenny Michaels
* JoAnn Navickas
* Jamie Orenstein
* Neil Ross
* Susan Shepard
* George Stamboulidis
* Laura Ward
* Andrew Weissmann

U.S. Attorney's Office, Southern District of New York

* David Denton, Associate U.S. Attorney
* Louis Freeh, Deputy U.S. Attorney
* Rudy Giuliani, U.S. Attorney
* Otto Obermaier, U.S. Attorney

AUSAs:

* Mike Chertoff
* Gil Childers
* Jerry Lynch
* Walter Mack
* John Savarese

Manhattan District Attorney's Office

* Robert Morgenthau, District Attorney

ADAs:

* Mike Cherkasky
* Pat Duggan

The FBI

* Jim Fox, Assistant Director, N.Y. Office
* Lou Schiliro, Supervisory Special Agent

Gambino Squad

* Jim Abbott
* Scott Behar, Special Agent
* Marty Boland
* Pat Colgan
* George Gabriel, Special Agent
* Bruce Mouw, Supervisory Special Agent
* Bill Noon, Special Agent

CAST OF CHARACTERS

* Frank Spero, Special Agent
* Matty Tricorico, Special Agent

Colombo Squad:
* Chris Favo, Special Agent

FBI/NYPD Joint Auto Larceny Task Force

Special Agents:
* George Hanna
* Bob Joyce
* Richie Mika
* Neil Moran

New York City Police Department

Detectives:
* Bill Burns
* Mike Falciano
* John Gurnee
* Frank McCann
* Vic Ruggiero
* Frank Shields, Sergeant

U.S. Drug Enforcement Administration

Special Agents:
* Eddie Magnuson
* Ron Melvin

U.S. Bureau of Alcohol, Tobacco, Firearms and Explosives

Special Agent:
* Billy Fredericks

United States Senators

* William Cohen
* John McCain
* Sam Nunn
* Willam Roth

Judges

Eastern District of New York:
* John R. Bartels
* Mark A. Costantino
* Raymond J. Dearie
* I. Leo Glasser
* Joseph M. McLaughlin
* Eugene H. Nickerson
* Reena Raggi
* Jack B. Weinstein

Southern District of New York:
* Kevin Duffy

Gambino Crime Family

Administration:
* Joe "Piney" Armone, Consigliere
* Paul Castellano, Boss
* Frank DeCicco, Underboss
* Aniello "Neil" Dellacroce, Underboss
* Joe N. Gallo, Consigliere
* Carlo Gambino, Boss
* John Gotti, Boss
* Salvatore "Sammy the Bull" Gravano, Consigliere and Underboss
* Frank Locascio, Acting Underboss and Acting Consigliere

Capodecinas:
* Tommy Bilotti
* Robert "Cabert" Bisaccia
* Sonny Ciccone
* Pasquale "Patsy" Conte
* Nicky Corozzo
* Joseph "Joe Butch" Corrao
* Roy DeMeo
* Robert "DiB" DiBernardo

* Lenny DiMaria
* James "Jimmy Brown" Failla
* Carmine Fatico
* Danny Fatico
* Tommy Gambino
* Pete Gotti
* Ralph Mosca
* Lou Vallario

Soldiers:
* Iggy Alogna
* Vinnie Artuso
* Dominic "Fat Dom" Borghese
* Thomas "Huck" Carbonara
* John Carneglia
* Mike Cirelli
* Jackie "Nose" D'Amico
* Armond "Buddy" Dellacroce
* Louie DiBono
* Johnny "Johnny G" Gammarano
* Eddie Garafola
* Gene Gotti
* Salvatore "Tory" Locascio
* Phil Modica
* Tony Plate
* Mark Reiter
* Angelo Ruggiero
* Sal Ruggiero
* Sal Scala
* Alphonse "Funzi" Sisca
* Arnold Squitieri

Associates:
* James Cardinali
* Norman Dupont
* Ralph Galione
* Manny Gambino
* Wilfred "Willie Boy" Johnson
* Anthony "Shorty" Mascuzzio
* Tony Moscatiello

* "Old Man" Joe Paruta
* Bosko Radonjich
* Anthony "Tony Roach" Rampino
* Joe Watts

Colombo Crime Family

Administration:
* Vittorio "Little Vic" Orena, Acting Boss
* Carmine "The Snake" Persico, Boss

Capodecinas:
* Patty Amato
* Michael Franzese

Soldiers:
* Jack Leale
* Tommy Ocera
* John Orena

Associates:
* Harry Bonfiglio
* Michael Maffatore
* Salvatore "Sonny Black" Montella

DeCavalcante Crime Family

Administration:
* John D'Amato, Underboss
* John Riggi, Boss

Capodecina:
* Gaetano "Corky" Vastola

Genovese Crime Family

Administration:
* Vincenzo "Chin" Gigante, Boss
* Venero "Benny Eggs" Mangano, Underboss

CAST OF CHARACTERS

Capodecina:
* Salvatore "Sally Dogs" Lombardi

Associates:
* Preston Geritano
* Barry Nichilo

Lucchese Crime Family

Administration:
* Vittorio "Little Vic" Amuso, Boss
* Anthony "Gaspipe" Casso, Underboss
* Alphonse "Little Al" D'Arco, Acting Boss
* Frank Lastorino, Consigliere

Bonanno Crime Family

Administration:
* Joe Bonanno, Boss

Capodecina:
* Jerry Chilli

Associate:
* Gus France

Bruno Crime Family

Administration:
* Phil "Crazy Phil" Leonetti, Underboss

Capodecina:
* John "Johnny Keys" Simone

Murder Victims

* Tommy Bilotti, Gambino captain
* Jimmy Bishop, painters' union leader
* Paul Castellano, Gambino boss

* Robert DiBernardo, Gambino captain
* Louie DiBono, Gambino soldier
* Frank Favara, next-door neighbor
* Albert Gelb, court officer
* Wilfred "Willie Boy" Johnson, Gambino associate
* Jack Leale, Colombo soldier
* Jimmy McBratney, Irish kidnapper
* Louie Milito, Gambino soldier
* Tommy Ocera, Colombo soldier
* Tony Plate, Gambino soldier
* Joh "Johnny Keys" Simone, Bruno Family captain

Defense Lawyers

* Ben Brafman
* Dave Breitbart
* Anthony Cardinale
* Roy Cohn
* Mike Coiro
* Bruce Cutler
* David DePetris
* David Greenfield
* Jeffrey Hoffman
* Susan Kellman
* Robert Koppelman
* Albert Krieger
* Ron Kuby
* William Kunstler
* Jimmy LaRossa
* John Pollock
* Rich Rehbock
* Michael Ross
* George Santangelo
* Jerry Shargel
* Barry Slotnick

AUTHOR'S NOTE

Even before Gambino Family boss John Gotti was found guilty on April 2, 1992, I knew this book had to be written. I was the lead prosecutor in that case. Together with other Assistant United States Attorneys in Brooklyn, and working with the Special Agents on the FBI's Gambino Squad, I not only brought down a notorious boss who'd stuck his finger in the eye of law enforcement, but we decimated an entire crime family and, in time, all of La Cosa Nostra.

John Gotti and I were way too bound up in each other. His rise and fall as Gambino Family boss coincided almost exactly with my ten years as an organized crime prosecutor. I came of age as a lawyer investigating and prosecuting him, members of his crew, and even his lawyer, and was appointed a federal judge because I finally succeeded in convicting him.

My two trials of Gotti on racketeering and murder charges were thus bookends for us both. His defense in the first mirrored the very public violence that catapulted him to the boss of the Family even as the case was underway, and the result cemented his status as America's celebrity don. The second was an even more hostile affair. They were sensational in different ways, and each was the most remarkable trial of its time.

THE
GOTTI
WARS

PROLOGUE

SPARKS

In mid-December 1985, Paul Castellano, the boss of the Gambino Crime Family of La Cosa Nostra, was on trial with nine other gangsters in the Southern District of New York. It was one of those lumbering, multi-defendant affairs that the Southern District then specialized in. It had been underway in the imposing courthouse on Foley Square in Lower Manhattan for more than three months, and there seemed to be no end in sight. Castellano was being defended in the case by Jimmy LaRossa, one of the best criminal trial lawyers of his day.

On Monday, December 16, the court wasn't in session. That afternoon Castellano and his driver, Gambino captain Tommy Bilotti, left their homes on Staten Island in a black Lincoln and stopped by LaRossa's Manhattan office to give Christmas presents to the women on his staff. From there they left to meet a group of Gambino captains and soldiers for dinner at Sparks Steak House on 46th Street, just east of Third Avenue.

They weren't the only ones out on the town that evening. Holiday cocktail parties are big in New York, and no industry or profession enjoys them more—or has as many—as law enforcement. December 16 is the height of the season, so by 6:00 p.m. that day just about every homicide or organized crime investigator in New York had a drink in hand somewhere in the city. At New York University Law School, G. Robert Blakey, author of the RICO Act, passed in 1970 to combat organized crime in the U.S., was holding a party before he delivered a lecture. All of a sudden, a beeper went off, then another, then another. The FBI agents and the prosecutors present huddled together in a corner before telling their host, "We can't stay—Castellano has just been shot." Within seconds, beepers were sounding all over town, the drinks were downed, and the rush to the nearest pay phones began.

Bilotti had driven the Lincoln uptown from LaRossa's office and turned right on 46th Street, heading east. Castellano was next to him in the front passenger seat. When they got to the light at Third Avenue, it was red. As they waited, they turned on the dome light and Castellano fumbled with some papers. The distraction cost them their lives. Had Bilotti glanced to his left while waiting to cross Third Avenue, he would have seen, less than five feet away, John Gotti and Sammy Gravano sitting in a parked car, waiting for them to arrive. Bilotti would have realized the danger and sped his boss to safety. Instead, Gravano used a walkie-talkie to tell the shooters to get ready, and as soon as the light turned green, Bilotti calmly crossed the avenue and pulled over to the right curb, into the no-standing zone directly in front of Sparks.

Castellano opened his door to step onto the sidewalk. The moment he was out of the car, the four men who'd been hovering near the door to the restaurant closed in. Dressed in identical double-breasted tan trench coats and dark hats, they pulled out handguns and let off a hail of bullets. Bilotti rushed out of the driver's door to help, but the shooters had already run around to where he was standing and gunned him down too. In less than ten seconds, both men lay dead—Castellano on the sidewalk and Bilotti in the middle of 46th Street. The gunmen walked in a group calmly but quickly to the east, toward Second Avenue, where getaway cars were waiting. Because it was rush hour in the holiday season, there were dozens of eyewitnesses. Nobody intervened.

Gotti and Gravano watched from inside the car across Third Avenue. After the light turned again, they too crossed the avenue and drove slowly past the dead men. Gravano was in the passenger seat, and he looked down at Bilotti's body on the way by. "They're gone," he told Gotti. The two men then drove east to Second Avenue and on south to Brooklyn, mission accomplished.

PART I

THE
FIRST
CASE

CHAPTER 1

"THIS THING OF OURS"

That night and in the days that followed, the vast network of informants that formed the backbone of law enforcement's fight against La Cosa Nostra unanimously blamed the murders on Gotti. Cops and federal agents weren't shy about sharing that information, and his photo was soon all over the television and newspapers.

In one sense, it was hardly news. Gotti and Castellano had been itching to kill each other for years. One thing had held them both back: underboss Aniello Dellacroce. Dellacroce, whose name translates sweetly into "Little Lamb of the Cross," was a gangster's gangster—shrewd, coarse, respected, feared. Only nepotism had prevented him from succeeding Carlo Gambino as boss in 1976, when Carlo passed over his second-in-command and instead anointed his cousin Paul Castellano. Even after that slight, Aniello Dellacroce remained, in effect, boss of part of the Family. The faction that stayed loyal to him after Castellano became boss was violent and unsophisticated. While the Castellano loyalists used the Family's corrupt relationships with union officials to siphon millions from the construction, carting, garment, and shipping industries, the people around Dellacroce were truck hijackers, loan sharks, drug dealers, and bookmakers. The most ruthless was John Gotti, the captain of the rough-and-tumble crew based in Ozone Park, Queens, at the hole-in-the-wall with the memorable name: the Bergin Hunt & Fish Club.

Gotti and the other half dozen captains loyal to Dellacroce deeply resented Castellano. As far as they were concerned, he'd divided the Family into the haves, wealthy through the easy work of labor racketeering, and the have-nots, tough guys who labored a lot harder to earn less, and who paid tribute to Dellacroce at the Ravenite

Social Club, at 247 Mulberry Street in Manhattan's Little Italy. That Castellano shared some of the income from the construction rackets with the Genovese Family boss, Vincenzo "Chin" Gigante, made matters worse. It infuriated Gotti and his crew.

For most of the last century there have been five Cosa Nostra Families in New York City and one in New Jersey. *Cosa Nostra* translates as "Our Thing" or "This Thing of Ours." The names of the New York Families today are Bonanno, Colombo, Gambino, Genovese, and Lucchese; across the Hudson River is the DeCavalcante Family. Territorialism reigned for most of that time, but the divides were only partly geographic in nature, since each Family, or "crew," operated throughout the city and in Jersey as well. The Gambino Family also had operations in Westchester County north of the city, Connecticut, and Florida. The more important territories were businesses and the unions that served them. Thus, if anyone tried to muscle into garbage carting in the city, they had to deal with Gambino captain Jimmy Brown Failla; the docks in Jersey belonged to the Genovese Family; the Lucchese Family had a lock on the painters' union, and so on. But they all shared the same structured hierarchy and reported up to the Commission, a governing body consisting of the bosses of the Five Families and the heads of the Chicago and Buffalo mobs.

All families have their schisms. John Gotti wanted to kill Castellano, but Dellacroce wouldn't let him. It wasn't because Dellacroce liked Castellano. He hated him too, but rules are rules. Dellacroce was old school, and he actually followed some of those rules, including the ones about whom you could and couldn't murder. You couldn't kill a "made" guy—a sworn member—of your Family without the permission of your boss. You couldn't kill a made guy in another Family without the permission of your boss and the boss of that other Family. You couldn't even ask a made guy in another Family to help you kill someone in your own Family without the permission of the other Family's boss. Finally, La Cosa Nostra even had a rule about whacking your own boss: you could do it, but only with the express consent of the other bosses on the Commission. So Gotti's desire to kill Castellano couldn't even be mentioned to Dellacroce. Gotti was his protégé, but Dellacroce would kill him before he allowed him to kill the boss.

Castellano knew all this. It was obvious, and embarrassing, that a third of the Family's captains reported to Dellacroce and not to him. It was just as obvious that Gotti had grown into a formidable threat in the years since Castellano became boss. Castellano wanted that threat extinguished, but just as Dellacroce had made it impossible for Gotti to kill Castellano, his presence made it difficult for Castellano to dispatch Gotti.

Even a boss can't order the murder of one of his captains just because he's afraid of him. He needs a reason. If Castellano were to kill Gotti without one, Dellacroce could go to the Commission and get permission to whack Castellano. So Castellano needed a justification, and just a few months before he was murdered he got one: the drug trafficking by members of Gotti's crew.

Another of the mob's rules was a prohibition against drug trafficking. This particular edict was the mob at its hypocritical best. All the Families had drug dealers, and tribute from that lucrative trade made its way to each boss just as reliably as the tribute from the mob's other illegal businesses. It was widely known that Castellano not only had drug dealers around him, but even had some in his own blood family. They weren't in danger of mob retribution, but still, the rule was there, and if Castellano could prove to Dellacroce that Gotti's crew had violated it then Gotti's days were numbered.

Gotti's best friend was Angelo Ruggiero, and both Ruggiero and Gene Gotti (by six years Gotti's younger brother) were soldiers in Gotti's crew. In 1982 the FBI planted a bug in Ruggiero's kitchen, and the famously loose-lipped Ruggiero talked to everyone who'd listen about his heroin trafficking. He, Gene Gotti, and about a dozen others were indicted in federal court in Brooklyn—the Eastern District of New York—some twelve months later. From the moment they were arrested, Castellano tried to get his hands on the incriminating Ruggiero tapes. He told Jimmy LaRossa to get copies of them from Ruggiero's attorney, but Ruggiero ordered his lawyer not to give up the tapes to anyone, especially LaRossa. For almost two years, LaRossa tried to get them without success.

Finally, in the summer of 1985, Castellano sent a message to Dellacroce: Ruggiero had broken a different rule—the one that states that every Mafia member must obey his boss. Castellano had demanded copies of the tapes, and Ruggiero had refused. That itself was a reason to whack him. Dellacroce summoned John Gotti and Ruggiero to his home on West Fingerboard Road in Staten Island, down the hill from Castellano's mansion on Todt Hill. It didn't matter that Castellano had drug dealers around him, Dellacroce told them (as the FBI listened in). "The boss is the boss," he growled, "give 'em the fuckin' tapes!" Both Gotti and Ruggiero objected, saying that Castellano was effectively turning them into informers, but Dellacroce was adamant. So in the fall of 1985, Ruggiero's lawyer finally gave a set of the tapes to LaRossa, who in turn brought them to Castellano. They were all the proof Castellano needed to put hits on John Gotti, his brother Gene, and Angelo Ruggiero for violating the rule against dealing drugs.

Timing is everything, though, and Castellano didn't move quickly enough.

On December 2, 1985, Aniello Dellacroce died, aged seventy-one, from cancer. John Gotti already knew he was in a whack-or-be-whacked situation, and with Dellacroce gone he could now do the killing. Just two weeks later, with the help of a dozen loyal followers, he orchestrated the hits outside Sparks, and within hours he declared that he was taking over the Gambino Family. Not a single member objected. In homage to his mentor, Dellacroce, he made the Ravenite his headquarters.

On the night Castellano and Bilotti were gunned down, I was a federal prosecutor in Brooklyn, an Assistant United States Attorney in the Eastern District of New York. I'd been in the job less than a year, having recently left a comfortable position at a prominent law firm. Even though I was a rookie, eight months earlier I'd been assigned to prosecute John Gotti on an entirely different set of charges, so I'd already become part of the criminal world in which the murders outside Sparks were a seismic event. Overnight, those deaths had a dramatic effect on the case I was working on. And over time they'd alter the course of my entire career.

CHAPTER 2

THE LURE
OF CRIME

I'd decided I wanted to be a federal prosecutor five years earlier, during the first couple of months of my clerkship. The judge for whom I clerked, Boyce Martin, sat on the United States Court of Appeals for the Sixth Circuit. He recruited his clerks from his alma mater, the University of Virginia School of Law, where I was a student. So after my graduation in May of 1980, my wife, Susan, and I headed off from our home in Charlottesville to his chambers in Louisville, Kentucky.

A law clerk for an appellate judge sits in an office all day reading briefs and advising his mentor how to vote when he or she meets with the two other judges on the case after oral argument. If his or her boss is the one to write the court's decision, the law clerk helps draft the opinion.

The civil side of the job was interesting enough. There were disputes over union elections and unfair labor practices, employment discrimination cases, contract disputes, antitrust claims, suits against police officers for excessive force, voting rights disputes. But the criminal cases were on a different plane altogether. Each one was a window into a criminal society from which I'd been completely sheltered, and I found that world fascinating. Once people decided they weren't going to obey the law, there were so many ways for them to get rich. In a way I couldn't fully explain, I found myself admiring these rule breakers' sheer audacity. My parents were quintessential law-abiders. They got W-2s for every penny they earned, paid their taxes, obeyed the system. As a result, they barely got by. I'd had no idea that there were all these people thumbing their noses at the same system, taking whatever they could and hoping to get away with it.

It was all so new to me, and so *human*. I could tell right away that, even though I liked the civil cases, crime was where I wanted to be. And the legal issues the criminal appeals raised gave me a tantalizing glimpse into the world of criminal investigations and trials. How do you make sure a lineup identification can be used at trial? When do Miranda warnings have to be given? Can a prior conviction be used as evidence? What are the things prosecutors can't say in summation? The learning curve seemed almost vertical, but the law was much more accessible and interesting than in the civil cases.

It wasn't as if the criminal cases gave me a burning desire to put criminals in jail. Even before law school, I'd pictured myself not as a prosecutor but as a criminal defense attorney. Like many people my age, I'd watched *The Godfather* so many times I practically had it memorized—and I'd long identified with Tom Hagen, the Corleone Family's soft-spoken, even-keeled consigliere, its voice of reason. But I could tell just from looking at the lawyers on our cases that the only way someone like me could get real experience in federal criminal cases was to become an Assistant United States Attorney. The AUSAs were nearly all young; the defense lawyers were a lot older, and when I asked around I learned that most had started out as prosecutors. That gave me two options: try to get a job as a gofer for a defense attorney or try to become a federal prosecutor and handle my own cases. It wasn't a real choice.

One problem, I soon learned, was that once my one-year clerkship ended I couldn't even apply to become a federal prosecutor. I'd be moving to New York City to be close to my mom, who wasn't well, and lawyers had to have at least two years' experience before they applied to be an AUSA in either of the two United States Attorney's Offices there. There were exceptions for Supreme Court clerks and other all-star applicants, but I was definitely not in that category. I'd have to work at a law firm for a couple of years first.

The conventional wisdom imparted to young lawyers is that you're supposed to choose a firm based on how you'd "fit" there. To me, this seemed ridiculous. The big firms had hundreds of lawyers, and I'd meet only four or five during my interview. I knew from the summer I'd spent after my second year of law school at Shearman & Sterling, a multinational law firm based in New York, that there are plenty of unpleasant people in any organization, and generally they're kept far away from applicants. I could fit in great with the lawyers at my interview and never see them once I went to work at their firm.

My approach to joining a practice was almost entirely mercenary: what I cared about most was having the best possible résumé when I applied for a job as an AUSA. I didn't care if I was miserable at the place so long as its name made me an attractive applicant after my two years were up.

In the end, my decision turned out to be easy—only one of the top-tier firms in New York even invited me for an interview. Yet it was arguably the best of them all: Cravath, Swaine & Moore, widely regarded as among the leading law firms in the world. My law school classmates bluntly expressed surprise that Cravath was interested in me. I hadn't made the law review, and instead of the impressive credentials many of them had, I'd spent my two years between college and law school as a professional housepainter.

The interviews at Cravath took a whole day, and I met with half a dozen partners and associates. During my conversation with David Boies, one of the star partners, we were interrupted by a call from Senator Ted Kennedy. Boies was on the phone for about ten minutes. Sitting there waiting for the call to end, all I could think was, I am sitting across the desk from a person who is actually talking to Teddy Kennedy. I would have taken a job as a messenger. When I got a call a couple of days later offering me a position as an associate, I accepted in a heartbeat.

Boyce Martin's clerkships, like those for most federal judges, ran from September to September. Toward the end of my year, Judge Martin asked me to stay on the payroll after I moved to New York and write a draft opinion for him in a complicated school desegregation case. I was flattered; I'd earned his confidence, which would serve me well in the years ahead. Also, drafting the opinion would give me a chance to learn the Supreme Court case law on the topic of intentional discrimination, which would be challenging. Those opinions were often deeply divided "plurality" opinions, in which many of the nine members of the court would write separately, agreeing with some of what the court's opinion said but not the rest. You needed a scorecard just to figure out what facets of the legal doctrine had garnered a majority of the justices. Another important dividend: I'd experience no gap in income between leaving the clerkship and starting at Cravath, and at that point in my life that was important. I happily agreed.

The extra few weeks working for Judge Martin turned out to be a godsend. It gave Susan and me some continuity in an otherwise traumatic move to New York City. We'd met in college at Georgetown, and we married when I was a housepainter. We were living in Northern Virginia at the time, then moved to Charlottesville for law school, and then to Louisville for the clerkship. Our combined salary in all three places wasn't enough to rent even the cheapest apartment in Manhattan, so we turned our attention to South Brooklyn, where we discovered Carroll Gardens. There were few gardens to be found there, but it was a clean and airy neighborhood.

Anyone who grew up in the New York suburbs of the 1960s and 1970s, as Susan and I did, would have thought Brooklyn a war zone. In the mid-seventies the city almost went bankrupt. Crime rates, especially those for violent offenses, skyrocketed. Not even the affluent areas in Manhattan were safe. Most of Brooklyn was dangerous at night, and since we weren't in a position to distinguish among neighborhoods, we assumed Carroll Gardens was as well.

On our first day there, after unpacking and returning the U-Haul truck, I needed to make good on my promise to my mother that I'd call to report how the day had gone. But we had no working phone. It was eleven at night, and I'd have to find a public one. Petrified of getting mugged, I ran as fast as I could down DeGraw to Court Street, where all the shops were. There was a pay phone a block and a half up Court, near Union Street. Out of breath but trying hard not to sound scared, I managed a hurried chat with my mom, then sprinted back home. The whole time my heart was racing from fear.

It was only a matter of days before Susan and I learned how little we had to worry. We lived in one of the safest neighborhoods in the city. The 76th Precinct, which was a block from our apartment, was a plum assignment for police officers because hardly anything ever happened there.

How come? We'd eventually have figured it out on our own, but a neighbor gave us the lowdown soon after we moved in. Carroll Gardens wasn't a safe neighborhood because it *lacked* criminals. In fact, they were all over the place. Shorty Mascuzzio had a club on Court near Sackett. Punchy Illiano owned a restaurant, Casa Rosa, on Court Street near President. Bobby Boriello and Preston Geritano ran a place over on Henry Street. Carroll Gardens was home to these and many other gangsters. They had their own way of dealing with crime, and it didn't involve calling the police. The ambient threat they'd created had proven to be so effective over the years that ordinary criminals chose other places to go about their work. The home burglaries that were the scourge of Brooklyn Heights at the time simply didn't occur where we lived. Street robberies were equally unlikely. I could call my mother from a pay phone anytime, day or night, and not have to worry or end up out of breath.

That didn't mean we didn't *hear* about crime. With so many criminals living in the neighborhood, talk of it was in the air. One night shortly after we moved in I was waiting for a pizza at Nino's, on the corner of our block. It was late summer and the doors to the street were propped open. A group of teenage boys were arguing over whether it was better to get a year or a year and a day.

"If you get a year, you don't get no parole," one said. "A year and a day, you get parole. You only do ten months."

"Yeah," another shot back, "but if you get a year, they keep you here. You do your time in Rikers. Your girlfriend can come see you. If you get a year and a day, they send you upstate."

To people in Manhattan and Brooklyn Heights, "upstate" means everything north of Yankee Stadium, up where the summer homes are. Carroll Gardens in the 1980s, though, was one of those neighborhoods in which "upstate" meant "in a prison other than Rikers Island."

"But they got yards upstate! They got no yard at Rikers. You get a year, you stay here. It's harder time *and* longer time!"

"I'd rather do the extra time here in Rikers. You know how far away Green Haven is? You can't get no fuckin' visits!"

And so it went. There we were, in a cozy neighborhood with pastry shops, outdoor vegetable stands, pork stores, and salumeria delicatessens. One of the local bakeries was Cammareri Brothers, soon to become famous in the movie *Moonstruck*. Most of the local merchants spoke only Italian. But our charming community also happened to be home to many of the city's prominent gangsters. In a few years, I'd get to know many of them all too well, but at the time I was just one of the many young urban professionals who were gradually gentrifying a Brooklyn neighborhood that was almost entirely free of crime.

To draft the opinion for Judge Martin I had to find a law library. Though the case was fact-intensive, my first task was to synthesize the Supreme Court's desegregation case law. I had six weeks to finish the draft, and looked around for a comfortable place to work.

Federal courthouses have their own libraries, and the United States District Court for the Eastern District of New York was up in Brooklyn Heights, near the entrance to the Brooklyn Bridge. The library was on its fourth floor, and the moment I walked in I knew I'd found what I needed. It looked out on a huge park, lined on each side by huge broadleaf trees that shaded wooden benches. My first visit was on a beautiful September afternoon, and I spotted young mothers with babies at one end of the park's playing field watching children from nearby Saint Ann's School.

The library was mostly empty of people. The stacks were against the wall and huge wooden worktables lined the windows that looked out over the park. I could spread out the briefs and the extensive trial records on one-half of a table and use the other half to take notes. When I looked up I wouldn't see a city; not even a car. Toward the end of the day, the sun set a rich orange behind the rows of sycamores on the far side of the park. It was perfect.

After a few days, the librarian politely asked me to identify myself. When he learned I was a law clerk for a federal circuit judge, life got even better. He privatized my table, allowing me to leave my books and papers spread out at all times.

I'd agreed with Judge Martin that I'd finish the opinion in time to start at Cravath on Monday, October 19, 1981. On Friday, October 16, I cite-checked the final draft, packed up my belongings, and returned all the books to their shelves. Beginning Monday there'd be no more walking to work; I'd be riding the subway and making my way through the canyons of Lower Manhattan to Cravath's offices at One Chase Plaza, set between Pine, Liberty, Nassau, and William Streets in the heart of the Financial District.

CHAPTER 3

CRAVATH

Cravath lawyers worked all the time. Days, nights, weekends, holidays, there were always lots of people there working. This was no doubt like any of the big firms on the top rung of the New York ladder, but the place had an intensity all its own. Associates boasted about "pulling all-nighters." Even the firm lore centered on how many hours people put in. An apocryphal story told how a partner once billed twenty-seven hours in one day. It wasn't fraud. He'd flown to the West Coast that morning, and had worked all twenty-seven hours until the clock struck midnight in California.

Though I'd chosen the place solely for how it would burnish my résumé, I found myself enjoying what I did, in large part because in my first week there I got lucky. Other firms assign associates to practice groups, where they work for all the partners in the group, but Cravath allocates new lawyers each to a single partner. You operated under that partner for at least two years, sometimes longer, and were employed by other partners only if loaned out. This had its risky side. Some partners demeaned the associates assigned to them. One of my friends was directed to bring a draft brief he'd toiled on all night to a country club tennis court in Westchester, where he had to wait patiently as the partner he worked for edited it between sets.

My stroke of good luck was that I was assigned to Ralph McAfee, the oldest active partner in the firm at sixty-six. A recovering alcoholic, Ralph had a gravelly smoker's voice and was regarded as a curmudgeon, crusty and profane. He enjoyed and cultivated this reputation, but he wasn't like the younger partners to whom my friends had been assigned. I got summoned to the country club too, but it was to play golf with Ralph. He found out I'd been a caddie for ten years at Whippoorwill Club in Armonk.

One Friday afternoon, after I'd been with him about six months, I picked up my phone and heard, "Hey, shithead, I want you to see what it's like to *have* a caddie rather than be one. I'll see you at Sleepy Hollow Country Club Sunday at eight." Click. Over the next two years he invited me to play so often that I had to come up with good excuses so I wouldn't hurt his feelings.

Ralph felt that Cravath lawyers labored so hard they should fly in comfort. As it wasn't right to charge a client more than the coach fare, he went into his own pocket to make sure I traveled first class. In countless other ways he treated me as if he actually liked me. He called me "shithead" often enough to keep up appearances, but I knew better.

A pivotal event took place my first week. It taught me a lot about the way Cravath operated. A prominent company had retained the firm to represent it in a commercial dispute. The matter wasn't yet a lawsuit, but the client was convinced it would be soon, and Ralph was the partner in charge of this new piece of business.

The first step was to get a fix on all the documents. Our client had a long relation-ship with the company on the other side and had a bank of file cabinets containing correspondence and draft contracts and the like. A senior associate, Mike Spencer, and I were dispatched to the client's offices to go through them and learn the documentary history of the case.

The in-house company lawyer who met us had something different in mind. There were no pleasantries or small talk. He showed us the file cabinets and told us to "sanitize" them. Once a lawsuit began, he explained, the law would forbid the destruc-tion of documents, so he wanted every piece of paper that would hurt the company's position destroyed before that would happen.

He explained all this so matter-of-factly that my first thought as he left the room was that I must be missing something.

"We can do that?" I asked Spencer. "Doesn't that violate something?"

"I don't know that we *can't* do it, legally," he answered, "but I know we *shouldn't*. And we're not doing anything until we speak to Ralph." Without even saying goodbye, we got right back on the subway and returned to the office.

Ralph seemed genuinely amused when we told him what had happened. "He's a shithead," he said quietly when we finished. Even as he spoke he was dialing the in-house lawyer's number. He talked to him on the speakerphone as Spencer and I sat there.

After confirming with the company lawyer that he wanted us to destroy harm-ful documents, Ralph told him, "We don't work that way. I could give you reasons why it would be lousy strategy: there'll be other copies of those documents; sooner or later what we did will come out; et cetera. But the fact is, even if we *could* get away with it and it would help us in this litigation, we wouldn't do it. It's wrong. If you want it done in this case, you'll have to find another law firm to represent you." Click.

Two and a half years after starting at Cravath I was more than ready for a move. It had taken almost two years after I sent in an application to just get an interview at the United States Attorney's Office, but by early 1984 I'd had two of them. The second was with Jerry Lynch, the chief appellate attorney, and it had gone well. I was called back for the final interview with the U. S. Attorney himself, Rudy Giuliani. Nothing was guaranteed, but once you reached the final interview, I was told, your chances were excellent.

Giuliani was about to celebrate his fortieth birthday and had taken up his new position the year before. His office featured prominently a couple of blue plastic seats from the old Yankee Stadium, salvaged during its renovation in the mid-1970s. He welcomed me to sit in one. I declined but seized the opportunity to say I was a diehard Yankee fan.

Giuliani began the interview by talking about the storied Southern District. Keen to litigate cases personally, he'd left the job of Associate Attorney General—the third-highest position in the Justice Department—to become just one of ninety-four United States Attorneys. "Any other office, it's obviously a step down, but not when it's the Southern District," he told me. "It was a promotion as far as I was concerned."

Within minutes he moved the conversation to the death penalty. Did I oppose it? Would I be willing to prosecute a capital case? It was an odd topic. There was no federal death penalty at the time, and the first of the laws that would produce federal capital trials in the 1990s was still five years away. Giuliani acknowledged that the issue was academic, but he obviously cared a great deal about it.

I thought I had a good answer. I wanted the job badly, so I began by emphasizing that I'd have no problem handling a capital prosecution. This wasn't entirely true, but since there was no chance it could happen I felt safe. Then I added, "If I were a legislator, I'd vote against it. Personally I'm opposed to the government putting people to death." This seemed safe ground. Our governor, Mario Cuomo, who was from the city and enormously popular there, had steadfastly opposed capital punishment and had vetoed legislation that would have returned it to New York. I thought Giuliani might even admire my parsing of the issue.

I thought wrong. He drilled into me. What if the victim were your mother? What if she were tortured? I assumed he was testing my commitment to principle, so I said of course I'd want to kill the guy with my own hands, but I really believed that the government ought to stay out of the business of snuffing out life—not because some people didn't deserve to be put to death, but because, on moral grounds, the government shouldn't be killing people.

The interview passed on to other subjects, and overall seemed to go well. As he walked me out of his office, Giuliani had his arm around my shoulder. "You have to tell Ralph McAfee I'll be calling," he told me. I'd listed Ralph as a reference on my application but written in bold type a request that they let me know before contacting him. It was a common and accepted way of saying, "Don't burn me at my current job with a reference check unless I'm really a contender."

"I'll wait till tomorrow before calling him so you have a chance to let him know," Giuliani said. He'd get back to me soon, he assured me.

Things did not go well the following morning. "What kind of a stupid goddam shithead idea is this?" Ralph growled. He wasn't a screamer, but was visibly angry. "Do you understand what you'd be giving up if you left this firm? You have a better chance of being made a partner here than anyone I've seen in a long time. Why would you walk away from that? What's the matter with you?"

"Nothing. I just want to do this. I've wanted to since my clerkship."

"I had no idea," he said, after a long pause. His anger was giving way to disappointment. We sat in silence in his office for an uncomfortably long time. I'd known he wouldn't be happy, but I hadn't expected such personal disappointment. He really wanted me to stay.

Giuliani didn't call that day, or the day after. In the meantime, Ralph had gotten some of the other litigation partners he'd loaned me to from time to time to lobby me to stay. None had ever set foot in my office before; at Cravath, the associates go to see the partners, not the other way around. But they came to me. Each was noticeably more circumspect than Ralph about whether I'd become a partner if I stayed. They'd obviously agreed to proclaim me "partnership material," a phrase each one used about twenty times, but they were plainly not assuring me that I'd get that promotion if I stayed.

After a week I asked Ralph to call Giuliani. He refused. "Listen, shithead, if he calls me I'll tell him you're an excellent young lawyer. I won't do anything to keep him from hiring you. But I'll be goddamned if I'm going to help you leave, because I think that would be a mistake. Besides, if he really wants to hear from me about you, he'll call." I knew he was right, so didn't press it.

The call never came. A full month after the interview, I got a one-line letter from Giuliani rejecting my application.

CHAPTER 4

BAPTISM BY FIRE

Before the Southern District turned me down, it hadn't occurred to me to apply to its neighbor across the East River. They were close geographically, with just the span of the Brooklyn Bridge separating them, but otherwise they were worlds apart. It was no knock on the Eastern District in particular. There was the Southern District—the flagship of the Justice Department, known as the "Sovereign District"—and then the ninety-three other U.S. Attorney's Offices, including the one in Brooklyn.

My years at Cravath made it especially unlikely that I'd have applied first to the Eastern District, even though it was within walking distance of my home and I'd had such a satisfying time early on working in the courthouse library. Public service wasn't what most Cravath lawyers aspired to, but there was plenty of talk about lawyers and law firms. An opposing attorney was sometimes described as a "former Southern District AUSA," and clearly that was a very positive attribute. And when one of our banking clients was victimized by a phony invoice scheme, I went with Cravath partner John Beerbower to the Southern District to present the case for prosecution. When they met with other lawyers, Cravath partners acted as if they owned the place—but this meeting was different. Even though we'd brought overwhelming evidence of a multimillion-dollar fraud scheme and offered the assistance of both the client and the firm in shaping the case, Beerbower assumed a hat-in-hand demeanor I hadn't seen before. We were the supplicants. And when Shirah Nieman, a young prosecutor, turned us away, we were doing the apologizing.

The Eastern District never came up in conversations at Cravath. I'd never heard a lawyer described as "a former Eastern District AUSA," and none of my contemporaries was even thinking of applying there. So it was a measure of my dedication to being an AUSA that the moment I got the rejection letter from Giuliani I did just that.

The application process was similar to the one I'd been through in the Southern District, so I was plenty nervous when after two rounds of interviews I was invited to meet the U.S. Attorney, Ray Dearie. That was the end to any similarities. Somehow Dearie knew that I'd been a starting guard on the Cravath team that won the Lawyers Basketball League championship that spring. We talked about basketball; and when that ended, we talked about golf, since my ten years as a caddie was on my résumé. The work of the office came up hardly at all.

It was July 1984, and after the interview I walked out of the courthouse into Cadman Plaza Park and sat on one of the benches. The late-afternoon sun was shining through the sycamores on the far side of the park. It was a beautiful and familiar scene, the one I'd enjoyed for six weeks from the fourth-floor library window when I first moved to Brooklyn. All I could think of was how much more pleasant it was talking with Dearie about sports than being grilled about the death penalty.

Just as with Giuliani, I'd been told in previous interviews that the job was mine unless I talked my way out of it. This time I managed to avoid that pitfall. A couple of days later I picked up my phone at work and heard Dearie's voice on the other end, offering me a position as an AUSA in Brooklyn. I accepted immediately.

On February 25, 1985, I was sworn in as an Assistant United States Attorney in the Eastern District of New York. It was 120 years to the day after Abraham Lincoln signed the law that created the district, carving it out of the "mother" jurisdiction—the Southern District of New York. Judge Eugene H. Nickerson, a descendant of John Quincy Adams, administered the oath in his chambers, and I had my photo taken with him and Ray Dearie. The judge was proper, handsome, dignified, gracious. His loyal courtroom deputy, an old Irishman named Bill Walsh, was fond of saying, "Look at him, that's the face of the people who took our lands." The judge made small talk as we waited for the photographer, asking me where I'd come from. He seemed genuinely interested in me and very kind.

I noticed, though, that his right arm hung limp. When we were introduced he angled his body to shake my hand with his right hand, which he was unable to extend. The arm had been withered by the polio that afflicted him just before he entered Harvard in 1937. An accomplished squash player in boarding school, he was so determined not to be derailed by the disease that he taught himself to play left-handed, becoming the best player at Harvard and captain of its team.

The U.S. Attorney's offices were on the fifth floor of the courthouse, one floor below the judge's chambers and one above the library where I'd worked for Judge Martin. There were large windowed offices on the outer side of the hallways that ran parallel to the exterior of the rectangular building. On the inner side were larger rooms, all windowless, occupied by four administrative assistants. Those rooms in turn had their own interior offices, dim spaces the size of large closets, each with a steel desk and chair. The windowless walls were all scuffed. I was assigned one of the closets.

My arrival pushed the previous occupant, George Daniels, out and across the hall into a windowed workspace, so he was delighted to see me. He introduced me to the assistants, then brought me to where I'd be based. The desk was cleaned out, but he showed me some business cards he'd left in the top drawer. "They can't switch phone numbers here," he explained. "Every time you move offices you get a new number. Since these cards already have your phone number, just cross out my name and put yours."

I was immediately assigned an appeal, defending the conviction of a drug dealer. By that afternoon my office was full of boxes. The surroundings were depressing, but the work was familiar; more than anything else, I'd written briefs at Cravath and handled several appeals. I spent my first week learning the case inside out.

Early in my second week, the Secret Service arrested Anita Ravenel, a cocaine addict, for passing a forged $300 money order. When they aren't protecting the President or other dignitaries, Secret Service agents are charged with enforcing an odd assortment of criminal laws. I'd come to learn that many agents tended to treat even minor criminals as if they were about to shoot the President.

Dave Kirby, the chief of General Crimes and therefore my boss, came by with Pat Convery. Convery was the Secret Service agent who'd made the arrest. Kirby introduced us and told me to handle the arraignment. He then left, leaving Convery sitting across from me.

"You know I'm new?" I asked.

"No, I didn't," Convery said. He was a big man with a huge mop of hair.

"Well, I am," I said, "and I don't have any idea what 'taking care of the arraignment' means."

"It means we go to court and she gets let out on bail," Convery said, smiling.

"Do we have to bring anything with us?"

"We bring the defendant and a complaint."

"Where's the defendant?"

"She's down in the Marshals' cellblock."

I didn't know what that meant, but I could tell Convery was in charge of the defendant.

"Great. So what's a complaint?"

Convery taught me what I needed to know: how to make the caption that read "*United States of America v. Anita Ravenel*"; how much description of Ravenel's crime was needed; what section of the United States Code to cite; and how to request that Ravenel "be dealt with according to law." He even knew where to find the preprinted file folders that AUSAs use whenever a new prosecution is opened. Within an hour, I was off to court. Convery went down to the cellblock to pick up the defendant. He'd meet me in the duty magistrate's courtroom.

I felt elated—only on the job a week, and here I was heading off to court to handle a case. There were partners at Cravath who'd never done that. Ravenel's forged money order was obviously small potatoes, but so what?

There were easily two dozen people in the courtroom. Most were AUSAs and defense lawyers, all gathered around a couple of long tables up near the judge's bench. Some were seated, others stood; they seemed to be involved in whispered negotiations as the judge handled the case before her. Back in the spectator section were agents sitting with their handcuffed prisoners. Others, whom I later learned were interpreters and pretrial services officers, were also milling about. I immediately sensed a problem. Stationed in the back with Ravenel, Convery was no longer in a position to coach me.

My pride turned to anxiety as I listened to what was happening in the other cases. After each was called, the judge would read the complaint, then ask the defendant's lawyer whether he or she had gone over the charges with the client. They all said yes and entered not guilty pleas. The first question the judge asked the prosecutor was the same every time: "What's the government's position on bail?" The problem was the AUSAs took a different position in every case. One asked for detention pending trial. Another asked for home detention with electronic monitoring. A third said, "I've spoken to defense counsel, and we agree, subject to your approval, Judge, on a $100,000 PRB, rather than an OR."

I could feel my body temperature rising. Part of it was the jargon—I knew they were referring to bail bonds, but I didn't know what all the letters meant. The judge read each complaint silently to herself, so I had no idea what these other defendants were alleged to have done. Even in the cases where there was disagreement about bail, neither side mentioned the charge, arguing instead about roots in the community, whether there were bench warrants, or whether the defendant had a job. Convery had said nothing about any of those things.

The other AUSAs at the tables were busy whispering among themselves. I could tell they didn't know I was a new colleague. In urgent need of advice, I followed one AUSA to the back of the courtroom after his case was finished, introduced myself, and asked if he could help me figure out what position I should take on bail.

"What kind of case is it?"

"A forged money order case," I said.

"Just ask for a $25,000 PRB," he said.

Primed (as I thought), when the courtroom deputy called, "United States versus Ravenel," I approached the bench and said, "Assistant United States Attorney John Gleeson for the government." Even though my heart was pounding, it felt great to say those words. I'd repeat them hundreds of times over the next ten years, and they never failed to give me goose bumps.

Ravenel had no money for anything, let alone for a lawyer, so one was appointed for her. Liz Fink, one of several disciples of the celebrated civil rights lawyer William Kunstler, caught Ravenel's case. I'd already heard of her, since she was litigating the long-running class action on behalf of the inmates who were injured or killed during the riot at Attica Prison in 1971. Fink was soft-spoken and friendly. She entered a plea of not guilty just before the judge turned to me to ask for the government's position on bail.

In time, I'd learn that almost all the judges in the Eastern District welcomed new prosecutors and defenders to the courthouse. Though the cases would naturally result in disagreements, sometimes even in acrimony, it was a community, and not a large one. Judges would ask where the new lawyers came from and wish them well. Many felt an obligation to teach young newcomers, and would assume an almost parental demeanor during an AUSA's or federal defender's initial appearance.

I wasn't before one of those judges.

"We request a $25,000 PRB, Your Honor," I answered confidently.

If all you had to go on was the look on the judge's face, it was as if I'd just asked that Ravenel be summarily executed. The judge stared at me in disbelief for about five seconds. "That's ridiculous!" she finally blurted. "Why? Why do you think this case, which involves one money order worth only $300, requires a PRB? Why shouldn't I release her OR?"

I was stunned. I not only had no idea what the answers were to her rapid-fire questions, I didn't even understand them. I just stood there, lost for words. But she was apparently waiting for some kind of response, so all I could think to do was say, "Judge, that AUSA," pointing to the back of the courtroom, "recommended that I ask for the $25,000 PRB."

"This defendant will be released on her own recognizance!" she declared, glowering at me.

The low-volume whispering in the courtroom had disappeared. A new AUSA was being baptized by fire, and everyone had stopped to watch.

The judge filled in some blanks on the bond then called out to the back of the courtroom, "Mr. Gold, should we schedule a preliminary hearing?" It turned out the AUSA I'd given up was named Mike Gold.

"Judge, this is not my case. It's Mr. Gleeson's," Gold replied.

"I know it is," the judge responded tartly, "but it's pretty obvious he has no idea what he's doing. So I thought I'd ask someone who does."

It was a different quiet now. The judge had gone beyond breaking in a new AUSA to humiliating one, and everyone present watched with the same rapt attention bystanders give a car crash. The judge finished the arraignment by speaking only to Gold. To his credit, he never came forward from the back of the courtroom, and kept repeating that it was my case, not his. He also said he was responsible for the position on bail that she'd found so objectionable, not me. But the judge would have none of it. She'd declared me incompetent and pretended I was no longer standing right in front of her.

When it was over, I walked back through the silent courtroom. The combination of the judge's cruelty and the look of complete devastation on my face drew a supportive crowd as I made my way to the door at the back of the room. When I got into the hallway outside the second-floor courtroom, everyone, including Liz Fink, tried to make me feel better. Apparently, many others had been subjected to similar treatment by that judge. I wasn't interested and quickly made my way up the stairwell to my office.

I called Susan and told her I'd had enough and would return to Cravath. "I didn't leave there to get humiliated," I told her. "I know they'd welcome me back."

"Let's face it," Susan told me, "you're not good at handling change. You never were. You can't quit. You'll look ridiculous if you go running back to Cravath. You've been looking forward to this job for four years. You finally have it, and you're going to quit after one week?"

She was right about me and change. Plus, there was something else about my distress that Susan nailed during our conversation. "Maybe this judge was meaner than she had to be," she told me, "but you went into her courtroom unprepared. At Cravath, you *never* did anything without being a thousand percent prepared. It's not enough just to *go* to court, you need to be on top of things once you're there."

CHAPTER 5

WILLIE BOY

On March 28, 1985, one month after I started as an AUSA, a woman named Diane Giacalone took down the Dellacroce case. She was one of the most senior lawyers in the office, having been there more than six years. Between her time in the office and a stint before that as a prosecutor in the Tax Division in Main Justice, she was also among the most experienced trial lawyers in the Eastern District. She knew her stuff.

Giacalone had grown up in the Richmond Hill section of Queens and attended Our Lady of Wisdom Academy in Ozone Park. She was a hard worker, a dedicated prosecutor. If there were significant others in her life, she kept them a secret. And despite a career that consisted solely of public service jobs, she owned a house in the upstate village of Hudson, where she spent a good deal of time in the summers. She had a life.

Nine defendants had been taken into custody, but Giacalone really cared about only one: Wilfred "Willie Boy" Johnson. It wasn't that he was the big fish in the case. That was Aniello Dellacroce, the underboss of the Gambino Family. The indictment also included three captains, or *capodecinas*: John Gotti, who at that point ran things at the Bergin Hunt & Fish Club in Queens; and Lenny DiMaria and Nicky Corozzo, who together were in charge of a crew based in the Canarsie section of Brooklyn. Of the others, three were made members of the Gambino Family: Gene Gotti, John Carneglia, and Dellacroce's son Armond, whom everyone called "Buddy." Willie Boy wasn't even a made guy. He'd never get made, for that matter, because he wasn't a full-blooded Italian.

Willie Boy wasn't even well known within law enforcement. In his fiftieth year,

he was five years older than John Gotti and had been in the Bergin crew since long before Gotti replaced Carmine and Danny Fatico as its captain in the late seventies. When
he wasn't in prison, Willie Boy was always around Gotti's club, and he was an "earner,"
for years steadily paying tribute to his captain from his gambling and loan-sharking
operations in Brooklyn. In sum, he was a loyal but junior associate in the Gotti crew.

On the day of the arrests, Willie Boy got all of Giacalone's attention because
the truth was he hadn't been quite as loyal as everyone believed. To the FBI, he was
5558-TE. "TE" is the Bureau's designation for its "top echelon" informants, its most
treasured assets in the fight against organized crime. Willie Boy had been regularly
meeting with the FBI for almost twenty years, a relationship that began when he was
in prison. The flip side of the oath of omertà is the mob's obligation to take care of
the family of a stand-up guy when he goes away. Back in the sixties Willie Boy had
been arrested, stood up, and went away, but nobody helped his wife and son, and they
struggled. This made him so angry he reached out to the FBI, telling them he'd be
willing to provide information. After he was released, that offer blossomed into one of
the most productive relationships in the history of the FBI in New York.

Willie Boy's value as an informant was the reason the FBI hadn't been involved
in his arrest or the other arrests earlier that day. Just before the case was indicted, the
Bureau approached Giacalone and the U.S. Attorney, Ray Dearie, to share some extremely confidential information: two of the defendants—Willie Boy Johnson and
Billy Battista—were sources, and Willie Boy was "TE." Neither Dearie nor Giacalone
had any idea; as far as the FBI was concerned, today's prosecutors were tomorrow's
defense lawyers, so the identities of sources were carefully kept from them.

When the agents told the prosecutors about Willie Boy and Battista (a low-level
truck hijacker with a much looser affiliation with the Gambino Family), they assumed
both informants would be removed from the indictment. But Johnson was going to
be charged with murder. In the late seventies, Aniello Dellacroce had been indicted
on racketeering and homicide charges in Florida along with an underling named Tony
Plate, who allegedly had killed a loan shark for his boss. Plate was a notorious tough
guy, and the evidence against him was plentiful. Dellacroce decided he'd have a better
chance of beating the case if Plate wasn't at the table with him, so Willie Boy went to
Florida and killed Plate. It worked; Dellacroce was tried alone and beat the case.

Now, six years on, Giacalone had enough evidence to charge Johnson with the
Plate murder. She told the FBI that rogue informants didn't get passes for murders,
no matter how valuable they were. She was backed up by Dearie, and together they

rebuffed the Bureau, and both Willie Boy and Battista were indicted. The FBI could do no more for their sources and walked away from the case for good.

Willie Boy's "209 file"—the mass of reports created from the information he'd supplied over the years—was literally two feet thick. Just about everybody in Gotti's crew had gone to jail at least once because of information Willie Boy had passed along. He'd told his handling agents about the crew's truck hijackings from Kennedy Airport as well as their loan-sharking operations and gambling businesses. He even gave up John Gotti for a murder in Staten Island, about which more later. In the jargon of his codefendants, Willie Boy was a rat, and had been very valuable to the FBI for a long time.

On the day of the arrests, Giacalone had him brought to her office so she could make a pitch to him. Susan Shepard, the chief of the Major Crimes Section, was also present. Giacalone wanted Willie Boy to become her witness.

Willie Boy was big and muscular, with a shock of greasy dark hair extending out over his forehead. He had a high-pitched voice that seemed out of place set against his imposing physical presence. After the handcuffs were removed, Giacalone got to the point.

"Mr. Johnson, the fact that you've been an FBI informant since 1966 will be made public in this case."

"You can't do that," he responded. "My whole family will be slaughtered."

"We are prepared to protect you."

"I don't want your protection. Why are you doing this to me? I was promised they would never tell anyone. Now you're going to tell John? I never would have met with them if there was any chance this could happen. You can't do this to me. I'm going to be killed. My whole family is going to be."

Giacalone laid out what was about to happen, and how Willie Boy could avoid it. In a matter of days, the informant file would be turned over to the defendants. He'd be detained pending the trial because the judge would know that if he were released on bail he'd flee rather than stick around to be killed. And if he remained in pretrial detention, the Gambino Family would try to kill him there as well, so he'd have to be housed in "the hole," the bleak solitary confinement the Bureau of Prisons euphemistically called "administrative segregation."

"You have two choices," Giacalone told him. "Choice number one is you cooperate and testify for me at trial. If you do, I'll tell the judge how much you helped out, and you'll probably get a much shorter sentence. I'll put you in the Witness Protection

Program, so when you get out of prison you and your family will have new identities in a relocation area. In the meantime, you'll be in the protective custody of the program, which is a lot more comfortable than the hole. Do you understand?"

Willie Boy was silent.

"Choice number two is you stay in the hole for a year until we try the case. If you get convicted, you'll get life for murdering Tony Plate. You'll spend the rest of your life in the hole for your own protection, because they'll always be looking to kill you, even in prison. If you somehow beat the case, John Gotti will kill you the moment you hit the street. So choice one is cooperate with us, do some time, and we'll relocate you and your family. Choice two is go to trial, and you'll either do life in the hole or get killed."

Willie Boy didn't even hesitate. "I will never testify against John Gotti. He's my friend."

"Mr. Johnson," Giacalone said, "my whole point is you really don't have any choice. If you don't cooperate, the best possible outcome for you is you'll spend the rest of your *life* in the hole. Twenty-three hours a day in lockdown; no contact with other people. That's what'll happen if you're convicted, and you *will* be. But if somehow I'm wrong and you manage to get acquitted, you know as well as I do you'll be killed as soon as you're out of jail. So, basically, you *have* to cooperate. It makes no sense not to take the opportunity I'm offering."

"No," Willie Boy said softly. "You can take me back downstairs now."

Giacalone was exasperated, but she could tell Willie Boy wasn't going to change his mind. The agents put his cuffs back on and escorted him out of the office. That afternoon the defendants appeared in court for arraignments. The indictment had been assigned to Judge Eugene Nickerson, who just over a month before had presided over my induction as an AUSA. Giacalone agreed to the release on bail of all the other defendants on various conditions, such as the posting of homes as collateral in case they skipped town. When it came to Willie Boy, however, she asked for detention.

"The reason is that Mr. Johnson has been an informant for the Federal Bureau of Investigation for a period of over fifteen years." The other defendants and their lawyers froze in disbelief: this was the first any of them had heard about it. Willie Boy was beside himself, but he'd known since his meeting with Giacalone that this was coming, and he'd frantically charted a course that he hoped would get him through it. He couldn't leave it to his lawyer, who was as surprised as all the others.

"Not true, Your Honor. I'm not no informant. I have talked to agents and everything, but I am not an informant."

It was an uncomfortable situation. Giacalone relayed to the court the conversation she'd had that morning with Johnson, in which he confirmed his relationship with the FBI and said he'd be killed if it were revealed. The judge ordered that Willie Boy be detained, agreeing that it was all too likely he'd flee if released.

To Jim Abbott, Willie Boy's handling agent at the FBI at the time, all this was a supreme act of treachery by the government. In exchange for Willie Boy's information, the FBI had promised him that his status would *never* be revealed. Now the same government that had made that promise had broken it. In Abbott's view, the pitch to Willie Boy was nothing less than extortion.

Abbott believed that Willie Boy should have been given an out. Even *had* he murdered Tony Plate—and Abbott didn't believe he had—Willie Boy could have been given the chance to plead guilty and do his time without his special status being revealed. Before sentencing, a message could have been sent to the judge that he'd been a TE informant—the FBI had done that before, without telling the prosecutors—and that would likely have shortened the sentence. A similar message could have been sent later to the Parole Commission. Willie Boy could even have continued as a valuable source, both in prison and when eventually released. Abbott believed, incorrectly, that the prosecutors had refused to consider that option because they needed Willie Boy's testimony so badly. As far as he was concerned, the session in Giacalone's office was more of a shakedown than an offer of a cooperation agreement.

I'd righted myself in the six weeks after my rocky start. With Susan's help, I'd taken something positive away from being humiliated at my first court appearance, and made it my business to be thoroughly prepared for everything I did. There were so many basics to learn: the Bail Act, the Speedy Trial Act, the Rules of Criminal Procedure, the Rules of Evidence. I'd immersed myself in all of it. I caught a couple dozen General Crimes cases, and everyone's written work—indictments, discovery letters to lawyers, letters and briefs to judges—had to be approved by supervisors. The feedback on mine had been overwhelmingly positive, which made me feel I was making the grade. It also resulted directly in an unusual assignment.

"I know you came here because you didn't want to be an associate anymore,"

Dave Kirby told me after calling me into his office that April, a few days after the arraignment in the Dellacroce case. He was in his typical position, feet up on the desk and a squash racket in his hand. "I know you want to try your own cases. But you're a very good writer, so I'm afraid I'm about to make you an associate again."

So began my participation in the Dellacroce case. Before it was over, it would come to be known as the Gotti case, the first of John Gotti's two federal RICO indictments. Kirby told me that Diane Giacalone needed help opposing a slew of pretrial motions. The defendants' lawyers had announced their plans to make dozens of challenges to the charges and the government's evidence. I was to write the brief opposing them. Diane also needed help reviewing hundreds of hours of wiretaps and bugs for more evidence. If the case went to trial, which was likely, I'd assist her, but that wouldn't happen for at least a year. In the meantime, I'd stop catching General Crimes cases so I'd have the time to focus on this one. I'd still pick up trials from other AUSAs who had scheduling conflicts, so the Dellacroce trial wouldn't be my first. It was clear I was being drafted, not being asked to volunteer. It was just as clear that this was a huge case for the office—Kirby said as much explicitly—and I'd have been crazy to resist. Still, he said that the office would be grateful if I took the job on and performed it well.

There was another dimension to Kirby's comments. More by his manner than through anything he said, he suggested that Diane wasn't easy to work with. Not everyone would be a good match for her, he told me, but he thought I had the personality to get along with her fine. But after an hour with Diane, I was wondering what Kirby was concerned about. Right off the bat I identified with her. Every horizontal surface in her office—desk, chairs, file cabinet tops, radiators—was covered with multiple stacks of paper. Most showed the discoloration and dryness that come with age, and the stacks were not neat. As she described the case to me, she'd occasionally begin casting about for documents. This involved navigating her way around several piles to a particular stack, then a methodical examination of the papers in it, beginning at the top and working her way down. She never finished looking through the stack or found what she was looking for, and even as these searches were going on she didn't stop talking about the case.

Diane was affable and gracious, with an easy smile and a good sense of humor. She told me she was a career prosecutor and more of a trial lawyer than a brief-writer, and needed someone who'd handle that side of things. She also wanted me to listen to months of 1981 wiretap recordings from a telephone in the Bergin Hunt & Fish Club and to the entire set of wiretap and bug tapes from Angelo Ruggiero's home in 1982.

"There are nuggets in those tapes," she said, "little pieces of evidence that will help our case. I want you to find them."

There were other tapes too. We'd use a Suffolk County gambling wiretap from the 1970s. George Foronjy, a loan shark victim who'd cooperated with the FBI and worn a wire, recorded a series of conversations with loan sharks who worked for two of our defendants. Finally, there were about six months of video recordings—hundreds of hours in total—that the New York City Police Department had taken from an apartment across the street from the Ravenite in the summer of 1979. One of my jobs would be to review them and make a composite videotape of gangsters entering and leaving the club on a regular basis as they paid respects and money to Neil Dellacroce.

Giacalone didn't say anything about my standing up in court and handling witnesses. That was fair enough. I'd never even seen a jury trial, so didn't feel slighted. And since I'd left Cravath only six weeks earlier, I still viewed myself as a support lawyer, whose job was to prepare others to do the actual talking. When I left Diane's office, I was excited, eager to roll up my sleeves in the fight against organized crime.

CHAPTER 6

WISEGUYSPEAK

Writing the brief in response to the defense motions was the most valuable learning experience I'd had as a lawyer. My friends in the General Crimes section were constantly picking up new cases and spending so much effort trying to get agents to meet with them and hustling from courtroom to courtroom that they had little time for anything else. There were briefing motions here and there, but everything was rushed and superficial. Most of us had come from big law firms, and we were all used to being much more thorough than our work as an AUSA permitted.

Once assigned to the Dellacroce case, I had the same luxury I'd enjoyed at Cravath. For six weeks I holed up in the same library in which I'd finished up my clerkship four years before. I made camp on the same long table, looking out on the beautiful park. Instead of the huge trial record from the school desegregation case, this time I surrounded myself with the indictment, Giacalone's lengthy prosecution memo, the huge pile of defense motions, and copies of every case they relied on.

My first task was to learn more about the charges. The history of La Cosa Nostra in New York is littered with stories of Irish guys—not Sicilians—doing stupid things, and one of the stupidest produced the centerpiece of our case. It was a scheme hatched in the early seventies to make money by kidnapping wiseguys' family members and holding them for ransom. Irish hoodlums would pull off the kidnappings by pretending to be cops.

In May of 1972, Manny Gambino became one of the victims of this ill-considered enterprise. Manny was Carlo Gambino's nephew, so in that sense he was Mafia royalty. The men who kidnapped him demanded a $300,000 ransom. They collected far less, as the family agreed to pay only $100,000. Then, as if impersonating cops to snatch gangsters' kids for ransom weren't risky enough, they killed Manny anyway.

Word spread among the wiseguys about the guys who were doing these kidnappings. It included the rumor that Jimmy McBratney, a Staten Islander, had been in on Manny Gambino's kidnapping and murder. John Gotti and Angelo Ruggiero saw the situation as an opportunity. What could be a better way to impress their boss than to whack the guys who snatched and killed his nephew? So on May 23, 1973, they walked into Snoope's, a Staten Island bar, with Ralph Galione, an associate from the Bergin Hunt & Fish Club. McBratney was seated at the bar. After a struggle, Gotti held one of McBratney's arms out to his side, Ruggiero held the other, while Galione shot the Irishman in the head.

The McBratney murder was one of the seven specific crimes Gotti was charged with in the Dellacroce indictment. He was also charged with two truck hijackings from JFK Airport in the late sixties, running a gambling business, aiding and abetting two armored car robberies in 1980, and loan-sharking.

It was clear from the first court appearance I attended that there was something special about Gotti. Dellacroce was the underboss, but he was old and frail and looked as if he'd been brought in from a nursing home. The other defendants all came across as ordinary guys, bewildered by the formality of the courtroom and off their stride. And they orbited around Gotti, who was confident, handsome, well dressed, completely at home in the courtroom, and in charge not only of the other defendants but their lawyers as well.

This was not a modern-day gangster. I'd already learned enough about the Mafia in New York to know that its bread and butter was labor racketeering. If you owned the right union, you could own an industry, or at least a big enough slice of one to siphon tens of millions of dollars a year out of it. And if you owned it for long enough, you didn't even have to threaten or kill to maintain your position. Everyone knew Gambino captain "Jimmy Brown" Failla owned Bernie Adelstein, the corrupt leader of Teamsters Local 813, and they'd known it for so long that no one ever dared to bid for commercial garbage-carting contracts in the city. The prices charged by the companies that were "with" Jimmy Brown were a little high, but the mob's presence was so entrenched there was never any need to tell potential competitors that if they bid against those companies they would get whacked. The same arrangements existed for pouring concrete on major construction projects, unloading cargo ships at the piers, moving racks of clothing around the garment center, plumbing and drywall work on new high-rises, and numerous other industries. The money flowed in, and the wiseguys in charge rarely broke a sweat and never got their hands dirty.

Gotti knew nothing about labor racketeering except it was happening on a large scale and his crew saw none of the riches from it. One of thirteen children, he was born in the Bronx on October 27, 1940, but the family moved when he was a boy to East New York, Brooklyn's roughest neighborhood. After dropping out of high school at sixteen, he joined the Fulton-Rockaway Boys gang, a breeding ground for Mafia members, where he met Angelo Ruggiero. An early job as a truck driver's helper prepared Gotti well for his first mob specialty: hijacking cargo trucks leaving nearby JFK Airport. That was big business back then, and it brought Gotti, Ruggiero, and Gotti's younger brother Gene into the Bergin and under the supervision of Carmine and Danny Fatico, who jointly captained a crew there. Surveillance photos taken outside the club in the seventies show the cocky, well-dressed John Gotti, looking like a character in *Saturday Night Fever*, using the reflection off the front window to brush his hair. The other members of the crew had the same attitude, giving the finger to the surveillance agents and dropping their pants for the cameras. They all hijacked trucks, and on the few occasions when they got caught, did short federal prison terms, and they could live with that. Then they expanded into running numbers and dice games, and the debts those businesses generated became their loan shark books. More than anything else, they were tough guys. When they were given "a piece of work," as John Gotti called a murder that was ordered from on high, they did it. There were made guys and even captains in the Castellano faction who'd never once killed, but for those around Gotti it was a given, a baseline requirement.

John Gotti married Victoria DiGiorgio, a half-Italian, half-Russian daughter of immigrants he met in a bar in 1958. They had five children and lived in the Howard Beach section of Queens, close to JFK. Their youngest son, Frank, was killed at age twelve in March 1980 when he drove a motorized bike into the street and was hit by a car. The driver, neighbor Frank Favara, disappeared a few months later, killed by members of the Bergin crew, which Gotti had taken over from the aging Faticos. By then the crew was also moving heroin. They were all tough guys, earners for their captain and for their underboss down at the Ravenite. Their loyalty to "Neil," as they called Dellacroce, was undiluted, as was their animosity toward Paul Castellano. Such was Gotti's world.

On paper, we had strong evidence of the McBratney murder. In 1975, Gotti and Ruggiero had pled guilty to the killing in state court in Staten Island. That they'd admitted to a homicide might seem strange, but it was a sweetheart deal. Even though the murder was an execution (and Galione, the shooter, was himself executed a few months later), Gotti was allowed to plead guilty to only attempted manslaughter in the second degree, for which his sentence was just two years in prison. Gotti had been represented by the infamous Roy Cohn, and informants reported that Cohn had bought the plea bargain with a bribe. This perversion of justice had an upside: Gotti's admission was a matter of public record, and we could use it at our trial. So was his admitting to the two truck hijackings for which he'd served three years in the late sixties.

The racketeering charge would be proven by establishing that Gotti had committed a series of other crimes—called "predicate acts"—as his way of participating in what was called an "enterprise," the legal term for an organized crime group. We'd use three of his prior convictions as predicates. They'd be easy to prove at trial, because we could offer in evidence the court judgments convicting him of those crimes as well as the transcripts of his guilty pleas. But there was a much bigger downside, which would be the jurors' natural reaction to our recycling old cases in this way. Sure, they'd be told that it was not "double jeopardy" to use old convictions as predicates for a racketeering charge. But just because the jurors would be told that it was *legal* to hold Gotti accountable again for crimes for which he'd already served prison time, that wouldn't make it *fair*. Juries value fairness. We were going to have that huge problem at trial, and it would outweigh the benefit of being able to prove three of our predicate acts so easily.

The charges against the other defendants were a similar potpourri of crimes committed over many years. Willie Boy Johnson was charged with killing Tony Plate and with the same gambling and loan-sharking John Gotti was charged with. John Carneglia, one of the biggest earners in Gotti's crew, was charged with the 1976 murder of a New York State court officer, Albert Gelb, in addition to a couple of airport hijackings and the two armored car robberies. Lenny DiMaria's racketeering acts were possession of untaxed cigarettes, loan-sharking, and gambling. Dellacroce, the underboss of the family, was charged with aiding and abetting everyone else's crimes.

As I worked through the motions and learned the case, the unifying theme of the various racketeering acts became clear. They fell into three categories. Some were the defendants' prior convictions. Others grew out of cases Diane had previously prosecuted against the defendants' underlings. Finally, there were crimes James Cardinali, Eddie Maloney, Sal Polisi, and several other accomplice witnesses would testify about at trial. They'd each told Giacalone about illegal acts they'd committed with—or heard about from—one or more of our defendants.

There were thirty-two separate challenges to our indictment and our evidence in the defendants' motions. The cream of the organized crime bar in New York consisted of highly skilled legal beagles, who knew the law and wrote great briefs, and also courtroom lawyers who'd stand in front of juries at trial. The papers I was responding to had been written by some of the best in the former group. I read and took notes on every case they cited. Then I went on to all the other cases—the ones they didn't cite—on the same issues, cataloguing each and carefully noting the differences not only in the outcomes but in the language they used.

The motions covered all the usual topics. The defendants moved for a witness list and a statement from us naming every one of the conspirators, even if they weren't charged as defendants. They challenged searches conducted by state and federal agents and wiretaps authorized by federal and state judges. They objected to joining the defendants and the separate crimes in one case, and argued for a large number of unconnected trials. They challenged the RICO statute itself on the grounds that it was unconstitutionally vague in every case and improperly used in this particular one. They asked for "bills of particulars"—that is, more precise statements from us as to what we claimed the defendants did, and who else was involved.

There were some unique motions as well. The dual status of Willie Boy Johnson and Billy Battista as both active members of the Gotti crew and active FBI informants created some tricky issues. We'd be offering at trial statements Willie Boy made to other people while they were committing crimes. A statement by a co-conspirator in furtherance of a conspiracy is exempted from the rule disallowing hearsay, meaning we could use it at trial. The theory is that each member of the conspiracy speaks as an agent for all. But, the defendants argued, Willie Boy was an informant, so he was an agent of the FBI at least as much as he was an agent of Gotti. He might have been talking to others in the Gotti crew just to generate information he could relay back to his FBI handlers. Why should those statements be admissible?

Willie Boy had his own arguments. If his FBI handlers knew all along that he was running a gambling business on Church Avenue, as charged, why wasn't that authorized by the FBI and therefore not a crime? Battista, who'd been charged only with truck hijackings and made bail on the day he was arrested, chose a different route. He jumped bail and became a fugitive, and if he's still alive he remains one to this day.

As I read on, it became clear that I wasn't learning all the governing law just for one case. I was getting an intensive introduction to areas I'd need to know my entire career as a prosecutor. Years later the research files I created would become the raw material for a treatise I wrote on federal criminal practice.

In addition to taking in all the basics, I realized that I'd need to learn the RICO law inside and out. By 1985 RICO had become the Babe Ruth of federal criminal laws. It allowed the government to charge in a single case, and include together in a single trial, defendants who previously had to be prosecuted separately. It also allowed the government to try in a single case all the crimes of a single defendant. Previously those charges had to be split up. Before RICO, our configuration of defendants and charges would have produced fifteen distinct trials, each involving only one or two defendants and a narrow slice of our evidence. In the courtroom, as in life, the whole is almost always greater than the sum of the parts, and RICO had become the bane of the existence of gangsters and their lawyers.

The Dellacroce indictment contained only two counts, and both were brought under the RICO law. Each defendant was charged in one count with participating in the affairs of an "enterprise" through a patchwork quilt of crimes; and in the other with conspiring to do so. As for the nature of the enterprise, instead of accusing the defendants of participating in the Gambino Family, the indictment alleged an enterprise consisting of only two crews and the underboss: Gotti's crew in Queens and the one captained by DiMaria and Corozzo in Brooklyn, supervised by Dellacroce in Manhattan. We'd have to prove beyond a reasonable doubt that this separate criminal organization operated within the Gambino Family. And it seemed clear that our defendants identified themselves as members of the Gambino Family, not some subset of it. Still, it would be odd indeed for a jury that decided our defendants had actually committed the crimes charged as part of their participation in organized crime to then acquit them because of a technical glitch in the precise definition of the enterprise.

Years later, long after the case was over, we'd discover how significant our charged enterprise turned out to be.

Once I finished my work on the motions (my brief ended up 136 pages long; my Cravath mentors would have been proud), my first job was to find as much evidence as possible in the various wiretaps and bugs. Since the scorched earth with the FBI over Willie Boy Johnson was still smoldering, I started with recordings we could get our hands on right away: the conversations intercepted at the Bergin by the Queens

District Attorney's Office back in 1981. There was a phone in the club, and the district attorney had had a wiretap on it for months. I spent a couple of hundred hours listening to the tapes, picking the conversations we'd use, then transcribing them.

On the bright side, it was a wiretap, so the audibility was great. When I switched to bug recordings later on, I'd have to listen to conversations over and over just to figure out what was being said. The beauty of a wiretap is that the words are spoken directly into a microphone.

I got steeped in mob language. For some reason I'd thought "youse" was a plural pronoun, but I quickly learned otherwise.

"Anybody else there?"

"No. I'm alone."

"Good. I'll come by youse in ten minutes."

The word "kid" connoted status, not age. To a made guy, an associate could be fifteen years older, but he would still be referred to as a "kid."

There were no "pleases" or "thank yous," and when a third person was needed to get something done, "I'll ask" was never part of the conversation. Not even "I'll get." "I'll *make* Frankie go over there and talk to him." Or "I'll make my wife bring that basket to his family."

The conversations had patterns. Ruggiero started almost all of his with food:

"Hey. It's Ange."

"Hey."

"J'eat yet?"

"Yeah."

"What'd j'eat?"

And predictable expressions. John Gotti was fond of "D'ya understand what I'm tryin' to say?" Sometimes it seemed unnecessary. "I hate that motherfucker. I'd like to fuckin' kill him. D'ya understand what I'm tryin' to say?" They understood all right. Other times it made sense. "I'm gonna be late because I gotta try to deal with this motherless fuck I spoke to that guy about at the other guy's place. D'ya understand what I'm tryin' to say?" Nope.

I learned the nicknames. "Ralphie Bones," "Georgie Butterass," "Benny Eggs," "Quiet Dom," not to be confused with "Skinny Dom," "Gaspipe," and on and on. Dozens of them. They didn't know each other's real names, so the nicknames could be used if they ever testified at trial. I figured we wouldn't need too much evidence to convict some of them, like "Pete the Killer." Anyone thinking of a life in the mob ought to consider their likely nickname ahead of time. When you're in front of a jury would you rather be "Good Lookin' Jackie" or "Mattress Face," "Sammy the Bull" or "Carmine the Snake"?

Except for a lot of illegal horse betting, there weren't many criminal conversations on the Bergin wire. Wiseguys, like all career criminals, are careful on the telephone, to the point where they sound as if they're talking about a crime even when they're not.

"Did you see that guy?" Angelo Ruggiero would ask Gotti.

"What guy?"

"The guy from over there. The one we saw last week."

"The tall guy?"

"No, the other guy! The one with the fuckin' . . . the guy who had the union beef last year."

"The guy from 86th Street?"

"No, not that guy! The other one, who we saw with what's his name from Canarsie!"

Every once in a while wiseguys ended up whacking the wrong guy. After all those hours listening to them, I found myself wondering why that didn't happen more often.

Though it didn't produce blockbuster evidence, the Bergin wiretap covered valuable ground. We had a gambling predicate, and since gambling is a minor-league crime it's okay to discuss by telephone. Literally thousands of bets were placed on or relayed over the Bergin phone each week. Most were on horses running at the Aqueduct Racetrack in Queens or at Monmouth Park Racetrack in Jersey—exactas, trifectas, quinellas, every kind of bet on a horse or combination of horses. I learned what they were, then picked about a hundred of the bets to play at the trial.

The Bergin wire also proved what a degenerate gambler Gotti was. He'd bet $10,000 on a single race. He was always being given tips, but they weren't very good, because he never won. If being a lousy gambler were a crime, we'd have had him dead to rights. Nor was he any good at paying what he owed. I listened to scores of state wiretaps of his bookmakers scrambling to "lay off" his bets. A normal bettor could be threatened or required to pay up front or have his debt converted into a loan shark loan, but this wasn't a normal bettor. So the bookmakers spread the risk among themselves.

The Bergin tapes also helped us prove that Gotti was the boss of the Bergin crew. In the memorable "Buddy My Balls" conversation—a blistering rant by Gotti directed at associate Tony Moscatiello (more about that later)—Gotti established beyond a doubt that he was the captain of the mobsters he'd inherited from Carmine and Danny Fatico.

Finally, the Bergin wire brought our case some levity. In one conversation an unknown caller asked for Frank "The Beard" Guidice, and when Guidice got on the phone the caller said he wanted to come to the club to "pay the vig on his loan." Vig is the exorbitant interest that makes loan-sharking so lucrative a business. Guidice yelled that he had no idea what the caller was talking about and slammed the receiver down. This was typical wiseguy behavior—horse-betting was one thing, but you don't talk about loan-sharking on the phone. And yet Guidice immediately picked up the same telephone and told a guy named Tony, "You won't believe what this fucking moron just did! This motherfucker just called and told me he was comin' down here to pay his fuckin' vig. Do you believe that? Just like that he said it, right on the fuckin' phone!"

Another source of levity was Detective Mike Falciano, an old-timer who worked on the Bergin investigation for the Queens District Attorney's Office. "The Falcon," as everyone called him, was well into his fifties. He supplemented what we learned from the wire by making "overhears" on the sidewalk directly outside the Bergin, where the real criminal conversations were happening. Wiseguys would naturally pause their conversations if any stranger, cop or otherwise, was walking or standing nearby. But the Falcon outfoxed them. One scheme he used to great effect was pretending to be a homeless person. At four in the morning he would hide a partially eaten sandwich under a pile of trash in the garbage can on the sidewalk outside the club. The next afternoon he'd stumble by, dressed in a stained old raincoat, and begin foraging. The wiseguys would watch in disgust as he discovered the sandwich, unwrapped it, and slowly ate what remained. But then they'd resume their talk of stolen loads or loan shark victims who refused to pay up. The Falcon got some pretty good overhears that way.

Our main contact with the Queens District Attorney's Office for this evidence was the Falcon's younger colleague, Detective Vic Ruggiero. Vic was a good and cooperative cop. By the time we started on the Dellacroce case, he had retired from the police department and joined a private investigation firm, but he was still helping us out and was our main witness when the defense asked for the Bergin wiretap to be suppressed.

Mike Coiro, who'd been house counsel to the Gotti crew for years, cross-examined Vic at the hearing, and began by saying, "Detective Ruggiero—I'm sorry, you're off the job now—*Mr.* Ruggiero . . ." Vic stiffened visibly on the witness stand,

and after the hearing ended he was furious. "There was no mistake there," he told me in my office. "He was telling me that I'm off the job so I no longer have the protection that comes with being a cop. That was a threat."

I hadn't perceived it that way at all—I thought Coiro had just misspoken—but figured Vic would know better than me. In any event, he was beside himself with anger and fear, which immediately made me worry whether we could rely on him as a witness at trial.

CHAPTER 7

THE CAST

One of the most interesting parts of putting our case together was meeting our "accomplice witnesses," a ragtag bunch of hoodlums who barely deserved to be called accomplices. They were criminals certainly, but low-level hangers-on to a man, and for the most part they hadn't even committed their crimes with our defendants. Still, each one of the six, Eddie Maloney, Sal Polisi, James Cardinali, Dominick LoFaro, George Foronjy, and Matt Traynor, was headed for a brief moment in the limelight.

Eddie Maloney was one of the Irishmen who, along with Jimmy McBratney, had been involved in the snatching of wiseguys' kids. He'd come to the government for protection after being shot multiple times in the Cozy Corner, a bar in the Maspeth section of Queens run by Phil Cestaro, a bookmaker and member of John Gotti's crew. It was amazing that Maloney had survived. When the final bullet was fired, it was from a handgun placed in the center of the Irishman's forehead.

When I asked Maloney how he'd survived, he said, "it only went in about this far," holding his thumb and index finger about two inches apart. I thought that even in a blockhead like his—his eyebrows were like wire brushes—there was some important stuff in that space. Whether it was from that adventure or not, Maloney was slow and difficult to prepare. More important, though he had damning testimony to give about Cestaro, he had almost nothing that was admissible against our particular defendants.

Sal Polisi was a colorful character from Queens who'd been to the Bergin and knew the people in Gotti's crew. He'd flipped a couple of years earlier after he was arrested for bribing a judge to help beat a drug case. The judge was named William

Brennan, but it wasn't the famous Supreme Court justice. This Justice Brennan was a corrupt trial judge in state court in Queens, and Polisi had testified in our office's successful racketeering prosecution of him.

As if being a drug dealer who'd bribed a judge weren't enough to damage his credibility, in 1974 Polisi tried to beat another rap by feigning insanity. Represented by Mike Coiro, Polisi pretended that mental illness rendered him unfit to stand trial. This earned him the Italianate nickname "Sally Ubatz"—Crazy Sally. He told us that after one of his court appearances he'd been driven home by Coiro, who made a stop at Roy Cohn's Manhattan townhouse. Gotti and Angelo Ruggiero were there, and according to Polisi they were celebrating Cohn's fixing a case involving Gotti. I had the docket sheet in Polisi's case, which showed that his court appearance occurred at the same time Cohn and Coiro had obtained the two-year deal for Gotti and Ruggiero for the murder of Jimmy McBratney.

At least Maloney and Polisi had provable connections to our defendants. James Cardinali, our most important accomplice by far, didn't. Cardinali decided to cooperate after being prosecuted for murder. In exchange for a manslaughter plea and a dramatically reduced sentence, Cardinali would testify that he'd been a regular at the Bergin from 1979 to 1981. He said that Gotti had told him he'd killed the kidnapper of Manny Gambino; Willie Boy Johnson had let it drop that he'd killed Tony Plate; and John Carneglia, the biggest earner in Gotti's crew, had freely shared that he'd killed a court officer. Cardinali's testimony was the fulcrum of the three murder charges in our indictment.

Cardinali wasn't even on law enforcement's radar screen before he flipped. There was no shortage of surveillance photos taken at the Bergin over the years, but he'd never been identified in any. After he flipped, the photos were all scoured again—and we found a couple of grainy photos that appeared to show Cardinali on the sidewalk outside the club. That helped, but he hardly seemed to have the sort of presence at the Bergin that would explain why everyone would be comfortable talking about any illegal activity with him, let alone murders. As Gotti would tell me to my face when Cardinali finally testified, he was a "motherfuckin' coffee boy" at the club, and it was unlikely that a jury was going to believe that everyone there confided in him.

Dominick LoFaro was in Captain Ralph Mosca's crew, and for the purposes of our case would contribute to our gambling charge against Gotti. Mosca was in charge of lucrative operations in Queens and upstate as well, and LoFaro worked in them. However, he made his real money selling heroin, and in 1983 he was arrested up in Orange County for drug trafficking. It was a big case at the time; LoFaro had distributed more than twenty-five kilograms of heroin, and the New York State Organized Crime Task Force seized $300,000 in cash from him when he was arrested.

LoFaro had known what he'd do if he ever got locked up for his heroin-dealing, and he didn't even want to be taken before a judge and arraigned. He cooperated immediately, agreeing to wear a wire to record a couple of years' worth of conversations with Ralph Mosca and others in Mosca's crew.

LoFaro had been allowed to keep $100,000 of the money seized from him. Because that was drug money, it would damage his credibility at trial. Also, when he started puffing about how valuable he'd be as a witness, he stretched the truth. He told the state prosecutors he was a made guy, and that he'd been sent on important missions to kill people for the Gambino Family, including one in which he killed five people with an Uzi. None of it was true.

LoFaro was our most forgettable witness. He talked slowly and seemed older than his fifty-six years. He helped Ralph Mosca run gambling businesses, and once he went with a carful of others to the Bergin to report to John Gotti about them. That was basically his entire contribution to our case. It's hard to make the world of organized crime seem boring, but LoFaro pulled it off. He was a one-man sedative.

George Foronjy was not, strictly speaking, an accomplice; he was really a victim. He'd come to the FBI because he was so far into the loan sharks and so unable to pay them back that he was about to get hurt. One of his creditors was Ralph "The Fly" Davino, an associate in the crew run by Lenny DiMaria and Nicky Corozzo. Turning to the FBI didn't get Foronjy away from the "shylocks," as Mafia loan sharks call themselves, at least not immediately. The FBI wired him up and sent him right back into them, hoping to record threats that would lead to arrests. Of all the proactive uses of cooperators, putting loan shark victims back on the street was one of the riskiest. The idea was to get solid evidence that they'd be roughed up without their actually getting beaten. We didn't need to worry too much about their getting killed. The whole point of any violence was to get debtors to cough up, and dead men don't pay.

Foronjy related some harrowing situations in ways that made us laugh. One of his loan sharks tended bar at the Georgetown Inn in Brooklyn, and Foronjy went there wired up to tell him he needed more time. The loan shark seemed fine with that news, and for a while they continued talking. Then all of a sudden on the tape Foronjy began mumbling loudly and continuously, and a careful listener could make out the word "gun." The bartender had put the business end of a handgun in Foronjy's mouth to make the point that he had to pay. Foronjy was trying to get the attention of the agents sitting outside in the car, who were caught napping. They should have hustled into the bar and arrested the loan shark.

On another occasion, Foronjy was about 150 feet from a daytime meeting on the street with a loan shark when the wire for his hidden microphone became unattached. Seconds from meeting an angry wiseguy with a gun, Foronjy looked down to see a twelve-inch piece of wire dragging behind him out of the bottom of his pant leg. Instead of freezing or trying to run, he unzipped his fly and started pissing on the sidewalk. The loan shark did an about-face and walked away. "Better off him thinking I was crazy than I was cooperating!" Foronjy said with a laugh.

He was a Brooklyn guy and had never even been to the Bergin. He helped us only against DiMaria and Corozzo, so his usefulness was limited; but he was a good witness.

Not all the colorful characters we'd lined up stayed on our roster. Matt Traynor had decided to cooperate after being convicted of bank robbery out in Nassau County. Like Cardinali, he'd been in and out of the Bergin, and he told us he'd been involved in some of the airport hijackings with the Gotti brothers. It was good enough testimony for us to rescue him from state custody and place him in a federal Witness Protection unit, where he was housed with Cardinali.

Traynor wasn't shy, and he was demanding. He wanted sneakers, commissary money, visits with family. Diane was good at saying no, which annoyed him, and in response to one of her no's he blundered, telling Diane that if he didn't get what he wanted he'd contact the defense lawyers and tell them that she'd asked him to lie. Faced with a witness who was both willing to give false testimony and trying to shake us down, we tore up Traynor's deal and crossed him off our witness list. Then, fulfilling our constitutional obligation to the defense lawyers, we told them they should interview him. We thought that was the end of him.

Most of our witnesses weren't accomplices. Rather, for one reason or another, they simply knew something useful. They ranged from people who happened to be in Snoope's Bar when McBratney was killed, to truckers whose loads got hijacked, to people with personal relationships with our defendants or their colleagues in crime. In canvassing what we had, I saw several instances of Diane's investigative brilliance. Much of our evidence about the armored car robberies was the result of what she called "girlfriend days" in the grand jury. Those robberies were committed by young men who hung around the Bergin. Our theory was that the proceeds of the robberies were shared with Gotti and others. Diane subpoenaed their present and former girlfriends to appear before the grand jury at the same time. Then she'd show up a half hour late, requiring them to sit together in the windowless, closet-sized waiting area next to the grand jury room. By the time she arrived to take their testimony, the women were eager to tell her terrible things about the men they'd been fighting over.

One of our pretrial issues required a road trip. It was an issue involving Barry Slotnick and his partner, Bruce Cutler, both on the defense team. Slotnick, a prominent mob lawyer in New York, represented Dellacroce, while Slotnick's protégé, Cutler, represented John Gotti. This situation presented a potential conflict of interest. The clash could be waived by the defendants, but that waiver had to be on the record and it had to follow a thorough explanation by the judge of the risks each defendant was taking. Dellacroce, according to his doctor's affidavit, was too sick to come to court, so we all made a road trip to his home on West Fingerboard Road in Staten Island.

The caravan across South Brooklyn to the Verrazzano-Narrows Bridge included Judge Nickerson, a deputy marshal, and a court reporter in one car; Diane Giacalone and me in another; and about four other vehicles bearing the defendants and their lawyers. When we arrived, Dellacroce's longtime girlfriend, Rosemary Connelly, was there to greet us. The home was immaculate, though a little disorienting because there were mirrors everywhere. Silver trays with Italian pastries were everywhere too.

Once everyone was present, we were ushered into Dellacroce's bedroom. A chair was brought in for the court reporter. The rest of us stood. Even at the time I realized how ridiculous the scene was. Crowded into the small room were Slotnick, Cutler, Gotti, the court reporter, Judge Nickerson, Dellacroce's doctor, Diane, and me. Dellacroce was lying in the bed, looking like death itself. The covers were not rumpled at all.

Waiver proceedings require a judge to explain to defendants all the ways that lawyers with a potential conflict of interest could screw their clients. While Judge Nickerson was in the middle of that, Dellacroce silently signaled his doctor, who asked the judge if we could take a break. Always the gentleman, the judge agreed, and we all trudged out into the living room. There weren't enough places to sit, so the judge and the court reporter took chairs while the rest of us stood awkwardly. Gotti seemed to make a point—both in the bedroom and in the living room—of holding himself especially erect. It was a military pose, arms folded in front, but he kept a smirk on his face.

The judge reached for a pastry and took a bite. There we were, in the living room of the underboss of the Gambino Family, and the silence was overwhelming. Judge Nickerson looked up at the group and asked politely: "Has anyone seen the movie *Prizzi's Honor?*" To this day that remains one of the best icebreaker lines I've ever heard, but the judge had no takers. About a minute later the doctor appeared and broke the silence, and we reassembled in the bedroom to complete the waiver proceeding.

Throughout it all, Dellacroce looked terrible. Giacalone and I were certain he was faking, and we even thought he'd been made up to appear paler than usual. Within a matter of weeks, a surprising revelation proved us at least partially correct. We learned that the FBI had a bug in his house. If they hadn't turned it off while we were there, it would have recorded Judge Nickerson's *Prizzi's Honor* line. And we'd also learn that, in a long conversation the day before, Dellacroce had kicked Gambino captain Mike Caiazzo out of the Family and mused out loud in his growling voice about whether to put him in a "fucking hole in the ground" for making the wrong guy the acting captain of Caiazzo's crew. The conversations recorded by the bug vindicated our suspicions, but not completely. Dellacroce was either truly ill or on the verge of being so; in less than five months he'd be dead.

The signs of dysfunction in our relationship with the FBI's Gambino Squad, which began when we burned Willie Boy, had already become too numerous to count. But this one topped them all, at least to that point—a court-ordered bug in the living room of our lead defendant in an indicted case, and we had no idea.

We were living with an FBI problem because Diane Giacalone had burned their informants, and by the fall of 1985 it was becoming increasingly clear we needed to put our two houses in order. It's hard to catalogue all that FBI agents typically do to help prosecutors. They serve subpoenas on uncooperative witnesses, bring cooperative ones in for pretrial prep, keep track of the physical evidence, prepare transcripts of recorded conversations, and do countless other tasks, all the while continuing to investigate right up to and during the trial itself. In the months leading to a major trial like ours, the prosecutors are in constant touch not only with the assigned case agent but with other agents as well.

Two features of our case made it particularly FBI-dependent. More than half a dozen of the predicate acts in our RICO counts had been prior FBI prosecutions. We needed everything from those trials: transcripts, minutes of guilty pleas, physical evidence, and witness statements. Though Diane served as prosecutor for some of those cases, which helped, we were almost entirely dependent on the Bureau for the others, including various airport hijacking cases from the 1970s.

Second, I'd be mining more than half a dozen wiretaps and bugs for evidence. I'd already begun doing that with the state wiretap at the Bergin, but two FBI bugs were especially critical. The 1982 bug in Angelo Ruggiero's home produced hundreds of hours of recorded conversations over several months. The recently disclosed bug in Dellacroce's home lasted only a month but produced dozens of hours of potentially useful conversations. The testimony about the various admissions our defendants made to our accomplice witnesses—especially James Cardinali—would need all the corroboration we could get.

Bug recordings were a logistical nightmare. The original tapes were kept on big reels that had been sealed up in boxes by the judge who'd supervised the electronic surveillance. They were preserved in the FBI's electronic surveillance storage space, or "Elsur Room." A court order based on an affidavit was needed to unseal them; duplicate tapes had to be made; the additional handling of the original reels had to be properly recorded on the chain of custody envelope containing each one; the monitoring logs had to be duplicated; the electronic surveillance orders and underlying affidavits had to be copied and produced; and the originals had to be taken back to court for resealing. It was a *lot* of effort even with an eager and dedicated FBI agent helping out. Without the Bureau's help, the hurdles could have been insurmountable.

Along the way we'd enlisted the help of the DEA, even though there were no narcotics allegations in the case. Their agents Ed Magnuson and Ron Melvin and NYPD detectives Bill Burns and Frank McCann assisted with subpoenas and witnesses. But there was no way those men would be able to bridge the gap between us and the Bureau. As excellent as FBI agents were in helping prepare for trial in one of their own cases, they were notoriously bad at cooperating with other agencies in the best of circumstances; the fact that Giacalone was the prosecutor made it impossible for the police department or DEA to get their cooperation.

That left *me*. I wasn't involved in the decision to burn Willie Boy. I was new to the office. I was thirty-one years old but looked ten years younger. And I found exactly the right path to what we needed: the Organized Crime Strike Force.

The Strike Force was a separate cadre of federal prosecutors in the same courthouse complex we were in. It was barely a tenth the size of our office—about twenty lawyers all told—and it focused solely on Italian organized crime within the U.S. Established by Attorney General Bobby Kennedy in 1967, the Strike Forces answered not to U.S. Attorneys but directly to the Organized Crime Section in Main Justice. In 1985 there were fourteen Strike Forces around the country, in all the places you'd expect, with a single exception: the Southern District of New York. Given how pervasively the Mafia was engaged in all sorts of crime, it was inefficient, to put it mildly, to have two sets of federal prosecutors in the same district competing to chase overlapping groups of criminals. The Southern District, always in its own mind first among equals and more powerful than any other U.S. Attorney's Office, had succeeded years earlier in forcing the Southern District Strike Force to merge with its U.S. Attorney's Office. In 1985 all the other Strike Forces were still in place. Within four years they too would be merged into their local U.S. Attorney's Offices, but in the meantime the Eastern District Strike Force would become very important to Diane and me.

The FBI's Gambino Squad worked hand in glove with the Brooklyn Strike Force. The two had worked together to bug both Ruggiero's home in 1982 and Dellacroce's in the summer of 1985, so when we needed recordings from these bugs in our case, I presented myself to the Strike Force. And when I did, the attorney in charge assigned Laura Ward to help me.

Ward was to the Strike Force what I was to the U.S. Attorney's Office—young, eager, full of innocence and dedication. She was my age, with a relentlessly upbeat personality. In addition, she seemed to know everyone. Part of it was her outgoing nature, but it was also because she'd literally grown up in the Southern District courthouse, where her father, Robert Ward, was a respected judge. Like me, Ward had come to the government from a large law firm, so we had the same enthusiasm for the real-world, in-court work we'd recently signed up for. Most important, neither of us cared about the squabbling that preceded us and had divided the Gambino Squad and my office. I needed the Ruggiero and Dellacroce bugs, and that was good enough for her. She got me duplicates of the applications, court orders, and monitoring logs, and gave me her own copies of the recordings.

Ward and I meshed well; whereas I was likely to forget and misplace things, she was meticulous and ultra-organized. As our relationship grew, she'd call to remind me of things I needed to do: disclosures to the defense; resealing orders; chain of custody requirements. For my part, I was spending hundreds of hours in my office on the opposite side of the courthouse complex, headphones on, listening over and over again to the recordings, finding ways, some big but mostly little, for them to beef up our case.

I was still new to the job, but I had a good feel for which conversations would be both accessible to a jury and add value to our cause. Once I found them, I'd spend long hours perfecting the transcripts, preparing excerpts that provided sufficient context to fend off claims of cherry-picking but still make a point crisply and without boring a jury. Ward made sure I tended to all the details I had to. We got along great, and since she was loved by all the FBI agents on the Gambino Squad, they began to take to me despite my association with Diane.

For her part, Diane was grateful for the relationship I forged with Ward. She watched it from a distance with great interest, as she knew better than anyone how difficult it is to prosecute high-level members of organized crime without the help of the FBI. She wanted the Bureau's help very much, but it wasn't in her makeup to try to rebuild the relationship. She was tough and believed the FBI had gotten too close to its informant and was now trying to protect him from being held accountable for murder. The Bureau was just as dug in, convinced she'd unnecessarily burned Willie Boy. That schism would never be repaired.

CHAPTER 8

INTO THE SPOTLIGHT

Neil Dellacroce died on December 2, 1985—of natural causes, in his bed, without ever serving a significant prison term, a rare trifecta for such a longtime ruthless gangster.

Within days, his death produced our first big break. Jerry Shargel, the lawyer for Buddy Dellacroce, was in our office telling us that Buddy would plead guilty to the racketeering conspiracy charge. We'd been aware that John Gotti needed Neil Dellacroce to protect him from Paul Castellano. When Jerry came to us, we realized for the first time that Buddy also needed Neil. We should have realized it. Buddy was a fun-loving, drug-abusing loser—everything his father wasn't. Once Neil was gone, there was no reason for anyone to lift a finger for Buddy, and his codefendants saw him as a liability because of his drug habit.

Through Shargel, Buddy offered to plead guilty to one of the two counts, meaning he'd face up to twenty years in jail. This was great news, as it would validate our case to have one of the accused admit the crime. It would also remove a defendant from a defense table that was already too crowded. Finally, it would remove Shargel from the trial, and he was hands-down the best defense lawyer in the case.

There were two catches. First, Buddy would plead guilty only if we agreed not to call him as a witness. Second, we'd have to allow him to be released from jail for the three months between his guilty plea and his sentencing.

The first catch was easy. There'd be no reason for us to call Buddy. For one thing, he wouldn't help our case. He was a gangster, and an unintelligent one at that. Also, he'd be petrified of the people he was testifying against. Besides, we wouldn't need him. If he pled guilty, we'd be able to use the transcript of Buddy's plea against the others at trial. There was a case from the Second Circuit, *United States v. Winley*, that allowed the guilty plea of one conspirator to be used at the trial of the others to prove the existence of the conspiracy. I was particularly eager to get Buddy's admission that the enterprise we'd alleged—two crews reporting to their underboss—existed within the Gambino Family. So we had no problem agreeing to Shargel's first condition.

The second was problematic. Releasing Buddy would turn the system on its head. Before his plea, Buddy had been presumed innocent and entitled to bail, but he'd blown that early on by violating the conditions of his bail. So we had someone already in custody on the grounds he was a flight risk who wanted to be sprung from jail after admitting he was guilty of racketeering. Usually, pleading guilty is what gets someone *into* jail, not what gets them out. However, the gift of a guilty plea, and the fact that we could use it against the other defendants, was too attractive to turn down. Diane and I persuaded our boss Ray Dearie that it was worth it.

On December 6, 2005, Buddy pled guilty and was released on a bond signed by several neighbors and family members, who posted their homes as "collateral" for him. He promptly absconded, and they lost the equity in their homes as a result.

Even though it gave us our first conviction, Diane and I were deeply disappointed by Dellacroce's death. He was our lead defendant, and our most important. Now we were stuck with a trial involving mostly low-level gangsters, as they appeared to us then. Everyone in law enforcement knew we'd indicted an important case, but its significance all but disappeared with Dellacroce's death. Also, we'd have to try a case about two crews reporting to an underboss without the underboss at the defense table.

Then on December 16 Sparks happened. It was a Monday evening. By the time the television programs were interrupted by news bulletins, it was about eight o'clock. I'd gotten home to my Carroll Gardens apartment about a half hour earlier and had fallen asleep in our bedroom. My wife, Susan, woke me to tell me to come out to the living room to watch what was happening because Paul Castellano was dead and John Gotti was going to be the new Gambino boss. Literally overnight—before the completion of a single news cycle—our case was transformed. For nine months our lead defendant had been an underboss no one outside of law enforcement had ever heard of. Now our lead defendant was a boss-in-waiting well on his way to becoming a household name.

We were still four months away from jury selection, so Diane and I took off Christmas Day. Susan and I spent it in Connecticut with my oldest sister, Kathy, and her husband, Chuck, who had assumed the roles of matriarch and patriarch after my mom died in 1982. My sisters Mary and Eileen and my brother Kevin were also there, all with their families. At the time they had eleven kids among them, so it was a happy and chaotic day.

The conversation away from the kids was all about Gotti. Everyone had known I'd become a federal prosecutor early in the year, and over the summer I'd told the family I was assigned to a Mafia case. But in the eight days since Castellano and Bilotti had been gunned down no one had made the connection between me and the media blitz.

"You're on *that* case?" Kathy asked, surprised and obviously worried, after I announced that John Gotti was my defendant.

"Well, we're not prosecuting the Castellano murder," I replied. "That crime is only nine days old. But Gotti is a defendant in the racketeering case I've been working on since April. And now he's the lead defendant."

I regaled them with stories about Gotti. He was a ruthless, violent, drug-dealing upstart from Queens, I told them, who took over the Gambino Family in a violent coup just before he was about to be whacked himself by the guy he'd killed. We were going to nip his career in the bud by getting him sentenced to life in prison.

My siblings, ever protective of their baby brother, were concerned, but they couldn't help being fascinated. All of a sudden, less than a year removed from the staid corridors of Cravath, their brother was a celebrity prosecutor.

I was flush with their attention. My brothers and sisters were an accomplished group. Our parents had one high school degree between them, but their seven kids excelled: advanced degrees; three college professors; the chief of pulmonology at a medical school; two other teachers; and me, the lawyer. They'd all nurtured me growing up—I couldn't have had a better or happier childhood—but with all they had going on no one had had any reason to notice me for anything other than being the baby. Now they were taking notice of something else, and I liked that more than I'd expected.

A couple of days later Mary called me at work. My brothers and sisters never did that, so right away I knew something unusual was up.

"Oh, Yonnie"—the nickname only she used for me—"I have to tell you something," she said. She was trying to be her usual upbeat self, but it was obvious she was distraught. The possibilities began popping into my head: she and Eddie were splitting up; one of them was gravely ill; something terrible had happened in one of our brothers' or sisters' families.

"What's the matter?"

"We knew all year you were on an organized crime case, but we didn't know until Christmas that John Gotti was one of the defendants."

"Well, hardly anyone did. But I don't understand why you're so upset."

"You're not going to believe this," Mary said, "and Eddie is sick about it."

"What?"

"They're related."

"Eddie is related to John Gotti?"

"Yes. They're cousins."

"'Cousins' covers a lot of ground," I said cautiously. "What's the exact relationship?"

"They're first cousins, Yonnie. Eddie's mom and John Gotti's father are brother and sister."

"Wow" was all I could come up with. I spent about ten minutes telling Mary not to worry, and that it wouldn't pose an issue at all. I'm sure it wasn't a very convincing effort, since I actually thought it was a huge problem.

"Well, who'da thought we'd have this snag and it would be *you*?" Ray Dearie said the next day when Diane and I went to his office. "Diane grew up Italian in Queens and walked past these guys' social clubs every day on her way to grammar school. If we found out she had some family relationship with one of these guys, that'd be one thing. But you? The Irish kid from Westchester? And your sister is married to Gotti's *first cousin*? You sure you want to stay on this case?"

I was. After my initial conversation with Mary, I spoke to her and Eddie together. He didn't know Gotti. The two strands of the family had stayed almost completely separate. Eddie's mom, Thomasina Gotti, had married Patrick Carvin, an Irish electrician, and moved to Mount Vernon, in lower Westchester, north of the city. Her brother John, the father of my defendant, stayed in Brooklyn, where they'd grown up. Eddie had been to the wake of one of their sisters, his aunt Connie, and Gene Gotti was there with some of his friends, but apart from that he never knew or saw his gangster cousins. He didn't care if I prosecuted them, and felt bad, even though he'd done nothing wrong, that he was causing me a problem.

I wasn't prohibited from staying on the case, but only barely. Before I told anyone, I'd hit the library to see if there were any rules about family relationships between prosecutors and the defendants they prosecute. There were, and they focused on the "degrees of consanguinity" between the two. Four degrees or less and you were toast. But I had five: me to my sister Mary, Mary to Eddie, Eddie to Thomasina, Thomasina to her brother John, and him to his son John, my defendant. I was free to prosecute my brother-in-law's first cousin.

"Not a word of this to anyone," Ray Dearie told us after he decided I could stay. "It will be on the front pages of the tabloids if it gets out, and Eddie's life won't be the same."

We now had a sprawling and sensational trial to prepare for, and less than four months to do it. Writing briefs wasn't new to me—that was all I'd done at Cravath—but trial prep was mostly uncharted territory. I'd managed to try three cases in the fall of 1985, before the Castellano murder, but they were all simple, with just a couple of witnesses each. The Gotti trial would include almost a hundred witnesses, some of whom Diane hadn't seen in ages, and others she'd never met at all. We had to find them, bring them in, talk to them about events that in most instances had occurred many years earlier, and prepare outlines for their direct testimony.

This experience was a revelation for me. I'd come into the job believing that prosecutors and agents were the good guys and that everyone felt the same way. I expected the people we were rounding up would admire what we were doing and be eager to play their part. Mistake.

One of my first witness prep sessions was with Miriam Arnold, and she quickly set me straight. Arnold had been in Snoope's Bar when Gotti and Angelo Ruggiero killed Jimmy McBratney. She remembered the details of the murder vividly, exactly as she had in the grand jury all those years earlier. But John Gotti was an unknown thug back in 1973, when she'd cooperated fully with the police and the district attorney. He wasn't anymore, and Arnold had zero desire to help us convict him of a RICO charge. She was furious with me. "Why can't you people leave me alone! I am *not* testifying about this again and you can't force me to!"

I was shocked. Why was she furious with me? I hadn't shot McBratney. I was going to put the guy who had in prison, where he belonged. The same naïveté that produced my surprise led me into a blunder. I thought I should answer her question, so I explained that even though we could technically prove Gotti's participation in the McBratney murder by reading his own 1975 guilty plea into evidence, we wanted to present a three-dimensional case. We wanted to re-create the scene in Snoope's through live witnesses.

I should have anticipated how badly this would backfire.

"You mean you don't even *have* to call me as a witness?" Arnold yelled. "You can spare me and my family, but you've just decided not to? Who the hell do you think you are? We're scared to death of these people!"

Civilians weren't our only problem. Vic Ruggiero, the former detective who'd helped with the Bergin wiretaps the summer before, wasn't returning our calls. Diane and I figured maybe he'd gotten too busy with his private eye work to bother with an unpaid stint as a witness, but when we checked with his former colleagues in Queens, they told us he'd decided he wouldn't be testifying. Vic believed that when Mike Coiro called him "Mr. Ruggiero" during the suppression hearing, he was telling Vic that he'd be treated like any other rat who testified against John Gotti. Vic had decided to make himself scarce.

The law has tools for dealing with witnesses who refuse to obey subpoenas to appear at a federal criminal trial, and I was learning how to use them. We filed an affidavit with Judge Nickerson telling him we had a material witness who'd indicated to us that he wouldn't be complying with a subpoena to testify at trial. "John, do you understand how unusual this is?" he asked after reading my request for a material witness warrant for Vic. "You need to arrest a former NYPD detective in order to get him to testify about the investigation he conducted while he was on the job? This is so bizarre. What's wrong with this case?"

Our problems with law enforcement weren't limited to former NYPD detectives. Diane and I had gotten used to the FBI's cold shoulder. I'd been able to figure out how the Bureau's bug recordings could help us, and with Laura Ward's assistance I'd done what we needed to do to get them into evidence. And Diane and I were able to cobble together the court files from the prior FBI cases that were predicate acts in our RICO trial. It was all ridiculously inefficient, but we got it done.

The Bureau's refusing to help was bad enough. In early 1986 that morphed into a more insidious situation: someone in the FBI teamed up with mob lawyers—people they hated even more than the mobsters they represented—to try to defeat our case.

Among the countless motions the defense lawyers were making was one to prevent us from using any co-conspirator statements made by Willie Boy Johnson or Billy Battista—the two informants Diane had indicted. I'd persuaded Judge Nickerson that unless an informant's handling agent explicitly authorized the informant to commit a crime, any statements during and in furtherance of that crime were co-conspirator statements, even if the agent was aware of the crime and even if the statements in question also furthered Johnson's or Battista's interests as informants. Still, we needed an evidentiary hearing to prove that the handling agents for Johnson and Battista had not explicitly authorized them to engage in criminal conduct with our defendants. The agents insisted they hadn't, but the defendants contended otherwise. And it was during that hearing that things got weird.

Willie Boy had been handled first by Agent Marty Boland, then by Jim Abbott. Boland and Abbott overtly hated Diane for burning Willie Boy, and believed that exposing him had set back the FBI's effort to combat organized crime many years. They were furious, and neither would even return our calls.

Battista, a far less serious criminal than Johnson and not nearly as valuable an informant, had been handled by Agent Pat Colgan. Colgan, unlike Abbott and Boland, was happy to cooperate with us. If he was upset that we'd burned Battista, he didn't show it.

The hearing into whether the FBI had authorized the informants to commit crimes was held in March of 1986. Colgan testified that he'd never given such authorization to Battista. During Jerry Shargel's cross-examination, the defense lawyer revealed that an anonymous male caller had provided him with material from Colgan's personnel file in the FBI. Colgan had been demoted two years earlier for improperly disseminating confidential information provided by an informant. Shargel used it to show "conflict between this agent and his brother agents," and to argue that Colgan was lying when he testified that he hadn't told Battista to commit crimes.

The judge believed Colgan and we won the motion, but he was visibly disturbed by how ugly the case was becoming. Someone in the FBI had crossed a bright line—the one between withdrawing from our prosecution of a mob boss and actively working against us to help that mob boss beat the case. That person had turned against Diane and me, and because Colgan hadn't done that he'd turned on Colgan as well.

The FBI wasn't the only federal law enforcement agency working against us. One of our witnesses was Sonny Black Montello, a Colombo associate who'd done some hijackings with the Bergin crew. He was in the Marshals Service's Witness Protection Program. Federal prosecutors don't know where relocated witnesses are, so all contacts with them must be made through the marshals. When Diane and I needed Sonny Black for trial we sent a subpoena to the DOJ's Office of Enforcement Operations for transmission to a deputy marshal in Montello's relocation area. That deputy would arrange for Montello's trip to New York, where he'd be in the protective custody of the Marshals Service until he completed his testimony.

"Sonny Black doesn't want to testify," Diane and I got told by the OEO. "He says he's finished cooperating with the government."

"We don't really care if he *wants* to testify," Diane snapped. "That's why God made subpoenas. And since when do we let witnesses decide their cooperation is finished?"

"All I can say is the local marshal tells me he's refusing to come."

Sonny Black's reaction wasn't unusual. Relocated wiseguys get settled in their new homes. They get jobs. They change their appearance. Another trip to New York can cost them those jobs and show the media what they now look like. In a high-profile case it can also result in media coverage. If someone back in the relocation area connected the dots and figured out who he was, Sonny Black would be required to relocate again, starting the process all over.

Diane asked me to take care of getting Sonny Black back for our trial, so I got a material witness warrant to arrest him. Judge Nickerson signed an order directing the Marshals Service to take him into custody and bring him to New York to testify.

When I went to his chambers to pick up the warrant, the judge called me into his office.

"John, why do you need an arrest warrant for someone who's in the program?"

"Because he refused to come in, Judge, like we wrote in the affidavit."

"But it's called the *Witness* Protection Program for a reason. If he refuses to be a witness, why don't they kick him out of the program?"

"I don't know, Judge." I was so far down in the weeds trying to get Sonny Black back that I hadn't thought about how unusual his situation was.

"There's something wrong with this," the judge said. "Jerry Shargel comes to sidebar to tell me that the FBI is helping *him* instead of you. You need a material witness warrant for a former NYPD detective. Now the Marshals are letting a witness in their own program refuse to testify in your case. You're not just up against the defendants and their lawyers. You're up against your own government."

We left it at that. I sent the warrant for Sonny Black to the OEO. A week later they called to tell me that the local marshal couldn't find him but would keep looking. I tried to get beyond that—Had they gone to his home? Had he skipped town? When had they seen him last?—but got no answer.

"This is called obstruction of justice," Diane said when I told her. "They're protecting him from us. They're not looking for Sonny Black. He's not missing or in the wind. He's where he's been all along. And there's nothing we can do about the fact that they'll help him stay away from our trial."

She was right. For the next year, until our seven-month trial ended, I got regular updates from the OEO on the alleged search for Sonny Black. The marshals were looking, I was told, but he was nowhere to be found. Then, a few months after the trial ended, I got a message that they'd found him. Along with the message was a request that I get the judge to vacate the material witness warrant; after all, the trial was over.

CHAPTER 9

FALSE START

Jury selection started on April 7, 1986. It never really got off the ground. The five hundred prospective jurors were petrified of Gotti, and it was hard to blame them. Just three months earlier he'd burst on the scene as the second coming of Al Capone. The media had already convicted him of masterminding the murders of Paul Castellano and Tommy Bilotti, and the fact that he was the new boss of the Gambino Family was common knowledge in New York. And because Diane and I had done nothing to try to alter the procedures used in typical jury selection, he now had in his hands the name and home address of every person on the jury panel.

As they were summoned one by one to be questioned by the judge, we saw the same look on all their faces. They each gave a quick glance at Gotti about fifteen feet away, then fixed their eyes on Judge Nickerson. Their look said, "You can't be serious. You can't really be asking me to serve as a juror in this case." Quite a few, men as well as women, started crying before any questions were asked. Some others got in a few answers before the tears came. But even when there was no crying, there was fear you could feel just by being in the courtroom.

Diane and I had discussed the possibility of asking the judge to empanel an anonymous jury. Such juries are rare, mostly because they're so harmful to defendants. When jurors are anonymous, their assigned number becomes their name throughout the trial. Their identities are kept from both sides, not just the bad guys, but they know early on that the defendants can't be trusted with their names. That's never actually said to them; a lie is used instead, the usual one being that anonymity is needed to keep the press from bothering them. But jurors know.

We believed that, before we could get Judge Nickerson to order an anonymous jury, we'd need strong evidence that Gotti had tried to obstruct justice in the past. We didn't have it. We had information that he and Angelo, through Roy Cohn and Mike Coiro, had bribed their way into the sweetheart deal in the McBratney murder case. And Gotti had just recently beaten a minor assault case in Queens because the complaining witness, Romual Piecyk, suddenly got amnesia on the witness stand, although we had no proof that he'd been intimidated. We weren't going to be able to make enough of a showing to get an anonymous jury, so we decided to not even try.

All the same, we seriously underestimated how much fear there'd be. We would need twelve jurors and six alternates, and after three full weeks of jury selection and several hundred in-court interviews, we weren't even halfway there.

Early in the morning on April 28, the fourth Monday of jury selection, Diane and I got summoned to the office of our new United States Attorney, Reena Raggi. Reena had become the Acting U.S. Attorney, pending a full-time appointee, after Ray Dearie was appointed to the bench.

On our way down the hall to Reena's office, I asked Diane if she knew what was up. People don't usually bother you early in the morning when you're on trial, not even the U.S. Attorney.

"Not a clue," she answered.

Reena was alone in her office, and she closed the door as soon as we entered. We sat down across from her at her huge desk.

"Do you have any basis to remand John Gotti?" she asked.

"I'm sorry?" Diane replied.

"If jury selection is suspended today, do you have grounds to revoke his bail so he is in jail when jury selection resumes in a few months?"

Diane and I looked at each other. We'd never once spoken to Reena about the trial.

"Not really," Diane answered. "He just recently beat that little assault case in Queens. The witness was obviously scared to death, but so far we have no evidence of intimidation. The witness could have clammed up because of what he learned on TV, for all we know. Why do you ask?"

"I was just curious. If for some reason jury selection were postponed for a few months today, it would be good if we could move to have John Gotti remanded into pretrial detention. That's all. It's almost nine-thirty, so you'd better be on your way up to the courtroom. Thanks."

When Judge Nickerson took the bench that morning, he read into the record an order suspending jury selection. We'd try again with a fresh jury panel four months later, on August 18. He gave us a date for us to state our positions regarding whether the next jury should be anonymous.

"How subtle can you get?" Diane whispered to me. "I guess we'll be moving for an anonymous jury."

After he finished the order, the judge looked up at Diane and me. Even we could figure this out.

"I think this is when we're supposed to move to remand Gotti," I told Diane.

"We sure are," she said. "Let's just hope he doesn't ask us right now on what *grounds* we're moving."

Diane stood up and asked nervously if we could appear the next day for a hearing on our application to remand John Gotti.

Despite the tedium of three weeks of jury selection, the courtroom was half full of reporters and court buffs. The motion brought an audible gasp, and the mood at the defense table went from delight at the postponement to outrage at our application. Bruce Cutler was furious, but luckily for us Judge Nickerson had no interest in discussing the details of our motion.

Diane and I quickly retreated to our offices. We had exactly one day to find grounds for claiming that Gotti posed such a danger of tampering with the judicial process that he had to be placed in jail until the jury announced its verdict.

If we could prove that Gotti had committed a crime during the thirteen months he'd been out on bail in the case, we could then argue that he could no longer be trusted to abide by his conditions of pretrial supervision, and therefore had to be remanded.

Gotti had just beaten a minor assault case out in Queens. Romual Piecyk, the complaining witness, had done a complete about-face on the witness stand, so we began by focusing on him. Proof that Piecyk was intimidated would serve double duty. First, witness tampering is a crime, and that would get us to first base. Second, we could argue that if Gotti was willing to tamper with witnesses in a trial as minor as that one—which was basically a dispute over a double-parked car—he obviously couldn't be trusted not to tamper with witnesses when charged with racketeering and murder.

The cops and prosecutors who lost the assault case were more than happy to help us. They believed that Piecyk's amnesia in the Queens courtroom—which produced the unforgettable *New York Post* headline "I Forgotti!"—happened because he had been "reached." As far as they were concerned, if we could prove that in our bail hearing and get Gotti remanded to prison because of it, it would be vindication for them.

The evidence they gave us wasn't great. It was based partly on Gotti's statements when Piecyk asked the cops to arrest him, partly on something Piecyk had said to the cops before he got amnesia.

The Queens prosecution was a bit lame to begin with. Piecyk, a refrigerator repairman, was driving in the Maspeth section of Queens when he found himself hemmed in by a double-parked Lincoln. He did what everyone in New York does in that situation: leaned on his horn. A man from the car then approached him and through the window slapped him in the face before going into a nearby restaurant. For good measure, he took some cash from Piecyk's shirt pocket. Piecyk called the police and pointed out Gotti, sitting at a table with about ten other guys. The officers went into the restaurant and told Gotti he was under arrest for assault. Gotti's response was "Does he know who I am? Let me talk to this guy." The statement mostly showed how conceited he was, but it also carried the implication that he was inclined to "talk" to witnesses against him.

As for Piecyk, he'd told Sergeant Anthony Falco before the trial that he had second thoughts about testifying because he was afraid. He added that since the indictment the brakes had failed on his van, and that he believed they'd been tampered with by "Gotti's people."

This was weak stuff. We had to show that Piecyk was intimidated by Gotti, not that he thought that he was intimidated by "Gotti's people," whoever they were. We wove it together with some informant information and surveillances that made it pretty clear Gotti had become the boss of the Gambino Family after Castellano's murder, but it was still far from compelling. The best thing we had going for us was a judge who seemed interested in putting Gotti in prison—so we went for it. Twelve witnesses in all, and it took more than a week, longer than most trials. When the hearing was over, Judge Nickerson said he'd get back to us with a decision.

On May 13, 1986, I drove to Providence for the day to watch my niece graduate from Providence College. Raymond Patriarca, Jr., the son of the boss of the New England La Cosa Nostra, was among the graduates. Can't get away from it, I thought. As I drove away from the Providence Civic Center, I heard a radio news report that Judge Nickerson had ordered Gotti to report to the Metropolitan Correctional Center on May 19. We'd won.

The news report included quotes from a live impromptu press conference called by Rudy Giuliani. The government was proud that it had successfully sought the remand of John Gotti, he crowed. I pulled the car over and looked for a pay phone. Diane was in her office when I called. "Congratulations to us," I said when she answered.

"Yes, I wished you were here when I got the call from chambers that we'd won."

"Did you hear about the press conference?"

"Yes," she answered. "Do you believe this guy? How shameless can you get? You'd never know from what he said that the case isn't even in his district."

Before he reported to the MCC, Gotti moved to reopen the detention hearing. His lawyers told Judge Nickerson they'd call Piecyk, who'd testify that he wasn't in fact intimidated by Gotti. We responded by saying that the best evidence Piecyk had indeed been tampered with was his "willingness" to now testify on *behalf* of Gotti. The judge would have none of it, and Gotti duly reported to the courthouse to be taken to the detention facility. He arrived with a seemingly chipper attitude, determined to show the crowd of reporters that he was unfazed at having to spend the rest of the case in pretrial detention. "I'm ready for Freddie," he crowed, smiling broadly, as he crossed the park to turn himself in.

CHAPTER 10

TAKE TWO

A lot was happening in the street in the six months after December 16, 1985, when John Gotti whacked Paul Castellano and took over the Gambino Family. Right away, Gotti had made Frankie DeCicco the new underboss. Since DeCicco had been close to Castellano and was one of the men inside Sparks whom Castellano was on his way to meet when he was gunned down, the promotion looked like a reward to Judas. In any event, DeCicco didn't enjoy his new role for long. On April 13, 1986, he visited Captain Jimmy Brown Failla at his club in the Bensonhurst section of Brooklyn. When DeCicco returned to his car, it exploded, blowing him to bits and injuring others nearby. His killers thought Gotti would be with him.

There was a message in how the murder was committed. One of the blood oaths every made member takes at his induction is not to use bombs to kill people. They're messy, and few things rile up law enforcement more than injuries to innocent bystanders. It was as though DeCicco's murderers were telling the street, "You want to break the rules by killing the boss? Well, we can break the rules too."

There were other changes. Gotti's being in the MCC made the process of selecting a new underboss to replace DeCicco more difficult. The elevation of DeCicco had signaled Gotti's preference for sharing leadership with someone from the Castellano faction. One obvious candidate was Robert "DiB" DiBernardo. DiB, a captain, had run the construction racket for Castellano for many years. The key to that business was Bobby Sasso, the president of Local 282 of the Teamsters. DiB owned Bobby Sasso.

Their corrupt relationship was as simple as it was lucrative. The only way a truck could get on a major construction site in New York City was if the on-site steward—a

Local 282 member who was usually in DiBernardo's crew—let the driver in. Because project schedules on those sites were so intricate, the ability to shut one down even for just a few hours conferred enormous economic power on the Gambino Family. Knowing that, the construction managers subcontracted to companies that were "with" the Family, even if their bids weren't the best ones submitted, just to keep the peace and the job moving. Concrete, rebar, drywall, electrical, plumbing—whatever the trade, the Gambino Family had a made member or associate in that business, and they'd reliably get the work.

DiB knew the construction business, and he'd controlled Bobby Sasso to great effect for Castellano. He played the central role for years in funneling to the mob $3 for every yard of concrete poured on major construction sites in New York City. One dollar went to Sasso, one to the Gambino Family, and, in a deal Castellano had struck with Vincenzo "Chin" Gigante, the boss of the Genovese Family, one went to Chin. Having to share the wealth with Chin rather than with the captains and soldiers loyal to Neil Dellacroce was one of the reasons Gotti hated Castellano so much.

DiB wasn't a tough guy. Like Castellano, he was more businessman than gangster. This made him a perfect, nonthreatening candidate to succeed DeCicco. But DiB also got whacked. It happened less than three weeks after Diane and I got Judge Nickerson to remand Gotti. It wasn't public and spectacular, like the hit on DeCicco. On June 5, DiB just disappeared, never to be seen again. It would take almost four years before Gotti himself would unravel it for us, but unlike DeCicco, who got killed for betraying Castellano and becoming Gotti's underboss, DiB got killed to *prevent* him from taking that position. In a guileful manipulation of both Gotti and Gravano, Angelo Ruggiero orchestrated DiB's death, and even managed to have the murder committed by Gravano, one of the people who liked DiB most.

In late June we got a new U.S. Attorney, Andy Maloney, whom Senator D'Amato had recommended to President Reagan. The AUSAs in our office responded to the news with a collective groan. Nobody had even heard of Maloney. He was an obscure defense lawyer who twenty years earlier had been an AUSA in the Southern District. Since we were constantly in skirmishes with them over which office would bring cases, we were afraid he would fail in the one quality we needed most from him—the courage to stand up to the Southern District.

Within a few days Diane and I met with Maloney to brief him on the Gotti case. He wanted to know why the FBI wasn't helping us. We told him about the schism over Willie Boy Johnson and Billy Battista. A West Point grad, Maloney made it clear to us that he'd never have pissed off the FBI like that, but what was done was done. He made no offer to help. We promised to keep him posted once the trial started in August.

The second jury selection took five weeks. Five hundred jurors were summoned to the courthouse on August 18, 1986. After being told briefly about the case by Judge Nickerson, they filled out sequentially numbered questionnaires, and this time they were anonymous; the number at the top became that juror's name.

The forms were designed to give us some information about the jurors but not enough to identify them. They wrote down only their neighborhoods, not their addresses; the nature of their employment, not their employers. Had they read about the case? If they had opinions about John Gotti, could they set them aside and be fair? What newspapers did they read? Had they ever been a trial witness or been questioned by the FBI? Almost half the pool was excused based solely on the questionnaires.

The first day of the rest of the process brought a media frenzy. There were reporters from all over the world, and they seemed to expect riveting action right away. Poor Romual Piecyk arrived as well. Gotti was in detention for tampering with him, and Piecyk once again came to tell the judge and the media that never happened. He'd been intimidated into coming to the courthouse to insist that he'd never been intimidated. Although he asked to see the judge, only the media gave him an audience.

The frenzy died down quickly. The five weeks of individual questioning, as important as it was, got tedious. Many prospective jurors didn't seem to understand the significance of judging Gotti until they found themselves in the same room as him. They wrote on the questionnaire that they could sit as jurors and be fair, but found themselves saying the opposite when they were sitting twenty feet away from a high-profile mob boss. For his part, Gotti did everything he could to maximize their fear. Always attentive, he looked directly at the jurors with a smirk on his face the entire time.

Other jury candidates would answer every question right, as if trying to get an "A" on a civics test. Diane and I found ourselves worrying about the people who seemed to be working so hard to get *on* the jury.

There were a few moments of levity. One prospective juror, an elderly woman originally from North Carolina, had checked "yes" to the question that asked if she'd ever been a witness at a trial. When Judge Nickerson followed up, she said the trial concerned the murder of her husband. The consummate patrician, the judge said, "Oh my! I'm very sorry. Do you mind if I ask you a couple of questions about it?"

"No, it's okay."

"Your husband was murdered?"

"Yes, sir."

"And you were a witness at the trial?"

"Yes."

"I'm extremely sorry," the judge said again. "This must be a terribly wrenching experience for you. But could you please tell us why it is you became a witness in the trial?"

"Because I'm the one who did it," came the response, without hesitation.

The woman had been charged with murdering her husband, testified in her own defense, and been acquitted. Her answers to a couple of follow-up questions suggested that the acquittal was likely based not on innocence but rather on a failure to prove guilt beyond a reasonable doubt. Defense counsel didn't agree with Diane and me on much during that trial, but we all agreed that, even in Brooklyn, there were certain life events that disqualified people from sitting as jurors.

Diane gave her opening statement on September 26, 1986, in a bright red suit. We'd been to court together many times, and we'd even been in front of juries together a lot, as Diane had supervised me during three small trials I prosecuted between jury selections. But I'd never seen this red suit before, or anything close. Sartorially, I was the typical male prosecutor. Diane was quoted by a reporter as saying, "John has two suits—one blue, one gray, both shiny," and she was right. But she was usually the same: dull, indeterminate clothing, and not a lot of variety. Nice clothes weren't her priority any more than they were mine. So the red outfit, which was as elegant as it was striking, drew double takes. Diane Giacalone had upped her already impressive game for the biggest trial of her life.

"Jimmy McBratney was a big man" were the first words she spoke, followed by a riveting description of his cold-blooded execution in a crowded Staten Island bar.

The packed courtroom was eerily quiet as she re-created the scene in Snoope's back in May 1973, when John Gotti, Angelo Ruggiero, and Ralph Galione went to kill McBratney. Inspired by the way McBratney and Eddie Maloney had kidnapped wiseguys' kids by impersonating cops and taking them into custody, the three gangsters announced themselves as police. Ruggiero pulled out a set of handcuffs and tried to place McBratney under arrest. The Snoope regulars knew cops when they saw them, and nobody was buying it, least of all McBratney, who was considerably larger than Ruggiero and Gotti. It became clear right away that removing McBratney to kill him elsewhere wasn't going to work, and to make matters worse one of the other customers got off his bar stool to help McBratney out. Jettisoning the plan to kill their victim somewhere private, Galione shot him dead in front of a bar full of witnesses.

After giving the jury a roadmap of the rest of our case, Diane finished strongly— even more so than we'd expected. She told the jury that in addition to the many recorded conversations and the testimony of witnesses, proof of the defendants' guilt would come right out of the mouth of another defendant who wasn't there in the courtroom. Buddy Dellacroce, she said, the underboss's son, had admitted that the charged enterprise existed and that his father was underboss, to whom the captains of the Gotti and the DiMaria/Corozzo crews reported. The jury would hear Buddy's sworn statement that the central allegation in our case was true.

The mention of Buddy's guilty plea got a huge rise out of the defense lawyers, who first caucused noisily, then formally objected. They'd spotted the vulnerability in our allegation of an enterprise-within-the-enterprise, consisting solely of two crews reporting to the underboss, and it was clear they hadn't expected us to use Buddy's plea to prove that element. They understood immediately that it would be much harder to deny the existence of that charged enterprise if a codefendant in the same indictment had pled guilty and admitted to it under oath before the trial began, and they went ballistic. But the judge, like us, knew the law, and their objection was overruled.

The temperature of the case had already risen considerably even before Bruce Cutler got up to deliver his opening statement. About a week before jury selection began, one of the defense lawyers, George Santangelo, had moved to disqualify both Diane and Judge Nickerson. Santangelo was new to the case, having come in to replace a far less aggressive lawyer for Nicky Corozzo. The motion was born dead; it claimed, ridiculously, that Diane had committed a federal crime when she told the clerk of court almost eighteen months earlier that the case should be assigned to Nickerson because it was related to two earlier cases before him. But it was intended to distract and inflame, and it succeeded. Then, just a few days before jury selection started, we'd gottten a call from an FBI supervisor. An anonymous caller had told the FBI that Diane wouldn't live to prosecute John Gotti. She acted unfazed, but these were dangerous people we were prosecuting, so we were both rattled.

Finally, right before we opened, *Time* magazine's cover was one of Andy Warhol's last works, a rendering of Gotti. It perfectly captured his trademark mannerism—buttoning his double-breasted suit jacket—and was next to the headline "Mafia On Trial." The inside story focused on Gotti but also mentioned the ongoing "Commission" case in the Southern District. The bosses of the Lucchese, Genovese, and Colombo Families were on trial together over there. The Mafia itself was in the nation's spotlight, and it was a testament to the star power of Gotti that our case—not the one across the river—was the lead story.

None of this had been wasted on Diane and me as we prepared for her opening statement. With the whole country watching, we naturally felt enormous pressure to bring home a conviction. The media attention was relentless, and Diane was having trouble ignoring it. She read all the press accounts and talked to certain reporters that she thought liked her. She tried to manage the stories, an impossible task in a case of such magnitude.

So the tension was already running when Bruce Cutler stood to make his opening statement. The captain of his college football team, Cutler was an imposing physical presence. He instantly elevated the pressure to another level entirely, setting the tone not only for the trial but for the rest of Gotti's career as a defendant. Right out of the box, he challenged the legitimacy of any prosecution brought by Diane and me. Voice booming, fist banging our table, Cutler declared that "the theme song of this prosecution is deception and manipulation!" Our evidence was "half-truths and lies"; we were creating a "fantasy world," a "secret underworld that doesn't exist." We had no decency, secretly planting a bug in Dellacroce's house "when he was dying of cancer."

Diane was his bull's-eye. Referring to her throughout as "the lady in red," Cutler accused her of indicting Gotti because "he was denied the country clubs, the fancy prep schools, and the Harvard business schools." That Diane and I had also been denied all those advantages didn't matter. "My God!" he shouted. "In this country, when you indict people for their way of life, there's something wrong!" The Bergin "is not some nefarious, behind-the-scenes location. People come in and out. Sanitation men, civil servants! Nuns, women, children!"

As intimidating as it was, it was hard not to laugh out loud. I tried to imagine Tony Roach or Willie Boy hanging out with nuns at the hole in the wall that was the Bergin. Cutler went on to liken our defendants to the Communists pursued by Senator Joe McCarthy in the 1950s. Pointing at the two of us, he yelled even louder: "They locked up in jail Japanese-Americans in California! They regretted it later. Sometimes the government does things that are wrong!"

Back and forth in the well of the courtroom he prowled, veins bulging. His suit was so tight on his big, muscular body that I could see the outline of his underwear on his butt, and it appeared as though the suit itself had squeezed all of Cutler's blood up into his head. He stopped short of saying McBratney got what he deserved, but he made sure to describe him as a "hoodlum, a bum, a lowlife! So when she says, *the lady in red*, that John Gotti went into this bar and upset things, that's not what you are going to hear!"

The peak of the performance was when Cutler alighted on his metaphor for the case—it was a stew with bad meat. "I ask you not to buy the rotten stew that the government is trying to sell you. It stinks! It's rancid! It's old! It's stale!" Then, walking up to the bench and grabbing the judge's wastebasket, "This is where it belongs! It's garbage!" He followed this with a slam dunk of the indictment.

The courtroom was stunned. In one respect, it was a tour de force. Cutler obviously idolized his client and appeared to believe everything he'd just said. But it wasn't lawyering. It was intimidation, pure and simple. There'd be no hiding behind the burden of proof or the presumption of innocence in this case, no mopey-looking defendants in rumpled clothes trying to blend into the background.

"When he sits there resplendent in his suit," Cutler bellowed at one point, "it's not out of being bold. It's out of pride. That's what made this country great!" There was no effort to shed even a glimmer of light on what John Gotti was proud *of*, nor any attempt to dispel the idea that he was proud of being exactly what we said he was. The opening statement made clear that Gotti's defense boiled down to this: "I'm the boss of the Gambino Family; what are you going to do about it?"

Judge Nickerson was known for running a controlled and dignified courtroom. He wasn't bashful when it came to telling lawyers what that entailed and expecting them to comply. In my few appearances before him, he'd admonish me whenever I failed to wear a white shirt in his courtroom, so we took it that his decision not to put an end to Cutler's theatrical table-pounding was tactical. He'd give Cutler and the other defense counsel all the rope they asked for, firm in the belief that they'd eventually hang themselves with it.

The problem with that approach wouldn't be apparent for months, but it should have occurred to us right at the outset. If neither the prosecutors nor the judge himself could tame an intimidating defendant, why should anyone expect a jury not to be intimidated?

CHAPTER 11

THE GRIND

The usual daily drill for in-custody defendants on trial is they change into their court clothes each morning in the Marshals' cellblock in the courthouse basement. At lunchtime they're taken from the courtroom back down to the cellblock. The Marshals give them lunch, and the fare is what one would expect: inexpensive, tasteless sandwiches. Then it's back to court for the afternoon session. At the end of the court day, the prisoners re-don their jumpsuits before heading to the MCC. Each defendant's lawyer provides clothes to the marshal each morning and picks them up at the end of the day.

This was not the routine for Gotti. The differences in how he was treated were considerable, and Diane and I had no idea how they came about. The handling of prisoners is the business of the judge and the Marshals; prosecutors aren't consulted. So we found out about the unusual routine only by observing.

The first change related to dressing for court. One morning toward the start of the trial I was delivering a brief in another case to a judge's chambers two floors below Judge Nickerson's courtroom. It was a half hour before the trial was to begin upstairs. As I was passing the judges' elevator, the door opened and Gotti, Cutler, and three deputy marshals got out. Cutler was carrying hangers holding Gotti's court clothes, which were covered with dry cleaner's plastic. He also had a large toiletry bag. They went down the hall and into a jury room. We soon learned that this process repeated itself every morning, using a different jury room each day. No quick-change down in the cellblock for the boss of the Gambino Family. He and Cutler spent quality time each morning primping. When the entourage entered the courtroom at 9:25, a strong whiff of aftershave and little clouds of talcum powder followed them.

The other change in routine began about a month into the trial, and it was even more dramatic. As I was wheeling our evidence cart out of the courtroom one day at the lunch break, I passed three men trundling steel carts into the courtroom, each loaded with caterer's trays. I couldn't see what was in them, but they were steaming and it smelled fabulous. When the courtroom doors closed behind them, deputy marshals locked them from the outside. Diane and I looked through the windows and watched. All seven defendants, their eight lawyers, and the guys who delivered the food were heaping the contents of the trays onto plates. Somehow the defense had persuaded Judge Nickerson to turn his courtroom into an Italian restaurant.

That process continued every day until the trial ended, the only change being that the delivery guys stopped waiting until Diane and I cleared out before wheeling in lunch. The moment the judge was off the bench, they were through the door. The same four carriers delivered the food every day, and I recognized the one who was in charge. His name was Anthony "Shorty" Mascuzzio, and he was from my neighborhood. He could be found every day on a folding chair outside Bravo Gelato, on Court Street near the corner of Sackett. He was never alone there, and the people around him were all men. I lived a block away and passed them on a daily basis. I knew right away that it couldn't be good to be a neighbor of the lunch bearer for the boss of the Gambino Family. Shorty didn't recognize me when he first started delivering to the courtroom, but I knew it was only a matter of time before he saw me in the neighborhood and realized who I was.

We called our first witness on September 29, and it took us four months to rest our case. In the first week, when we put Sal Polisi on the stand, we felt the impact of having indicted so many defendants. Seven on trial meant seven cross-examinations, which can make a trial drag even in a tightly run courtroom. Polisi contributed only slightly to our case, but he was on the stand for six days.

The content of the crosses hurt us even more than their length. Polisi's baggage included his efforts to write a book, and there were thirty hours of recorded conversations he'd had with a ghost writer a couple of years earlier. They were laced with racist views, and included use of the N-word multiple times.

Also, Polisi had not only used his mental illness gambit to beat cases and get reduced sentences, he'd called on it again to get disability benefits from the Veterans Administration. Over a twenty-year period, he defrauded the VA out of more than $300,000.

Dominick LoFaro was even more of a disaster. He helped us only on a gambling charge, and it came at a ridiculous cost. LoFaro admitted that during the three years he was cooperating with prosecutors upstate, he was still selling heroin. And though the grandiose hitman stories he'd told to sell himself as a witness were false, he had in fact committed two murders—one of a woman he shot in the face—for which the state authorities who arrested him had agreed he wouldn't be prosecuted. We were sorry we called him.

I also quickly discovered that I'd gone overboard on the gambling wiretaps. One of our several Public Morals detectives was on the stand for three days as we played hundreds of fifteen-second telephone conversations in which someone bet on a number or a horse. We'd play an hour or two of calls, then he'd testify about the search of the particular "wire room" that was being recorded. We'd move on to the next wire room and repeat the process. The whole thing was mind-numbing.

The defense kept us busy throughout, helped by the fact that they outnumbered us eight to two. Each afternoon we'd be required to tell them which witnesses, or which recorded conversations, we'd be presenting the next day. Almost invariably, someone on the defense team would object to at least parts of the testimony or recordings. The judge would then ask for a letter from us in response, to be filed before court began the following morning. Whichever one of the two of us wasn't preparing the witnesses that evening would have to draft the letter. We needed another lawyer on the team, and could have had one for the asking. Not wanting to suggest I couldn't keep up, I never said anything to Diane. I figured she thought we were doing all right, and that the effort necessary to bring someone else up to speed would outweigh the benefits.

After Cutler set the tone in his opening statement, the atmosphere in the courtroom remained toxic, especially as it related to Diane. The defense lawyers hated her. All the characteristics that would have led them to consider a male prosecutor tough led them to refer to her, openly in the courtroom no less, as a "bitch." Cutler called her a "tramp" on the record, which only in retrospect we recognized as a warning sign of what was to come.

A chronic source of friction was the defense lawyers' habit of misrepresenting statements we'd made to them. One of the lawyers would ask us after court to consider a request, and the next morning they'd tell the judge we'd agreed to it. It got to the point where I refused to speak to one lawyer in particular except on the record in court.

On an occasion when the judge wasn't in the courtroom Diane called George

Santangelo out on one of his misrepresentations. It immediately escalated into a disagreement about who'd said what, and when Diane repeated what Santangelo had said, she pointed her index finger at him.

"Take that finger and shove it up your ass!" Santangelo snarled, as the press corps listened enrapt.

The witness examinations were of a piece with everything else the defense was doing. In his cross of Sal Polisi about his attempt to beat a 1974 case by faking insanity, Willie Boy's lawyer asked, "And you pulled everybody's chain when you were doing your psychological routine? *You were jerking everybody off?*"

I whispered to Diane, "Did he just say that?" She nodded.

When Bruce Cutler crossed Eddie Maloney about the conversations he recorded while cooperating, it went like this:

> Q: "You used expletives like 'fucking cocksucker' and 'bum' on the tape quite often, didn't you?"
>
> A: "Yes."
>
> Q: "Is that what you are?"

Judge Nickerson was usually the personification of courtroom decorum, and in every other case he'd overseen the proceedings had had a special dignity. That the defense lawyers could ask one witness if he was jerking everybody off and another if he was a cocksucker and get no reaction at all from the bench showed how badly the courtroom behavior had deteriorated, and how much the poisonous atmosphere had worn down the sixty-nine-year-old judge. He'd been on the bench ten years, but the way this case was being defended was new for everyone involved. And federal judges don't have bosses to help or enable them to course correct. Judge Nickerson, who was fiercely independent by nature, had chosen a laissez-faire approach that was close to making his court a free-for-all, and there was nothing anyone could do to reverse it.

CHAPTER 12

WORDS IN COURT

For the first four months of the trial I enjoyed an unexpectedly warm relationship with the defendants. Lenny DiMaria, one of the captains at the defense tables, was naturally outgoing and particularly friendly, and I learned to like him. Each day at lunchtime I'd push our evidence cart out of the courtroom just as Shorty Mascuzzio's guys were wheeling in lunch, and Lenny always asked me to join them. More than once he told me that if I ever left the U.S. Attorney's Office I'd have a job with them.

The most striking interactions were the ones I had with Gotti. In every other case, defendants in custody were taken back into the Marshals' pens when the judge was off the bench, but Judge Nickerson let Gotti stay in the courtroom. During the fifteen-minute breaks we took midmorning and midafternoon, he'd talk to me. The seven defendants and their eight lawyers occupied two long tables that formed an "L." Combined with our table in front of the jury box, and then the judge's bench, they formed a square. There was a large carpeted area in the center, and Gotti would walk into it during breaks and engage me in conversation. Cutler didn't like his doing this at first and tried to stop it, but Gotti waved him off.

Our exchanges were almost always easy banter. His mood was consistently upbeat, as if he didn't have a care in the world. He asked about my family a couple of times and I changed the subject. I tried not to reveal the anxiety such questions produced, and avoided thinking about what would happen if he knew my sister Mary was married to his first cousin.

A recurring theme of our talk was how low-level the witnesses were. In Gotti's view, Polisi was a "nobody," Cardinali a "coffee boy," Eddie Maloney an "Irish faggot" he'd never even met. LoFaro had come across him one time, in a large group. "How can youse rely on these people?" Gotti asked me repeatedly. When he first said this, it was during Cardinali's testimony, and I said, "All right, I get your complaint about our witnesses. But tell me this, are we wrong about who you are? Are we wrong about you being the boss and about these crimes?" He just smiled.

Only twice did our exchanges get serious. The first was about the Buddy My Balls recording. Ever since Tony Moscatiello phoned the Bergin back in 1981 to return Gotti's call, Buddy My Balls had become a legend within law enforcement, not because the recording was significant evidence—all it showed was that Moscatiello answered to Gotti—but because the ninety-second tape was a window into Gotti himself. He was intimidating and controlling, to be sure, and Buddy My Balls made that clear. But he was also an out-of-control hothead, and his diatribe put that on full display.

When Willie Boy, who answered the phone at the Bergin, handed it to Gotti, Moscatiello opened with, "Hi, buddy."

"Buddy my fuckin' balls!" Gotti raged. "What—do I gotta reach out for you three days in ad-fucking-vance?"

Moscatiello replied by blaming his wife for not passing along the message.

Gotti: "She said she told you yesterday!"

Moscatiello: "She didn't tell me yesterday, John."

Gotti: "She did so! You tellin' me your wife's a fuckin' liar now?"

Just when it seemed as if he couldn't possibly be angrier, he stepped it up a couple more notches: "And don't let me have to do this again, 'cause if I hear anyone else calls you and you respond in five days I'll fuckin' kill you!" This was clearly not hyperbole. The conversation ended with Gotti, still in the height of fury, promising to tell Moscatiello's wife that her husband called her a liar and to find out from her if she passed along the message. Before slamming down the phone, he ended ominously, "We'll call her and ask her! Maybe youse are all fuckin' liars!"

At the next break Gotti shot to the center of the courtroom square like a boxer coming off his stool.

"Why did youse have to play that call?" he asked. He was furious, and though we'd seen lots of anger from the lawyers, this was the first time it came from him.

"I don't understand," I said. "That conversation is one of our least powerful pieces of evidence. It doesn't even suggest a crime, let alone prove one. All it shows is Tony answers to you. There's no real dispute that you were in charge at the Bergin. Why are you so upset?"

He looked right at me, his anger subsiding. He was obviously weighing whether he should answer my question.

"Look," he said, "I have an image. That call with Tony is bad for my image."

Our second serious exchange came after another disconcerting tape. We took a short break just after playing a conversation between Angelo Ruggiero and Gene Gotti from the 1982 Ruggiero bug. As coworkers often do, the two of them viciously complained about their boss, Captain John Gotti. Ruggiero referred to him as the guy "your mother shit out," and Gene had some equally choice words for his big brother. Gene was sitting there as a codefendant, and it was awkward, to say the least, when everyone pulled off headsets to take a break.

John Gotti approached me with a smile. "You know one good thing about this trial?" he said. "Youse've taught me a lot about the people I have around me." As he said this, he was making a circular motion with his forefinger, in a manner that made me think he would eventually stop and point it at someone. Given the context, I thought it would be his younger brother, who'd just vilified him for all the crowded courtroom—and soon the tabloid-reading public—to hear.

I was half right. His hand motion stopped and his finger pointed at one of his codefendants. But it wasn't Gene Gotti; it was Willie Boy Johnson.

Willie Boy was such a marked man it was ridiculous. John Gotti kept paying Rich Rehbock, a B-team mob lawyer, to represent Willie Boy—no doubt to keep him from flipping any further—but otherwise he was on his own. He sat at the defense table right next to Gotti. No one, not even Rehbock, talked to him. When he wasn't in the courtroom, he was in the hole in the MCC for his own protection. His wife was destitute. Willie Boy was allowed to make a single phone call per week, and one week, out of desperation, he called his son and set up a drug deal. The line was of course recorded, so when the MCC brought the tape to our office and asked us to prosecute, we got an indictment for an attempted "telephone count" (using a telephone to facilitate a drug deal). We could have charged Willie Boy with something more serious, and his son as well, but we actually felt sorry for them.

Unlike Gotti, Cutler was all intimidation all the time. He told the judge at the outset he wanted no sidebar conferences because only lawyers are allowed to go up to the judge and John Gotti wanted to be involved in everything. He beat up on witnesses in ways that were obviously unprofessional, and he refused to be held in check, even when the judge tried, which wasn't often. In a loud voice Cutler asked Polisi to confirm that he was a "thief, a yellow dog, and a pimp," and when Judge Nickerson tried to shut him down he went on, in a louder voice, to ask him again, without reprimand.

Three weeks into the trial Diane's frustration boiled over. In crossing a witness who'd been in Snoope's when McBratney was killed, Cutler violated a court order. Although Gotti had done two years for the McBratney homicide, there was no double jeopardy problem with us including that murder as part of our RICO charge. Cutler had been directed not to suggest otherwise to the jury, but his last question to our witness was "Did you ever hear of someone going to jail twice for the same crime?"

Diane immediately moved for an order of contempt, and the ensuing argument was revealing in multiple ways. It was still early in the case, but the relentless abuse was getting to her. She argued that Cutler was "attempting to take this courtroom and turn it into a music hall for Mr. Cutler. I believe, Your Honor, that the government cannot have a fair trial if Mr. Cutler continues to perform a vaudevillian act before this jury." The argument seemed odd and disconnected from the conduct that we were objecting to.

For his part, the judge seemed naïvely to believe he could modify Cutler's behavior by appealing to his self-respect.

"I don't think I am going to hold him in contempt, but the questions were plainly improper, and have been with respect to several of the witnesses." Then, in a bizarre exchange in which Cutler repeatedly interrupted him, the judge went on: "I have never held an attorney in contempt. I am very reluctant to hold people in contempt or to admonish people because I expect people to act in my courtroom as they uniformly have—almost uniformly—in a professional manner."

With Cutler talking over him throughout, it was hard to imagine that the judge actually believed his lecture would work. If he did, it was only for an instant, because when he finally officially let Cutler speak, the lawyer said, "You want to know what I think? Ms. Giacalone doesn't like the way I question people because I show the jury the scum that they are," pointing at us. Before our trial, people rarely talked like that in Judge Nickerson's courtroom, and when they did they were scolded. But the wince that passed over the judge's face was all that remained of that.

Diane and I failed to fully appreciate it at the time, but Cutler's disrespectful soliloquy was a harbinger of worse behavior to come: "For Ms. Giacalone to get up and talk about sanctions, is she really serious, Your Honor? Judge, witnesses call me and tell me what the government does to them. Witnesses call me and tell me how Ms. Giacalone threatens them, how Mr. Gleeson threatens them. And then they get up here in a nice little dress and a nice suit and say, in front of the press, John Gotti is going to influence witnesses."

The judge denied Diane's application, which prompted the other defense lawyers to put on their own show. Barry Slotnick, in a shameless attempt to suck up to Gotti, who'd cast him aside in favor of Cutler when Dellacroce died, said the judge "should be offended" by Diane's application, and should consider sanctions against her for improperly seeking sanctions against Cutler. "With regard to the questioning of witnesses," Slotnick said, "the reports we get in terms of what witnesses were told by the government, how they were told to testify and what to testify to, we will open it up."

We got the first taste of what they were talking about that afternoon. Our next witness was to be Miriam Arnold, who had been present in the bar for the McBratney murder and had testified against Gotti and Ruggiero in the Staten Island grand jury back in the 1970s, when they were no-name hoodlums from Queens. But Arnold had made it clear during our prep session that she had no intention of testifying against Gotti now that he was a notorious crime boss. She'd at first managed to dodge our efforts to serve her with a subpoena, but we'd finally managed to serve her just a few days earlier. When she arrived at our office that morning, she told the detectives working with us that she would "take care" of us when she got on the witness stand. Taking that as a threat that she would testify falsely and claim not to recall facts she'd remembered clearly just a few months earlier, I told her we were no longer confident she'd testify truthfully, so she wouldn't be testifying and could go home. As annoyed as I was, I felt sorry for her. She was genuinely terrified of Gotti, and as a result had apparently decided to testify that she couldn't remember facts no one could forget. It would be Romual Piecyk all over again.

Arnold didn't get out of the courthouse quickly enough. When we returned to court after the lunch break, she was with Cutler. He reported that "the government attorneys were pressuring her and destroying her, harassing her and threatening her with perjury and contempt because she couldn't recall with specificity what happened thirteen and a half years ago." He asked Judge Nickerson to allow testimony from her about what he called my abusive handling so the court and the press could become "aware of what unfettered power can do." Arnold was sitting right there, and I was trembling at the thought of what they might force her to say. Thankfully, for once the judge would have none of it, and we got back to the trial.

One afternoon the three Southern District prosecutors who'd just finished trying the Commission case stopped in. They were on something of a victory lap, having all received the John Marshall Award, the highest honor the DOJ bestows, for their work on that case, in which three bosses were convicted. I saw Cutler whisper to John Gotti who they were, and at the next break, as I was back in the spectator section saying hello, Gotti walked over. Because he was in custody, he couldn't leave the well of the courtroom, but he was only about fifteen feet away, and he had everyone's attention.

"Chertoff, Savarese, Childers," he said, pointing at each in order. "I'm John Gotti. Now we all know each other." He was smiling, and looked like a man who knew there was literally no chance he'd be convicted. His cocky introduction over, he went back to his seat.

With only Diane and me at our table, I was both junior prosecutor and paralegal. At the end of each day one of my jobs was to gather up all the evidence we'd used and return it to where it belonged. Each photo and document had its own plastic sleeve, marked with its exhibit number, in huge loose-leaf binders. The same was true of the tapes. "Clearing the beach" we called the process of placing them all in the proper plastic containers, and it took from fifteen minutes to a half hour after the courtroom was evacuated.

The defense team had its own evidence cart and copies of every government exhibit, so someone had to do the same tidying for them. They had no paralegal either, and somehow the task fell to John Carneglia. Probably the toughest of all in Gotti's crew—which was saying something—Carneglia had become a stronger and quieter presence as the trial progressed. He and his brother had a huge junkyard on Fountain Avenue in Brooklyn, where they chopped and crushed cars. The FBI was certain that plenty of guys whose bodies had never been found had ended up in one of those metal cubes that came out of their compressing machines. But for the seven months we were on trial Carneglia finished the days as a paralegal. Alone together in the courtroom, he and I would take off our jackets and silently get to work on the piles of photos, documents, and cassettes that littered the tables. I noticed right away corroboration of Sal Polisi's statement that Carneglia carried a handgun tucked into his pants in the small of his back—always available but with no bulge for cops to see. He'd never take a gun into the courthouse, but it appeared as though he needed something to fill the void; as Carneglia stacked away the evidence I noticed he always had a large hairbrush in the exact spot where Polisi said he carried his gun.

One evening I was at our table matching cassettes to their containers, and Carneglia was doing the same on his side. There was a constant clacking noise as cassettes were inserted and plastic boxes were snapped shut and then placed in stacks. We were facing the front of the courtroom when Carneglia looked to his left and we made eye contact. A smile slowly spread across his face and he said, deadpan, "You gotta protect da integrity of da tapes!" I laughed out loud. It created a little paralegal kinship between us for the rest of the trial.

Our case was a patchwork of three different elements—old convictions of our defendants, disparate crimes Diane had convicted others of committing for the benefit of our defendants, and accomplice testimony. One day we'd have testimony about the raid of a dice game in Brooklyn, the next the focus would be on truck hijackings from the airport, and then we'd switch to loan-sharking. A helpful aspect of the RICO law is the way it allows disconnected crimes to be prosecuted in a single case, but that risks a trial with no center, and ours seemed to lack one.

The core charges were the three killings. We could get RICO convictions without proving them—only two predicate acts have to be proved for a defendant to be found guilty. The jury could convict Gotti even if the only predicate acts we proved were the two gambling charges, or two hijackings. But his sentence in that event would be much shorter, and we correctly felt that a failure to get guilty verdicts on the murder charges would mean we'd lost the case.

This was how James Cardinali became, almost by default, the centerpiece of our case. He was an unlikely candidate for such a starring role. A heroin addict who got jammed up on a murder by the Brooklyn DA, Cardinali flipped to avoid spending the rest of his life in prison. But that was long before the Castellano murder, and he had every reason to believe his cooperation would stay below the radar.

Cardinali had already buckled once under the enormous pressure after Gotti became boss. Like Traynor, with whom he was incarcerated when they were both on our witness list, he tried to leverage his enhanced value by demanding extra privileges. When they were denied, Cardinali said he wanted out of our case and out of the Witness Protection Program. He even filed a request to be returned to state custody. Then after a couple of weeks came another change of heart. He realized what life would be like for him in Attica or Green Haven. Backing out of testifying wouldn't alter the fact that he was a rat, and unprotected rats don't fare well in state prison. Unprotected rats who gave up John Gotti made out even worse. So Cardinali rescinded both his requests—to be taken off our witness list and to be returned to state prison. Because he hadn't tried to shake us down, as Traynor had, and because we needed him so badly, we took him back, and Cardinali resumed his critical role in our prosecution.

His direct testimony lasted three days and went as well as we could have expected. The heart of it—the testimony about the three murders—lasted less than half an hour. Though Gotti had admitted his role in the McBratney murder when he pled guilty twelve years earlier, Cardinali's testimony was what made that crime a RICO predicate. Gotti had told him that he took part in the killing in order to become a made member of the Gambino Family. As for Willie Boy Johnson, he confessed to Cardinali that he'd killed Tony Plate to enhance Dellacroce's chances of beating a case in which Dellacroce and Plate were codefendants. And finally, Carneglia confided in Cardinali that he had killed Albert Gelb, the New York State court officer, to keep him from testifying against Carneglia's brother Charles. Gelb was in a Queens diner one night when Charles passed him on the way to the restroom. Gelb saw a firearm tucked into the small of his back, followed him, and placed him under arrest. As the trial approached, Gelb received anonymous threats that he'd be killed if he testified. Undaunted, he remained a witness, and John Carneglia murdered him in his car late one night a few days before the trial.

There was one big problem with Cardinali's testimony: it flew in the teeth of the typical wiseguy practice of never talking to anyone about past crimes, let alone to coffee boys about murders. Cardinali seemed credible on direct, but the crosses were lengthy and effective—he'd spend a total of nine days on the stand—and they altered the course of the trial.

Cardinali himself handed the defense a gift. During the period between when he temporarily decided to jump ship then decided to climb back on board, he'd called Bruce Cutler. In a long conversation that Cutler recorded, Cardinali talked about Diane. He told Cutler that she'd boasted to him that Judge Nickerson treated her like a daughter, and that she got whatever she wanted in court while the defense lawyers got nothing. I was present when Diane had said to Cardinali that, compared to how he treated the hostile defense lawyers, the judge treated her like a daughter. That was all she'd said, and I hadn't thought anything of it at the time. It was true. But when the words came out of Cardinali's mouth on cross-examination, one of the most important lessons all trial lawyers must learn was seared into me forever: never say anything to a witness you're not comfortable hearing repeated in open court. Diane was mortified and the judge was visibly upset. As the trial proceeded, the testimony would further impair his ability to keep control of the courtroom.

The worst was yet to come, though. Cardinali wasn't any better at dealing with a tough woman prosecutor than Cutler himself, or the other defense lawyers. So his rant about her on the phone to Cutler dovetailed nicely with their misogynistic defense.

Cutler began his explosive questioning: "I don't want to go into it in front of the court and jury," but that's exactly what he was doing, and there was nothing he wanted to do more. "You did indicate to us," he continued, "that the image she projects in the courtroom has nothing to do with reality. I see her out of the courtroom and—in your word, not mine, and I apologize to the jury—she is a slut, did you say that?"

"I might have said that, yes," a smiling Cardinali answered.

Leading him along with questions based on Cardinali's own rant and getting agreement from his witness at every step, Cutler tore into Diane. His feigned queasiness at embarrassing her evaporated. Diane was a "powerful, treacherous woman" who'd not only threatened Cardinali but Matt Traynor too. Mocking Cardinali for mending fences with her, the cross went on:

"You made up with Ms. Giacalone, did you?"

"Yes, sir."

"So she's no longer the same individual you described in May of 1986, is that correct?"

"That's correct."

"In other words, she's no longer a slut. Is that right? In your mind?"

"Correct."

"She's no longer a blow job in your mind?"

"Correct."

"She's no longer a liar, isn't that right?"

"Correct."

"She no longer puts words in witnesses' mouths, is that right?"

"Correct."

"She no longer harasses, threatens, and accuses witnesses, does she?"

By this time Cutler was screaming, and the judge interrupted him: "Please keep your voice down." But it had no effect.

"She no longer threatens and harasses and intimidates witnesses, is that right?"

"As far as I know."

And on and on. All of it might have been excluded as a sideshow, but a successful objection by us would only have proved the charge that the judge favored Diane, so we had to let most of it go. As for me, I was repeatedly thrown into questions as "her helper, Mr. Gleeson."

Next to me I could feel Diane unraveling. It was so raw and bizarre and personal. And most of all it was so *public*. As debilitating as it was to hear in a packed courtroom, we both knew it would be described to a very wide audience in the morning papers. As strong as she was, Diane was being beaten down, and the blows were having their effect. She spoke less, and was beginning to look tired.

Cutler's intense hatred of her was on display throughout. "Did you remember that question she asked with that sweet smile?" he asked.

Determined to get before the jury Cardinali's statement that Diane and I wanted to introduce "dirt" into the trial, Cutler refused to obey a ruling that he couldn't.

The Court: "The objection is sustained. Please don't do that."

Cutler: "That's the same kind of dirt, isn't it?"

Diane: "Objection."

The Court: "Sustained."

Cutler: "Object a hundred times! That's also sustained, Your Honor?"

The Court: "Please, Mr. Cutler, please."

As the judge was losing control of Cutler, Diane was losing her patience. Cutler accused her of lying to the Bureau of Prisons so Cardinali could get a visit from a woman. He kept referring to her in his questions as "she" and "her," and Diane finally lost it:

Cutler: "It suited her purpose to suit your purpose, isn't that right?"

Diane: "I have a name!"

Cutler: "Isn't that right?"

Diane: "I have a name! I'm not a she or her!"

The Court: "Yes."

Cardinali: "That would be right."

Cutler: "It suited her purpose and it suited your purpose?"

Diane: "I have a name, and I'd like it if he would refer to me by my name!"

Cutler: "I have, Judge. I like her name very much. I mention it very, very much."

The jurors wore their hatred for Cutler and their sympathy for Diane on their faces. It was obvious that he knew it and didn't care. Any other trial lawyer would want a jury to like him. Cutler wanted this jury to fear him.

Cardinali finally finished testifying a week before Christmas. We still had a couple of dozen witnesses left, but most were quick: surveillances, some more gambling evidence, records custodians, and the like. Between them and the week off for the holidays, it took us until mid-January to complete our case.

Even in a normal trial, four months is grueling. We'd presented seventy-eight witnesses and hundreds of exhibits, and the prep work had been relentless. After spending all day in court we'd spend another six hours preparing for the next day. Add to the normal wear and tear the nonstop hostility and abuse, and we were worn out. We hoped for a defense case that would give us time to prepare a great summation, so we were relieved to learn that they'd call some witnesses.

CHAPTER 13

TRAYNOR

The defense's first witness was Matt Traynor. As corrosive as the atmosphere had become during our direct case, it seemed like child's play once Traynor's testimony began.

He testified that when Diane (to whom he was allowed to refer throughout as "Mama Giacalone") and I first talked to him, he'd told us he'd never committed crimes with our defendants. We wanted him to testify otherwise, he said, and to implicate John Gotti in murders. He claimed that to get him to commit perjury my wife, Susan, and I arranged for him to get Tylenol with codeine from a corrupt psychiatrist at Beth Israel Medical Center, where Susan worked.

We'd had no idea this was coming, so it landed hard on me. When I was at Cravath, Ralph McAfee told me many times that all a lawyer has to offer is good judgment and integrity, and without both you're sunk. And there I was being accused in open court of suborning perjury and distributing a narcotic in my effort to succeed. Making matters worse, the day of Traynor's direct examination happened to be the one day Susan chose to come to court to watch the trial. I'd had other trials, but she was busy building her career as a psychiatric nurse and this was her first visit to observe me in action. Within minutes of taking a seat in the back of the courtroom she heard Traynor accuse us both of crimes, and she promptly left, never to attend one of my trials again.

I was still reeling from that when we discovered that Traynor was letting me off easy compared to what he'd do to Diane. He testified that I acquired drugs for him whenever he asked for them, and when he requested some sex, Diane took over. She gave him a pair of her panties so he could, as he put it, "facilitate" himself in prison. Diane was motivated, Traynor testified, by her experiences walking past the Bergin as a schoolgirl. The wiseguys had ridiculed her for being skinny, and according to Traynor she'd go to any lengths for revenge, including trading her underwear for some false testimony.

At the outset of his testimony, while it was underway, and after it was over, we told Judge Nickerson that Traynor's testimony should never have been permitted, and once it happened we asked that it be stricken from the record. The defense argued that if the jury believed Traynor, it could infer that we also got our other witnesses to lie. On that theory every allegedly dishonest thing Diane or I had ever done would be fair game.

We contended that even if that made sense, the value of Traynor's testimony to the defendants was far outweighed by two compelling facts. First, the most effective way for Diane and me to rebut Traynor's allegations would be to get up on the witness stand and deny them, but the ethical rules prohibit a lawyer from being both a witness and an advocate in the same trial. The defense had known what Traynor would say months before the trial started. If they wanted to present that testimony, they were obligated under the law to say so before the trial began. If the judge decided at that time to allow it, we could have preserved our right to testify by getting other AUSAs to prosecute the case. We obviously couldn't switch prosecutors now. The defense decision to surprise us with this testimony, we argued, forfeited their right to use it.

Second, Traynor's testimony created a huge trial within the trial. Traynor didn't just savage Diane and me. He trashed every federal agent and cop he'd ever come into contact with. We had dozens of reports, going back ten years, in which he spoke to detectives and agents about committing crimes with people at the Bergin, including several of John Gotti's brothers. Those reports were the reason Traynor had become our witness in the first place. Now, to fit the defense narrative, all those agents and cops had to be liars, and that's what Traynor was claiming. He never committed those crimes, and he never told anyone that he had. Diane and I were certainly attacked the most viciously, but more than a dozen others in law enforcement were accused of creating phony reports. We told the judge that allowing a witness we didn't even call to vilify so many of us would derail the trial we'd almost completed and begin a new one, a trial about law enforcement's handling of Matt Traynor over a period of more than a decade.

We were right on both our arguments. But Cardinali's testimony that, according to Diane, the judge treated her like a daughter had complicated things. Rulings in our favor might strike the jury—and the appeals court if we convicted the defendants—as confirmation of that. Whatever the reason, Judge Nickerson appeared to us to be avoiding any suspicion that he was partial to the government. Traynor's testimony steered an already bizarre trial into an alternate universe. Diane and I returned to our offices downstairs and tried our best to wrap our heads around what had just happened. The panties-for-perjury accusation was so beyond the pale that we just sat in Diane's office and looked at each other. We'd been hoping to sum up the case and get our convictions in a matter of days. Now we had this. Tabloid fodder for a tabloid case. More than anything else, we were physically and emotionally exhausted.

Andy Maloney, our new U.S. Attorney, came by to talk about how we should respond. He began by asking Diane how she felt about my doing the cross. She objected immediately.

"He can't do it," she said, "he's not up to it. If it were Brian Maas, fine, I'd agree, but he's not." Brian was an experienced AUSA and one of Diane's friends. Then she and Maloney spoke about my ability to cross Traynor as though I weren't sitting right there. Diane's criticism, and her decision to express it so bluntly, was hurtful, but at least Maloney was saying I'd do a great job.

Traynor had trashed me too, and in any other setting that allegation—trading drugs for perjury—would have been spectacular. But it was a measure of how brutal his direct had been on Diane that we acted as though all he'd accused me of was being late to court. In any event, *one* of us had to cross him, and eventually Diane agreed with Maloney that it couldn't be her.

The cross lasted two days. I walked Traynor through every interaction he'd had with law enforcement officials and asked him about every statement he had made over the years about committing crimes with members of the Bergin crew. Over the course of the examination it became clear that either Traynor was a world-class liar or there was a long list of otherwise honorable people who didn't know each other and yet had conspired to falsely record his admissions to crimes. Still, he never stopped pushing back, telling the jury at one point that "the average juror would never understand how underhanded" Diane and I could be.

Shortly after Traynor's testimony ended, Susan received a phone call in her office at Beth Israel Medical Center. The voice on the other end said she was "calling from the law offices of Susan Kellman." Kellman was one of the defense lawyers for Lenny DiMaria. The caller asked "Is this Susan Gleeson?" and when Susan said yes, she hung up. The defense promptly served Beth Israel with a subpoena for my wife's entire personnel file. Word quickly spread throughout the hospital that Susan's records had been subpoenaed in the ongoing, high-profile trial of Gambino boss John Gotti. It'd been bad enough when Gotti's vile defense implicated her the one day she'd come to the courtroom. Now the fabrication had permeated her workplace, and she was understandably not happy.

I was livid. The ostensible basis for the subpoena was that the forensic psychiatrist who'd prescribed Tylenol with codeine for Traynor also worked at Beth Israel, so the personnel file would supposedly shed light on the defense's claim that I offered Traynor drugs in exchange for perjury. But I knew raw intimidation and harassment when I saw it.

The trial wasn't in session the next morning, but I insisted on seeing the judge with defense counsel. I made no effort to conceal my anger, and I inadvertently made it clear to the judge that it wasn't directed solely at defense counsel.

"Even by the standards in this trial," I argued, the personnel file of my wife was "so beyond the pale of relevance, of admissibility" that the court had finally to do something.

"The only plausible basis for the service of this subpoena is harassment," I went on in a long diatribe. "Diane Giacalone and I have been subjected to a torrent of harassment in this courtroom for the past six months or so, that we've withstood, not happily, but we've withstood it. Now that harassment has reached outside the courtroom to someone very close to me. We would ask the court to exercise its discretion to exert some control over the manner in which this case is proceeding."

If Judge Nickerson was upset by my criticisms, he didn't show it. Rather, he was at last supportive. After listening to defense counsel, he said, "It's just so off the wall, completely off the wall. I will quash the subpoena on my own motion. This case is not going to turn into any more of a circus than the defendants' attorneys have already made it."

"Maybe we should have gotten angry at him sooner," Diane said to me when I reported what had happened.

When the defense rested their case, we faced an important decision. Traynor had accused Diane and me and more than a dozen law enforcement officers of various forms of criminal activity. It seemed impossible that the jury would believe him. But if we went right into summations, the defense would argue that his testimony had gone unanswered. We couldn't testify ourselves, but we could call those dozen witnesses, many of whom now lived far from New York. If we did that, it would prolong the trial by weeks, and doing so also ran the risk of dignifying Traynor's testimony.

We decided we needed to put on a rebuttal case, and that I would handle it alone. So we settled in for several more weeks of trial. After sixteen witnesses, many of whom flew to New York on almost no notice, we rested. It went well, with one agent after another telling the jury about the various crimes Traynor said he'd committed with the Gottis.

The downside was that it became exactly what we'd told Judge Nickerson he should have avoided—a trial within a trial. In my ten years as a prosecutor I would personally try twenty cases. With the exception of my two trials of John Gotti himself, the rebuttal case in the first of those trials was longer than any of the others.

The case gave everyone involved in it unprecedented access to the press. The defense lawyers shamelessly used it to try to influence our jury. Just as Traynor was about to take the stand to make his allegations about Diane and me, Barry Slotnick had given a speech at New York Law School. The jurors, he said, should look upon Gotti "as a symbol of oppression." He went on: "When they look at John Gotti, what they're really looking at is Salem, where they burned witches."

For every absurd comparison like that there was also a public attack on us. After Traynor's testimony, Cutler told a *Newsday* reporter that the jury needed to hear from Traynor so it could see that "he was treated in a typical, unethical way by these overzealous, ambitious, vindictive federal prosecutors."

It was not finished yet, of course. The summations were quite a spectacle. Bruce Cutler repeated the main themes of his opening statement almost half a year earlier. He described our allegation that there was any such thing as a Gambino Family as a "fantasy." The only reason the case was brought, he argued, was that the government didn't approve of John Gotti's "lifestyle." If only he hung out at a country club, Cutler argued, rather than the Bergin, he'd never have been indicted.

He also added a new theme, saying twelve separate times that Diane and I represented "a new breed of prosecutors." Jeff Hoffman, Gene Gotti's lawyer, called the prosecution a "rebirth of McCarthyism," and likened our effort to imprison Gotti and his codefendants to the internment of Japanese-Americans in World War II. George Santangelo compared the trial to Nuremberg, as though the postwar trials of major Nazi criminals bore some logical similarity to McCarthyism and the Japanese internment camps.

"Do you believe this?" Diane whispered to me while Hoffman was waxing on about civil liberties. "What juror in his right mind could possibly buy this shit?"

Once deliberations began, the jury was sequestered in a hotel. Deputy marshals guarded them, and they also monitored communications with family members or anyone else in the outside world.

A couple of days into their deliberations I ran into Chief Deputy Marshal Mike Pizzi in the garage in the courthouse basement. He complained to me about the jurors. They could watch movies in their rooms, and a couple had ordered pornographic films. Since deputy marshals had to go rent them, it was awkward. More troubling, one juror was an alcoholic. The rules of the sequestration limited them to two drinks each at dinner. Juror Number 11, whom we referred to as "Oil Terminal Operator" because that was his job, was angry about the limit and had complained to the judge to get more.

"The guy's a fuckin' drunk," Pizzi told me. "We're worried about him getting the DTs. Between him and the porno people, you have some lowlifes on this jury."

Though that report gave us pause, the view from the courtroom itself was more comforting. You could tell from the jurors' notes, which requested evidence and readbacks of testimony, that they were proceeding systematically through the verdict sheet, considering each predicate act in order. When they were brought into the courtroom for readbacks of testimony or supplemental instructions on the law, they looked relaxed and harmonious. All the trauma of the Traynor testimony and our monthlong case rebutting it seemed a distant memory. Diane and I grew more confident each day.

On the afternoon of Friday the 13th of March, 1987, after deliberating for a full week, the jurors announced that they'd reached a verdict. As they walked into the packed courtroom, I glanced at Gotti. He was smiling, as was so often the case, and seemed relaxed. You'd never know from looking at him that we were about to learn whether he'd be spending the rest of his life in prison.

Because he was the lead defendant, the first of the verdicts delivered by the foreperson was on the RICO count against Gotti.

"Not guilty."

There were at least as many gangsters in the courtroom as there were press and prosecutors from our office, and they let out a muffled cheer. There was still the RICO conspiracy count, so Gotti wasn't yet off the hook, but before that verdict would be read, the foreperson had to say how all the other defendants had fared on Count One. Gene Gotti? Not guilty. Willie Boy Johnson? Not guilty. As each verdict was announced, the din went up a notch. By the time all seven defendants had been acquitted on Count One, everyone in the courtroom could feel what was coming.

Finally, "How do you find the defendant John Gotti on Count Two, racketeering conspiracy?"

"Not guilty."

The courtroom erupted.

Diane and I knew immediately that even if we lived another fifty years, we were experiencing what would be the lowest point of our careers. The seven grueling months on trial, the enormous work put into it before it began, and the very public and embarrassing allegations—all would have been worth enduring had there been guilty verdicts. The alternative was so bad that we had never really allowed ourselves to contemplate losing. But now it was happening, and we sat dumbfounded.

Even worse, we were trapped. Between us and the courtroom doors were dozens of wiseguys and an equal number of print and broadcast reporters. Some were rushing in from the hallway, others through the swinging doors into the well of the court. The wiseguys were yelling and wanted to get close to Gotti. We weren't going anywhere with that crowd in the way.

As bad as that was, Gotti decided to make it worse by being a graceless winner. As he made his way through the crowd, he turned and pointed at Diane and me and yelled, "Shame on them! I'd like to see the verdict on them!" All the reporters were scribbling in notepads, so we knew his exit line would be all over the newspapers the next morning.

The judge's law clerk approached us and said to come with her out the judge's door behind the bench. We did, and a stairwell just outside that door took us down to our offices. We met with Andy Maloney, and could hear the press gathering outside his office as we spoke. Andy was upbeat, a remarkable feat in the face of such a high-profile humiliation. He told us we had to speak at least briefly to the media at some point, and asked if we'd agree to do it right away.

Diane said she would, and after the press filed in and set up their cameras and microphones, she was the picture of grace.

"We presented the evidence as best we could," she said. "We accept the jury's verdict."

The reporters pressed her for a comment about the personal attacks on her.

"A jury verdict is the end of the case," she said, evenly and firmly. "My personal feelings are mine."

Andy announced we were done, and the reporters packed up their gear and left. When we were alone again, he said he was proud of us, and that he'd visit Rudy Giuliani the next morning. He wanted a promise from the Southern District that we would get the next Gambino Family RICO case against Gotti. If they could indict him for the Castellano homicide, fine; otherwise Andy would insist that we were first in line. He meant well, but the possibility that some other AUSAs might succeed where we'd just failed was cold comfort.

A few minutes later Diane and I emerged from his office to see the entire Criminal Division crowded into his reception area. It was a large space, but there were more than a hundred AUSAs there, and they spilled out into the corridor. Cases of Budweiser were stacked on the receptionists' desks. It was all hugs and congratulations and beer for the next hour.

We were still reeling from the acquittals, but being in that crowd was far better than being by ourselves. At one point Diane turned to me and said, "Imagine what it would have been like if we'd won."

For good reasons, sworn allegations that federal prosecutors tried to suborn perjury do not get ignored. John Gotti didn't know it when he pointed at us as he walked out of the courtroom and declared that we should be investigated, but the Justice Department's Office of Professional Responsibility was required to do just that.

Judge Nickerson also felt obligated to address the issue, and did so five days after the acquittals, in a memorandum to the chief judge, Jack Weinstein: "Having listened to and observed Traynor I find his testimony that the prosecutors sought to suborn perjury to be deliberately false and wholly unbelievable. Moreover, I find completely credible the government's rebuttal witnesses who refuted Traynor's statements."

The judge was trying to help us out, and Diane and I saw a tinge of guilt in it. Matt Traynor should never have been allowed to testify, and by the time the month-long rebuttal case was finished, nothing could have been clearer. The rules of evidence empower judges to avoid distracting sideshows like Traynor's, and we'd asked Judge Nickerson to use that power. He was wrong when he denied our request, and the ensuing circus had proven it. He also had every reason to believe that Traynor's perjury was a central reason for the acquittals.

Almost five more years would go by before we'd learn that John Gotti had walked free for another reason entirely.

PART II

THE INTERLUDE

CHAPTER 14

HANNA

In that summer of 1987, a few months after the acquittals, I ran into Willie Boy in Cadman Plaza Park. He was on his way into the courthouse on the minor drug case we'd brought against him during the Gotti trial.

We shook hands and I asked him how he was. "I'm good," he said in that unsettling high voice of his.

"Aren't you worried?" I went on. "Don't you think you're in danger, now that everybody knows you were an informant for all those years?" It was remarkable he was still alive.

"Nah, Mr. Gleeson, I don't think so," he said. I could tell he'd had this exact conversation many times, but he wasn't the slightest bit impatient. "I think I'm okay with him because I didn't testify against anyone." He didn't have to say who "him" was.

"Willie, you're kidding yourself. They *have* to make an example out of you. Do you really think they want to send a message that it's okay to be an informant as long as you don't become a witness?"

"Nah, I don't think I have a problem." He was smiling. "But thanks, Mr. Gleeson. I really appreciate it." He was pleasant and polite, and seemed genuinely unworried. As we walked into the courthouse together, I wondered if he'd really convinced himself that he'd been forgiven.

Willie Boy wasn't the only player from the trial I encountered that summer. I kept bumping into Shorty Mascuzzio, the Gambino associate who'd organized the lunches at the trial—running into him not by the courthouse, but down in Carroll Gardens, where we both lived. Shorty hung out around the Bravo Gelato storefront on Court

Street, a block and a half from our apartment. He and his crew sat in folding chairs on the sidewalk. I'd also seen him in Monteleone's, a bakery on Court a block closer to Carroll Park, an asphalt playground.

Shorty didn't have the grace to ignore me or just nod silently when I passed by. His side had triumphed in the trial, but it wasn't in Shorty's nature to win generously. He couldn't just let the verdict drift into the wake for both of us.

"Heyyy, Johnnnnn," he called from his folding chair the first time I saw him that summer, dragging out each word. "Who you acquittin' now?" There were three or four men sitting with him, young guys in wife-beaters. They all laughed as if Shorty had said the funniest thing they'd heard for weeks. I just ignored him. That same scene repeated itself, essentially verbatim, on another three or four occasions. Even with some time to think it over, Shorty couldn't come up with anything better than "who you acquittin' now?" Finally I changed my route home, but there was no avoiding him completely because Court Street was the commercial hub of our neighborhood, so on weekends I'd still see him now and then. I got used to his taunt, but it irritated the hell out of me that he kept repeating it in front of the younger tough guys, who otherwise wouldn't have had any idea what I did for a living.

I didn't always share these experiences with Susan. Part of my reasoning was to spare her from worrying. Part of it was selfish. We'd bought a co-op apartment there when I was at Cravath, so we'd dug into the Carroll Gardens neighborhood. Then I'd lopped off more than half my income to take a government job. And now my position was arguably putting us in physical danger. Susan had every reason to wonder why, exactly, I was value added to our marriage. Her support of me never wavered even slightly, but I saw no need to test its limits.

Shorty Mascuzzio and Willie Boy weren't the only reminders of the trial. I had an unusual visit that summer from Murray Cutler, Bruce's father. Murray was a former New York City police officer, but he'd spent most of his career as a criminal defense lawyer. He was a gentleman, and we got along well.

Murray had come to meet with another AUSA, and he stopped in my office on his way out.

"Please don't get the wrong impression of Bruce," he told me. "He's a good boy."

"Murray, why are you telling me this?"

"I just want you to know what I'm telling you. I know he behaved badly in that case."

No kidding, I thought. I had no doubt Bruce Cutler had been responsible for

Traynor's outrageous perjury. And now he'd become Gotti's press secretary, telling any reporter who'd listen how Gotti hated drugs and had cleaned up his Queens neighborhood of dealers. One article had even quoted Bruce as saying that if he had a son he'd want him to grow up to be like John Gotti.

"I want you to understand," Murray told me, "when Bruce was a homicide prosecutor, he hung around with homicide detectives. He talked and acted like them. It was as if they filled in a little piece of who he was. Now I see that same thing happening with these hoodlums. It's not him. He's a good boy."

"Murray, don't worry about it," I replied. "That one client of his brings out the worst in everyone who ends up in his orbit. I know Bruce isn't a bad guy at heart. And I very much appreciate your coming by."

Murray was visibly relieved. When he'd first put his foot into my office, he acted as though he'd expected me to throw him out. And in truth I'd failed to appreciate how much Bruce's newfound notoriety could affect others who had no responsibility at all for what he was doing. Not long after my conversation with his father, Bruce's younger brother applied to be an AUSA in California. They wanted to hire him, but before they did so I was called and given the opportunity to prevent it from happening. Maybe I was influenced by the fact that my brother-in-law was Gotti's first cousin, but it made no sense to me that other members of Bruce's family should be punished for what Bruce had become. I kept quiet, and the younger Cutler got the job.

Shortly before the Gotti trial Dave Kirby had become chief of the Appeals Division, and right away he recruited me to be his deputy chief. Then, in the summer after the acquittal, Kirby enjoyed his Vermont vacation so much he decided to stay there. So all of a sudden, after less than two and a half years as an AUSA, I was chief of appeals.

Diane had been appointed chief of Special Prosecutions after the trial ended. Even though we were each supervising a significant section of the office, within a few months it was clear our careers were headed in opposite directions. The parts of Diane's personality that empowered her to stand up to the FBI and to build the most important prosecution in the country were admired by her colleagues and superiors while that case was underway, but it had ended badly and now people viewed her differently. She remained tough and assertive and someone who refused to suffer fools, but instead of receiving deference, she now got mostly eye rolls. Within a year of the acquittals, she left her new job to take up a position in the legal department of the Metropolitan Transit Authority, which runs the city's subways and buses.

I found myself on the receiving end of compliments for having "put up with" Diane. Had we won, it would have been all kudos all the time for us both, but the loss brought blame, and it landed exclusively on her. Of course, she'd been lead counsel, but there was more going on than that. Women who lose huge cases don't get second chances.

As chief of appeals, I had it in my power never to try another case. But despite the disaster of the Gotti trial, something was drawing me back. As bad as the blowout had been, there were still some silver linings. I grew up as a lawyer in that one case. Such a process usually happens over a series of trials, not just one. But seven-month trials are rare, and ones with only two lawyers presenting the case rarer still; criminal trials of any length without a single law enforcement agent or even a paralegal at the prosecution table were unheard of—until ours.

Of the ninety-four witnesses, I'd examined seventy. My cross of Traynor lasted two days, and my rebuttal summation took four hours. Tensions had grown as the trial progressed, as had the nastiness directed at Diane, but my confidence increased along with them. The uncertainty and nervousness I'd felt during my six brief general crimes trials gave way over the seven months to a natural ability to frame questions without a script and to adapt to unexpected testimony. I knew how to get exhibits into evidence and how to engage in court with opposing lawyers on the fly. Confidence is a big part of trial lawyering, and now I had it.

So in September of 1987, six months after the acquittals, I decided to try another case. I teamed up with the joint auto larceny task force, an FBI and NYPD combination based in the FBI offices in Rego Park, Queens. Car crimes weren't exactly gripping, but I'd heard there were some good investigators on that squad. My case agent, Bob Joyce, was thorough and determined, and the other FBI agents, I would come to learn, were among the best in New York. One was George Hanna, a larger-than-life character who worked auto crimes to great effect but had more and better informants in organized crime than any other agent in the city. It was impossible not to like the guy. He was full of street sense and comfortable around prosecutors. Not one to stay behind a desk, he worked his informants round the clock, and visited our offices all the time, usually unannounced and always carrying a big bag of coffees from Cranberry's, a local deli.

Hanna was a legend in the FBI before he even started working. All new agents get a week off between graduation from the academy and reporting for duty, and Hanna spent his in Brooklyn. One morning he walked into a local bar to say hello to the owner and discovered an armed robbery in progress. One man put a gun to Hanna's head and told him to sit at the far end of the bar. The other had a gun to the bar owner's head, and he and the owner headed down the basement steps to get the bar's money. The upstairs robber told Hanna that after they got the money he'd be required to strip naked and be locked in the freezer. This didn't sound attractive to the young agent, so when he heard footsteps coming up the basement stairs he stepped away from the bar, identified himself, and pulled his weapon. He ordered the gunman to drop his, and when he refused and raised it to fire, Hanna shot him dead.

On the stairs with the bar owner when he heard the shots, the other robber rushed back into the basement. "Come on, I don't want to have to kill you too," Hanna called down to him. Over a tense few minutes, he talked him into giving himself up.

That began a storybook thirty-year career. Hanna accomplished as much in the fight against organized crime over that period than anyone else in the FBI or any other agency. He never again fired his weapon.

Hanna's partner on the car squad when I first met him was an Irishman named Neil Moran. They were close friends but couldn't have been more different. Hanna was from an Italian neighborhood in Brooklyn, Moran from the Bronx, where the Irish identify themselves by their parish rather than their neighborhood. The perfect Odd Couple, Moran was Felix Unger to Hanna's Oscar Madison. Moran was an excellent investigator but also a consummate worrier. Hanna, on the other hand, simply wanted to catch criminals, and had little patience for the paperwork requirements that kept agents behind their desks.

The investigation I worked with the car squad involved a chop shop out in the Rockaway section of Queens. The vehicles involved weren't cars but trucks, and they weren't used but brand new. The shop's operator, James Watts, paid people to steal the tractor half of tractor-trailers, right off new truck lots. They were hot-wired and driven to a fenced-in yard in Rockaway, where they were dismantled and sold for parts.

Half the car squad ended up testifying for me, and only one had an unhappy time of it. Special Agent Richie Mika testified as an expert on vehicle theft, explaining to the jury how thieves break into and start cars and trucks, switch VIN plates on them, and find buyers for stolen parts after the vehicles are taken apart. He was a real pro and the jurors loved him. He even gave pointers to the jury about how to avoid having their own cars stolen. I finished Mika's direct just before we broke for the day. When he left to go home, he discovered that his car had been stolen from a spot right in front of the courthouse while he was testifying. The next morning I decided it sufficiently undermined his expertise that I ought to disclose it, so I reopened the direct examination to have him tell the judge and the jury, who all got a kick out of it. Mika was good-natured about what had happened, and his ability to laugh at himself made him an even better witness.

The trial, my first before Judge Joe McLaughlin, couldn't have gone better. Watts was obviously guilty, and the jury convicted him quickly. The defense lawyer, who had been at Cravath when I was there, wasn't the type to pull stunts. No one accused me of distributing illegal drugs to suborn perjury. I felt I was back in the saddle, ready to try more cases. In addition, the auto larceny squad shared space out in the FBI's Queens office with the Gambino Squad. The agents were close, in large part because of George Hanna and his wide-ranging cadre of organized crime informants. It was the beginning of a new relationship between the FBI and me.

That same month Matt Traynor pled guilty to perjury. In a sworn statement given in the Nassau County Jail, he said Bruce Cutler had directed his false testimony, instructing him to blurt out the lie that Diane had given him her underwear, at which point Cutler would attempt to cut him off and say the topic was inappropriate. The plan called for Traynor to forge ahead anyway, and Cutler would ask the judge to order him to stop. Basically, Traynor testified that Cutler arranged things so it would look as if he were valiantly trying to save Diane from the humiliation that Cutler himself had scripted.

Traynor admitted his intense hatred of Diane, but he was also motivated by fear. He said Cutler had told him that providing the false testimony in Gotti's defense would make up for his having been at one point a rat, and would enable him to stay alive in prison.

Fortunes vary. While Willie Boy Johnson was still in the street in the summer of 1987, Tony Roach Rampino, one of the other codefendants in the trial before Judge Nickerson, wasn't as lucky. Rampino had fallen on hard times over the seven months, and he needed to earn. One of George Hanna's many informants called him that summer to say Rampino had agreed to sell him four ounces of heroin. Hanna teamed up with the Brooklyn District Attorney's Office, got some "buy money," and arrested Rampino the moment he handed the heroin over to Hanna's informant.

Rampino panicked. "John will kill me," he wailed. Everyone knew Rampino was both a drug user and a small-time dealer, but he'd grown up under Gotti's wing at the Bergin, so he was safe. Now, however, he'd been caught selling heroin, and based on his reaction, he was toast as far as Gotti was concerned.

Rampino knew he'd never make bail without Hanna's help. He was facing a state case brought under the ultra-harsh Rockefeller laws, which would send him away for at least twenty-five years. The case against him was airtight. A judge would let him out while the case was pending only if Hanna asked, so Rampino dangled John Gotti in front of him.

"I'll wear a wire back to the club," he promised, "and I'll tell you the other shooters in the Castellano murder."

Hanna asked if he could help the FBI seize the guns used by the hit team outside Sparks.

"Maybe" was the answer.

It was tempting, but Rampino reeked more of fear than anything else. His close friend for decades was now the boss, and though in truth he remained loyal to Gotti, he convinced Hanna and the Brooklyn District Attorney's Office that he was now scared stiff that Gotti would kill him. Firm in the belief that the release of Rampino would be far more likely to result in his becoming a fugitive than a government witness, Hanna refused the deal and opposed bail. Rampino was detained, went to trial, got convicted, and was sentenced. He would serve twenty-five years upstate before getting any chance at parole.

CHAPTER 15

THE RUGGIERO BUG CASES

In August of 1983, two years before Diane indicted Gotti, the FBI's bug in Angelo Ruggiero's kitchen had resulted in Ruggiero being indicted. The dozen defendants included not only Ruggiero but also Gene Gotti and John Carneglia. The case was assigned to Judge Mark Costantino. Everyone knew immediately that meant everything would be on a slow track.

Judge Costantino wasn't known for keeping long hours on the bench. His criminal cases tended to get bogged down in protracted pretrial hearings. The first of the five trials the Ruggiero case produced didn't start until four years after the indictment was handed up. Gene Gotti and Carneglia were already defendants in that prosecution for two years when they became defendants again in the case Diane and I had tried. When our indictment drew Judge Nickerson in 1985, there was no question, despite all that was involved, that the trial would begin in about a year, and it did. After spending seven months in that courtroom, Gene Gotti and Carneglia had only two months off before resuming their daily commute to the courthouse for the Ruggiero trial.

In one respect, Judge Costantino's slow pace saved their lives. The extensive narcotics conversations recorded on the bug in Ruggiero's home were all Paul Castellano needed to kill John Gotti and his entire crew. If the case had proceeded on a normal track, those conversations would have played in open court long before Neil Dellacroce died. As long as Dellacroce was alive, John Gotti couldn't kill the boss; but between the extensive delays in Judge Costantino's courtroom and Ruggiero's refusal to turn over copies of the tapes, it took Castellano more than two years to get the proof he needed to eliminate Gotti. Before he could arrange that murder, Dellacroce died and Gotti beat Castellano to it.

The only thing slower than pretrial proceedings in Judge Costantino's courtroom was the trial itself. The case was the perfect storm: extensive bug recordings, ten separate cross-examinations of each government witness, and absurdly short trial days. When James Watts was sentenced in October 1987, the Ruggiero trial had been underway for almost seven months. Everyone involved except the judge himself was fed up and eager for it to end.

Then, within days of the completion of my trial of James Watts, came the informant information that Ruggiero, Gene Gotti, Carneglia, and a fourth defendant, Eddie Lino, had identified five members of the supposedly anonymous jury in the Ruggiero trial and were busy fixing the case. An informant reported that one juror was already in the bag.

The double jeopardy clause forbids the government from appealing an acquittal, so Andy Maloney didn't want verdicts from a jury the FBI believed was tainted. However, one can't just walk into a trial that is entering its eighth month and ask for a do-over based on information from unidentified confidential informants. So Andy asked me to start a grand jury investigation and see if we could gather some evidence that the defendants had tampered with the jury.

The grand jury occupies a unique role in our federal criminal justice system. Rooted in centuries of Anglo-American history, the Fifth Amendment to the Constitution says that no one can be required to answer to a felony charge—that is, be bound over for trial before a petit jury like the ones we see on television—except upon indictment by a grand jury. Ideally, then, the grand jury serves as a kind of buffer between the government and the people. But in reality it's no buffer at all. A grand jury presentation can consist entirely of information that would be inadmissible at trial. A prosecutor can use illegally obtained evidence to get an indictment, and if the prosecutor has other evidence in his or her possession that indicates innocence, the prosecutor can withhold it from the grand jury. The prosecutor need only establish probable cause, not proof beyond a reasonable doubt, that the target committed the crime. Most important, there's no one else there but the prosecutor and the grand jurors. The target and his lawyer aren't even allowed in the room, let alone permitted to question the evidence.

That grand juries don't act as a check on prosecutors doesn't mean they're useless. They're enormously useful to the prosecutors themselves, and indeed are one of the most powerful tools they possess. A grand jury has nationwide subpoena power, and can summon witnesses and documents to the grand jury room. Guided by the Assistant U.S. Attorneys who bring their investigations to them, the grand juries' awesome powers become their powers. And because everything grand juries do is shrouded in closely guarded secrecy, those subpoenas, which are prepared by prosecutors and served by federal agents, are ominous indeed, and strike fear in the hearts of those who receive them.

Since the Gambino Squad was staffing the trial itself, it was walled off from my grand jury investigation, as were the AUSAs trying the Ruggiero case. Two agents from the Lucchese Squad were assigned to work with me. They were based in the Queens FBI office, next to both the Gambino and the auto larceny squads. The agents on all three were close.

Grand jury secrecy is so strict that even now, more than three decades later, it would be unlawful to disclose what occurred in that grand jury room in 1987. But subsequent proceedings in the public trial of the Ruggiero case revealed that, within a month, we established that the defendants had retained the services of a former NYPD detective, who admitted encountering one of the jurors in the garage near the courthouse, where the juror parked his car. The ex-detective denied any wrongdoing, but the admission dovetailed with the informants' report that he'd used his contacts in the police department to run the license plates of the jurors. This wasn't exactly powerful evidence, but it wasn't negligible either.

Then, on December 9, 1987—seven weeks after our investigation began—we got lucky. One of the jurors, Gary Barnes, told the judge he needed permission to come in late the next day. When asked why, Barnes said he needed to attend his naturalization ceremony. Since only citizens may sit as jurors, this was a surprise. In a curious twist that was telling only in retrospect, the defendants *objected* to the excusal of the juror despite his legal ineligibility to serve. But Judge Costantino excused Barnes from jury service, as the law required.

The following day, Barnes returned to his job at a large brokerage firm in Manhattan. After he arrived at his desk, he received a phone call from a coworker. Barnes didn't know the man, who asked to speak to him in person about a matter he refused to discuss on the phone. When they met, he said he was a good friend of Gene Gotti, and asked how the trial was going. He also asked what kind of cars Barnes liked, unaware that Barnes was no longer on the jury. The ex-juror, terrified that the gangsters had tracked him down even though he was supposed to be anonymous, called the FBI and told them what had happened.

Because it was a brokerage house, all the phone calls in Barnes's office were automatically recorded. We pulled the call to Barnes, and clearly the caller was making a criminal overture. It was a weird situation. He thought he was approaching a sitting juror to influence him—a crime—but in fact he wasn't. However, that could still amount to an *attempt* to commit jury tampering. Also, if the wiseguys had discovered Barnes's identity and were trying to reach him, that corroborated our informant information that they were trying to corrupt other jurors as well. So, even as the trial entered its ninth month, our investigation into whether tampering was underway became white-hot.

We listened to the other calls the caller made on his work phone that day, and the one immediately after he spoke to Barnes caught our attention. He'd dialed a Manhattan number, and, when the call was answered, he said, "I just met with him." The man on the other end answered, "I'm waiting for you here." We pulled the subscriber information for the number, and it was the telephone at the bar in Johnny Gammarano's place in Lower Manhattan. "Johnny G," as he was known throughout law enforcement, was a Gambino soldier.

When we served a subpoena on the caller, he immediately reached out for Charlie Carnesi, a mob lawyer from Brooklyn. Not coincidentally, Carnesi was also representing the former NYPD detective who was identifying jurors, and both Carnesi and the former detective had met with Ruggiero in the MCC during the time our investigation was underway. Barnes's coworker was trying to fix the Ruggiero jury for the Gambino Family.

A month later, I was still using the grand jury to follow other leads and wanted more time, but AUSA Bob LaRusso was about to rest the government's case. So Andy Maloney and I walked into Judge Costantino's courtroom and told him the government wanted a mistrial because there was reason to believe the defendants had tampered with the jury.

It was impossible to determine who was most surprised. LaRusso had had no idea we were coming. We'd isolated him and the Gambino Squad from our investigation. The judge was a deer in the headlights. The ten defendants and their lawyers were just as stunned, but within moments they were angry as well. They'd been sitting in the courtroom for nine months, and now they were hearing the entire trial had to be done over.

Their lead lawyer was Ron Fischetti, who shot out of his chair, outraged. He said the motion was a smoke screen for the government's belief that the trial wasn't going well. I'd told the judge that our investigation had uncovered significant evidence that the defendants had tried to tamper with the jury, and that we wanted a hearing to present that evidence. Fischetti claimed that there was never a bona fide grand jury investigation at all, and the court should deny the motion.

Judge Costantino refused that request, and I duly put Barnes and an FBI agent on the stand. Although the defendants crossed them both, most of their efforts were directed toward the media, which broadcast their allegation that the only basis for our motion was that we were about to lose the trial.

A lethargic trial had suddenly morphed into a high-stakes showdown. After the hearing, we asked Judge Costantino to speak individually to the jurors, three of whom told him they could no longer be fair. Since only two alternates remained, a mistrial was unavoidable. The only issue left couldn't have been bigger: Were our actions justified, in which case we would have a new trial? Or not, in which case that was it, and ten high-ranking members of the Gambino Family would walk free?

Judge Costantino, who'd often brag that he'd never once read a brief in more than thirty years on the bench, was in over his head. The lawyers in his courtroom were obviously not the only ones who noticed, because on January 20, 1988, the day after we filed our post-hearing memorandum, a new judge took over. There is no law or rule or practice that permits this, and indeed it violates a core principle of Article III of the Constitution: the independence of federal judges. Yet that didn't seem to matter.

The new judge was the chief: Jack Weinstein, a legend in the federal judiciary. He'd never allowed an absence of authority to stop him. Many years before, in response to the use of the Agent Orange defoliant in Vietnam, which produced health problems for tens of thousands of soldiers, he invented what is now known as "mass tort" litigation so they could all be compensated in one case. He defied harsh mandatory sentencing laws—refusing to impose what the law required him to mete out. He often got reversed by the court of appeals, but he didn't care. He reckoned that he knew what was right, and if the law hadn't yet figured that out he'd do it anyway, firm in the belief that his view would eventually prevail.

Weinstein was also famously protective of the court he led. The media had been loudly reporting for two weeks that we were lying when we said we had conducted a legitimate grand jury investigation. Not willing to leave that incendiary allegation solely in the hands of Judge Costantino, the chief judge now ordered us to disprove it to the entire court. All the judges would sit en banc in the ceremonial courtroom the next day, and I was told to bring eleven sets of my entire grand jury presentation, one for each judge.

Friends in the office suggested that I challenge the order. Courts of appeal can sit as a group to resolve important issues, but district courts can't. It had never happened before, anywhere, in the history of our country, not least because there was no law or rule or case that authorized it. Chief Judge Weinstein had simply made it up.

"Look, I don't know if he's allowed to do this or not," I told my colleagues. "I assume he isn't. All I know is that he's done it, and it's going to happen tomorrow morning. And we're in the right—it *is* a bona fide investigation, and I've got two feet of transcripts that prove it. I'm not going to look defensive by challenging his authority."

The next morning, a ten-defendant criminal case, allegations of jury tampering, and the Gotti name brought a circus atmosphere into the huge courtroom that had previously been used solely for ceremonial functions and naturalization proceedings. When the eleven judges had filed in, I received permission to distribute my stack of transcripts. Ron Fischetti tried to speak for the ten defendants, hoping to engage with Chief Judge Weinstein, but the judge wasn't biting, and the proceeding was over almost immediately.

The next day the en banc court issued its findings:

1. The grand jury proceedings investigating possible jury tampering in *United States v. Ruggiero* were appropriate.
2. There was good reason for the United States Attorney to have brought to the trial judge's attention the possibility of jury tampering.
3. Any publicity arising from the United States Attorney's application, which may have led some jurors to doubt their ability to decide the case fairly, was not the fault of the United States Attorney.

The full court left it up to Judge Costantino whether to grant a mistrial, and he promptly did. The Gambino Squad didn't know how to react. They'd been on trial for nine months, all of which was now a big waste. On the other hand, as they listened to our evidence, they'd become persuaded that the jury had been compromised, so they were visibly relieved that the case wouldn't be going to that jury. And they were especially relieved to be out of Costantino's courtroom.

One other outcome was unambiguous: the agents on the Gambino Squad were pleased with me. I was no longer tarnished by my association with Diane Giacalone and by our loss in the John Gottti case.

I still hadn't worked directly with those agents, but shortly after the mistrial I got my chance. One of my close friends, Larry Shtasel, had a drug case that had its origins in the bug in Ruggiero's kitchen. Shtasel's defendants were Arnold Squitieri and Alphonse Sisca, an inseparable pair of made guys universally referred to in law enforcement circles as "Arnold and Funzi." They were close to John Gotti, and Squitieri in particular was a tough guy who'd racked up a homicide conviction as a young man. The Gambino Squad's informants had reported that both men were involved in the murders of Castellano and Bilotti. The Gambino Squad was staffing the joint Southern District/Manhattan DA investigation into those murders, but it was going nowhere. The squad, looking for a break, thought if it could jam up Arnold and Funzi on heroin trafficking charges, one might flip and help jump-start the investigation into the murders at Sparks.

In addition to the tapes on which Ruggiero discussed selling them heroin, there was a cooperating witness. A small-time drug dealer named Richie Pasqua had flipped. Pasqua had grown up in East Harlem with Arnold and Funzi. He claimed during his debriefings to have bought a kilogram of heroin from them at the Red Oak Diner in Fort Lee, New Jersey, in 1982, around the same time that Ruggiero was blabbing that they were his customers.

Driven by the desire to flip Arnold and Funzi, Shtasel indicted them in New Jersey, where the sale to Pasqua had taken place. The case was assigned to a judge in Camden. It was a bleak venue to try a case, and two hours from New York City, but I didn't care. When Shtasel told me he was leaving the office, I jumped at the chance to work directly with the Gambino Squad, so as soon as the mistrial was declared in the Ruggiero case, I turned my attention to Arnold and Funzi.

My case agent was Bill Noon, and we spent about a week isolating the conversations from the Ruggiero bug that would best prove our charge. Then we visited Richie Pasqua, who'd been placed in the Witness Protection Program. His testimony was direct and simple: he'd bought a kilogram of heroin from Arnold and Funzi at the same time they were being supplied by Ruggiero.

In June 1988 Noon and I checked into a Philadelphia hotel for our three-week trial across the river in Camden. The jurors were not only *not* anonymous, but a week before the trial began the clerk of court sent their names and home addresses to me and defense counsel. The judge in the case clearly didn't like the fact that an out-of-town prosecutor had come into his courtroom. A couple of times each day he'd say, "Well, I don't know how it's done in Brooklyn, Mr. Gleeson, but . . . ," then go on to describe some weird local practice that always worked to my disadvantage.

The defense lawyers were a humorless pair, Dave Breitbart and Bob Koppelman.

They acted annoyed the entire time. Just before opening statements, with no heads-up to me at all, Breitbart told the judge he'd be offering into evidence Matt Traynor's testimony about me from the Gotti trial. "If Mr. Gleeson is accusing our clients of being drug dealers, it's only fair that we be able to prove that he also dealt drugs," Breitbart argued.

Most judges would not only have denied the request but would have chewed out Breitbart for even making it, but I was being home-jobbed, so the judge acted as if of course we should simultaneously try the case about the defendants dealing drugs and the case about me. For some reason, I had with me the transcript of Traynor's statement that his testimony at Gotti's trial was false. The judge decided he had to keep Traynor's testimony out, but he made it clear that, had Traynor not recanted it, he'd have let it in. I resolved never to enter a courtroom again without a copy of Traynor's statement.

Arnold and Funzi, unlike their lawyers, were pleasant to be on trial against, and we got along great. During breaks we talked in the courtroom. They were close to Gotti and knew I'd been the junior prosecutor in his big acquittal, so they asked me lots of questions about that case.

During one of our conversations, we were all back in the spectator section of the courtroom. Funzi had his feet up on the back of the bench in front of him and his hands behind his head, looking up at the ceiling. He said, "John, how old are you?"

"Thirty-four."

"Thirty-four. Let's see, where was I when I was thirty-four? Thirty-four . . . Leavenworth! I was in Leavenworth." Then he talked about the inmates with him at the time, including several prominent wiseguys. It was as if we were shooting the breeze over a drink in a bar.

At one point Arnold and I visited the men's room together. We were standing at adjacent urinals when he said, "You know, I only have one 't' in my name."

"Is that right?" I said. We'd spelled his name "Squittieri" in the indictment, and our heavily litigated case had produced hundreds of court filings with that spelling. The judge had issued published opinions that would be cited for years with those two "t"s.

"Not anymore," I told him, and he burst out laughing.

The judge remained angry with me the entire trial. Just before summations, some Genovese soldiers were indicted in Newark for conspiring to kill John Gotti to punish him for whacking Paul Castellano, and the arrests naturally produced newspaper reports. Because Gotti's name had come up often during our trial, the judge thought the publicity might prejudice Arnold and Funzi in the eyes of the jury, and he called me into chambers to chew me out.

"I can't believe you took that case down yesterday! Why couldn't you wait until next week when this trial will be over? Why shouldn't I declare a mistrial?" I explained that Sam Alito, the U.S. Attorney in New Jersey (and of course since 2008 a justice on the U.S. Supreme Court), had not consulted me, a young line assistant from another district who happened to be trying a case in Camden, about when to bring his indictment up in Newark. The judge eventually decided to let the case go to the jury, a great relief to me because I'd just as soon have had acquittals than start over in front of him again.

I summed up on the Tuesday after the long July 4 weekend. It was a strong, tight case. In addition to the other evidence, Pasqua had testified that he talked to the two defendants about the one-kilo deal at his mother's wake; when we retrieved the guest book from the funeral home, Arnold's and Funzi's signatures were in it.

Though I didn't need it, as soon as I sat down I got some help from the defense. Over that weekend a U.S. Navy warship in the Persian Gulf, in the mistaken belief it was being attacked, shot down a passenger plane, killing 290 people. President Reagan immediately acknowledged the blunder. Dave Breitbart began his summation by solemnly telling the jury that sometimes the government makes mistakes. Just this past weekend, he said, it had made a grievous mistake that cost hundreds of innocent lives. "This prosecution, ladies and gentlemen," Breitbart said grimly, "is such a mistake."

It was a monstrous comparison, and the jurors rolled their eyes in unison, and they soon made short work of coming in with a guilty verdict. Despite the references during the trial to Gotti and the Gambino Family, and knowing full well that Arnold and Funzi knew their names and addresses, the jury exuded nothing but confidence when they individually confirmed their decision. I thought maybe we should try more gangsters in Camden—but not before that judge.

CHAPTER 16

DELROY

The spring and summer of 1988 brought some changes. Buddy Dellacroce, who pled guilty and immediately became a fugitive, was finally found, dead of an overdose, up in the Pocono Mountains of Pennsylvania. Shorty Mascuzzio, my neighborhood nemesis, was suddenly no longer a problem. He was shaking down a disco owner in Manhattan at two-thirty one morning when the crowd upstairs heard the sound of gunshots from the basement. Shorty had pistol-whipped the owner, who responded by taking the gun from him and shooting Shorty in the neck and back, killing him. Manhattan District Attorney Robert Morgenthau's office took the case to a grand jury, but the disco owner testified that he was acting in self-defense, and the grand jury refused to indict him.

The shoe finally dropped on Willie Boy Johnson as well. Other crime families had complained to Gotti, wanting to know why he was taking so long to kill him. What was going to keep others from flipping if Willie Boy were allowed to live? Part of the reason for the delay was that Willie Boy had done a few months on the minor drug case we'd made against him, but it had been almost a year and a half since the acquittals before Judge Nickerson. Gotti finally gave the contract to Eddie Lino. Lino was close to Angelo Ruggiero, and was one of the dozen codefendants in the drug trafficking case based on the Ruggiero bug.

At 6:20 in the morning on August 29, 1988, Willie Boy was leaving his home in the Flatlands section of Brooklyn to go to a construction job on Staten Island. A couple of young men Lino had given the job to were waiting outside. At some level Willie Boy must have been expecting them, because as soon as he saw them he bolted. But he was too bulky and, at fifty-two, too old to outrun his killers. They left nothing to chance, shooting him six times in the head and twice in the back. They were well aware that law enforcement knew it was just a matter of time before Willie Boy was whacked, and they may have suspected that they were not the only ones watching him that morning. Before driving away, they spread jack-shaped spikes on the street behind them to puncture the tires of any pursuing car.

I was on vacation on Long Beach Island with my sister Mary and brother-in-law Eddie when Willie Boy met his fate. Eddie was an early riser, and he'd go out to get bagels and the tabloids each morning. Willie Boy was on the front pages, just as he'd been when his informant status was revealed more than three years earlier. He'd chosen that life and made choices that he knew could result in a death sentence. Still, as I sat on the deck of our rented beach house, looking at the gruesome photos of the murder scene, I felt bad for him. He'd committed plenty of crimes, but all his troubles began once the mob refused to take care of his wife and son when he went to prison. He stood up, but then his bosses let him down, so he ended up selling information to the FBI. Then, when Diane Giacalone wanted him to become her witness, he stood up again, just like he was supposed to do. Now he was on the front pages in a pool of his own blood.

When I returned from vacation, I felt like a veteran prosecutor, but while I'd learned how to present a criminal case, I had only a vague idea how to build one. Federal prosecutors spend much more time investigating crimes and "making" cases before the grand jury than they do presenting them at trial. Except for my investigation into the jury tampering in the Ruggiero case, my experience consisted mainly of trying cases others had indicted. That was about to change.

By the mid-1980s, crack cocaine was taking over Brooklyn. Guns were everywhere, the crack trade was extremely lucrative, and, in substantial part because of drug-related violence, the city's murder rate had exploded. Crack reigned supreme, and the undisputed King of Crack was a ruthless operator called Delroy Edwards. Delroy—no one ever used his last name—was from Jamaica, and he surrounded himself with young fellow countrymen who helped him distribute the drug all over the borough.

His business model was simple. Lock a worker—usually a teenage addict—into a "spot," a decrepit ground-floor apartment with a small hole in the door. Give him $1,000 worth of vials containing small rocks of crack, either in $5 or $10 sizes. His job was to collect the cash the addicts on the other side of the door pushed through a hole and give them the right number of vials in return. A "runner," sometimes protected by an armed enforcer, would return a few hours later to collect the money and resupply the spot. If the worker was "short," usually because he'd smoked some of what he was supposed to sell, he'd be shot. Not dead, but shot; a flesh wound and a lesson. If another crack dealer opened a spot too close to one of Delroy's, he'd be shot too. Dead.

Delroy rode that simple model to great financial success. After opening spots in all the rough neighborhoods in Brooklyn, he expanded to Philadelphia and Washington, D.C. The detectives assigned to the Brooklyn North Homicide Squad were overwhelmed by the number of murders and other acts of violence that their street sources reported were Delroy's doing.

Sergeant Frank Shields was in charge of Brooklyn North Homicide, and had a working relationship with Billy Fredericks, a local Alcohol, Tobacco and Firearms agent. They'd worked together on a number of weapon seizures, and the two decided that there was a need to look into Delroy's organization. They approached Jonny Frank and asked him to do it.

Jonny was a year ahead of me in the office and had distinguished himself by conducting complex investigations. But he didn't care for courtroom work and had no interest in trials. Still, when he was asked by Shields and Fredericks to turn street chatter about Delroy into a RICO case, he was intrigued. Knowing he'd eventually have to prosecute any case he managed to build, he looked around for someone who'd take the lead in a trial. That brought him to my office, and my acceptance landed me on the ground floor of an investigation that involved several law enforcement agencies.

Jonny taught me that the first order of business was to organize hundreds of bits of crime-related information into "episodes" and build a separate file for each. Every routine drug arrest at one of Delroy's crack spots, every gun possession, every murder we suspected him of, was an episode. Within weeks we had a few dozen, and once we started arresting low-level members of Delroy's organization the number increased exponentially. They were basically kids, and they all hated Delroy, a brutal boss, so they flipped on the spot. The Brooklyn North Homicide detectives had an encyclopedic knowledge of local murders, especially the unsolved ones. Someone would say they had heard Delroy brag about shooting some American Blacks on Sterling Place between Buffalo and Ralph, and the detectives immediately knew what case it was, and had the homicide file on our desks the next morning.

We moved fast when a new name came up, wanting to arrest that person before he fled back to Jamaica. The hurry-up offense placed in sharp relief how the different law enforcement agencies worked. One of our cooperators told us about a murder we'd already been aware of, but he gave us a new target: a guy nicknamed "Bigga" had driven the getaway car. As soon as the cooperator left our office, we decided Bigga had to be found right away, but all we had besides the nickname was the Brooklyn neighborhood he lived in.

First to arrive the next day were the federal members of our team. They had printouts from FBI and DEA databases showing all arrestees that had Bigga as an alias, which they'd cross-referenced with the national NCIC database. Using an age-range to winnow the search further, they'd narrowed it down to about a dozen guys. About a half hour later the Brooklyn North Homicide detectives arrived. They had no paperwork, but they hadn't come empty-handed.

"We went out to the neighborhood," one said, "and we found four guys named Bigga. We have them all in a van downstairs, and they're ready to talk."

In the end, Jonny and I culled from more than a hundred episodes the ones we could prove beyond a reasonable doubt. There were still way too many to impose on a jury, so we selected the most serious cases we had and made them predicate acts in the first RICO case against a street gang: six murders, more than a dozen other shootings, multiple gun counts, and drug trafficking charges.

In the spring of 1989, during the run-up to Delroy's trial, Gene Gotti and John Carneglia were being prosecuted once again on the narcotics charges based on the 1982 bug in Angelo Ruggiero's home. There were big changes this time. Ruggiero, the lead defendant, was in prison dying of cancer, so the case against him was severed. Also, after the mistrial based on jury tampering, the charges against the other two men were severed from the rest of the indictment and reassigned. The retrial landed in the courtroom of eighty-nine-year-old Judge John Bartels. When he was nominated by President Eisenhower, the only criticism of Bartels, aged fifty-six at the time, was that he wouldn't serve long enough. He showed them, serving on the Eastern District bench for forty-three years.

Another significant change was the length of the government's case. The first iteration of the trial had lasted nine months. This time, Andy Maloney asked me to consult with AUSA Bob LaRusso with an eye toward streamlining the case, as I'd done when trying Squitieri and Sisca. The trial began on April 17, 1989; less than a month later LaRusso was summing up.

After six full days of deliberations, the jury reported that one juror was refusing to vote or even discuss the case. When the juror was summoned in front of Judge Bartels alone in chambers, he reported that two men had approached him late at night in his driveway and made it clear that they knew he was on Gene Gotti's jury. The juror was afraid, so the judge excused him. Over the virulent objection of counsel for Gotti and Carneglia, an eleven-person jury promptly convicted both defendants of trafficking in narcotics.

The two felt railroaded, and during the several-week period between the jury's verdict and the sentencing, John Carneglia violated one of the cardinal rules of pre-sentence behavior: never say anything negative about your judge *before* sentence is imposed. He told a tabloid reporter that he didn't think he'd get too much time, and that he looked forward, once out of prison, to "pissing on the judge's grave."

On the day of sentencing in July 1989, the judge's law clerk came out before the judge took the bench. He walked over to the defense table and told Carneglia's lawyer that he had a message for his client.

"The judge wants Mr. Carneglia to know that his probation officer hasn't been born yet," the law clerk said. A few minutes later, Gene Gotti and John Carneglia were sentenced to fifty years.

We'd indicted twenty-five people along with Delroy Edwards, and every one except him and his girlfriend pled guilty. I'd tried and convicted the girlfriend by myself, and Jonny Frank and I tried Delroy together in the summer of 1989. The trial was mind-numbing from all the details of violence. There were so many murders, shootings, and beatings, and it was all so routine and casual.

By the time we got a verdict, the national media was paying attention. The jury's final two notes to Judge Dearie were delivered simultaneously. One was the typical "we have reached a verdict." The other made it onto *Newsweek*'s "Quotes from the Week" page. It said, "Now that we have rendered our verdicts, what steps will be taken to protect us from the defendant?"

I persuaded the judge to take the jury's verdict before providing the answer to its question, which of course was "none." Criminals know, even though jurors do not, that there's no profit in threatening or killing a juror after the verdict is in.

CHAPTER 17

MIKE COIRO

Mike Coiro was the original New York mob lawyer. He'd grown up in the profession defending John Gotti, Angelo Ruggiero, Gene Gotti, and the other regulars at the Bergin, and it was a good living. In the late 1960s and '70s all the young gangsters there were hijackers. Everyone who could hop onto the running board of a tractor-trailer and put a gun in the driver's face was stealing from nearby John F. Kennedy International Airport. John Gotti was convicted in the Eastern District in 1967 for hijacking a load of women's apparel from the cargo area of Northwest Airlines. His younger brother Gene was found guilty along with him, as was Ruggiero. Gotti picked up another hijacking conviction the following year. John Carneglia, one of the toughest members of the crew and later its biggest earner, had several airport convictions as well.

Stealing truckloads of goods from the airport became so routine that thieves would often do it without knowing what they were stealing. After ditching the driver, they'd bring the truck to a "drop," a warehouse where they could store the hot goods until it was safe to sell them. There was excitement when they discovered what they'd stolen—carpets, televisions, frozen shrimp, clothing—sometimes followed by anxiety as they scrambled to find buyers for merchandise they'd never handled before. As the Bergin crew were also active in gambling, loan-sharking, and narcotics, they kept Mike Coiro busy, and they grew to trust him. In 1973, when John Gotti and Ruggiero graduated to murdering McBratney, Coiro represented them in that case as well, along with Roy Cohn.

Everyone liked Coiro, including the prosecutors he squared off against. Like many old-time mob lawyers, he was a screamer and a chair-thrower when a jury was in the room but a friendly and fun-loving adversary at other times. I first met him in 1985, when I was a brand-new AUSA and he'd come to my office, supposedly to inspect evidence before the Gotti trial. Diane Giacalone had warned me that Coiro was more likely to joke around than actually look at any of it, and sure enough he spent the first ten minutes asking about me. "Whoa! I never met a *Cravath* lawyer before!" he bellowed. "You're in for a treat, because you're gonna meet some characters in this case you'd never run across if you stayed at the big firm." He then regaled me with stories about the Bergin and himself.

Coiro told me how his clients thought he was lucky because his wife and his girlfriend were both named Stephanie. They were envious because he never had to worry about slipping up by saying the wrong name. But shortly before Valentine's Day one year, Coiro went to a jeweler near his home on Long Island and ordered two gold pins, each engraved with an "S." One was much larger than the other. Coiro's wife happened to be in the store in early February, and the jeweler, who didn't know about the girlfriend, gave her a sneak preview of both pins. So when Valentine's Day came and Coiro gave her only the little one, he was busted. "So much for my good luck!" he roared, his eyes disappearing behind narrow slits above his big, toothy laugh.

Coiro felt more loyalty to his clients than he did to the ethical rules of his chosen profession, so it was only a matter of time before he became a defendant himself. He got his opportunity in 1982, when the Gambino Squad put the bug in Ruggiero's kitchen.

In the eyes of federal law enforcement, Ruggiero and his younger brother Sal were exact opposites. Sal was smart, discreet, and great at what he did, which was dealing in large quantities of heroin. When in the mid-1970s the FBI finally made a case against him and an Eastern District grand jury indicted him, Sal promptly skipped town. The FBI searched for him the world over while he lived for years under an alias in Franklin Lakes, New Jersey, less than an hour's ride from New York City, still actively engaged in large-scale heroin trafficking.

Angelo wasn't as smart as Sal and was famously indiscreet. For years he showed up wherever law enforcement had a wiretap or bug, speaking freely about the various criminal schemes he was part of or was planning. He also talked about others, and got more people indicted with loose talk than anyone else in the mob. Our disastrous seven-month trial two years earlier had not included Angelo as a defendant, but his voice regularly filled the courtroom as we played conversations from half a dozen wiretaps and bugs over the previous decade. On a break during that trial, John Carneglia produced one of its few light moments by handing his lawyer a quarter and saying, "Here, go out to the pay phone in the hallway and dial any seven numbers at random. There's a fifty-fifty chance Angelo will answer."

The Ruggiero bug was the beginning of the end of the Gambino Family, for it exposed the heroin trafficking of John Gotti's crew. The conversations it recorded had already convicted his brother Gene and Carneglia. The bug also led directly to the murders of Castellano and Bilotti. But among its other, lesser-known accomplishments was how it captured the essence of Mike Coiro. Meeting regularly for coffee in Ruggiero's kitchen, he'd keep his clients abreast of the various investigations that affected them. As a young prosecutor listening to those tapes for hundreds of hours more than three years after they were made, I'd laugh out loud at his dry sense of humor. "The IRS agent who served the subpoena put off our meeting," he reported one morning. "He has to go to the firing range." Pause. "Needs to stay sharp in case he needs to shoot some taxpayers."

Those tapes also showed Coiro's darker side. He'd relay to Ruggiero and Gene Gotti reports from the hooks he claimed to have in the Nassau County District Attorney's Office, the Queens District Attorney's Office, and even my own office, in the Eastern District.

On May 6, 1982, Salvatore Ruggiero's six-year run as a fugitive ended. The FBI didn't catch him. Rather, his private plane crashed into the ocean off the coast of Georgia, killing both him and his wife. After the plane went down, Coiro was overheard in Angelo's kitchen coaching him on how to mislead the Eastern District grand jury that was searching for Sal's assets. Coiro even offered to lie to the grand jury himself to help Angelo avoid a charge that he'd harbored his fugitive brother.

Those conversations put Coiro on the radar screen as a potential defendant, but they might not have been enough to bring a case. Boasting about law enforcement hooks didn't prove that he'd actually bribed anyone. He could even have been making up the fact that he had those corrupt sources, just to make himself appear more valuable to his clients. Besides, Coiro benefitted from the problem prosecutors always face when they consider charging criminal defense lawyers for committing crimes along with their clients. There's a built-in defense: they're not only allowed to talk about crimes with their clients, they're *supposed* to. The more they know about their clients' misdeeds, the better they can defend them. So Coiro might have avoided a criminal charge if it hadn't been for two conversations.

In the first, Ruggiero and Gene Gotti asked him to convert cash into checks.

In explaining why he needed Coiro to take control of the money, Ruggiero said the words that made Coiro a money launderer and a federal defendant: "I might as well put the heroin in my fuckin' hands as the money, same thing."

"I know," Coiro said. "You could get caught in a bad situation."

Ruggiero's use of the word "heroin" placed Coiro in a very bad situation. It was also highly unusual. An agent can spend a career investigating drug traffickers without ever hearing that word used by a suspect. Ruggiero's use of it revealed his inexperience. It also put Coiro at the defendant's table and would haunt the Gotti crew for a decade.

The other conversation came at the end of a discussion about Coiro's law enforcement sources. One morning in the spring of 1982, sitting around Ruggiero's kitchen table, Gene Gotti became nostalgic about the long association between the members of his brother's crew and Coiro. "Mike," Gotti said, "you're not our lawyer. You're one of us as far as we're concerned."

"I know it, Gene," Coiro answered, "and I feel that way too. That's an honor." The first part of Coiro's remark is not what did him in. Sitting in Ruggiero's kitchen with men he knew and had loved for many years, what was he supposed to say? "No, Genie, you guys are the criminals, and I'm just the lawyer" would hardly have been a likely response, even if it were true. A jury would understand that. But Coiro's last three words would hurt him badly. A jury would forgive him for not insulting his gangster friends over coffee, but it was something else to say it was "an honor" to be considered a gangster rather than an attorney. It would make it much easier for them to find him guilty of the obstruction charges he was indicted on.

Indicted in 1983 with Ruggiero, Gene Gotti, and nearly a dozen others, Coiro was the last defendant standing in what had become the longest-running federal criminal case in the country. Years earlier, his attorney, Jerry Shargel, asked that Coiro be tried separately. The motion was granted, and by the time the other defendants had completed their various trials it was the fall of 1989. For more than six years, Coiro wore two hats in the Eastern District: he was an indicted defendant, presumed innocent of the serious charges against him, and he was also a practicing defense lawyer, vigorously representing the same people with whom he'd been charged with committing crimes.

By 1989, all the players in Coiro's case had changed except the defendant himself. The case had been reassigned to Judge Joe McLaughlin, the garrulous former dean of Fordham Law School before whom I'd tried the Watts case two years earlier. When he scheduled the case against Coiro for trial in November 1989, Shargel backed out for unstated reasons. Bruce Cutler replaced him. During the years Coiro was under indictment, Cutler had also replaced Coiro as house counsel for the John Gotti crew of the Gambino Family. Cutler, not Coiro, played the role of chair-thrower in our 1987 trial. And when Gotti and all his codefendants were acquitted, it catapulted Cutler into national prominence.

At the same time that Cutler replaced Shargel, I learned that the case needed a new prosecutor. Bob LaRusso had had enough. I'd just finished the Delroy trial, and the prospect of a rematch with Cutler appealed to me, so I volunteered.

I got ready to prosecute Mike Coiro with Bill Noon, the same agent who'd helped me convict Squitieri and Sisca. In the meantime, other agents on the Gambino Squad, working with other prosecutors in my office, were trying to place three bugs in 247 Mulberry Street, the building that housed the Ravenite Social Club. The Ravenite consisted of two small rooms, railroad style, on the ground floor. They'd been John Gotti's headquarters since he took over as Gambino boss in December 1985.

In September 1989 Gotti was once again under indictment. Bob Morgenthau, the Manhattan district attorney, had charged him with ordering the Westies, an Irish mob under the Gambino Family's wing, to shoot John O'Connor. O'Connor was the business agent of Local 608 of the carpenters' union. A new restaurant, Bankers and Brokers, had been built downtown near Wall Street, and O'Connor had the place destroyed because nonunion carpenters had built it. But he hadn't asked around enough to know that the owner of the restaurant, Phil Modica, was a made member of the Gambino Family. Made guys are allowed to go nonunion. The shooting would not be fatal, but would teach O'Connor a lesson. The Westies did it by shooting him in the butt.

By the fall of 1989 O'Connor was fully recovered, but he was still plenty scared, and was definitely not helping to bring those responsible to justice. Even though it was just an assault charge, the O'Connor case was potentially a big problem for Gotti, whose criminal past made him a "persistent offender" under New York law, which would land him in state prison for at least twenty-five years if convicted. He was forty-nine years old. His career would be over.

But the case wasn't what Morgenthau had hoped it would be. A couple of Westies would testify, but they were a drug-addled and murderous duo with insuperable credibility problems. The case was going to stand or fall on a tape-recorded conversation at the Bergin in which Gotti supposedly ordered the shooting. "Bust 'im up," he allegedly said, referring to O'Connor. The problem was that only a wishful thinker could make out *any* words on the barely audible tape, let alone such a convenient sound bite.

No one in federal law enforcement believed Gotti would be convicted, so the FBI and the prosecutors in my office were busy trying to make the next case. The conversations to be intercepted in 247 Mulberry Street would be the centerpiece. However, they already had competition. Morgenthau was still pursuing Gotti for the murders of Paul Castellano and Tommy Bilotti and had teamed up with the Southern District to prosecute those killings. For almost four years, they'd been trying to make a case against Gotti, and weren't having much luck.

Because Little Italy is in Manhattan, placing bugs in the Ravenite required the permission of a federal judge in the Southern District. AUSA Lenny Michaels and Special Agent George Gabriel of the FBI left the Eastern District's offices in the federal courthouse in Brooklyn Heights, crossed the bridge into Manhattan, and entered the stately Southern District courthouse in Foley Square to present an application. Michaels, a careful lawyer, had touched all the necessary bases before a judge could approve the extraordinarily invasive tool of listening to private conversations. His application took up 145 pages. After reviewing it and having a friendly exchange with Michaels and Gabriel, the judge authorized the installation of three bugs at 247 Mulberry Street.

One of the bugs was already in place. Agents had installed it the previous year, but had turned it off when their authorization expired. Michaels and Gabriel didn't expect much from it. Putting aside the audibility nightmare created by fifty verbose gangsters all talking at once, wiseguys were far too careful to talk about crimes in a social club, an obvious spot for a bug. Still, the agents hoped that snippets of conversation from inside the club might shed some light on conversations intercepted by the better-placed bugs they planned to install.

Michaels and Gabriel expected more from the hallway bug. The main entrance to the Ravenite was on Mulberry Street, in full view of the FBI surveillance team based in a rented apartment up the street. The team videotaped everyone who came in or exited through that street entrance, but there was another door leading from the club's back room into the interior of the three-story building. Gotti would summon people into that hallway for conversations he didn't want overheard. With linoleum floors, plaster walls, and bare wooden steps leading to the upstairs apartments, the hallway's acoustics made electronic eavesdropping very frustrating. The slightest shuffling of feet made scraping noises that reverberated around the space. Footsteps even a few feet away sounded like rifle shots. And then there was the constant din coming from the crowded club.

In September, October, and November of 1989 a few conversations were intercepted, but they were nothing to start a case on. Even worse, on several occasions the agents could hear Gotti and others continue their conversations as they walked up the stairs. The agents knew where they were headed: to Apartment Ten on the second floor. The tenant was Nettie Cirelli, the seventy-four-year-old widow of Mike Cirelli, a Gambino soldier. Norman Dupont, the Gambino associate who acted as caretaker of the club, would run upstairs and give Nettie money to go out shopping or to eat. With her gone, Gotti would use her living room.

The Cirelli apartment was ideal. Indoor meetings, particularly right in the same building that housed the Ravenite, posed the obvious risk of being bugged, but Gotti, who'd been educated over the years in the finer points of electronic surveillance law, had reason to feel safe. First, the government can't try to bug a meeting place it doesn't know about, and though Ravenite regulars knew that Gotti would sometimes bring people into the hallway to talk, few were aware that he'd occasionally head up the stairs, and hardly anyone knew where he went when he did. Second, Gotti knew that it's one thing to get permission to install a bug in a social club, an office, or a restaurant, but quite another to install it in someone's home. A judge would naturally hold the government to a higher standard if it wanted to bug the home of an innocent old lady. Third, even if a judge's permission were given, such an installation requires physical intrusion, and Nettie Cirelli almost never left her apartment. When she did, it was in the middle of the day, for brief shopping excursions. Entering the building then was out of the question. For decades, the residents of 247 Mulberry Street and the surrounding buildings had been the eyes and ears of the gangsters in the Ravenite. One day in 1979, a stranger parked his car directly in front of the club, and we filmed Mike Cirelli as he smashed the car's windows and opened the nearest fire hydrant. He filled the car up to the broken windows with water. Special Operations agents were very good—even legendary in law enforcement circles—but they couldn't sneak into Nettie's apartment during daytime hours.

The first of Gotti's reasons to feel comfortable was short-lived. As of September 1989, the Mafia's code of silence had worked well in keeping members of crime families off witness stands, but it hadn't kept them from talking. Willie Boy Johnson was dead and Billy Battista was in the wind, but there were other confidential informants everywhere, in all the families. One was close enough to Gotti to give up Nettie's apartment as his secret meeting place, so when the judge authorized electronic surveillance, the third bug he gave his blessing to was to be in Mrs. Cirelli's home.

The government had more difficulty overcoming the other protections the apartment gave Gotti. The only way to avoid arousing the suspicion of the neighbors was to enter the building to plant the bug in the middle of the night. But the apartment was tiny. What if Nettie woke? The entire project would have to be scrapped, because Gotti would no longer use the place. And that would be the least of it. If there was one threat the residents of 247 Mulberry Street didn't have to worry about, it was people breaking into their homes in the dead of night. With all the gangsters around, they didn't have to depend on the police for their peace of mind. The front door to the building didn't even have a lock. What if Nettie woke up and died of a heart attack because two G-men dressed in black were skulking around? Gotti had already beaten two cases, and his lawyers were actively working on an overarching theme that the government was getting so desperate to convict him that it would stoop to anything. Frightening an innocent old lady to death would fit nicely into that narrative.

For almost three months, agents monitored the club itself and the hallway, but not the apartment. They listened helplessly as Gotti began conversations in the hall, only to head up the stairs. Knowing full well that a discussion that could end Gotti's career was about to occur in a room they couldn't bug, the agents agonized as the voices faded away.

The agent in charge of ending this situation was George Gabriel. At first blush, he was an odd choice in such an important case. He was only thirty-three, with relatively little experience investigating La Cosa Nostra, having come to the Gambino Squad only two years earlier from an FBI office in the suburbs. In drug or stolen property cases, two years of work can make an agent a veteran, but organized crime investigations are notoriously long-term. Agents have to learn the structures of various Families, the relationships among them, and who controls the unions that help the mob earn. Informants have to be recruited and nurtured so the agents can decide whom to investigate, and for what. It takes time and patience.

Gabriel distinguished himself right away. He enthusiastically studied the FBI's warehouse of information about the five New York Families and the DeCavalcante Family in New Jersey, and he absorbed it quickly. Gregarious and outgoing, he also got along well with gangsters in the street and with prosecutors. He was an especially good cook, having learned as a teenager in the Long Island diner owned by his father, a Greek immigrant. At his backyard barbecues, Gabriel would simultaneously prepare shish kebab, grape leaves, steaks, chicken, hot dogs, and burgers, all the while joking with his friends and their kids. People who knew him wanted to spend as much time with him as possible.

Gabriel was determined not to blow the opportunity created by Gotti's use of Nettie's apartment. The special operations people wouldn't go in until he told them to, and he was prepared to wait. In September, when the bugs were authorized, Gabriel got the judge to sign a separate order allowing the FBI to put a pen register on Nettie's telephone. It didn't intercept conversations, so there was no need for a warrant, but it showed when Nettie's telephone was off the hook and which numbers were dialed from it. In the autumn of 1989, Nettie used her telephone consistently to call her friends, and she made occasional calls to her son in California.

On November 19, the pen register went silent. The following morning, Gabriel, feeling it was safe to do so, called Nettie's number, and there was no answer. A surveillance team reported that she hadn't left the building that morning. Gabriel figured she'd left the day before, perhaps for a Thanksgiving trip to visit her son. It was time to go in.

Late that night, agents slipped through the unlocked front door to 247 Mulberry Street, walked up to the second floor, and picked the lock to Nettie's apartment. There was little doubt where the bug should go. Around a coffee table in the center of the tiny living room were a couch, two stuffed chairs, and a lamp on an end table. Within minutes, they installed a tiny piece of equipment and were gone.

Ten years earlier, Detective John Gurnee had believed he'd accomplished a similar mission by installing a bug downstairs in the Ravenite. He'd had to deal with Duke, a vicious German shepherd who stayed in the club at night, so he came armed with a container of his wife's meatballs, liberally laced with tranquilizers. He slipped them through the mail slot one by one until the dog fell over. It worked perfectly—Gurnee picked the lock, planted the bug, and left undetected. The following morning he was back in the observation post across the street. Finally ready to listen instead of just watching and videotaping, Gurnee was full of excitement when Norman Dupont arrived and opened the door to let Duke out to relieve himself on the sapling in front of the club. But instead of bounding out in his usual fashion, Duke staggered out like a drunk to his usual spot and lifted his leg. Incapable of maintaining his balance on only three legs, he flopped over. Later that day, Dupont and several other low-level associates tore the club apart until they found Gurnee's bug.

Gabriel didn't have to worry about Duke, long since gone, but in the days following the agents' break-in, he was concerned that someone in the building might have seen or heard them and reported it. He monitored every available source of information to determine if the apartment bug would go the way of Gurnee's. But informants were reporting nothing. The video surveillance of the front of the club showed business as usual. The bug in the club itself maintained the same level of activity. Although the Gambino Squad wasn't intercepting any criminal conversations, they were hearing the same degree of chatter that they'd been intercepting for months. The slightest suspicion of a break-in would have altered the pattern. At the least, no one would have talked in the club. Within a couple of days, Gabriel was convinced they were in the clear.

Nettie returned after Thanksgiving, and on November 30 the Gambino Family used the apartment for the first time since it was wired. Gotti, consigliere Sammy Gravano, and acting underboss Frank Locascio exited the rear door of the club and walked up the stairs to Nettie's apartment. They sat down in the living room and had a conversation that was transmitted so clearly that the agents listening in could barely contain themselves. The noisy chaos of the club was gone. So were the harsh, echoing sounds in the hallway. Other than the voices of their top three targets, the only sound the agents could hear was soft music that a Hollywood director might have chosen as the background for a scene in which a mob boss is talking to his underboss and consigliere.

CHAPTER 18

THE BUG OF ALL BUGS

At exactly the same time that Gotti, Gravano, and Locascio were going up the stairs to Nettie Cirelli's apartment, Mike Coiro's jury was filing into Judge McLaughlin's Brooklyn courtroom to announce its verdict. When the foreman pronounced Coiro guilty of racketeering, Bruce Cutler groaned loudly and put his forehead on the table. Coiro himself was stoical. As Judge McLaughlin was polling the jury, I looked over at the defense table. Coiro met my gaze with a forlorn smile and shrugged. He mouthed the word "congratulations." It was an odd feeling for me. I'd known Mike for almost five years, but more as a friendly adversary than a defendant. Even during the case Diane Giacalone and I had tried, Mike had remained friendly and gracious throughout.

The spectator section of the courtroom contained a dozen Assistant U.S. Attorneys who'd come to watch the verdict. There was an equal number of defense lawyers there to support Coiro. Several spectators on both sides said later that anyone who didn't know the players would have believed Cutler was the one who'd been found guilty.

Judge McLaughlin gave the jurors some canned remarks about the sacred public trust invested in them, thanking them for their service. As the last juror filed out, the judge stood up and headed for the same door, which also led back to his chambers. As he walked, he said, "Unless there are outstanding motions or things to take care of—"

"Yes, I have a motion, Your Honor," I said. "I have a motion to remand the defendant."

Sentencing wouldn't happen for months, and I wanted Mike Coiro in jail immediately. I wanted to flip him. The jolt of a jail cell following the impact of a RICO conviction would help me do that. The disorienting effect, especially on a man who'd never spent a night in prison, would make him vulnerable.

As the judge returned to his chair, I glanced back over to the defense table. Coiro's gaze had turned to ice. Cutler was livid. I started to argue why Coiro should be imprisoned immediately. I didn't even try to suggest that he was a flight risk. He was a danger to the community, I argued, not because he himself would commit acts of violence, but because the people he served would.

The judge denied my motion, and seemed annoyed I'd even made it. He knew that, at bottom, I was motivated more by a desire to soften up Coiro than a concern for the safety of the community, but he did grant my backup request that Coiro be ordered to stay away from members of the Gambino Family. By the next day I was to submit a list of the people with whom Coiro couldn't associate.

After the judge left the bench, I walked over to the defense table and shook hands with Cutler. He'd recovered from the verdict and was buoyed by winning the bail motion. I extended my hand to Coiro, but he turned away. I learned later that for the rest of his life he resented my effort to have him jailed. The conviction was deserved; he bore no grudge from that. But he thought my attempt to remand him was over-reaching.

Cutler and Coiro did not immediately leave the courthouse. Cutler had an important mission. He'd been instructed to bring Coiro to see John Gotti, so the order prohibiting Coiro from associating with members of the Gambino Family posed a problem. The list of the names I would supply to the court the next day would obviously include Gotti and just about everybody else down at the Ravenite. Cutler knew that if Coiro went down to the club that evening, I'd be back in court the next morning asking to revoke his bail for brazenly violating the judge's order. *That* motion would be granted. So before Cutler could bring his client to the Ravenite, he needed Judge McLaughlin's permission. While Bill Noon and I were still in the courtroom, Cutler and Coiro went to get it.

Cutler brought Coiro down the back corridor behind the courtroom to the judge's chambers. He rang the bell and they were let in. Coiro respected the jury's verdict and the judge's order, Cutler explained, but he wanted to impose upon the court in one minor way. He wanted to say goodbye to his friends. All he wanted was to make one last trip to the club to bid farewell to people he'd known for almost his whole adult life.

Judge McLaughlin was moved. He didn't care for Cutler, and he'd openly ridiculed his ignorance of the rules of evidence during the trial, but he felt bad for Coiro, so he granted the request. By the time Bill Noon and I were wheeling our evidence cart out of the courtroom, Cutler and Coiro were in a car heading to the Ravenite.

Before they arrived, the administration of the Gambino Family began the first of the apartment conversations that we recorded. Gotti, Locascio, and Gravano were talking about what the agents would soon learn was Gotti's favorite topic: investigations into him. On this night, Gotti was worried about the murders of Castellano and Bilotti. The most audacious double killing in mob history was approaching its fourth anniversary. Gotti had received information from one of his law enforcement sources that he'd be indicted under a relatively new federal murder law, the one that outlawed murders that "enhanced" the defendant's "position" in a racketeering enterprise, in Gotti's case the Gambino Family.

Gotti had also learned that Jimmy Brown Failla had been subpoenaed to appear before a federal grand jury. Failla was the Gambino captain who dominated New York City's commercial carting industry. He also happened to be one of several high-ranking Gambino Family members inside Sparks who'd been waiting to meet with Castellano and Bilotti the night they were murdered.

Gotti wondered out loud who was behind these efforts to make him a defendant again, for the fourth time in five years. "They hate me, them fuckin' prosecutors," he growled. "If this is Gleeson again, this fuckin' rat motherfucker . . ."

After a pause, Gravano said, "You think it's gonna be him? I don't think it's gonna be Gleeson or Giacalone. I think it'll be Mack, or somebody with more brains."

"Think we'll go Southern District," Gotti said. "I think it'll be the Southern District."

"I think somebody with more brains," Gravano continued. "They don't want to lose this case."

"Exactly, Sam," said Gotti.

As soon as Cutler and Coiro arrived, Coiro was escorted up to Nettie's apartment by an underling who didn't go in with him. Cutler remained downstairs.

If Coiro thought Gotti, Gravano, and Locascio had summoned him to give him sympathy, he was mistaken. "I knew you was guilty there. I didn't guess it, I knew it," Gotti said as Coiro sat down. "I don't think you're gonna go away before the appeal. So you got a fuckin' 'nother year on the street, maybe." Gotti had been around the system long enough to be an expert on who got bail pending appeal, and he'd figured Coiro's sentence as well: "I think he's gonna give you ten years. And maybe look for you to do about three or four."

"I'll do it, John," Coiro said.

"You know, Mike, you got no choice," Gotti said. There was an edge in his voice. Coiro's assurance that he'd do his prison time had implied there was another option. And in fact there was: everyone in the room knew that he could avoid a lengthy sentence—even avoid prison altogether—by cooperating with me. But Coiro wasn't about to discuss that option with Gotti, and he knew he'd made a mistake even suggesting it existed.

Gotti couldn't contain his contempt for his former friend Ruggiero, whose conversations in his own kitchen had convicted Ruggiero, Gene Gotti, John Carneglia, and now Coiro. Ruggiero was sick from cancer, having recently been moved from prison to a hospital bed, and he'd be dead within a week.

"I hate to talk about people that are dying," Gotti complained. "But I gotta call him a cocksucker. A guy was telling me this morning. 'All your trouble came from two places,' he says, 'Willie Boy Johnson and Angelo's house.' Willie Boy Johnson, and Angelo Ruggiero decided he wanted to be a big-shot operation. That's all our trouble. Not mine, *all* our troubles."

Turning to the business at hand, he told Coiro about a meeting he'd had with one of his own hooks. "Mike, what I get told, you forget here, ya know what I mean? I've been told by a source that that pinch is coming down. It's gonna be a joint pinch. The state, it's for murder, conspiracy to murder. The feds, they got a new statute, enhancing your position—commit murder to enhance your position."

Gotti said he'd been given a couple of names besides his own who'd be defendants in the case. Turning to Coiro, he added, "Ya gotta find out the rest of these fuckin' names now. Supposed to be a group of skippers. I got some names, but I wanna hear if they coincide."

The agents monitoring the bug were beside themselves. In a matter of minutes during the very first interception on the apartment bug, Gotti was conspiring to bribe a law enforcement officer. He didn't even know the identity of the person he was conspiring to bribe: "You gotta grab this guy. You gotta tell him, listen, give us the motherfuckin' names. Mike, we've been good to him in the past, we'll be good to him in the future. Give us the names. I never once asked you who he is. Did I ever ask you once?"

"Never!"

"And I won't! I give you my word. Give us the names."

The rest of the conversation conveyed why Gotti wanted the information. "Listen to me," he told Coiro. "If you're away even for three years, everything'll be status quo. Whatever we got, we got. If *I'm* away, status quo. But if we're *all* away . . ."

"Then we're in trouble," Coiro said.

"Listen! Not only we're in trouble. If only we're in trouble, so be it. A lotta things in here, people will be in trouble. And that we don't want." Gotti thought the Gambino Family couldn't survive if the entire administration was locked up, so he was preparing for that possibility. He wouldn't become a fugitive; he couldn't, really, because by then he was a national celebrity. But someone else in the room—his underboss or consigliere, or both—would, *if* they were going to be charged. Safely on the lam, they'd be able to run the Family while the case against Gotti and the others to be charged was pending. As Gotti put it, Coiro's mission was simple: "Mike, fuck the charges and everything. We already know all that. Who's getting arrested, and when."

"You got it, John," Coiro assured him. "I'll go see him tomorrow."

Bill Noon and I were in Stub's bar near the Brooklyn courthouse when Noon's pager went off. It was Bruce Mouw, the supervisor of the Gambino Squad. When Noon called his boss back, Mouw wanted to speak to me.

"Congratulations on the conviction today," Mouw said.

"Thanks, Bruce. Congratulations back at you. It was a great team effort. My only regret is I couldn't get the judge to put him in. I really want to flip him."

"That's the main reason I'm calling," Mouw said. "I can't tell you why, but could you please stop trying to do that?"

"What?"

"Could you please stop trying to put Mike Coiro in jail?"

"Why? We like guys like him in jail. That's why we do what we do."

"I can't tell you why. Also, Bill tells me that tomorrow you're supposed to file a list of people he can't be with. Can you please not do that?"

A long pause. Even I could figure this out.

"It sounds like there's something going on that I'd love to know about," I said.

"Yep."

"Any chance you're gonna tell me?" I asked.

"Sorry, John."

"Maybe someday?"

"Maybe." I could tell he was enjoying himself.

"It also sounds like the most important thing I did today was not winning the trial but losing the bail motion."

"You got it," Bruce answered.

"Okay," I said, "happy to be of service. Have fun."

Gotti's source was wrong. Morgenthau and the Southern District weren't even close to charging him with the Castellano murder. They were trying desperately, but they were failing. And Gotti was wrong in thinking I might be involved in the ongoing investigations. On November 30, 1989, the day of the first apartment conversation, I knew nothing about the Ravenite bugs.

In less than a month, I'd be in charge of the investigation, but on the evening of Coiro's conviction I was ignorant and blissful. Coiro was an important defendant and his racketeering conviction was significant. Even better, the very next day Delroy Edwards received seven consecutive sentences of life without parole, to be followed (just in case he had eight lives) by a consecutive 585 years in prison. In short, I was feeling pretty good.

So, for different reasons, were George Gabriel and the agents on the Gambino Squad. The apartment bug was off to a spectacular start. The acoustics were great, and they'd already intercepted a crime in progress. They were full of hope for something more dramatic, something that would put Gotti away for good. By the time I was installed as the lead prosecutor three weeks later, they'd have it.

Within a span of eighteen months, I'd tried Squitieri and Sisca, Delroy Edwards, and Mike Coiro. I thought I was ready for something different, so I agreed to supervise Special Prosecutions, the unit in our office that investigated corrupt government officials.

There were seismic changes at the time, both in our office and in law enforcement generally. Attorney General Dick Thornburgh took a dim view of the Justice Department's Organized Crime Strike Forces. There were still fourteen strewn around the country. They'd been created by Attorney General Bobby Kennedy and were centrally controlled by the Organized Crime Section in Main Justice in Washington. Thornburgh had clashed with one when he was the U.S. Attorney in Pittsburgh and regarded them as unnecessary competition. It made no sense, in his view, to have separate federal prosecutor's offices operating in the same places, fighting with each other for cases. So he decided to get rid of the Strike Forces by merging them into the local U.S. Attorney's Offices, effective October 1, 1989.

The merger in Brooklyn was anything but seamless. The problems started with the different cultures of the two offices. The attorneys in the Brooklyn Strike Force were almost all former state prosecutors. Most had worked under Morgenthau in the Manhattan District Attorney's Office. Assistant District Attorneys are courtroom lawyers. They generally start their legal careers as prosecutors and spend their time mainly in court. They try lots of cases, but they don't do much legal writing. Now they'd have to learn.

The Eastern and Southern District U.S. Attorney's Offices hired from a different pool of lawyers. Most AUSAs had gone to top law schools, clerked for federal judges, then spent a few years at one of the large law firms. Many, like me, had known nothing about criminal cases when they were hired and had never stood up in court. The U.S. Attorney's Offices' thinking was to hire the best young lawyers in the city and teach them how to prosecute; the Brooklyn Strike Force's policy was to hire the best local prosecutors in the city and make them feds.

It wasn't flagrant, and there were exceptions, but resentment ran in both directions. Strike Force lawyers tended to regard AUSAs as eggheads who couldn't try their way out of a paper bag, while the AUSAs regarded Strike Force lawyers as good on their feet but unable to think or write well.

A few of the Strike Force lawyers found jobs in the private sector soon after the announcement of the merger. But then Andy Maloney turned a trickle of departures into an exodus. Early on, a reporter asked for his reaction to the departures, and Andy handled it badly. It was fine with him, he said, because his AUSAs could "try circles around" the Strike Force lawyers. This of course infuriated those remaining; if there was one indisputable advantage they had as a group over the AUSAs in our office, it was that they were more experienced—and better—on their feet in court.

So two events were unfolding simultaneously. First, the Ravenite investigation of

Gotti was starting up. If the bug turned out to be a success, the intercepted conversations would require extensive grand jury investigations to flesh out what Gotti, Gravano, and Locascio were talking about; it would basically be a full-employment act for organized crime prosecutors.

Second, all the original prosecutors were leaving. Ed McDonald, the Strike Force chief who was to play himself in the 1990 movie *Goodfellas*, had been among the first to leave when Thornburgh's merger plan became public. His replacement had departed in August, along with five of the remaining thirteen. As the office stumbled toward the merger, it was beginning to look as if there'd be no one left to merge into the U.S. Attorney's Office.

By the time AUSA Lenny Michaels brought the Ravenite bug application across the river for approval, the Brooklyn Strike Force office was a ghost town. Michaels himself had already accepted another job and was just a caretaker. Of the twenty lawyers who'd been prosecutors just a year earlier, only two would survive the merger for more than a few weeks—Laura Ward and Pat Cotter. Ward I knew well already. Though I didn't know Cotter, I'd seen him in court a few times when our cases overlapped. He was short and ruddy-looking with a reddish beard. He looked as Irish as Paddy's pig, as my father would've said. I'd heard he'd come to the Strike Force not from the District Attorney's Office—the typical path—but from the Legal Aid Society, where he represented indigent defendants in state court. One of the proceedings that I happened upon was a detention hearing before Judge Nickerson in the case against "Frankie the Bug" Sciortino, a made guy in the Colombo Family. In the middle of it the judge was leaning toward releasing Sciortino, and Cotter decided he'd step up his arguments a notch. That can backfire in the dignified atmosphere of Judge Nickerson's courtroom, but Cotter managed to nail the right combination of scrappiness and respect. I could tell the judge enjoyed listening to him, and Cotter eventually turned him around.

The merger was becoming a political crisis for the DOJ. Some prominent members of Congress—including Senators Ted Kennedy and Joe Biden—had opposed it, warning that the government's fight against organized crime would be weakened. The exodus of prosecutors in Brooklyn also attracted press attention. It was starting to look as if the federal effort to investigate organized crime in New York was being abandoned rather than merged.

In mid-December Andy Maloney summoned me to his office. When I arrived, Lenny Michaels was there but Andy wasn't. I hadn't been told why my presence was required, so I was surprised to see him.

As soon as I sat down, Michaels closed the door and started whispering to me.

"We have a bug in the apartment above the Ravenite," he said. "We've only been up for two weeks but we've already gotten two fantastic conversations."

"Lenny, why are you whispering?"

He shrugged. "You never know," he said. "The first conversation happened right after you convicted Mike Coiro. Gotti asked Coiro to contact one of his law enforcement hooks. The second happened a couple of nights ago, and you're not going to believe it when you hear it."

"Why?"

"He says he whacked Robert DiBernardo. Just like that, that simple, he says he whacked him."

I was still absorbing this news when Andy joined us.

"I know I just asked you to run Special Prosecutions," he said to me after he sat down, "but now I want you to run Organized Crime." Michaels obviously thought I'd known this was coming. I hadn't, and was stunned. I'd been heading Special Prosecutions for just a few months, and was nearly getting the hang of pursuing allegations of official corruption. It was paper-intensive work, and even though the crimes were important—I was currently investigating a prominent elected official—they didn't engage me the way the wiseguys had.

"Of course I'll do it," I said. "You know I love that stuff."

We talked about the Ravenite apartment. Michaels insisted on still whispering everything, and since Andy's hearing wasn't great he kept telling him to speak up, but Michaels refused. I got it all, though. We already had Gotti on an obstruction count based on his conversation with Coiro on November 30, and he'd explicitly admitted to two murders, not just DiBernardo's, less than two weeks later. It was an extraordinary development.

Andy wasn't an excitable person. He still had a West Pointer's military bearing at sixty years of age and generally kept his emotions in check, but he was clearly worked up. He reminded me that on the day after the acquittals two and a half years earlier, he'd gone over to the Southern District and won a promise from Rudy Giuliani that we'd do the next RICO case against Gotti.

"They've got the rights to the Castellano murder," Andy said, "but it doesn't look like they can make that case. Sparks happened almost four years ago. This case we're making looks like it will be the next prosecution of Gotti. Ever since those acquittals, I've really wanted us to be the ones to convict him."

The meeting was late in the afternoon and when it ended I set off for home. All I could think about on the long walk down Clinton Street to Carroll Gardens was that I might get to try Gotti again. Andy and I hadn't discussed that specifically, and I knew he and others could decide that the first trial had been so ugly and personal that it would make no sense to have me lead the second. We had plenty of good trial lawyers, so why burden this new case with predictable accusations from the defense that it amounted to a sore loser's vendetta? If I were the U.S. Attorney, I wouldn't take that risk. But I wasn't, and I had every intention of leading the case. Even though I knew it might not work out, I fantasized a bit about how the trial might go. There were thousands of prosecutors who spent their entire careers hoping to work on a case that important. Here I was, less than five years into my time in the Eastern District, about to start working on my second, against the same defendant. It seemed way too good to be true.

When I got home, I told Susan about the lateral move to chief of Organized Crime. I thought it might upset her. She'd liked my recent move to Special Prosecutions, no doubt in part because the nastiness we'd both gone through a couple of years earlier had no chance of repeating itself in the milquetoast world of official corruption. But instead she was happy for me. She knew investigating and prosecuting gangsters was what I wanted to do more than anything else, and that meant more to her.

Special Prosecutions had its own offices on the sixth floor of the courthouse, away from the rest of the U.S. Attorney's Office down on the fifth floor. The next morning I told the four AUSAs in my section that I'd be leaving them to become chief of Organized Crime. Before I finished, Bruce Mouw and George Gabriel arrived unannounced.

I already knew Mouw. He'd been the supervisor of the Gambino Squad for many years. He was old-school FBI and had been livid when the office had burned Willie Boy Johnson four years earlier. But a lot had happened in between, and I'd earned his trust. Gabriel I had never met. The three of us crammed into my small office and Mouw closed the door.

"Congratulations on being named chief of OC," he said.

"Thank you. I assume you had something to do with it."

"Yep. And now we're here to ask you for something."

This was Gabriel's cue. He told me about the bugs at the Ravenite and what they'd already recorded. The audibility was better than any bug they'd ever had, and the first two conversations by themselves would support at least three predicate acts, including two murders.

"Even if we go down on the bugs today," Gabriel said, "we will definitely have a RICO case against the administration—Gotti, Sammy Gravano, and Frank Locascio."

"Good for you, and congratulations," I said. "What's your request?"

"We want you to lead the case," Mouw said. "This is obviously going to be an important trial, maybe the most important one in our lives. The squad has gotten to know you, and we like what we've seen."

I couldn't have asked for better support than I'd gotten in my two trials with Bill Noon, and told them so. We talked some more about the December 12 conversation, which was barely a week old. Gabriel said there were a lot of construction-related statements by Gotti we'd need to investigate in addition to the two murders.

"What about the Castellano case?" I asked Mouw. His squad was supporting the joint investigation being conducted by the Southern District and Morgenthau.

"We were hoping this bug would put us over the top on that one, but, if you listen, Gotti actually denies any involvement in the Castellano hit."

"He *denies* it? You're kidding."

"Nope. Says Castellano deserved it, but he doesn't know who did it."

"Yikes. What have you come up with in your investigation in the Southern District?"

"Not much. Dozens of eyewitnesses, but except for one guy who puts Gotti across 46th Street just before the murders, nothing."

By the time they left, I knew I'd be trying Gotti again. Even if Andy were concerned about my baggage, that would be outweighed by the FBI's request that I lead the team. I would never mention that baggage myself, and no one from the government raised it either. I expected my history with Gotti would fuel one of the central defense themes at the trial, but that would be infinitely preferable to watching from the sidelines. I was back in the ring.

PART III

THE
SECOND
CASE

CHAPTER 19

THE MOTHERLODE

Just before Christmas 1989, George Gabriel brought me copies of the first two Ravenite conversations.

He'd warned me about the first. "You're not going to like this one," he said with a smile. Happily, I was alone when I first heard Gotti and Gravano say the Department of Justice would never entrust the next case to me, but would get someone with more brains," from the Southern District no less. I'd learn to laugh at it soon enough, but that wasn't my first reaction.

I was eager to hear the murder admissions made in the second conversation. The first topic discussed was Robert DiBernardo. "DiB," which the wiseguys pronounced "Dee Bee," had disappeared on June 5, 1986, about three weeks after Diane and I got Gotti remanded in the first case. There was no question he'd been murdered, but we never found the body. He was a captain in the Family, and when Castellano was in charge DiB ran the Family's construction racket by working with Bobby Sasso, the president of Teamsters Local 282. It was widely known in law enforcement that Gravano had taken over the Family's construction interests after DiB was killed, but we were nowhere near solving DiB's homicide until that December 12 recording.

Gotti was complaining to Frank Locascio about Gravano, who wasn't present. The complaint: Gotti had allowed Gravano to take over DiB's role, and Gravano was now using that power to enrich only himself and the people around him. The rant began with a startling admission: "When DiB got whacked they told me a story. I was in jail when I whacked him. I knew why it was being done, I done it anyway. I allowed it to be done anyway."

And DiB wasn't the only one: "Where are we going here? Every fucking time I turn around there's a new company popping up. Rebar, building, consulting, concrete. And every time we got a partner that don't agree with us, we kill him. You go to the Boss, and the Boss kills him."

So Gravano was amassing wealth and power in the construction racket by getting Gotti's permission to kill anyone else in the Family who got in his way. On a roll, Gotti continued. When Castellano died, Gravano was "nothing." Then Gravano told Gotti that "DiB cried behind my back"—was disloyal—and now DiB was killed on Gotti's order and Gravano "got all that . . . got Bobby Sasso." So Gotti's explanation to Locascio of what happened to DiB was this: Gravano sent word to Gotti in the jail that DiB was bad-mouthing him, always a good reason to whack someone. Gotti ordered the hit, allowing Gravano to take over the construction racket, and now Gravano was enriching himself and those around him.

Anger does different things to different people, and apparently it induced Gotti to admit ordering murders. The rant about DiB included the answer to another of our mysteries. Louie Milito had been a soldier in Gravano's crew when Gravano was a captain. Milito had a company called Gem Steel. He didn't formally own it, but it was "with" him, and it made both him and Gravano a lot of money. Then on March 8, 1988, Milito suddenly disappeared. His wife, Linda, was distraught. Gravano assured her that he'd find out who was responsible and extract revenge. Twenty-one months later, here was Gotti telling Locascio that Gravano himself had been the killer, with Gotti's blessing. "I took Sammy's word," Gotti fumed, that Milito had "talked about me behind my back." "Louie had Gem Steel," and now Gravano "got Gem Steel."

Still on the warpath against Gravano, Gotti complained that Gravano *wanted* to kill Louie DiBono, another Gambino soldier, and that DiBono had wanted to whack Gravano. The two apparently had a beef: "Louie DiBono opened up a business for him. He hates Louie, Louie hates him. Why did they go together, Frankie? You know he hates—he wanted permission to shoot Louie DiBono. Louie DiBono wanted permission to get him shot. Why did they go partners, Frankie?"

Gotti's point was that the wrong people were getting rich as a result of the power he'd allowed Gravano to accumulate. The ability to shut down a job site, for which Sasso was paid handsomely by the Gambino Family, was supposed to enrich the entire family. Instead, the people around Gravano were making millions while "the rest of the *borgata*" was starving.

When it came to specifics it was clear that Gotti was actually concerned more about his own wealth than anyone else's. "Jesus motherfuckin' Christ," he railed at Locascio, "I'm with some people today, Marine Construction . . ." Marine was "with" Gotti; when it made money he got a big piece of it. But because of Gravano, Marine "got nothing! They got no job! If Angelo was handling Bobby Sasso, would they have a job? You tell me. Right or wrong?"

"They would get *all* the jobs," Locascio answered loyally.

Gravano was "creating a fuckin' army inside an army." In an obvious reference to the situation that led to Castellano's murder, Gotti told Locascio that Gravano "ain't gonna create a fuckin' faction. No. That, that shit, I saw that shit here. I saw that shit and I don't need that shit." And on and on it went. The tirade lasted almost an hour. All the Teamster stewards at the sites were now from Gravano's crew. He was "taking work out of other people's mouths . . . using my fuckin' flag to conquer the whole fuckin' market," and turning "the whole fuckin' industry into a private playpen."

"He's gotta cut it out!" Gotti repeated three times at the end.

Was he planning to whack his own consigliere? The recordings were unusually clear, the voices crisp. I'd spent years struggling with inaudible tapes that had to be listened to over and over again. By contrast, these apartment conversations made me feel as if I were sitting on the couch next to Gotti. There'd be no need to "enhance" what we had or for an expert to "explain" Gotti's admissions, no need for accomplice witnesses.

I was also struck by how much Gotti's world had changed since Judge Nickerson's courtroom. For twenty years prior to that trial, he'd had his Bergin crew around him. They were unsophisticated, but they stuck by each other. As I listened to Gotti, it occurred to me that was all gone from his life: Angelo Ruggiero had died of cancer; Gene Gotti and John Carneglia were each serving fifty years; Willie Boy was dead; Tony Roach was doing twenty-five to life.

Not only was Gotti surrounded by a different set of gangsters, but almost all had been on the other side of the schism that divided the Family when Neil Dellacroce was alive. John Gammarano, Danny Marino, Jimmy Brown Failla, even Gravano himself— they were Brooklyn and Staten Island guys. They'd never hung out at the Bergin and had rarely been seen at the Ravenite when it was Dellacroce's club. And they were much more savvy criminals, experienced at using unions to siphon money out of the city's industries rather than operating gambling businesses or loan shark books or selling narcotics. Gotti, despite being boss, was clearly out of his element, both in terms of the people around him and the crimes they were committing. He didn't know the construction business. He bragged that Gravano was bringing him $100,000 in cash each month, but he had no way of figuring out whether he was being cheated, so he simply assumed he was. Besides, it was he who'd betrayed the previous boss, Paul Castellano, to whom all these lifelong criminals had at one point been loyal. Despite all his swagger, he could hardly expect loyalty in return.

Gotti, Gravano, and Locascio used the apartment only three more times in the six months we had our bug in place, and all the conversations occurred right away. The first, on January 4, 1990, was dominated by a discussion about whom the Gambino Family would put up to become made guys. In that one tape Gotti gave us all the evidence we'd need to prove the enterprise in the case against him.

A made guy is *amica nostra*. The literal translation is a "friend of ours." If a gangster introduces someone as a "friend of mine," his fellow gangsters can do what they want with or to him. But if he introduces him as a "friend of *ours*," that guy is a big deal. One must respect, and can never double-cross, a made guy.

Getting made involves a ceremony. The associate is brought to a secret location. One or more members of the administration are present, as well as some captains, and always the sponsor of the guy getting made—the captain of his crew.

"Do you know why you're here?" is the first question.

"No" is the only permissible answer. So the ceremony starts with a lie.

Next the boss, or if he's not present whoever is presiding, says, "This is a society, and you are about to become a made member of a Cosa Nostra." Then they go over the rules. The guy getting made promises to put the "Family" before his own family, to kill for the boss, not to sell drugs, not to raise his hand to another made member, not to screw around with a made guy's wife, not to kill people with bombs, and a few others. The anti–drug trafficking rule was the direct result of harsh sentencing laws like New York's Rockefeller laws. The rule wasn't meant to keep anyone from dealing drugs, because it was a lucrative business and all the Families were in it. But the long sentences tempted those who got caught to flip. So the rule allowed for murder by the Family of anyone who got arrested. Dead men don't talk. The rule against car bombs was a risk-aversion measure. Car bombs can kill innocent passersby, which ignites law enforcement in ways that the "mere" murder of a gangster doesn't.

At that point, the guy getting made has to show his trigger finger. The finger is pricked until it bleeds, and he has to hold a crumpled-up saint card—the kind they give out at Catholic wakes. Someone lights the card, and the guy getting made has to cradle it in his hands, juggling it back and forth to keep from getting burned, and say, "If I divulge any of the secrets of this secret society, my soul should burn in hell like this saint."

Then, with the exception of the newly made guy, everyone locks hands, followed by unlocking and locking them again, this time with him included. There is a lot of kissing, and the new member is officially made.

The January 4 and January 17 apartment conversations focused on the process that leads up to this ceremony. Before it can happen, Families have to circulate to the other Families a list of the guys they plan to make. It's a custom designed to ensure no Family makes a rat, or worse yet an undercover cop. The Bonanno Family almost made Joe Pistone, an FBI agent who used the name Donnie Brasco, and as a result the Family was "put on the shelf"—unable to make anyone for years.

Gotti pontificated to Gravano and Locascio about the guys they were putting up. "This is gonna be a Cosa Nostra till I die. Be it an hour from now or be it tonight, or a hundred years from now when I'm in jail. It's gonna be a Cosa Nostra. A Cosa Nostra!"

The five guys they were putting up, Gotti said, will "be here forever. They won't be havin' the secret fuckin' parties when people won't be around." Coming from someone who whacked his own boss, the concern for "secret parties" made sense. It also explained Gotti's rule that everyone regularly report to the Ravenite. The made guys groused about having to schlep into Manhattan several times a week, but the Family under Gotti wasn't going to fracture as it had under Castellano, not if John Gotti could help it.

Gotti also talked about the possibility of fixing a juror. He was in state court at the time, charged with ordering the Westies to shoot the union leader John O'Connor. Jury selection was underway, and Gotti told Gravano and Locascio that he wanted to reach one of the prospective jurors, an Irishman who worked for the telephone company. That part of the conversation brought George Gabriel to my office. "Should we tell Morgenthau?" he asked me. "What if that guy makes it onto the jury and they succeed in reaching him?"

It was clear Gotti wanted to do just that, but not clear that he could. More important, they were still picking the jury, so there was more than an even chance their man wouldn't get picked. I decided we weren't going to run the risk of burning our bug by telling Morgenthau. He might use it to try to get Gotti remanded or act in other ways that could alert the defendants. Also, his trial team included the New York State Organized Crime Task Force, a state office based up in Westchester County, and I had no intention of sharing our surveillance with two law enforcement agencies. The risk of a leak was too great.

"You know they'll be through the roof when they eventually find out, right?" said Gabriel.

"I know," I said. "We'll deal with it then. I'll take the heat." Andy Maloney agreed: we weren't going to burn a bug that could take down an entire Family—and maybe other Families as well—on the outside chance that it might save Morgenthau's shaky assault case.

There was one other significant development in the January 4 conversation. Before Locascio joined them, Gotti reiterated to Gravano that he would be in charge of the Family if Gotti was imprisoned. "This is my wishes," Gotti said, "if I'm in the fuckin' can this Family is gonna be run by Sammy." In light of that plan he asked Gravano, who at the time was consigliere, if he'd rather be underboss. A grateful Gravano accepted. From that point forward Gravano was the second-in-command of the Gambino Family. Locascio, who had been the acting underboss, performing the role of imprisoned Joe "Piney" Armone, became the acting consigliere, and Piney became the consigliere.

The January 24 conversation touched on many topics, but the one that consumed the most time was the conspiracy to murder Corky Vastola, a captain in the DeCavalcante Family over in New Jersey. If La Cosa Nostra protocol were a college course, the effort to kill Vastola would be a good final exam question: If the Gambino Family boss wants to whack a DeCavalcante Family captain, but the only person the DeCavalcante captain will meet with is a Genovese Family associate, how does the Gambino boss get the job done?

It turns out that the answer is *very* complicated.

Gaetano "Corky" Vastola was a huge earner. For many years he'd had a hand in construction rackets in both New Jersey and Brooklyn. He'd been close to both Frankie DeCicco and Robert DiBernardo before they were killed. That long-standing association with the Castellano faction was reason enough for Gotti to hate him. In January of 1986, four years before our bug in the Ravenite apartment and just a month after the Castellano murder, a bug in the Bergin Hunt & Fish Club recorded Gotti complaining about Vastola's involvement with a concrete plant and calling him the "biggest bullshit artist in the universe."

I had run across Vastola several times while prosecuting Arnold Squitieri and Funzi Sisca two years earlier. He was facing RICO charges before the same judge, and many of the pretrial court appearances were held back-to-back. He always looked and dressed more like an investment banker than a gangster. So I had a visual image of him as I listened to Gotti arrange his murder.

Gotti was hot to kill Vastola, and he wasn't bashful in listing the reasons why. "I was in the can with him. You asking me how he does time? The worst I ever saw in my life!" Vastola complained too much about being in prison. Even worse, according to Gotti, was the fact that he'd been convicted in Jersey but had been released pending his appeal. Gotti saw that as evidence that he was cooperating. Never mind that Squitieri and Sisca were also convicted, and the same judge had also released them pending appeal: Vastola was a rat. Finally, for two years Vastola had refused to "come in" when called by John Riggi and John D'Amato, the boss and underboss of the DeCavalcante Family. Coming in when called was another cardinal rule. When you were needed to kill someone, you had to come in to get the order. If they'd decided to kill you, you still had to come in, so they didn't need to do it in public. "I don't know if he's a rat now," Gotti told D'Amato. "Is he gonna be a rat someday? Yeah."

Gotti needed the DeCavalcante Family's blessing to kill Vastola, and he had his own way with words to make his point: "If you think the guy's a rat, or he's weak, you're jeopardizing a whole *borgata*, a whole Cosa Nostra for this guy. If I know a guy's weak and I let him go running around the street, and you get locked up, I'm a fuckin' rat too!"

D'Amato was persuaded, so Gotti turned to Gravano and told him to "whack this fuckin' kid."

That was impossible, Gravano explained. Vastola "a hundred percent knows" he could get killed, so for two years the only person he'd meet with was Barry Nichilo, a Genovese associate in Sally Dogs Lombardi's crew. Vastola and Nichilo had some construction business together in Brooklyn. "He won't come in to nobody," Gravano said.

"This motherless fuck!" Gotti fumed.

But Gravano had already spoken to Nichilo, for whom he had nothing but praise. They also knew each other from the construction business. As a favor to Gravano, Nichilo agreed that he'd ask to meet Vastola at "the farm," where Nichilo would kill him. The farm part had us scratching our heads—these were Coney Island guys—but the rest was pretty clear.

There was a problem with using Nichilo, however. He was with the Genovese

Family. "Imagine if a guy told us he wanted to use one of our guys without telling us?" Gotti explained to Gravano. "Can't do that." They concluded that if they used Nichilo without permission, Nichilo would then be killed by members of his own Family.

In principle, the path to killing Vastola was clear, but it still had to go through Nichilo's boss, Chin Gigante. Gigante hated Gotti, and the feeling was mutual. One of the reasons Gotti had murdered Castellano was the latter's decision to share money from the construction rackets with Gigante. And Gotti knew Chin's people had plotted in 1988 to kill Gotti because Chin never forgave Gotti for killing Castellano without a formal go-ahead from the Commission.

With Chin unlikely to grant any request by Gotti, the Gambino Family schemed some more. They could approach Benny Eggs Mangano, Chin's underboss, whom Gravano knew well and liked. But Benny Eggs (his mom had run an egg store) would likely need to run it by Chin. So as an alternative they talked about having John Riggi, the DeCavalcante boss, make the request and pretend the whole idea was his.

If all these machinations weren't about shooting someone in the head, they would have been a riot. Who knew whacking someone could be so complicated? But one thing was clear: to prove a conspiracy to murder Vastola all we needed was evidence of an *agreement* to kill him, and we had plenty of that. "All I know is, he's got to get hurt," Gotti said, to everyone in the apartment's explicit agreement, and it had to happen soon, before Vastola "died of old age."

CHAPTER 20

THE TEAM

The five apartment tapes were brimming with conversation about the affairs of the Gambino Family. Gotti talked incessantly about incoming "tribute." Money flowed in from garbage carting, construction, the docks, gambling operations, loan-sharking, the garment center. Twenty-four thousand dollars a week arrived in cash from construction alone. Gotti bragged about getting "pieces" of businesses, shares of "scores" every week at the docks from captain Sonny Ciccone. Even the Connecticut gambling operation earned him $1,600 a week. His calculations sometimes left us perplexed: "Frankie, the guy gives Joe Watts $9,000 every two weeks. He takes a third, and I get two-thirds. Don't I get two thousand a week?"

Whacking people was a constant topic. When Gotti discussed with Gravano and Locascio who should be made, he emphasized that even though having done a "piece of work" was a requirement, it wasn't enough: "I want guys that done more than killing." They talked about whether anyone would try to do to him what he'd done to Castellano. Gotti was unworried: "Who's gonna challenge me? Who's gonna defy me? What are you gonna do? Take a shot, like I did to that other guy? I'd welcome that, Frank. I'll kill their fuckin' mothers! Their fathers!"

A member of the Sicilian Mafia who'd flipped in a Southern District case "gotta get whacked," he fumed. "You want to challenge the administration, you're going, you motherfucker!" For every conversation that was clearly about a crime, either planned or already committed, we had a dozen others that probably were, but we lacked sufficient information to be sure.

I needed a team, and there was no question my first recruit would be Laura Ward.

The agents on the squad loved her, we'd worked effectively together on the first case under much more difficult circumstances, and we now had almost five years' experience as prosecutors. There couldn't have been a more obvious candidate, and she was delighted when I asked.

My other choice was Pat Cotter, the only other remaining member of the Strike Force. In the few weeks I was chief of the section, I'd gotten to know and like him. It probably helped that we were both from big families that were seriously Irish. Maybe that was the reason we also had a similar sense of humor.

Cotter wasn't happy about the abolition of the Strike Force and the departure of everyone except him and Ward. His resentment surfaced in a way that posed a problem for me: a refusal to handle "arraignment duty," an administrative task AUSAs had to perform. When a drug courier was stopped at an airport at night and the Customs agent needed authorization to arrest, the call went to the AUSA on duty. If another agent thought he or she had probable cause to search a car, the AUSA on duty would get the call at whatever hour, listen to the facts, and either approve the search or not. Cotter had come to the Eastern District to be part of an elite group focused solely on La Cosa Nostra, not to handle the underbrush that arraignment duty dishes up. He felt he should be exempt.

No one enjoyed having dinner interrupted for a phone call with an agent, let alone being woken up at two-thirty in the morning to decide if a set of facts amounted to probable cause. But all the other AUSAs in the section were on the duty list, and there was no legitimate reason to give Cotter a pass. So I took him to lunch right after I became chief and told him I needed him to suck it up and do arraignment duty like everyone else. He pushed back hard but respectfully. I pushed back just as hard and appealed to the egalitarian in him. In the end I told him we were in the first months of the new Organized Crime Section, which I was determined would be a success, and asked him to spare me an unnecessary management problem. When he agreed, it made an impression on me.

There were good reasons for choosing Cotter. As a former defense lawyer, he brought a perspective Ward and I lacked. Prosecutors who've never defended a case tend not to see weaknesses as readily as a former defense lawyer can. Also, prosecutors rarely get to cross-examine witnesses. Cotter had crossed hundreds at Legal Aid and would naturally be better at that than us. Our ultimate indictments would include charges, including homicides and gambling, that are normally the stuff of state court prosecutions, and Cotter was familiar with the NYPD's practices and forms, how it used the property clerk to store evidence, and all the little things that would help him work with the police officers who'd assist our investigation and trial. Finally, given the political opposition to the abolition of the Strike Forces, I didn't want any more departures, and putting Cotter on the Gotti team would definitely keep him around.

There was work to do. We had all those apartment conversations, and, in many of them, we'd need to figure out what they were talking about. One of our main tools was the grand jury. Investigating grand juries have enormous power in our system, with nationwide subpoena authority to obtain documents and testimony from anyone. So right away we empaneled the Gambino Family special grand jury—twenty-three citizens drawn at random from the district. They'd meet in secret in the courthouse whenever we summoned them. I wanted a continuous group of grand jurors that would help us gather evidence, not just for the case against Gotti but for all the other cases we'd bring based on the Ravenite recordings. Special grand juries can sit for three years. By the time we were finished, the members of that one would know more about the Gambino Family than the Gambino Family knew about itself. The experience would bind them together for years. Long after the grand jury expired, they gathered for annual reunions in the diner across the park from the courthouse, and occasionally I'd join them. Years later, after I became a judge, one of the grand jurors asked me to preside at her wedding, and I did.

While we were still up on the Ravenite bugs, we had to observe a few basic rules. First, the grand jury itself would be told nothing about them. There'd come a time when all the key recordings would be played for them, but that wouldn't happen until after we shut down the bugs. I had no particular reason to suspect any of the twenty-three members of our jury, but history had taught me to be ultra-careful. One of the few cases we had inherited from the disbanded Strike Force involved a grand juror who leaked what was happening in the jury room to Colombo Family captain Michael Franzese.

Second, the things we learned solely from the bugs couldn't be the subject of questioning in the grand jury while the bugs were still up. We had to assume that Gotti would know about every single question we asked of a lay witness. If it got back to him that we'd grilled Mike Coiro in the grand jury about his law enforcement "hooks," Gotti might remember that he'd summoned Coiro to the Ravenite apartment minutes after Coiro was convicted of racketeering and ordered him to find out who was getting indicted. End of conversations in that apartment.

This left plenty to investigate. Gotti reported to the IRS his income from Arc

Plumbing out in Queens as a plumbing salesman, and he also claimed to be a zipper salesman for Albee Trimming, a company in the garment center. With a criminal tax count against him in mind, we used the powers of the grand jury to track down all his expenses. We knew what he spent on suits and shirts, and to have his hair "coiffed," as his barber put it, every single day in the club (we found ourselves wondering how much got snipped each time).

Another fundamental rule of investigations is when you've got a great wiretap or bug in place, use it. And there's no edict that says law enforcement has to sit around waiting until wiseguys decide to talk about their crimes. You use your other tools of investigation to get them talking. And so it happened that I decided to subpoena Tony Roach Rampino into our grand jury.

Tony Roach got his nickname because, sad but true, he looked like one. He was fifty-one years old, tall, gangly, and slightly hunched over, with sunken eyes in a pock-marked face and a really bad combover. He had a solid reputation as a tough guy who'd been intensely loyal to Gotti for decades. Surveillance photos from the Bergin Hunt & Fish Club featured him hanging around on 101st Avenue outside the club back in the early 1970s. He was widely believed to have helped kill Frank Favara—Gotti's next-door neighbor who in 1980 had accidentally run over and killed Gotti's twelve-year-old son, Frank.

Rampino had been a defendant in the disastrous trial before Judge Nickerson. I came to like him. I'd see him in the elevator and occasionally in the park across the street from the courthouse. He was shy and self-conscious. He had a lot to be self-conscious about, with that combover and the shiny sharkskin suits he wore, which had definitely come off the back of a truck. But Tony Roach was courteous and respectful. He'd always have a quiet "Good morning" and a slight smile for me when we entered the courtroom together, and he'd even quicken his pace so he could open the door for me and my evidence cart.

Rampino was a lifelong heroin addict and dealer. Shortly after the first trial ended in 1987 George Hanna learned from an informant that Rampino had offered to sell him heroin. Hanna saw an opportunity for a break in the Castellano murder investigation. Under his watchful eye, the informant bought four ounces from Rampino, and Hanna swooped in and made the arrest. Tony panicked, and in a roundabout admission to the Castellano and Bilotti murders, he promised to tell Hanna the names of the "other shooters" if he were released. But he was not released, he refused to flip, and got twenty-five to life.

I thought I might stimulate some conversation at the Ravenite if I brought Rampino from his upstate prison to our grand jury room. As soon as I put in the request with the warden, I got a call from Dave DePetris, who'd represented Rampino in the trial before Judge Nickerson and in the state drug case Hanna had made against him. Gotti had paid DePetris's fees both times and had retained him again to represent Tony for his grand jury appearance.

"I hear you're bringing Tony Roach down from upstate," DePetris began. "What's it about?"

"Castellano and Bilotti," I answered. There had been a *Daily News* column in 1988 about Tony Roach's "other shooters" statement, so DePetris didn't need any more explanation than that.

"You know he's gonna take the Fifth, right?" he said.

"Yes, of course. But still plan on half a day at least. I'll have an immunity order waiting." I could take away Rampino's Fifth Amendment right by getting such an order, which would prevent me from using his grand jury testimony against him in any way if I ever wanted to prosecute him for the Castellano murder. Since he was already over fifty and doing twenty-five to life in state prison, I wasn't giving up much. Besides, with respect to the Castellano killing, there was no way he was going to admit either his involvement or anyone else's anyway.

"There'll be a few other areas I'll question him about, but the gist of it is John Gotti and the murders of Paul Castellano and Tommy Bilotti."

"Okay," DePetris said. "Thanks. See you next week."

I had no illusions about Rampino. He was a stand-up guy, and a possible perjury charge from my grand jury wasn't going to scare him. He'd also have the option of remaining silent even though the immunity order would take away his Fifth Amendment right to do so. That would amount to contempt, likely to get him a couple of extra years, which wasn't going to panic him either. But John Gotti's obsession with all investigations of John Gotti made it a good bet that my exchange with DePetris would be followed quickly by some conversation down at the Ravenite.

Sure enough, the next day Gotti summoned Bruce Cutler and brought him into the Ravenite hallway. "They're gonna give him immunity," he told Cutler immediately, and "they're gonna hit him with the question" about the "shooters." Gotti also said that he'd heard that law enforcement believed that the shooters Rampino was referring to were Gene Gotti and John Carneglia.

Gotti and Cutler had a short but remarkable conversation about which crime

Tony Roach should commit. Should he testify and lie, or should he refuse to testify despite the immunity order and be guilty of contempt? Cutler reasoned that Rampino could testify falsely and get away with it because he hadn't been under oath when he spoke to Hanna. Gotti instructed him to meet with DePetris to decide which road Rampino should take. Either way, Gotti said—in a reference to James Cardinali—"Tell him we don't need another phony junkie battin' against us."

Just in case Cutler's role in the family wasn't already clear, Gotti added another assignment: all communications to and from the Patriarca Family—New England's La Cosa Nostra—would be made exclusively through Cutler. "In the future, this Jack Cicilline," he said, referring to Raymond Patriarca, Jr.'s, lawyer, "whatever the fuck his name is I'm gonna send him a message that if I ever want to get a message to them, or from them, we'll do it through you. You'll call him or he'll call you."

Cutler responded that he'd never heard of Cicilline. Gotti told him, "He's a lawyer. Not much of a lawyer. Like you."

On February 9 our job got harder. Gotti was acquitted in state court on the charge that he'd ordered the shooting of John O'Connor. The jurors made short work of the case, which depended almost entirely on an inaudible snippet of recorded conversation. Most juries have many rounds of voting among themselves before reaching the required unanimous decision. This one took a single vote before announcing its verdict. The *New York Times* called Gotti "an icon of the underworld and the nation's top Mafia boss," adding, "law-enforcement officials conceded glumly that the acquittals would magnify Mr. Gotti's reputation for legal invincibility." The tabloids anointed him "the Teflon Don." He'd faced criminal charges three times in four years—our RICO case, the assault charge in Queens involving Romual Piecyk, and now Morgenthau's case—and no one could get any of them to stick.

Gotti had indeed become an icon of the underworld *in the media*. In the underworld itself he enjoyed no such reputation. His insistence on celebrity status was unique and a finger in the eye of law enforcement, whose response was to up its game against *all* the Families, not just Gotti's. The FBI had a squad for each Family, and those squads got bigger and busier after Gotti became the Gambino boss. The other Families, and even many members of his own Family, were furious at his refusal to realize that he was a gangster, not a media star, and he was hurting the entire Mafia as a result.

Unlike most other bosses, who'd been in charge for decades, Gotti had been in the position for only four years. In that time he'd shown by his own flaws that there was more to running a Cosa Nostra than being a tough guy, a killer surrounded by killers. A mob boss had to run a conglomerate of businesses, and Gotti never had the requisite acumen. Within the mob, Gotti was perceived as a dangerous loser.

Gotti was a media icon because the American public has always glorified outlaws: Robin Hood, Jesse James, Bonnie and Clyde, and, in the Mafia world, the Corleones and Tony Soprano. It doesn't matter that art hasn't done a good job of imitating Mafia life. To pick one example, mob bosses don't listen patiently to disputes among people in the community and, Solomon-like, dispense justice. And the popular belief that they might have become CEOs if only they'd had the right upbringing is ridiculous. Their success has nothing to do with business acumen; it happens because the people they do business with know they'll get a bullet behind the ear if they resist. But the American public sees what it wants to see. A handsome gangster in a thousand-dollar suit thumbing his nose at authority is a surefire recipe for celebrity status, and that's what Gotti had achieved.

In early March Mike Coiro was sentenced. We hadn't overheard an apartment conversation since January, but we were still hopeful, and I didn't want to burn our bug. That meant I couldn't tell the sentencing judge that within an hour of the verdicts Coiro was up in the apartment committing another crime. This didn't affect the sentence, because the judge gave him fifteen years—considering Coiro's age and physical condition, a big chunk of the rest of his life.

After the sentencing, Cutler went across the river to report to Gotti. He did it in the club itself, on the first floor of 247 Mulberry. Gotti was surprised to learn that Coiro had refused to say anything when given the opportunity to address the judge. We didn't really need any more enterprise evidence, but Gotti gave us some anyway, this time about the oath of omertà.

"For a guy like me to get up and say something," Gotti explained to Cutler on the tape, "it's like humbling yourself. Even when we're a hundred percent innocent, we're sworn not to say nothing. And you sit there and take it on the chin. But he's not."

Since I represented the government at the sentencing, the conversation drifted around to me. "Gleeson's the boss now," Cutler reported. "Giacalone went to the subways, and Gleeson's the boss."

One of the many chilling conversations recorded in the apartment was about who would represent Gotti in the next case. Bruce Cutler had gotten him acquitted in our RICO case, had represented him in the Piecyk assault case, and was his counsel again in the O'Connor assault trial. However, it didn't take an expert to understand that Bruce wasn't a complete lawyer. He could beat up an accomplice witness on cross-examination and he had no qualms about calling a prosecutor a "tramp" or bellowing in summation that a witness was a "yellow dog rat!" but that was about the extent of his forensic skills. He didn't know much law, couldn't write a complete sentence, and was devoted to the idiotic defense that the Mafia was a figment of law enforcement's imagination.

Gotti was planning to enlist someone better than Cutler in what he knew would be the case of his life. So he told Gravano and Locascio that he wanted Jimmy LaRossa. He realized this would be tricky. LaRossa had been the longtime attorney for Paul Castellano and the two had become close. It would be awkward for him to defend Gotti at all, let alone against a charge that Gotti had killed LaRossa's friend and former client. So Gotti explained that the approach would be indirect at first. "I'm gonna send him a feeler ahead of time," he said. But there was no doubt that LaRossa would be required to put aside any queasiness over representing his friend's killer. "Then I'll ask him. If he says no," Gotti went on to explain, "I'll kill him."

CHAPTER 21

TURF WAR

We spent the spring putting witness testimony and other evidence into the grand jury. There were gambling businesses to prove, loan-sharking operations, labor racketeering, obstructions of justice, and of course murders. Tony Roach Rampino's testimony was anticlimactic: once immunized, he denied any knowledge of who killed Castellano. We didn't believe him, but there was no way I could prove beyond a reasonable doubt that he'd committed perjury. By the middle of the summer our indictment was taking shape, with a well-rounded set of charges. The Ravenite recordings gave us overwhelming evidence of the Gambino Family, our RICO "enterprise," and the leadership roles of Gotti, Gravano, and Locascio. As for the predicate acts, we'd charge two completed murders (Roberto DiBernardo and Louie Milito), one conspiracy to murder (Corky Vastola), and even a rare "solicitation to murder" charge, based on Gravano's unsuccessful request for permission to kill Louie DiBono.

Beyond that, we decided on two separate gambling predicates, one for the Connecticut operation and another for Brooklyn and Queens. We lumped all the loan-sharking evidence into a single conspiracy count. There were two obstruction of justice counts, one for agreeing to stonewall the Tommy Gambino trial and the other for paying Coiro and others for inside information about the Castellano murder investigation. Finally, we charged Gotti with defrauding the IRS by claiming to be a low-paid plumbing salesman when he actually raked in millions. Because he discussed his tax situation with Locascio during the December 12 diatribe about Gravano, we charged Locascio in the tax count as well. We tried hard to make a tax case against Gravano too, but he'd filed returns and declared quite a lot of income, so we failed.

There were so many references on the tapes to other criminal activity that we could have added a dozen more predicate acts, but the goal was to go only with the strongest cases. I was determined not to run the risk that the jury would think we'd overcharged. The defense theme would be that the government was desperate to convict the invincible John Gotti, and even a single weak count could feed into that. Still, even being conservative, we had a classic RICO case. The crimes covered the entire period Gotti had been a Mafia boss and reflected the breadth of the Gambino Family's criminal activities. I worried a little about lack of depth; our case would consist almost entirely of recorded conversations. No accomplice witnesses, no victims, no eyewitnesses, just tapes. On the other hand, you can't cross-examine a tape recording, so our evidence was unshakable. Thank goodness for Nettie Cirelli, for her lovely little apartment, and that she liked to go shopping.

One day that summer, as we were nearing completion of the prosecution memo, Andy Maloney called me to his office. He told me that the Southern District and Bob Morgenthau were planning to indict Gotti for the Castellano and Bilotti murders. Their case was a stinker, he said. After years of investigation, Walter Mack and Pat Duggan had come up with almost nothing. Of the dozens of eyewitnesses to the murders, only one was able to place Gotti on the scene moments before the shooting. He said Gotti was pacing back and forth on the north side of 46th Street, directly across from the front door to Sparks, looking nervously toward Second Avenue. And the witness claimed to have heard Gotti say out loud (even though he was alone), "What the hell are they doing up there? They'll be here soon." The Southern District's theory was that Gotti was annoyed that the shooters were late getting into place.

The witness identified Gotti only after first being exposed to the media blitz that followed the murders. The news reports included dozens of photos of Gotti, casting him as the mastermind of the hit as well as the new boss of the Family. That was bad enough; Gotti's defense would be able to say that the witness was identifying the man he saw accused on television, not the man he saw on 46th Street. But the Southern District made the problem worse by staging an actual identification that couldn't have been made in more suggestive circumstances. There was no lineup, no photo array, or steps taken to hide from the witness exactly whom the detectives wanted him to finger. Rather, in 1986, when Diane Giacalone and I were trying Gotti, the detectives took the witness into the spectator section of the courtroom and asked him if he could identify the man he'd seen on 46th Street. Not surprisingly, he picked out Gotti, who was seated at the head of the defense table. It was arguably the worst identification procedure in history. A motion to suppress it as unnecessarily suggestive would have a high likelihood of success.

The only other witness the Southern District team had was Phil Leonetti, the underboss of the Bruno Family in Philadelphia. Leonetti had flipped three years earlier and cooperated against his boss and uncle, Nicky Scarfo. Leonetti told the FBI that he and Scarfo met with Gotti in New York in February 1986, two months after the Castellano murder. According to Leonetti, Gotti assured Scarfo that he'd obtained permission from the Commission to whack Castellano.

That was the sum of the Southern District's case. There was plenty of evidence that Gotti hated Castellano, but the only proof of Gotti's involvement in the actual crime was the shaky identification and the testimony of Leonetti, whose desire to get his forty-five-year prison term reduced gave him a powerful incentive to say whatever the FBI wanted to hear.

To make matters worse, Gotti had repeatedly *denied* killing Castellano on our Ravenite tapes. On three separate occasions, he said he wasn't involved in the murder. For our part, we never doubted his involvement, and we knew that his having *not* gotten the Commission's permission for the killing gave him good reason to deny responsibility, even when the only audience was his underboss and consigliere. But Gotti's lawyers would argue persuasively that the government wanted it both ways: when Gotti admitted crimes in secretly recorded conversations, it must be true, but when he denied them, it must be false. Heads the government wins; tails Gotti loses.

Andy was certain the Southern District would fail at trial, and that another government defeat would enhance Gotti's aura of untouchability even more. The media had already made such a big deal over his beating three cases in a row. Andy was afraid that the Castellano case would be such a high-profile loss that it would overwhelm anything we put together.

The option of going first wasn't available to us. The Southern District was ready to indict, and the five-year statute of limitations for their single-count charge was approaching. Even if we indicted right away, the pretrial proceedings for our multi-predicate RICO indictment would inevitably take longer than a straightforward murder case.

"They can't stand the idea of Gotti being convicted over here in Brooklyn," Andy said. "They'd rather roll the dice with a lousy case, even if it runs the risk of making him untouchable, than let us convict him." Andy had worked for Bob Morgenthau decades earlier, when Morgenthau himself was the Southern District U.S. Attorney. He was also close friends with Otto Obermaier, the current Southern District U.S. Attorney, and had served with him as an AUSA in that office under Morgenthau. Basically, Andy was a charter member of the Southern District alumni club, and now that he was the U.S. Attorney in Brooklyn he was getting his first taste of what it was like to be the outsider.

We had two options. The first was to get in line behind the Castellano murder case. If the Southern District won, ours would be irrelevant; if they lost, our case would be all the more important but also more difficult. The second option was to try to join the cases together.

"Why don't we try to persuade them that their shaky case would draw strength if we made the Castellano hit another murder predicate in our indictment?" I suggested. "RICO cases are always stronger than the sum of their parts. We have very strong evidence that Gotti had DiBernardo and Milito killed, and that's bound to rub off on the Castellano predicate."

But Andy didn't want our case to be tainted by the Castellano murder charge. He felt that Gotti's recorded denials were poison pills, not just for that charge but potentially for the whole case. He was afraid the jury might be so upset at our charging Gotti with a murder he'd denied in conversations with close friends that it would express its disapproval by acquitting him of everything. But the more we discussed how invincible Gotti would become after another acquittal, the more convinced we became that we should take a crack at folding the two cases together.

"We could invite Mack and Duggan onto our trial team and keep them in charge of that predicate," I told Andy. "They might not want that, and, if they accept, it would be a bigger crowd at our prosecution table than I want, but we'll need to offer that as a courtesy if we really expect them to give up their case."

Andy agreed and called Obermaier to ask for a meeting. I would make a presentation of all we had and show them how embedding the Castellano murder charge into our case would strengthen both. The resulting indictment would be prosecuted by all three legal teams—the Eastern District, the Southern District, and the Manhattan DA's Office.

A week later Andy and I crossed the river for a meeting in Obermaier's conference room. The upper echelons of both our rival offices were there in force. Manhattan District Attorney Morgenthau had Mike Cherkasky, his chief of investigations, and

Pat Duggan, chief of rackets. Southern District U.S. Attorney Obermaier had David Denton and Louis Freeh from his executive staff, Criminal Division chief Jerry Lynch, and various others from his Organized Crime Section.

After exchanging pleasantries, Andy said I would explain why we should add the Southern District's murder charge to our RICO case, and I tried to start with a little levity. "I feel like I'm about to sum up to a jury," I said, and it did feel as if the Twelve Angry Men were seated before me.

"This is the toughest jury you'll ever face," Morgenthau said immediately, without a hint of levity. We were in the large conference room adjacent to Obermaier's office, but there was no doubt that Morgenthau was in charge of their side of this turf war. He was an imposing presence. Tall and thin, with a long face full of vertical lines, he looked and sounded severe. Son of President Kennedy's treasury secretary, former U.S. Attorney in the Southern District, and longtime District Attorney in Manhattan, Morgenthau was both political and law enforcement royalty. I had no idea what he was like with his peers, if he had any, but when it came to someone like me he was not one to hide his gravitas under a bushel. He weaponized it. His response to my effort to be casual was meant to throw me off.

I proceeded to lay out our case, weaving the Castellano murder into it. As it turned out, it fit pretty well. Much of our evidence related to the rift between the two factions in the Family—one loyal to Castellano, the other to Dellacroce. Whenever Castellano came up in Gambino conversation, Gotti castigated him as a selfish and hypocritical boss. Also, the Castellano murder had taken place just six months before Gotti and Gravano killed DiBernardo, and the two deaths were linked. DiBernardo had been loyal to Castellano, and Gotti had admitted on tape that he'd whacked DiBernardo for his "subversive" talk after the Castellano murder.

I laid out our other predicate acts as well, complete with excerpts from the Ravenite conversations. I concluded that even if the jury didn't buy the Castellano evidence, it was extremely unlikely that they'd react by acquitting him across the board. However, if the Southern District lost an extremely high-profile case charging only the Castellano homicide, our follow-up indictment would be cast as another desperate attempt to bring down an underworld figure who by then would be considered a Houdini and something of a hero.

As soon as I finished, the meeting broke up. I'd expected questions and at least some discussion, but Obermaier and Morgenthau just thanked Andy and said they'd get back to us. My presentation wasn't reviewed at all. The only person who said anything to me was Jerry Lynch. As we all got ready to go, he came around the table and shook my hand. I told him we'd met six years earlier during my unsuccessful effort to get Rudy Giuliani to take me on. Lynch didn't remember that, but he praised the arguments I'd just put forward.

"Looks like you have a great case," he said. "Good luck with it."

Two days later Andy summoned me to his office. He was ashen.

"You made a pretty good pitch there," he said. "Otto just called to say they agree, there should be one case."

"That's great," I said evenly. "So what's the matter?"

"They say the one case should be theirs. They demanded all of our evidence so they can indict the whole thing in Southern. If we don't agree, they're going to ask Main Justice to order us to give them our case."

He seemed surprised by the audacity of Obermaier's demand.

"What happened to the promise Giuliani made to you that the next Family-based case would be in Eastern?"

"They're reneging on it."

"Just like that? They don't deny making it?"

"Just like that." He still looked stunned, and for a few moments said nothing.

"Andy, I know you idolize Bob Morgenthau and you're friends with Otto, and you're all Southern District guys. But you're out of those circles now. These people think they're better and smarter than everyone else, and they know no shame."

More silence, so I kept going. "Can you imagine making a promise that the next case would be theirs, then when it comes along saying you won't honor that promise? But none of this surprises me and it won't surprise a single AUSA in this office. These friends and idols of yours feel the Southern District of New York is entitled to everything it wants. If we don't dig in and fight them tooth and nail, they're going to get exactly what they want here, and we'll watch them try our case. Welcome to the Eastern District."

Andy's silence did not mean he wasn't listening. He'd been double-crossed and was clearly stung, but as that subsided it was clear he wouldn't take it lying down. He'd been a boxer at West Point. He'd fight his longtime friend Obermaier and his old boss Morgenthau.

All of a sudden we were litigating against our fellow law enforcement colleagues. The judge: Bob Mueller, then Assistant Attorney General in charge of the Criminal Division in Main Justice. Instead of gathering evidence against criminals, we were now absorbed in drafting letter-briefs arguing over who should prosecute the Teflon Don.

The Southern District's briefs were as shameless as Obermaier's telephone call. Morgenthau and Obermaier each submitted one. Morgenthau's began by acknowledging "that an agreement was struck in the fall of 1986 between the SDNY and the EDNY that the next 'Family' case against Gotti would be brought in the EDNY." But the SDNY should not, in his view, be bound by its own promise: "This agreement should be put aside and is not in the best interest of law enforcement." I'd heard this "best interest of law enforcement" line before. I'd had several turf battles with Morgenthau's office over the years, and it was the stock line used by his ADAs. If they were to be believed, the best interests of law enforcement were *always* served by the Manhattan DA getting what he wanted.

Once they got beyond the problem that they were going back on their word, they still had to justify why we should be ordered to hand our entire investigation over to them. Both letters chose the same bizarre argument: the Southern District had better jurors. Theirs were Wall Street executives; ours were mostly criminals. Citing figures from the 1988 census report, Obermaier wrote: "The crime rate in the Eastern District is 3,912 per 100,000 population while that in the Southern District was 1,445. This is totally consistent with our thesis."

The letters also claimed that the Southern District and the Manhattan DA were "equipped with the most knowledgeable and skillful" prosecutors, an obvious slight to my whole team. There was an oblique reference in Morgenthau's letter to the inclusion of attorneys "from all three offices" on the team that would try the case. Andy told me that both Morgenthau and Obermaier had let him know orally that they'd include me. It was cold comfort: I'd have to pack up an investigation that Laura Ward and Pat Cotter and I had been working on for almost two years, bring all our evidence across the river, become the junior member of their trial team, and tell Ward and Cotter thanks, but goodbye.

The briefing to Bob Mueller was followed by an oral argument. When on November 8, 1990, Andy and I boarded the shuttle at LaGuardia for the forty-five-minute flight to D.C., I wondered what the public would think if it knew that officials from three separate offices were spending taxpayer money to fight among themselves over who would prosecute a Mafia murderer. I believed that competition among prosecutors in New York was good—it elevated everyone's level of performance—but this dispute was law enforcement at its selfish worst.

Mueller was gracious in his role. I spoke first, and started with an updated version of the pitch I'd made in Obermaier's conference room. I emphasized how nicely the Castellano murder charge fit into our broad-based RICO indictment, and how much stronger it would become in that context. I also explained that more than 90 percent of the evidence and more than 90 percent of the predicate acts in the combined cases arose solely out of our investigation. We'd made the case, and we knew it inside out. It could be brought soon, and if DOJ really wanted to win the trial it would make no sense to turn everything over to prosecutors who'd have to learn the details from the ground up. Just as important as getting the convictions was the need to consider the equities; it would be unfair to let the Southern District move in and take our case. It would be crippling for the morale of our entire office.

Morgenthau and Obermaier jointly made the Manhattan DA/Southern District argument. No one asked why Morgenthau, who despite his storied history was just a state prosecutor, even had a seat at the table. It was testimony to the clout he wielded in law enforcement generally. He and Obermaier focused almost exclusively on their claim that the Southern District had higher-quality people in their jury pool. Obermaier in particular seemed obsessed with the higher crime rate in our district. He made it sound as if we'd be busing in our jurors from Rikers Island.

One significant change in the months since the debate began was that Walter Mack, the AUSA in charge of the Castellano murder investigation, had left the Southern District for the private sector. Mueller asked Obermaier whether Mack could be persuaded to return to try the case if it were "awarded" to the Southern District. I found the implications of the question disturbing for obvious reasons. Obermaier looked surprised and hesitated, but Morgenthau immediately piped up: "If you give us the case, I guarantee Mack will be back." I couldn't help but admire his audacity. Here he was, a state prosecutor, sitting at the table in Main Justice, where only federal prosecutors were allowed, and promising that someone who'd never worked for him would return to a job in someone else's office on almost no notice. It was quite a performance.

Mueller reserved judgment and we all packed up to head back to New York. Morgenthau and I were the first ones to make it out into the grand marble hallway outside Mueller's office, and he immediately pulled me aside. "John, you did a great job in there, good enough to win. I want you to promise me something, though, no matter how this turns out: let us prosecute whoever killed Jimmy Bishop." Bishop was the former head of the painters' union and a Queens Democratic district leader. He'd been under the control of the Lucchese Family for years. He'd been killed the previous

May in Queens, which was not even in Morgenthau's jurisdiction. This was the first one-on-one conversation I'd had with Morgenthau, and I was caught off guard. Placed on the spot, I said yes, and even though I had no idea why he wanted the favor, I immediately knew I'd made a mistake.

Andy and I shared a cab to National Airport. He was cautiously optimistic, but I couldn't stop thinking about Morgenthau's move outside Mueller's office. He had taken advantage of my inexperience and his own stature within law enforcement. I decided it was best not to tell Andy I'd just conceded what might turn out to be our next turf battle. Fortunately for me, it turned out well. I found out later that Bishop had been cooperating with Morgenthau's office when he was murdered by the Luccheses, so Morgenthau had a score to settle. The killers were prosecuted in our courthouse in Brooklyn by both offices working together.

I too felt optimistic about the meeting. Mueller was a good listener, and he seemed especially receptive to the arguments that we'd lived the case and knew it inside out and that it would be a terrible blow to the entire Eastern District to let the Southern District swoop in and take it. Plus, I'd essentially summed up our case twice—once in Obermaier's conference room and now down at Main Justice—and I was liking it more and more. When I got home, Susan asked how the argument had gone. I told her I was confident we'd win the turf battle and that we'd convict Gotti, his underboss, and his consigliere. She of course wanted me to prevail against the Southern District and succeed in convicting Gotti, but I couldn't help thinking that from her perspective, the prospect of my trying John Gotti again was at best a mixed bag. Traynor's perjury about us in the first trial had left scars on us both. Two days later Andy summoned me into his office. "Mueller just called. The case is ours."

"Fabulous. But he'll be second-guessed to death if we lose it."

"Well, he made the right call. He was impressed by your presentation," Andy added generously. "He said you obviously know the case and believe in it and are persuasive. You inspired confidence in him." This was nice to hear.

"Do we have to take on Mack and Duggan?" I asked.

"No. They were given the option but declined. I'm sure they have no desire to work under you, and you're the lead prosecutor. The whole thing is ours, Castellano murder and all."

Now we just had to win.

CHAPTER 22

THE ARRESTS

When the old Strike Force units were eliminated, all their lawyers were given the option of becoming Assistant U.S. Attorneys. This wasn't limited to being an AUSA in the district where their Strike Force office was located—they could work as AUSAs anywhere. The New Jersey Strike Force had a young lawyer from Queens who'd been hired straight out of his clerkship. In October 1989, shortly after his arrival in Newark, the chance to be an AUSA in Brooklyn came his way, and he jumped at it. Which is how I ended up with George Stamboulidis.

Had he applied directly, he probably wouldn't have gotten the job. He had no prosecutorial experience and his credentials on paper were ordinary; he'd gone to Temple Law School and clerked for a district judge there in Philadelphia. But Bob Stewart, the widely respected Strike Force chief in Newark, had seen great potential in him and hired him right off the clerkship.

The potential lay in the combination of several striking characteristics. Stamboulidis was supremely confident without the slightest whiff of arrogance. Even when he wasn't sure what he was doing, which was not infrequent, he acted like he owned the place. But he was guileless, and pulled it off without offending anyone. And he impressed everyone with his earnestness, willingness to help, and good cheer. These qualities also made him very teachable, and he worked hard to make sure he was taught.

I learned early on that I needed to be clear in what I asked him to do. He came to our office to take on organized crime work, but he knew hardly anything about how to be a prosecutor, so we treated him like any new AUSA and assigned him to some minor cases in the General Crimes Section to cut his teeth. After he'd put in a year there, I took him into the Organized Crime Section. When he sat down in my office for the first time, I asked him what baggage he'd brought with him, and he said he still had a handful of cases to finish up.

"Well, get rid of them," I said. "We have real criminals to chase here." I wanted him to plead out his current workload, with favorable plea bargains if necessary, so I could get him involved in our work as soon as possible.

A couple of days later he told me he'd cleared all his cases. I was pleased, but slightly surprised, as I'd thought it would take him longer to arrange the deals. When I asked him how he'd managed it so fast, he said he'd presented the cases to the grand jury and got them to "no true bill" them.

"You did *what?*"

"I got them to refuse to indict."

This was bad. "No true bills" are rare in the federal system. The easiest part of the job is getting an indictment, and it's embarrassing to fail even once in a career, let alone on multiple cases simultaneously.

"Why did you do that?"

"You told me to get rid of my cases. That's what I did."

Okay, so this kid takes direction well, I reflected; I just needed to be careful in giving it to him.

It was late November of 1990. We finally had the go-ahead from Main Justice to bring the case ourselves, and Pat Cotter, Laura Ward, and I had finished our presentation to the grand jury. The indictment was drafted and we were set to go, but there was one problem: Gravano wasn't around. He hadn't been seen at the Ravenite for several days, and informants were reporting that he wasn't in Brooklyn either.

This news made me anxious. I recalled that up in the Ravenite apartment they'd talked about Gravano going on the lam. When Mike Coiro had been summoned there after his conviction and they'd asked who was going to be arrested and when, the reason was so Gravano could abscond and run the family while Gotti fought the case. Now Gravano had disappeared. We were never able to identify Coiro's hook, and I couldn't help wondering whether someone in our office had tipped him off that we were about to indict.

I wanted to know whether Gravano was out of town temporarily or had actually absconded, so I called Jerry Shargel and asked whether he'd accept a subpoena for a voice exemplar from Gravano. Such exemplars help juries identify the speakers on recordings; they can listen to a defendant on the exemplar and compare it to the voice in the recorded conversation. I didn't really need one at the time, but the answer to my question would give me Gravano's status. Criminal defense lawyers *always* accept subpoenas directed to their client. They don't do this as a favor. If they refuse, an agent must serve the subpoena in person, which provides direct access to the client, usually when the lawyer is not around to protect him.

On the other hand, if Gravano had taken flight, Shargel wouldn't accept service, as it would obligate his client to show up to provide the voice exemplar on the date I gave him. If he failed to appear, I could get an arrest warrant for him. Shargel would never commit his client to something if he couldn't speak to him about it first.

Jerry asked me for a day to get back to me and an assurance no one would try to subpoena Gravano in the meantime. That was a sign right there. If Gravano were around and reachable, I had no doubt Shargel would accept service. In any event, he called me back the following day and said he wouldn't. So I had my answer. Gravano was gone.

For a week we all went into a funk. It wasn't just the prospect of multiple trials that upset us. With Gravano absent, we'd have an empty chair at the trial. That would give the defendants an advantage, as they'd be free to blame him all they wanted.

We weren't prepared to postpone our case a long time for Gravano. Nine months earlier Gaspipe Casso, the underboss of the Lucchese crew, had also bolted just before we indicted him, and he still hadn't turned up. I talked to Andy about waiting until after the holidays before arresting Gotti, on the theory that maybe Gravano would come home for Christmas. I suggested that we go forward with the indictment but keep it under seal for a while. That way we'd have arrest warrants ready to go and could take action the moment Gravano showed up.

We were mulling this over when on December 9 George Gabriel called. "Sammy's back," he said. "Time to move." We immediately went into the grand jury and asked them to vote on the indictment. Prosecutors have to leave the room while the jury deliberates, but it took only a few minutes before I was summoned back in.

"Okay, we voted it," the foreman told me. He was excited. They all were. Our Gambino Family special grand jury had already been meeting frequently for almost a year. They were a cohesive group, and they knew this was going to be a blockbuster case. Their sense of pride in their role was palpable. I said thanks to the foreperson and asked him to come with me to the duty magistrate judge's courtroom to "hand up" the indictment to the judge. As we were walking out of the grand jury room I noticed we had a small problem. The last line of every indictment is a signature above the word "Foreperson," and it was blank. I stopped and asked the foreman to complete the indictment. He froze.

"I have to sign it?"

"Yes, that's what the signature line is for."

"Will it become public?"

"Yes."

His mood suddenly changed. It dawned on him that it's one thing to be part of the prosecution of a mob boss while in a private room in the courthouse, but another to be identifiable. Panic was welling up inside him. It occurred to me that it was lucky for us he wasn't aware of all this before they voted to indict.

"There's no law that says your signature has to be legible," I told him. "Pretend you're a doctor." This piece of pragmatic lawyering led to a huge sigh of relief and some unreadable chicken scratch above the signature line. We proceeded on our way to the duty magistrate, whose eyes widened at the names Gotti, Gravano, and Locascio in the caption of the indictment.

By early evening the administration of the Gambino Family was in the Ravenite. When George Gabriel walked in with half the squad behind him, the scene almost looked staged. In the rear room of the club was a round table with a white tablecloth. Above it were framed artist's sketches of Neil Dellacroce and John Gotti. Beneath them, sitting at the table, was the man himself, flanked on either side by his underboss and consigliere. All three were taken into custody. "Teflon Don Arrested!" shouted both the eleven o'clock news anchors that night and the tabloids the following morning. Another media circus was about to begin.

The following day, December 12, 1990, at 3:30 in the afternoon, Gotti, Gravano, and Locascio were brought up from the Marshals' cellblock to a courtroom overflowing with journalists. We'd been focusing on these men so intently and for so long it was a relief finally to have them in court.

The case was assigned to Judge Leo Glasser. He'd been on the bench less than a decade but was sixty-four years old. A former law professor and dean at Brooklyn Law School, Judge Glasser had an almost Talmudic approach to the law and decision-making. Whereas some judges decide how disputes should come out and then have their law clerks find some justification for the result, Judge Glasser always began by reading every relevant judicial opinion. I'd had a two-defendant narcotics trial before him a year earlier, and in many respects he was still a law teacher. If I cited a case in a letter or a brief, I had to be ready to give its facts, the court's decision, and the reasoning behind the decision, just as if I'd been in a law school classroom. "A judge's last refuge is the law," he was fond of saying, and of all the fifteen judges in the courthouse he was far and away the most rigorous in learning the applicable law and following it. This made him impossible to categorize as either pro-government or pro-defendant.

When we learned the day before that he'd preside, Bruce Mouw and George Gabriel were a little disappointed, precisely because he wasn't reliably pro-prosecution. I had a different take, which I shared with them. Right out of the box we were likely to make a controversial motion to disqualify Gotti's lawyers. That motion would be on firm legal ground, but of course it would be criticized both in and out of the court-room. Frustrated at three consecutive failures to convict Gotti, the media would say, the prosecutors are now trying to separate him from the lawyers they couldn't beat. We needed a judge who'd faithfully apply the law. Judge Glasser fit the bill.

At our first appearance, I told him we wanted the defendants detained pending trial. This was arguably the most important motion in the entire case. If Gotti made bail, he'd have a year as a free man to influence public opinion, and he was one of the few defendants who commanded the kind of media attention that would enable him to do so. The press fawned over him when he gave a homeless man a $50 bill during his trial for the John O'Connor shooting. I had no desire to allow him such leeway again. I also wanted all three defendants to feel the pressure that pretrial detention imposes. Locascio, who was quite a bit older than the others, was looking after his ninety-two-year-old mother. If we got him detained, he might flip.

I told the judge we were moving to remand them on two grounds: they posed a serious danger to the community as a whole and a specific risk to witnesses and jurors. We brought to court a detention memorandum, complete with "greatest hits" excerpts from the Ravenite bugs. We'd been working on the motion for weeks, and the composite recording, with dozens of snippets about violence and obstructing justice, was compelling. I asked for a hearing at which we could play the excerpts, and Judge Glasser scheduled one.

At the end of the proceeding came a moment of high drama. The law requires prosecutors to inform trial judges of potential conflicts as soon as possible, so I said that the defense lawyers "have themselves been overheard on the electronic surveillance," and that we might move to disqualify counsel.

When moments later the judge left the bench, they descended on me. Which of them was recorded down at the club? What was said? When could they listen to the tapes? When would I decide whether to move to disqualify? More striking than the questions was the tone. Up till then each of them had been purely antagonistic. That very afternoon Cutler had mocked me in open court for my inability to convict Gotti, saying that I was trying to make Gotti do "life on the installment plan" by repeatedly indicting him and moving for pretrial detention before he was acquitted. That had got some laughs from the reporters. But now he suddenly acted friendly. He asked what he was recorded talking about, and for a meeting to go over those tapes. The others were just as anxious and inquisitive. I refused to discuss the issue, telling them to stay tuned.

The detention hearing was held four days before Christmas. Our pitch was simple: the defendants together managed a huge criminal organization; they were killers and so a threat to the community; and they were also known witness- and jury-tamperers and therefore a danger to the justice system itself. The centerpiece of our evidence would be excerpts from the bug in the Ravenite apartment.

Our written presentation was a narrative interspersed with those excerpts. At the hearing itself, I would provide the backdrop for each of the excerpted sections, then play them. We were fired up. The audibility of the recordings would surprise everyone. More important, we had discussions on tape about La Cosa Nostra and making new members of the family, admissions to past murders, the scheming to whack Corky Vastola, and about a dozen instances of obstruction of justice. We'd use only the clearest excerpts; my goal was to do as little talking as necessary and to tell Judge Glasser that the defendants' own words compelled a decision that they be denied release.

Before the hearing even started, however, our case changed dramatically.

We were scheduled for 10:30 that morning. We'd had the courtroom wired for sound the day before and wanted all the speakers and headphones checked before we began. I stayed in my office to prepare the oral presentation and asked George Gabriel, Laura Ward, and Pat Cotter to do a sound test. Carmine Russo, the Gambino Squad agent who'd prepared all our transcripts, had come along to assist as well.

They were gone for a while, but at 10:00 all four rushed into my office. Gabriel, Ward, and Cotter couldn't contain their excitement. "We have another murder!" Cotter blurted out. "It's clear as a bell! You're not going to believe what we missed."

Ward was talking over him about needing to revise the presentation that was scheduled to begin in half an hour. At the same time, Gabriel was talking about how quickly we could get a superseding indictment. All three were ecstatic. What they proceeded to describe was an extreme example of how what you know can affect what you can hear.

When Gotti spoke to Locascio during the December 12, 1989, apartment conversation about the murders of DiBernardo and Louie Milito, he explained why he'd ordered the killings. He'd been told that DiB and Louie had talked "subversive" behind his back. Our transcript, the result of hundreds of repeated listenings, included the following:

> **Gotti:** "DiB, did he ever talk subversive to you?"
>
> **Locascio:** "Never."
>
> **Gotti:** "Never talked to Angelo, and he never talked to Joe Piney. I took Sammy's word that he talked about me behind my back. Louie, did he even talk to any of you guys?"
>
> **Locascio:** "No."
>
> **Gotti:** "I took Sammy's word. Louie (IA)."

The "IA" stood for "inaudible," and the last attribution, which lasted about fifteen seconds, was given that designation because Gotti dropped his voice to a whisper. We knew there was something more he said about Louie, but no matter how many times we replayed the tape we couldn't make it out. Given the context, we assumed it was about Louie Milito.

By the late summer of 1990 we'd completed almost all the transcript work. As of the morning of the detention hearing, we hadn't listened to the December 12 conversation in nearly three months. During that time, on October 4, 1990, Louie DiBono had been whacked. DiBono had known he was in trouble—Gravano had a huge beef with him over money from DiBono's drywall business. So DiBono obviously wouldn't come in when he was called. Having infuriated the man who was now the underboss, he figured that the order to come in was for the purpose of killing him. This meant that Gravano and crew had to complete the job wherever they could, and in DiBono's case that meant the underground parking lot of the World Trade Center, where his drywall company had a gig. He was shot to death and left in his car.

Armed with the knowledge that DiBono had been murdered only ten weeks earlier, my team discovered during the sound check that the whispered part of the December 12 conversation wasn't about Louie Milito at all. Rather, in words that were quiet but so unmistakably clear that no one would ever challenge they were said, Gotti was talking about Louie *DiBono*. Where Carmine Russo had put "IA" in the December 12 transcript, in fact Gotti whispered: "Louie DiBono. And I sat with this guy. I saw the papers and everything. He didn't rob nothing! You know why he's dying? He's gonna die because he refused to come in when I called. He didn't do nothing else wrong."

So Gravano had had a business dispute with DiBono, whom he accused of stealing from him. He asked permission to kill him but was denied it, and Gotti concluded DiBono hadn't stolen from Gravano after all. That was DiBono's good news. The bad news was he hadn't come in when ordered to do so. Sometime before the December 12 conversation Gotti had ordered DiBono's death because he had flouted his authority. Ten months later, DiBono received his punishment.

We had a new murder count. Gabriel and Ward left to prepare the revised transcript we could hand up at the detention hearing. Cotter was in the hallway telling everyone else in the section about our discovery. Russo was still on the couch in my office, looking as if he'd seen a ghost.

"Carmine, what's the matter?" I asked after everyone else had left.

"I feel so bad," he said. "Those words are so clear. I don't know how I missed them."

"Forget it," I said, "we all missed them, not just you. It's no big deal."

"No, you don't understand. I know all that. I'm sad because I feel responsible for DiBono's death. We would have warned him. He might be alive today if I'd done my job right."

I explained that DiBono knew full well that his life was in danger, which was why they had to kill him in a public place. DiBono wasn't going anywhere no matter what the FBI told him. But Carmine wasn't buying any of it. A deeply devout Catholic, he was taking responsibility for the murder while the rest of us were exulting.

We went back to court for the hearing, and it couldn't have gone better. Our presentation was a smorgasbord of reasons why the boss, underboss, and consigliere of the Gambino Family couldn't be trusted not to kill people, not to run the Family's construction, carting, docks, and other rackets, and not to obstruct justice, if they were released pending trial. Each point I made about the enterprise they ran and the various crimes they committed while running it was illustrated by a recording from the Ravenite. All three defendants were detained.

One of our many illustrations of Gotti's penchant for violence was his statement that if Jimmy LaRossa refused to represent him in the next case, Gotti would kill him. Though the recording itself was still sealed, I described the incident in open court. A reporter found LaRossa and asked him to comment. The lawyer immediately responded that Gotti was only joking. But we had the recording, which LaRossa would not hear for months. Unfortunately for him, there was no laughter or lightness when Gotti said he'd send LaRossa a feeler, then ask him outright, and LaRossa could either say yes or be killed. On topics like that, Gotti did not make jokes.

CHAPTER 23

MARY JO

A lot of our evidence at trial would include the activities of Bruce Cutler and Jerry Shargel. By talking so much about them and to them, Gotti had made his lawyers part of our case. The law is clear that a lawyer can't be a participant in a crime or a necessary witness to one and also be the lawyer in a trial involving that crime. We had to decide whether to ask the judge to kick Shargel and Cutler out of the case.

Mouw and Gabriel together had first mentioned a motion to disqualify defense counsel to me long before the indictment. It wasn't the sort of suggestion FBI agents typically make. Such motions are rarely presented, and are usually denied. Also, they almost always emanate from lawyers, not agents. So back in the spring of 1990, during one of my regular visits to the Gambino Squad out in Queens, I was surprised when the two agents suggested that we should try to keep Cutler and Shargel out of a case we hadn't even brought yet.

Mouw had personal experience with the topic, and it involved Shargel. Six years earlier he'd taken a bag of cash from Roy DeMeo, a Gambino captain, to pay the fees for the defense of two members of DeMeo's crew. Shargel wasn't going to represent either one—he was representing a third gangster in the same case—but was using DeMeo's cash for the other two, to retain lawyers he could trust not to allow their clients to cooperate against DeMeo.

A highly respected judge in the Southern District disqualified Shargel from that case, ruling that he'd become "house counsel" to the DeMeo crew and had helped hire lawyers who could be counted on to represent others in ways that wouldn't harm

DeMeo. Shargel's activities had become evidence of an organized crime enterprise—that is, proof of the criminal association involving DeMeo and his crew.

Mouw and Gabriel believed we had an even stronger case. We had one recording of Gotti fuming that he had to pay Shargel $300,000 in a single month for the defense of others in the Gambino Family, and another in which Shargel himself whispered to Gotti in the Ravenite hallway that he'd given $200,000 of Gotti's money to a lawyer to defend Gotti's codefendant in the O'Connor assault trial.

It was true that we had a strong motion on that ground, but we were going to need more. Atmospherics matter, and we had a poisonous environment for a motion to disqualify counsel. The so-called Teflon Don had beaten three cases in four years, and Bruce Cutler had been by his side for each of those victories. Now the government, in its fourth shot, was trying to get Gotti's lawyers kicked off the case? We'd look vindictive just by making the motion. It wouldn't matter that Cutler would be almost useless in this particular trial; the only talent he had was for cross-examining accomplice witnesses, and we had none of those. But that nuance would be lost in the knee-jerk reaction to our motion. In the court of public opinion, we'd make Cutler look like Clarence Darrow.

The biggest obstacle to making the motion was we couldn't afford to lose it. If we moved to disqualify and failed, it would be front-page tabloid news. Our trial jurors would know about it, and Cutler and Shargel would figure out ways to remind them over and over. We'd not only look weak and afraid, we'd also look ineffectual.

My desire for a power move pulled me in the opposite direction. The detention hearing already had me planning what I felt would be a winning strategy: flipping Frank Locascio. I had several reasons to be optimistic. The charges against him were relatively benign; he had a strong desire to care for his mother; and he was from the Bronx, so wasn't a longtime friend of his codefendants. Flipping a consigliere was obviously a long shot. No one at that level or higher had ever cooperated. Also, Locascio's son Tory was a made guy, and his life in the mob would likely be over if his father flipped. Even so, there were ways to deal with that. All I needed was to get the word to Frankie that we'd love him to work with us.

Short of moving Locascio from their table to my witness list, the best power move I could make would be to separate Gotti and Gravano from Cutler and Shargel. It would knock them back on their heels. Cutler had come to personify Gotti's fighting cases through intimidation. We wouldn't miss his in-your-face antics.

In every big case there's a lull for the prosecutors after the detention hearing. We'd turned over all the Ravenite bug applications at the arraignment and notified counsel of the various other bugs and wiretaps we'd be using at trial. The defense lawyers needed a couple of months to digest it all and to examine our exhibits before making pretrial motions, but that meant I'd have an unencumbered January to work on the case, and I planned to use it to figure out this disqualification business.

I asked George Gabriel to bring me every scrap of information we had about the lawyers: every reference to them on the tapes, and every time their voices were heard. We asked Carmine Russo to make a log of all the occasions Cutler and Shargel were seen entering or leaving the club, and to listen carefully again to every club and hallway recording while they were there.

While I waited for the evidence, I read cases relating to disqualification till I knew the law inside and out. During the week after Christmas 1990 that was all I did.

We could trump the right to counsel of choice in several ways. One was the situation Shargel had found himself in five years earlier—where the lawyer acts as "house counsel" to the racketeering enterprise charged in the indictment. Another disqualifying conflict arises when the lawyer is present during an event to be proved at trial. A lawyer cannot be both an advocate and a participant in such a key event. If his version of what occurred becomes relevant, he needs to be available to provide it, and he can do that only under oath from the witness stand, where he can be cross-examined.

The third category is when a thorough job of defending a case might shine a light on criminal conduct by the defense lawyer himself. If the lawyer helped commit the crime, he may pull punches rather than run the risk of exposure.

Finally, a conflict arises when a government witness is a former client of defense counsel. A lawyer's duty to his client continues even if that client later becomes a witness for the prosecution. The lawyer can't use the information learned when representing the former client to cross-examine him at trial. I intended to call Mike Coiro as a witness at trial, and both Shargel and Cutler had represented him in the case I'd tried before Judge McLaughlin. They couldn't ethically cross him.

Between Christmas and the New Year Gabriel brought me a box of cassettes he'd put together. The recorded conversations either included the lawyers or were about them. Most were from the Ravenite, although some were from the earlier bugs in the homes of Neil Dellacroce and Angelo Ruggiero.

By the end of two weeks I knew we'd be making the motion to disqualify. I spent a third week drafting it. The eighty-nine-page brief began: "Shargel and Cutler are faced with virtually every type of actual and potential conflict of interest that can arise in a criminal case. Several of these conflicts would warrant disqualification standing alone. When viewed in the aggregate, it is difficult to conceive of more compelling circumstances for the relief we seek."

The motion against Shargel was a slam dunk. Gotti had told a group in his club that Shargel was a "lowlife motherfucking rat" until he instructed members of his crew to retain him. And in the previous ten years Shargel had represented a dozen people around Gotti, including Gravano, Ruggiero, both Carneglias, Arnold Squitieri, and Buddy Dellacroce. Gotti complained bitterly about all the money he paid "under the table" to Shargel and to Cutler to represent other people. It was bankrupting the Family, at least according to Gotti, who then went on the rant that made all the tabloid front pages once the Ravenite tapes were unsealed: "Gambino Crime Family? This is the Shargel, Cutler, and Who-Do-You-Call-It Crime Family!"

Gotti complained that these under-the-table payments affected his lawyers' performance. "You get a guy like Melvin Belli," he said, referring to the notorious King of Torts, "who pays his taxes, and he gets in there and tells the judge, 'Go fuck yourself!'" But Shargel and Cutler couldn't afford to piss off people, he said. "You don't wanna do it because, you cocksucker, you know and I know that *they* know that you're taking money under the table. Every time you take a client, another one of us on, you're breaking the law."

Taking Gotti's complaint at face value, Shargel and Cutler would at least have committed tax crimes. Other recordings suggested additional breaches. Gotti stated that he had instructed Shargel to direct others to commit contempt of court instead of testifying at the trial of Tommy Gambino, an instruction that was one of our charged crimes.

Our motion wouldn't be based solely on Gotti talking *about* Shargel, however. Shargel couldn't stay away from the Ravenite, and by going down there he placed himself right in the middle of one of the obstruction of justice counts.

We knew the identity of one of Gotti's hooks: Bill Peist, a detective assigned to the elite Intelligence Division of the New York City Police Department. In 1984, Peist and his wife were driving into Manhattan from Brooklyn to go shopping when they got a flat tire on the Manhattan Bridge. When Peist got out to change the tire, another car hit him, and it cost him a leg. He applied for the generous disability pension reserved for officers who are injured in the line of duty, but since he wasn't on duty the request was denied. So Peist had to learn how to live life with an artificial leg while still working as a detective. It was difficult, and he was furious at the NYPD. His wife's cousin was an associate in Gambino captain Joe Butch Corrao's crew, and for the next five years Peist got back at the police department by going on Gotti's payroll in exchange for top-secret police information.

On November 29, 1989, Gotti got a report from Peist. An on-the-job-detective could never go near the Ravenite, so the intelligence was delivered by Joe Butch Corrao. Gotti called Corrao out of the club into the Ravenite hallway, where he duly whispered his message. Gotti next summoned Shargel, who joined them. With Corrao standing right there, Gotti said he'd just received word that he and others would be arrested in a federal case for killing Castellano. Shargel had put himself in an obstruction of justice crime scene. The next evening Gotti would commit the crime again by summoning Mike Coiro up to the Ravenite apartment and directing him to find out who would be arrested and when.

The more I immersed myself in the recordings, the worse it got. Gotti had also told him "It must've been a ball" to kill Castellano, and Shargel laughed. That statement would be part of our proof that Gotti had committed the murder. If Shargel was planning to put a spin on that conversation, he'd have to do it from the witness stand, not in a summation.

The recordings were almost as bad for Cutler. He too couldn't steer clear of the Ravenite, and as a result he'd not only made himself a witness to some of our best evidence, he'd actually helped create it. After Coiro's sentencing, Cutler reported to Gotti in the club. The information caused Gotti to talk about the oath of omertà, and why Coiro, who wasn't bound by it, should have asked for mercy from the judge. So there was Bruce Cutler, who'd denied the very existence of the Mafia in the first trial, listening to the boss of the Gambino Family talk about one of the Mafia's cardinal rules. How would he handle that if he were Gotti's lawyer at the next trial? Would he tell the jury that when Gotti said directly to him "we're sworn not to say nothing," he was referring to something other than the oath of omertà? If so, I'd have the right to cross-examine Cutler, and a defense lawyer can't also be a witness.

And just as the recordings showed that Shargel had been Gotti's instrument for obstructing justice at the Gambino trial, they revealed that Cutler had been his instrument for obstructing our grand jury investigation. Less than twenty-four hours after I'd told Tony Roach Rampino's lawyer that I'd be immunizing Rampino and questioning him about the Castellano hit, there was Cutler, right on cue, in the Ravenite hallway, strategizing with Gotti over whether Rampino should lie or refuse to testify.

By mid-January, I'd finished drafting the motion. I brought it to Mary Jo White, our new chief assistant U.S. Attorney, apologized for how long it was, and left. This was my first serious collaboration with her and I was anxious about it. Mary Jo was another Southern District alum, so there was a collective groan in the office when Andy Maloney brought her in as his number two. She was a Columbia Law School alum as well and, among other talents, even though she was only about five feet tall, was an extremely able tennis player. When Andy asked her to join our office she was a partner at the elite Manhattan law firm Debevoise & Plimpton. Southern District, Columbia, tennis, and Debevoise painted a picture: from all outward appearances Mary Jo had never even set foot in the Eastern District of New York, let alone had any connection to its U.S. Attorney's Office. I'd convinced myself that we had to move to disqualify the lawyers and was concerned that she and Andy would be so afraid both of the adverse publicity and of losing the motion that they wouldn't allow me to file it.

My anxiety was unfounded. The next day Mary Jo and I spent an hour together. Her first words to me were "There is no way this motion can be denied." She had some suggestions, all of which made the brief better. She was a superb lawyer and a gifted writer.

On January 18, 1991, I filed the motion to disqualify not only Cutler and Shargel but also a third lawyer, John Pollock, whom Gotti had paid for many years to do the brief-writing for most of the men in his crew. Pollock was "who-do-you-call-it" in Gotti's complaint that his *borgata* ought to be called the "Shargel, Cutler, and Who-Do-You-Call-It Crime Family."

A month later we argued the motion in Judge Glasser's courtroom. The hearing lasted most of the day. Shargel and Cutler had their own lawyers to argue their side, which was a mistake. We'd prefaced our motion by saying it wasn't about whether Shargel and Cutler had done anything wrong. We insisted that the only people we'd accused of illegal conduct were Gotti, Gravano, and Locascio, and our essential point was that if Shargel and Cutler were allowed to speak to the jury about conversations and events they themselves had participated in, we couldn't receive a fair trial. But when the two lawyers got their own attorneys, and sat quietly at the defense table alongside their clients while others made their arguments for them, they made themselves look like defendants too.

Even worse for them, their counsel were unprepared. Shargel had retained Herald Price Fahringer, an old-timer known in the New York criminal bar as "High Priced Fahringer." With his thousand-dollar suits, silk pocket handkerchieves, and perfectly coiffed white hair, High Priced looked impressive, but it ended there. After

I'd spent more than two hours providing dozens of specific examples of how Shargel and Cutler were entangled in our trial evidence, Fahringer began his argument by saying he'd "parsed" an "adroit sentence" from an opinion by Justice Thurgood Marshall in one of the relevant cases. Before he could share the results of his parsing, Judge Glasser pointed out, "I should add that that's a dissenting opinion." After this shaky start, Fahringer, instead of addressing the concrete examples of how Shargel had made himself part of the evidence, wove an over-the-top argument from judicial opinions about the presumptive right to counsel of choice. At one point the judge interrupted again to say that if Fahringer were correct, no lawyer could ever be disqualified. It was an abysmal performance, and we left the courtroom feeling confident.

The spring and summer of 1991 were a busy time in the Organized Crime Section. The offenses we'd charged as predicate acts had to be prepared for trial, and since almost all included participants besides our defendants, those other gangsters had to be charged too. I had separate teams of AUSAs getting the indictments against them ready. George Gabriel and Bruce Mouw did the same on their end by assigning those cases to agents on the Gambino Squad.

So while my trial team and I worked with Gabriel on the Vastola murder conspiracy against Gotti, Gravano, and Locascio, I assigned Neil Ross and Jamie Orenstein to make the case against the others involved. Ross was very comfortable on his feet in the courtroom; we'd hired him out of the Brooklyn DA's office, where he impressed us during the Delroy case. Orenstein was his closest friend but also his opposite, a brilliant technical lawyer and brief-writer. The case included John Riggi and John D'Amato, the boss and underboss of the DeCavalcante Family, so it was a big deal. I teamed up Geoff Mearns, a young star in the office and once a world-class marathoner, with Laura Ward to work the Connecticut gambling case against Tommy Gambino and others. JoAnn Navickas, one of our most junior colleagues, who'd recently come from a big firm, was assigned to work the Joe Butch Corrao piece. Since that case also involved Detective Bill Peist, I decided I'd do it with her. Cops are a nightmare to prosecute; the blue wall of silence puts the oath of omertà to shame. Mike Considine had come into my section at the outset almost two years earlier, when we had almost no AUSAs and no cases. He'd helped me build the section, which now had twenty lawyers. Mike took the Queens gambling indictment. Gambling is not a serious crime, but the main defendant, Ralph Mosca, was a captain of long standing in the Family, so it was a priority assignment.

We had cases against other Gambino captains—Jimmy Brown Failla, Robert Bisaccia, Sonny Ciccone—who were some of the most powerful criminals in New York. On top of that, we had more made guys in our sights than we could count. Spreading them among the AUSAs in my section and the agents on the squad was a necessity, given all the work we needed to do, but it was also great for morale. It gave everyone, including those who wouldn't make it into the courtroom during the trial, a piece of that case. They'd work with us and our agents on the same crimes we'd be proving against Gotti, and these spinoff cases were hugely significant in their own right.

George Gabriel and I saw a lot of each other that year. He'd occasionally appear in my office with a cassette containing a single conversation. When I was writing the disqualification motion, those cassettes included either the voices of the lawyers or conversation about them. One day he showed up particularly excited.

"Listen to this," he said as he slipped a cassette in the player on my desk. It was short, and I could tell it was from the Ravenite hallway. Gotti could be heard saying, "Congratulations," someone whose voice I didn't recognize then said, "*Grazie*," and there was a sound of a kiss. At that point George shut off the machine. He was beaming.

"Okay, what are you so proud about?" I asked. "Who's he talking to, and what's it about?"

"It's Fat Dom Borghese, and John is congratulating him on getting made that day. I thought we'd play it at trial."

"Cool. How do we know what he's congratulating him for?"

"They had a ceremony that day. January 19," George replied.

"How do we know that?"

"Three informants told us about it. One was there."

"Fantastic," I said. "We'll put them on the stand and then play the tape."

"You can't call them," George said. "They're CIs," meaning confidential informants. "I can't even tell you who they are."

I knew this, of course. I was just needling him. "Look," I said, "this is the difference between information and evidence. We have great and reliable information that the reason Gotti is congratulating Fat Dom is Fat Dom just got made, but unless one of those informants takes the stand at trial, we have no *evidence* of what they're talking about. The judge won't let it in. So this tape, interesting as it is to you and me, is worthless at trial."

As I was speaking, I was taping the Fat Dom cassette to the dingy tin wall of my office, just above my conference table. For the next six months I used it as a symbol of the difference between evidence and information, a distinction even the best agents find elusive—but which prosecutors worry about every single day.

CHAPTER 24

BRUCE'S CRUCIBLE

On July 16, 1991, the Metropolitan Correctional Center put John Gotti in the hole. They'd received an anonymous call saying certain prisoners, unidentified, were out to kill him, so they had him moved to "Nine South"—a cell in solitary confinement, the same maximum security unit in which Willie Boy Johnson had spent almost two years.

The hole was a miserable place. It was used to discipline inmates, and when Gotti was originally detained the prior December he'd been put there, no doubt to convey to him who was in charge of the place. His lawyers immediately challenged the placement. There are procedures that must be followed before "administrative detention," as they call it, can be used, and the MCC hadn't followed them. When we went to court to argue the challenge, I knew we'd get grief from the judge, the ultimate procedure-follower, so I had Pat Cotter defend the MCC. We lost, and sure enough the judge blasted Cotter. I stood well away from him as he went down swinging.

"I get it," Cotter said with a smile as we returned to our offices, "I'm the stunt lawyer on this team. I guess every team needs one."

This time putting Gotti in the hole was technically more defensible. The MCC is responsible for the safety of its inmates, so when a threat comes along, the natural reaction is to err on the side of protection. If there's no clue about which prisoners pose the threat, the only way to protect someone is to separate them from the other inmates. As a practical matter, though, putting Gotti in the hole was silly. There was no one safer in jail than the Don. The other prisoners worshiped him, and waited on him, Gravano, and Locascio hand and foot. Permission was required—from other gangsters who protected them—for other inmates even to approach them. There was no way Gotti would be harmed.

Bruce Cutler got me at eight-thirty at night at my desk, starting the call all outraged by the MCC's move but calming down when I told him I agreed with him. He accepted that Gotti should sign a waiver of any liability on the part of the MCC if something happened to him, which I figured would satisfy the warden's only real concern. As long as Gotti signed such a waiver, I'd join Cutler in recommending that his client be placed back in the general prison population. I told him I'd try to get that accomplished immediately.

Miraculously, I was put through to an actual live person at the MCC. It was normally impossible to reach a staff member after four in the afternoon, but I got lucky by punching in the extension for the legal counsel's phone. The person there wasn't able to help and certainly wouldn't give out the home number of anyone who could, but when she heard it was about John Gotti she agreed to phone a deputy warden at home and give him my number.

The deputy warden called a few minutes later, and I told him I understood the desire to avoid civil liability, but Gotti was willing to absolve the MCC of any liability in return for being let out. They could draft the broadest possible waiver and he'd sign it. The deputy warden said they'd have to do a threat assessment and could release Gotti from Nine South only if the threat was found to be nonexistent.

"Look," I said, "that whole procedure is designed to protect the inmate and cover the Bureau of Prisons in case anything happens. But Gotti doesn't want protection."

I still got resistance, because liability waivers weren't in the MCC's repertoire.

What finally persuaded him was a threat. "If you insist on keeping him in the hole, you know he'll bring another challenge in court. And when he does, you'll have to send one of your lawyers this time because we'll be joining Bruce Cutler on this one. It'll be John Gotti and the U.S. Attorney against the MCC. The last time we defended your decision to put him in the hole we got chewed out because of your mistake. I have no intention of having the prosecution team take any of the heat for this."

"Okay, I'll see what I can do," he said finally. I got back to Cutler that night and told him I thought we had the issue solved without having to get the judge involved. We'd find out for sure in the next day or so.

"John, I appreciate it, I really do," Cutler said, genuinely grateful. He'd obviously gotten an earful from his client.

Gotti was out of the hole two days later. Cutler apparently got another earful anyway, because he was all over the tabloids on July 20 about the death threat and confining Gotti to the hole.

"There's no danger, there're no threats," the *New York Post* quoted him as saying. "The only danger is from the government. This was done by Gleeson and his cohorts. John Gotti is the most loved person in the city."

"Christ, this guy is something else," Pat Cotter said when the trial team met the following Monday. "He has our help getting Gotti out of the hole, then he blames us for putting him there! Doesn't he realize that's the last time we'll lift a finger for him on anything?"

"I think he does," I replied. "But Bruce isn't in charge here. He's a completely different lawyer when he's representing Gotti. I got along fine with him in the Coiro trial. He did nothing remotely like this."

"I agree that it's all coming from Gotti," Laura Ward said. "He told Bruce to get him out of the hole, and when he got out he told Bruce to blame it all on us. Bruce isn't going to tell him you helped. In fact, he'd probably get in more trouble if Gotti knew he'd called you."

When they left, I called Cutler. All I got was his voicemail.

"Bruce, it's John Gleeson," I said. "I'm a little bewildered, to say the least, over what I read in the *Post* Saturday. If we're gonna go forward in this case like professionals, we need to talk about that. Give me a call." He never did.

I really wasn't angry, partly because the *Post* article had been on a Saturday and two days had passed. Mostly I felt sorry for him. Cutler was a grown-up and had chosen whom he'd represent, but he was in a tough spot. Despite his public expressions of love and admiration for his client, he was afraid of Gotti.

I wasn't angry at Cutler, but the judge was. He summoned us all into court two days later and warned him to "stop trying the case in the newspapers." He specifically called out Cutler for accusing me of having Gotti placed in the hole. Cutler showed no sign of backing down, saying that I controlled the MCC "from the basement to the top floor. If he doesn't want John Gotti in solitary, he won't be there."

The judge didn't leave it at that, but went on to blast him for violating the rule that prohibited him from making public statements that could influence the jury pool, and threatened to hold him in contempt.

On July 29, Ethel Cohen, Judge Glasser's secretary, called to say the judge had entered an order in the case. I went down to the first floor, crossed the lobby into the courthouse side of the building, and took the elevator up to the fourth floor. Ethel buzzed me in and handed me a single piece of paper. All it said was the motion to disqualify Cutler and Shargel was granted.

When Jimmy LaRossa asked to meet with me, the request came from his law partner, Mike Ross. I'd known Ross from a couple of cases we'd had together. He was about twenty years younger than LaRossa and an even better lawyer. He said the two of them wanted to talk to me, and while he didn't say what they wanted to talk about, he didn't have to.

I asked Andy Maloney to join me in my office, as I figured that if they didn't get what they wanted they'd go to see him anyway. After an exchange of pleasantries, LaRossa got to the point. Gotti had asked him to get involved in the case, but LaRossa also represented Jimmy Brown Failla, and had for many years. "I know you can't tell me where your investigation is going," LaRossa said, "but if Jimmy Brown is eventually going to be indicted, it makes no sense for me to come in now for someone else." He went on some more about how he'd like to represent Gotti, but not if it would jeopardize his ability to represent Failla if we later added him to the indictment. "So if there's any chance you'll indict Jimmy Brown, I won't come into the case now," he finished.

We all understood what was actually happening. LaRossa was looking for help. He wanted to stay out of our case against Gotti without getting killed.

I had no sympathy for him. "Jimmy, I don't get it," I said, even though I got it perfectly. "This is the first time I ever heard of any defense lawyer asking a prosecutor's advice about whether to come into a case. You know full well we can't tell you who'll be indicted and who won't. If you want to represent John Gotti, go ahead. Are you really asking for our blessing here?"

This was followed by silence. LaRossa wanted to be able to tell Gotti that he couldn't come into the case because of me. But I was in no position to help him even if I'd wanted to.

"Can't you give me something to tell him?" LaRossa insisted.

I couldn't resist. "Jimmy, you told the whole world he was only joking when he said he'd kill you if you refused. What are you so worried about? If you don't want to represent him, just tell him no."

Andy was more sympathetic. He asked me whether we might need testimony from LaRossa at the trial. A key piece of our timeline on the Castellano murder was the date that Castellano received Angelo Ruggiero's tapes. It was LaRossa who'd given them to him.

Andy had a good point. Unless Gotti agreed to stipulate at trial that Castellano finally got copies of the tapes in the fall of 1985, we would need to call LaRossa as a witness. And Gotti never stipulated to anything. I had zero interest in taking LaRossa off the hook, but our need for his testimony seemed clear.

"Do you intend to subpoena me to testify at trial?" LaRossa asked.

"No, I don't," I said. "If Gotti refuses to stipulate, I know you'll show up voluntarily if we ask, so there's no need to serve you with a subpoena."

After LaRossa and Ross left, Andy said he thought I was insufficiently sensitive to the problems lawyers have with clients because I'd never been a defense lawyer. He genuinely felt bad for LaRossa.

"Andy, he has only himself to blame," I said. "Before he even listened to that conversation where Gotti said he'd kill him, he'd decided to defend him in the media, saying it was a joke. Nobody forced him to do that. Now he's obviously listened to that recording and he sees he's in deep shit with a very dangerous man, and he wants us to bail him out by handing him a subpoena he can show Gotti? Sorry. He chose to get in bed with Gotti. He can get himself out."

I was certain that the intimidation tactics that had worked for Gotti five years earlier would be used in the upcoming trial as well. The disqualification of the lawyers accelerated them. Fresh from being removed from the biggest case of his career, Bruce Cutler promptly gave an interview in GQ magazine in which he went after Judge Glasser. "He is like the Jews the Nazis used to lead the death camp inmates into the gas chamber," he was quoted as saying. I winced. The judge was deeply religious, and this was intended to inflame him. Cutler was using his own and Gotti's favorite trope—the evil of cooperating with the authorities against your own people in order to save yourself. He'd attacked Judge Nickerson, Diane, and me from the well of the courtroom in our first trial. Deprived of the ability to do the same in this one, he would attack in the media instead. "They've thrown the Constitution out the window when it comes to Mr. Gotti," he told one reporter. The trial was a "witch hunt" led by "sick and demented" prosecutors, an "example of McCarthyism."

The *GQ* article was accompanied by a photo of Cutler. It showed almost all of him, as he was wearing only a violet Speedo and a visor. He was sweating heavily. It was an odd photo to accompany a piece about a lawyer—striking, but not in a good way.

In early August, George Stamboulidis walked into my office with FBI agent Chris Favo. Favo, who was on the Colombo Squad, was the agent version of Stamboulidis—young, extremely hardworking, and as earnest as could be.

Stamboulidis explained that Favo was working with Michael Maffatore, an informant. Maffatore had told Favo that he'd helped bury Tommy Ocera, a made guy in the Colombo Family. He was willing to cooperate with Favo. He'd wear a wire.

"Who's he going to talk to first?" I asked.

"A guy named Harry Bonfiglio," Stamboulidis said.

"Who's he?"

"Another nobody like Maffatore," Favo said. "We'd never heard of him before this. He's an old guy. Definitely not made."

"Was he involved in the murder?"

"No," Favo went on. "Bonfiglio helped Maffatore bury Ocera's body in Forest Park in Queens. Neither was in on the hit itself. But Maffatore says Vic Orena ordered it."

Now we were really getting somewhere. Orena had been running the Colombo Family since Carmine Persico was sentenced to a hundred years in the Commission case a few years earlier. Even though Persico would die in prison, he refused to step down as boss, so Ocera was his "acting" replacement in name only. He was the number one guy in the Family.

"How does Maffatore know Orena gave the order?"

"Maffatore and Bonfiglio were with Jack Leale, a made guy," Favo said. "They drove Leale to a meeting with Orena. They stayed in the car while Leale took a walk with Orena. When they got close to the car on their return, Maffatore heard Orena tell Leale that he had to 'take care' of something. Maffatore didn't hear what that something was, but Leale got back in the car and said he'd just been given a contract to whack Tommy Ocera."

"Who shot Ocera?" I asked. "Leale?"

"He wasn't shot," Favo replied. "They lured him to Patty Amato's house, where Leale garroted him. Amato was there." Patty Amato was a captain in the Family.

"Does Maffatore know why they killed him?"

Favo explained that Orena and Amato had ordered the hit to stay out of jail. Ocera had a restaurant—the Manor—out in Merrick in Suffolk County. Vic Orena and his associates in the Colombo Family met there on Monday nights. Ocera, among other things, was a loan shark, and in early October 1989 the Suffolk police executed a search warrant at the Manor and seized Ocera's records.

Ocera urgently wanted them back, and sent his girlfriend to the police in an effort to retrieve them. The problem wasn't just that the records implicated him. They also showed payments he'd made up the line to Amato and Orena. If Ocera flipped, the records would corroborate his testimony against them. Both Amato and Orena were worried enough that he'd implicate them that they decided to whack him.

I had to make a decision. Orena and Amato were significant targets, but this was a long shot. Even if Maffatore was telling the truth and turned out to be a viable witness, no case could be made with just him. If we wanted to get to Amato and Orena, we'd have to flip Leale. But Maffatore wasn't close enough to Leale to have a wired conversation with him. The only person he was likely to have confide in him was Bonfiglio. To start making a case, we'd have to persuade Maffatore to get Bonfiglio to admit helping to bury Ocera's body. Next, we'd have to prosecute Bonfiglio and get him to flip. Then, if both men were good witnesses, we might be able to use them against Leale, and any charge would have to stick if we were to have a chance at turning Leale. Lots of things had to go right for us just to win a prosecution of one made guy, let alone the captain and their boss.

It was the exact opposite of what we were doing in the Gambino Family investigation. The ultimate targets were the same—the boss of a Cosa Nostra and as many other members of that enterprise as possible—but ours was a top-down approach. We'd recorded the boss, underboss, and consigliere and were working our way down from there. Stamboulidis and Favo were starting at the bottom—it didn't get any lower than Maffatore—and hoping to make it all the way up to Orena. Quite a climb.

"All right," I said, "it's a long shot, but Orena is a boss and Amato's a captain. So let's see if Maffatore can get Bonfiglio to talk about burying Ocera's body. We'll go from there."

"Well, there's a little problem," Stamboulidis said. "Maffatore's in the Nassau County Jail. He's been in on a drug charge for three months and he's got nine more to go."

"You're kidding, right?"

They weren't, of course. It was why they'd come to see me. Maffatore's being in jail turned a long shot into a pipe dream. First, he was in state custody, not ours. We couldn't just ask a federal judge to order the Bureau of Prisons to turn Maffatore over to our agents for a day. We were going to have to deal with state and local corrections people, and they weren't eager to let convicted felons out of jail.

Worse yet was the fact that Bonfiglio knew Maffatore was in jail, and had been sentenced to a year. All of a sudden Maffatore was going to show up at his door nine months earlier than he was due to get out—wouldn't Bonfiglio be a little suspicious? And then, out of nowhere, Maffatore would start to reminisce about a two-year-old murder and how they buried the body? Criminals are so leery of their fellows co-operating they don't talk even about minor crimes, let alone murders. This looked like a ton of work to pursue a potential dead-end lead—but I couldn't help admiring Stamboulidis and Favo's enthusiasm.

"Too much work, too little chance of reward," I said finally. "If you guys want to wrangle with the state people for a month to try to arrange for a one-in-a-hundred shot with Bonfiglio, go ahead, I'll sign off on it. But if something more promising comes along in the meantime, this will be the first thing we put on the back burner." Off they went, but with a determined look in their eyes.

CHAPTER 25

LAWYERING UP

At the next court conference in the Gotti case we could tell straightaway it was going to be a circus. It had been set for 9:30 a.m. on August 7, 1991, and when we arrived at 9:20 the place was packed. The media presence, which had been heavy all along, had swelled even more because of the disqualifications of Cutler and Shargel. The reporters now filled not only the spectator section of the courtroom but the jury box as well. The Marshals already had Gotti, Locascio, and Gravano at their seats. They were conferring with Shargel, Cutler, and a couple of other lawyers. It looked like the run-up to any court appearance, except that at 9:28 all the defense lawyers abruptly left the room. "Oh boy, here we go," I said to George Gabriel, Laura Ward, and Pat Cotter, who were with me at the prosecution table.

The defense lawyers weren't required to leave. Even Shargel and Cutler had been barred only from trying the case, not from the pretrial proceedings, so they could have stayed. But Gotti had decided to put on a show, and that required everyone on the defense bench to solemnly march out just before the judge entered. It said a lot about Gotti's hold on the lawyers that he'd not only managed to order his own team out of the room but Gravano's and Locascio's as well. David Greenfield, an honorable and dedicated attorney who was representing Locascio, hadn't been disqualified, yet at Gotti's whim he did what he must have regarded as unspeakable: left his client unrepresented in the court-room. The reality was, lawyers were afraid of Gotti, and Greenfield was no exception.

When on the dot of 9:30 Judge Glasser took the bench, he immediately noticed that there were only defendants at their table. His face suggested he wasn't pleased.

The courtroom deputy called, "United States against John Gotti." I got up and said, "John Gleeson for the government." That was followed by an awkward silence, as no one announced an appearance for any of the three defendants. Finally, the judge said, "Mr. Gotti, do you know whether Mr. Cutler intends to be here this morning?"

Gotti stood up. "He said you said he's not my lawyer anymore."

"I said at trial," the judge responded. "I didn't disqualify him from pretrial proceedings."

A pause. "Could you explain that to me?" Gotti asked.

The way he said it made clear that it was not really a question. This was a confrontation. Judge Glasser had firm views on how people should behave in court and gangsters taking him on in a packed courtroom wasn't in his playbook. He had a temper too, so this was a recipe for a blowout.

But the judge surprised us. He patiently explained that Cutler and Shargel could do everything but participate in the trial itself. Gotti knew all this already, of course, but he'd asked for an explanation, and that's what he got.

"I want you to clarify a few things for me," he persisted. "Why can't I have my counsel, Bruce Cutler?"

"I made that clear in a decision, Mr. Gotti," the judge answered, still calm as could be. He had filed a written decision explaining the disqualifications a few days earlier. "I'm sure Mr. Cutler has explained it to you."

Gotti said Cutler had been his only lawyer for seven years, and then, pointing at me, added: "I've been his only defendant for seven years. He says he welcomes a good fight. He says he wants a fair trial. He can't handle a good fight and he can't win a fair trial."

The judge still wouldn't bite, and tried to steer the proceeding back to Gotti's efforts to replace Cutler, but now it was Gotti who wouldn't budge. If Cutler couldn't try the case, he argued, then Gleeson shouldn't be allowed to either.

Giving up on Gotti for the moment, the judge turned to Gravano and asked him how much time he needed to replace Shargel. "I have no idea," Gravano answered. "Jacoby and Meyers don't come to the MCC." This was a good line, delivered in a perfect deadpan. Everyone in the courtroom, even the judge, broke out laughing.

Seeing an opening, I suggested that we adjourn the case for a week to give Gotti and Gravano more time to hire trial counsel. The judge agreed and set a date, but Gotti wasn't finished. He asked why the judge had recently given Cutler and Shargel a "Dutch uncle" lecture about not making statements to reporters, only to turn around and kick them off the case. Again, the judge wasn't biting, so Gotti returned to what was beginning to look like his favorite subject: berating me. He asked the judge to explain the court rule that limits certain statements to the media by lawyers in a case, but before the judge could answer, Gotti pointed at me and snarled, "It only pertains to me? Or to this bum too?" He said the disqualification of Cutler was based on "the phony tapes and phony transcripts from Lord Fauntleroy here."

Even in the context of such a bizarre proceeding, this was new territory. Defendants don't talk much in court to begin with—that's what their lawyers are for—but when they do, they're generally not allowed to call the prosecutor a bum. Coming from a murderous crime boss whose legendary anger was visibly rising before our eyes, it created a chill in the courtroom. The Lord Fauntleroy comment, at least on the surface, wasn't in that category. It was just weird. It left us wondering whether Gotti knew what that was a reference to. In any event, I was scratching my head at the allusion to the little rich boy in a velvet suit and lace collar.

The judge ignored it all. He was trying to bring a troubling and flammable court appearance to an end, but before he could do so Gotti had one more beef he wanted on the record, and it went a long way toward explaining why he was so angry with me. He had the following exchange with the judge:

"I had a lawyer sit here and they subpoenaed him two weeks after he came in."

"I haven't the vaguest idea what you are referring to," the judge said.

"I'm talking about Mr. LaRossa, my friend."

"I haven't got the vaguest idea what you're referring to," the judge repeated.

"Ask him," Gotti said, pointing at me again. "He knows."

"These proceedings are concluded," the judge said, and quickly left the courtroom.

So there it was. Evidently, after his meeting with me, Jimmy LaRossa had falsely told Gotti that he'd agreed to enter the case as his lawyer, but he also told him that my response had been to serve a subpoena on him. Gotti bought it; as far as he was concerned, he'd successfully persuaded LaRossa to represent him, and I promptly subpoenaed him to kick him off the case. First I disqualified Cutler, then I disqualified LaRossa.

"Well, boss," Cotter said when we got back to my office, "the good news is we don't have to worry anymore that Gotti's gonna kill Jimmy LaRossa. The bad news is it looks like he's gonna kill you instead."

In the ensuing weeks a parade of high-profile defense lawyers entered the MCC to be interviewed by Gotti. Once again, he was about to become the main defendant in the highest-profile trial in the country, so there was no shortage of applicants.

For his own lawyer, Gotti chose Albert Krieger. Krieger's office was in Miami and he had national stature, not least for having represented Joe Bonanno, the boss of the Bonanno Family, in the 1970s. He had a shaved head and a deep, booming voice. Maybe most important, he was highly respected both within and without the defense bar. Judge Glasser would be relieved by the selection. The contrast with the street-fighting Cutler would be good for the judge and good for Gotti as well.

Shargel had been Gravano's go-to lawyer for years, but he had no role in replacing him. Gotti made that selection as well, choosing Ben Brafman, a prominent New York attorney whose career was on a steep upward trajectory. Brafman was disliked within the defense bar, and many lawyers complained openly about him, even to me. Still, he was an effective courtroom advocate. Gotti had no doubt gotten good advice in making his selections, and he had chosen well.

One morning in early October, when I was alone in my office, reworking the trial outline yet again, Bruce Mouw called. "Are you sitting down?" he asked.

"That's all I do these days. What's up?"

"Sammy Gravano wants to cooperate."

My heart stopped. Of all the possible turns the case could have taken, this was the one nobody had even speculated about. Six weeks later, when Gravano's cooperation became public, dozens of smart-alecks all of a sudden had known he'd flip. He was too Machiavellian not to, they said. He'd never done a long prison term. He'd never forgiven Gotti for killing Paul, some said, overlooking the fact that Gravano was part of the murder team. There were as many reasons as there were people who claimed to have known it was going to happen. But before it actually did, nobody had even whispered the possibility.

"What happened?" I asked.

"We have been approached by an intermediary."

"Who is he, Bruce? And don't tell me you're not going to tell me."

"It's not a he," Mouw said. "It's Debbie. She says Sammy'll testify, but only if he gets immunity."

I couldn't decide which was more preposterous: that the underboss of the Gambino Family would use his wife to approach me, or that he expected I'd give him immunity in exchange for his testimony.

Using Debbie as the intermediary was contrary to one of the basic instincts of a true mobster—to keep a strict separation of family from the Family. A made member's wife was supposed to have nothing to do with the life. At his initiation ceremony, a made guy promises to put La Cosa Nostra first. The wife is not told about Family business, and knows not to ask. As Gotti's wife famously said when a reporter asked what her husband did for a living, "I don't know what he does. He provides." Since court cases were part of the business, wives had no place there either. It was no more appropriate for a wife to attend a trial than it was for her to be present at the shakedown of an extortion victim. Family members of real wiseguys weren't even permitted to sit in on sentencings, even though their mere presence might weigh in favor of leniency.

If he were simply going to flip, Gravano hadn't needed to get his wife involved. At one of his many court appearances, he could have whispered to a deputy marshal that he wanted to cooperate. We'd have separated him from Gotti and Locascio, arranged for him to get a lawyer he could trust, and found a safe place to keep him in custody pending trial. Gravano had known that option was available. The fact that he'd reached out through Debbie revealed that he'd thought his idea all the way through. He'd realized that the worst possible outcome for him would be if he *tried* to cooperate but failed, and Gotti *knew* he'd tried. Gravano was aware that we might reject his offer. If we did, he'd still be considered a rat for having made the effort. He'd be sent back to jail and for his own protection placed in the hole. He'd then be no different than Willie Boy Johnson. Even if he beat the case, he'd be killed in the street.

Gravano knew he needed someone he could absolutely trust to keep his overture secret, and the only person who fit that description was his wife.

"Tell her that immunity is out of the question," I told Mouw. "If that's a deal-breaker, then forget it. But Bruce, he's a savvy guy, he has to know that. He's charged with three murders and a murder conspiracy. People like that don't get immunized."

"I agree," Bruce replied. "But what do I tell her?"

"I don't know. It's not like I've thought about this. I can't imagine that we could give Gravano anything better than a twenty-year cap. If he does any better, it's going to have to come from Judge Glasser at sentencing. And even the offer of a twenty-year cap would be subject to him giving us a 'proffer'"—that is, a session that determines whether a would-be witness will become an actual witness. "We've got to find out what he can do for us, whether he's truthful, and if he's ready after all these years in the mob to give people up. For all we know, he's going to come in and say they're all innocent, and Chin killed Castellano. We have to meet with him."

"He won't meet with us now. He wants Debbie to meet with you to see if he can trust you."

"*Debbie's* gonna decide if Gravano can trust me?"

"John, he wants this meeting. Let's give it to him."

"Fine, but first you have to tell her immunity is off the table. It's a complete waste of time if he's really serious about that."

"Can I pass along the twenty-year cap?"

We both knew it was a vital question, and I should have taken longer with my answer. Weeks later, in retrospect, it was clear to me that I could have offered Gravano a higher maximum sentence than the one I ended up giving him. He would have signed on with a twenty-five-year cap, and maybe even with no cap at all. But I wanted to get Gravano on our side. This was the underboss of the most powerful Family in the country, a man who'd been in the mob for three decades. No one anywhere near his stature had ever flipped. It would be an enormous blow to the Gambino Family and to all of La Cosa Nostra in New York and New Jersey. Most of all, it would be the ultimate power move against Gotti, just ten weeks before trial.

I thought about Mouw's question long enough to decide that I didn't have the time or the desire to start a back-and-forth with Gravano. We had less than three months before trial and a lot of work to do. If we signed up Gravano, the case wouldn't be delayed but it would have an entirely different look. We'd go from a presentation resting almost entirely on recordings to relying on an accomplice witness with the tapes as corroboration. The witness list would change dramatically. If Gravano testified that he'd killed DiB and Louie Milito, for example, we'd no longer have to call the dozen or so people needed to prove circumstantially that the two men were dead. If Gravano was part of the Castellano and Bilotti hit, it might eliminate the need to call the onlooker who'd identified Gotti at the scene. The focus of the trial would switch from the tapes to Gravano. That prospect was fine with me; in fact, I welcomed a case with greater depth, but accomplice witnesses take a ton of time—to sign up, to debrief, to prepare for trial—and I had hardly any. I wasn't going to use up the hours dickering with Gravano over the terms of a deal.

"Yes, you can pass along the twenty years. But Bruce, you have to emphasize two things. First, tell Debbie to tell him not to think twenty is our starting point, like immunity was for him. It's our end point. I don't have time for offers and counteroffers. He has to agree to a twenty-year cap. Second, it's not an offer yet. We have to meet with Gravano and hear what he has to say first."

"Okay, I'll get back to you," Bruce said. "John, we have to keep this quiet. On our end only Matty, Frank, George, and I know. Nobody else can." Matty Tricorico and Frank Spero were the agents Debbie Gravano had approached. They were inseparable legends in the New York office of the FBI. Older than most of the other agents, they'd known each other for decades and kept to themselves. They lived and did much of their work on Staten Island, where Gravano lived. They'd been investigating him for years and had developed a good relationship with him.

When Bruce said no one else could know, he was referring to Andy. In the excitement, I hadn't thought about the issue I was about to face. The FBI wanted me to start down the road to what might be the most important deal in the history of the Eastern District without telling the United States Attorney. It wasn't that Andy's heart wasn't in the right place. The problem was, as most people in federal law enforcement in New York knew, Andy made an appearance just about every night at the University Club, where he met with friends. One was Jerry Finkelstein, the publisher of the *New York Law Journal*. Others included some of the most respected criminal defense attorneys in New York, men Andy had known when they were all Southern District AUSAs in the sixties and seventies, and who were now the lions of the city's defense bar. The Gotti case was the talk of the town, especially as the trial approached, so no doubt Andy was being asked about it over drinks every night. Mouw was right to question his ability to keep the news about Gravano to himself, and if it leaked and made it into the paper there'd be no possibility of a deal.

I thought about the trial team. "Bruce, if I don't tell Andy, I can't tell Laura, Pat, and Jamie either. Andy will kill me if he's the *only* one we keep in the dark. He's the U.S. Attorney."

"So don't tell anyone."

CHAPTER 26

THE OVERTURE

As soon as I hung up, my excitement turned to anxiety. Before I could strike a deal with Gravano, I needed to meet with him. We had to talk about his crimes, and what he could give us. I had to see if he'd make a good witness. This gave me a glaring Sixth Amendment problem. I could speak to Gravano only if his lawyer consented. Legal ethics said the same thing. If I met with Gravano without his lawyer's consent, I could lose my license.

There was no way Gravano would see me if his lawyer had to be notified. Ben Brafman may have been his attorney, but Gravano hadn't retained Brafman, Gotti had. If Brafman were told that Gravano wanted to meet with me to discuss cooperation, Gotti would know immediately. Gravano could easily be killed and so could his family. At the least, the meeting would not happen.

Still, there was no way I wasn't going to see Gravano. I had plenty of respect for the Sixth Amendment and no qualms about following the code of professional responsibility, but I believed in my bones that neither could sensibly prohibit the meeting. Gravano wanted to discuss an option that he believed might be in his best interest— pleading guilty and cooperating with the government. Normally, his attorney's obligation would be to act in his client's best interests, but this wasn't an ordinary case. Gravano had good reason to believe that Brafman would not be on his side if he were asked to explore cooperation. It wasn't just Brafman's connection to Gotti. He was a mob lawyer and collected big fees from his clients. If one of them testified against other gangsters, that business would come to a screeching halt. A big-time gangster is not going to retain or direct the people under him to retain a rat lawyer. Cooperation might be in Gravano's best interest, but it would definitely not be in Brafman's.

The Sixth Amendment and the ethical rule had a common purpose—to ensure that an attorney can protect his client's best interests. If they prevented Gravano from going around his attorney and reaching out directly to me when he believed Brafman would betray him, then the law and the rule made no sense. There had to be exceptions to both provisions when the client believes he'll be killed if he tells his lawyer what he wants to do. Although no such exceptions were recognized by the courts I had little doubt that, if I had to, I could convince Judge Glasser and the court of appeals to create one.

The first Gotti trial had taught me to consider how everything I did would look if viewed in the worst possible light. I began to consider the ways in which meeting with Gravano could blow up in my face. As long as our interview eventually led to a cooperation agreement, I was in the clear. The only person who could complain about a violation of Gravano's rights would be Gravano. If he became my witness, he obviously wouldn't claim that I'd violated his rights by meeting with him and his wife.

Nor was I concerned about the possibility of contacting Gravano and failing to reach a deal. He'd just go back to the MCC and we'd proceed to trial. He'd have no interest in broadcasting the fact that he'd tried to become a witness.

The worst-case scenario for me was the same as for Gravano: if we didn't reach an agreement and word got out that we'd talked. Then, to explain to Gotti why he'd met with the government's lead prosecutor in the first place, Gravano would accuse me of violating the Sixth Amendment and the no-contact rule. Gleeson, he'd say, was so desperate to salvage a shaky case that he'd brought one of the defendants to his office to make a pathetic and illegal pitch. I could imagine how it would go: "He was trying to shake me down—just like they did to Willie Boy in the first case. I told him to go fuck himself and that we'd see him in court. He didn't even tell my lawyer. He should be disbarred."

I tried to imagine how that scenario would play out. I'd explain to Judge Glasser that the only reason I'd spirited Gravano out of the MCC was because he wanted to see me, not the other way round. He'd believe me over Gravano, but still it would be a very unusual situation. I decided that if meeting with Gravano or his wife was going to blow up in my face, the fact of it wasn't going to be a surprise to Judge Glasser.

The judge's chambers had the feel of a home. Ethel Cohen, his assistant for many years, welcomed visitors into a waiting area with a powder-blue carpet. From the visitors' chairs just inside the door, Ethel was framed by green plants on the credenza behind her, and beyond that by a sweeping view of Midtown Manhattan. The Empire State Building was centered perfectly in one of the floor-to-ceiling windows behind her.

Always friendly, she was ready for the couple of minutes of courthouse chatter that always preceded the business at hand. On this occasion, however, her eyes fixed on the tape recorder I held in my hands. She sensed right away that this wasn't a cursory visit.

"I'll see if he's ready to see you."

The middle area of Judge Glasser's large office, between the imposing conference table at one end and the oversized desk at the other, was basically a living room. A couch and armchairs surrounded an elegant wooden coffee table. The western wall of windows that lit Ethel's area gave the judge's chambers a similar lightness that contrasted dramatically with the somber, windowless courtroom in which he presided. The same welcoming air was true of the judge himself. Out of his black robe, in his trademark white shirt and bow tie, he seemed much less imposing.

"Come in, John, sit down."

"Hi, Judge." I sat in one of the armchairs and put the tape recorder on the coffee table.

"What brings you here?"

"I want to place something on the record, but I want your permission to do that by making a tape myself, rather than ask a court reporter to join us. It's not that I have any reason to distrust the court reporters—I don't even know which one is assigned to you this week. It's just that what I want to tell you is so singular and so sensitive that I believe you'll agree that the fewer people who know of it the better."

"All right. Go ahead."

I turned on the tape.

"Judge, I wanted to inform you that Salvatore Gravano has reached out to the government through an intermediary. He wants to discuss the possibility of cooperation. The intermediary is his wife, Debbie Gravano. I intend to meet with her tomorrow afternoon in a hotel in New Jersey. Depending on how that goes, I will arrange a secret meeting with Gravano himself in order to get a proffer from him. I will keep the court apprised of my contacts with Gravano and his wife. I will seal this tape in an envelope and maintain custody of it. If Gravano eventually becomes a government witness, it will be disclosed to his codefendants."

I was nervous, and staring the whole time at the recorder. When I turned it off I looked up. Judge Glasser was smiling. I got to my feet, said thanks, and started to leave.

As I reached the door, the judge said, "John, you didn't make an application."

"Excuse me, Judge?"

"Lawyers come to judges for relief. They make an application, give reasons for it, and the judge either grants it or denies it. You haven't asked for any relief." He seemed to be enjoying himself.

"Yes, sir, that's true." I was not about to ask for permission to speak to Gravano's wife. If I did and was turned down, meeting with her would place me in contempt of court, even if the judge incorrectly denied the request. I wasn't going to take even the slightest risk that Judge Glasser would prohibit me from doing something that neither the Sixth Amendment nor the ethical rule should prohibit. I really wanted to get out of his office before he took it upon himself to decide the issue, even though I hadn't asked him to. But he wasn't finished.

"John, who knows about this?"

"Just me in my office. In the FBI, Bruce Mouw, George Gabriel, and Matty Tricorico and Frank Spero, who are also on the Gambino Squad."

"Not even the U.S. Attorney?"

"Just me."

"Keep it that way."

"Yes, sir." I opened the door and hastened past Ethel, anxious to get out of chambers before the judge could say anything else.

It took them a month, but George Stamboulidis and Chris Favo finally got permission from the New York State Department of Correctional Services to "borrow" Michael Maffatore from the Nassau County Jail. The plan was to take custody of Maffatore and have him meet with Harry Bonfiglio. Maffatore would try to get Bonfiglio to admit on tape that he'd helped bury Tommy Ocera in Forest Park. Then we'd arrest Bonfiglio and try to flip him.

The conditions set by the state were strict. We'd have Maffatore for only twelve hours. If it turned out Bonfiglio was unavailable that day, all the effort over Maffatore would be wasted. And even if we succeeded in getting them together, Maffatore would have to work fast. Normally, he'd have several meetings with Bonfiglio before attempting to insert memories of a murder into the conversation, but with only twelve hours to work with, there'd be no opportunity for him to ease his way back into Bonfiglio's confidence.

Obviously, the state prison people worry about escapes when they lend out prisoners. The agreement to turn Maffatore over to Favo and Stamboulidis was conditioned on their ability to make sure he couldn't skip. This took some doing, as Maffatore would have to be provided with a car in order to meet Bonfiglio. Since surrounding Maffatore with FBI vehicles wouldn't be conducive to getting an admission from Bonfiglio, Maffatore's car was fitted with a kill switch that Favo could trigger remotely. He and a surveillance team could monitor Maffatore from their own cars blocks away. They'd hear everything being said. If there were any reason to be concerned, Favo could disable the car's engine in an instant.

"Okay, let me see if I have this right," I told Stamboulidis and Favo when they reported all of it to me. "Maffatore will just show up at Bonfiglio's house, without any notice, after not seeing or speaking to him for months. Then he'll get Bonfiglio to drive somewhere with him. And while they're driving Maffatore will casually bring up the fact that they buried Tommy Ocera. That's the plan?"

"That's the plan, boss," Stamboulidis said, smiling broadly. "You don't sound too optimistic."

Maffatore had told them that he and Bonfiglio had been instructed by Jack Leale to bury Ocera's corpse in Queens' Forest Park, but they'd had a tough time getting the body into the trunk of the car. Rigor mortis had set in, and the cadaver kept springing up each time they tried to close the lid.

"He thinks he can get Bonfiglio to laugh about it now," Stamboulidis said.

"Well, don't expect an admission, that's for sure," I said. "In fact, if Bonfiglio doesn't start yelling 'What are you talking about!' when Maffatore brings it up, I think you can call it a success."

For our meeting with Debbie Gravano, Bruce Mouw had reserved a suite in one of the hotels just outside Newark Airport. When he, Matty Tricorico, and Frank Spero picked me up at the courthouse, they didn't come inside as they usually would. If Laura Ward or Pat Cotter saw me leaving with them, they'd ask us what was going on and we'd have to lie. It was bad enough sneaking around behind their backs. So I arranged to meet them on Tillary Street, around the corner from the courthouse.

On the way over to New Jersey, Matty and Frank were more talkative than usual.

"All Debbie wants is to meet you. We already told her you're not going to double-cross him," Frank said. I wondered how I could possibly double-cross Gravano. What did he think I could do?

"Gravano told her she had to meet you in person before we could arrange a meeting with him," Matty added. "We think she wants your guarantee that nobody will ever know about your meeting with Gravano."

"And, God forbid we do meet with him and there's no deal, nobody can know it happened," Frank added.

"Is this what she's already told you guys?" I asked.

"Pretty much, John," Matty said. "Except, to tell you the truth, she says everything like she's memorized it, like she don't even understand it. She's *very* nervous."

When we got near the airport, Frank couldn't figure out how to get to the hotel. We could see the place, but kept passing it, trapped in the maze of elevated roads and ramps where I-95, I-78, and Routes 1 and 9 all meet. We continued going in circles around the hotel. Frank was obviously embarrassed. He was a fabulous agent, not the type to get lost anytime, let alone on his way to a vital appointment, and let alone with his boss, Bruce Mouw, sitting in the backseat. The fact that we kept passing within a hundred yards of the hotel only made matters worse.

"Why don't we just park right here and rappel over the side," I said as we passed by the hotel on an elevated roadway. I was trying to inject a little levity into the situation, but had no takers.

When Frank finally figured it out and we pulled into the hotel parking lot, Matty spotted Debbie's blue Pathfinder.

"She's here, Frank," he said, pointing to the car.

"Good." Frank had a tight smile on his face and was clearly relieved. We'd all been considering the possibility that the biggest breakthrough in the history of the fight against organized crime might be missed because we couldn't get to a building we'd been circling for half an hour.

Debbie Gravano wasn't what I'd expected. There was no makeup, fancy hair, jewelry, or gum-chewing. She was exactly my age, which made her seven years younger than her husband. With short hair, and dressed in jeans and a cotton sweater, she was the archetypal girl next door. She could have passed for any one of about fifty girls from my suburban high school class.

Nervous as Debbie was (she would smoke during the entire meeting), her relief at seeing Matty and Frank was palpable. She'd been alone in the suite waiting for us and had evidently worked herself into a state. After she let us in, she led us to a living room, where she spoke softly with Matty and Frank while Bruce and I stood off to the side. The conversation was about logistics: what Debbie had told her children about where she was going; when she was expected back; when she was planning to see Gravano again at the MCC. I was struck by all the first names they used. Matty and Frank had plainly spent a lot of time with her and she seemed to trust them completely.

After a few minutes, Debbie turned to me and I put out my hand. "Hi. I'm John Gleeson."

Debbie said hi but wasted no time with pleasantries. "Sammy is willing to cooperate with you. He's willing to testify at the trial but he wants to meet you first, and he wants immunity. He also wants a one-year limit on cooperating, like Michael Franzese got, and he won't testify against his friends." She said it mechanically, with no inflections. Just as Matty had said in the car, it was as if she'd memorized her lines.

I had the sinking feeling that this entire exercise might be nothing more than a diversion, intended to distract us from getting ready for trial. I looked at Bruce, who was supposed to have passed along the message that immunity was out of the question. I could tell he was annoyed, and that he had in fact passed the news along, to no avail.

The so-called Michael Franzese Memorial Cinderella Clause was even less likely to come Gravano's way. Franzese was a young, handsome, college-educated captain in the Colombo Family. He'd gotten jammed up in the late 1980s on a gasoline excise tax scam. Franzese was prosecuted by the Brooklyn Strike Force in 1989, in its waning days before it was merged into the United States Attorney's Office. Except for Laura Ward and Pat Cotter, the members of that office had one foot out the door when Franzese offered to cooperate. They made a deal that only a prosecutor about to leave government service would make: Franzese agreed to testify, but only in cases that were indicted within one year of his agreement.

From the point of view of a cooperating witness, especially a gangster, the one-year limit made all the sense in the world. It meant that Franzese's obligation was finite and short-lived. Since the law required the court to bring indicted cases to trial within a matter of months, he could expect to be finished testifying—and to begin his new life—in about eighteen months.

From the government's perspective, the one-year time limit was ridiculous. If Gravano told me a Lucchese Family soldier had come to him in need of urgent assistance in getting rid of a body, and that Gravano had assigned a member of his crew to the task, that wouldn't be enough to make a case. However, if two years later a Colombo associate flipped and told us about a murder by the same Lucchese soldier, and that he and one of Gravano's guys buried the body, that was another matter. I might learn the name of the murder victim or, with luck, even be able to dig up the body. With the combined testimony of Gravano and the Colombo associate, I might have a good case against the Lucchese soldier, the member of Gravano's crew who helped bury the body, and maybe others as well. A deal with Gravano that allowed him to refuse to testify in those circumstances was out of the question.

If there was a silver lining to the ill-advised bargain struck with Franzese, it was that he didn't give up much information anyway. Although he'd risen to the rank of captain, he claimed not to have been involved in any murders. In fact, he could offer no help on any type of violent crime. When I took over the Organized Crime Section in January 1990, Franzese's window of obligation was closing fast. I read all the debriefing reports and found only one plausible case: an obstruction of justice charge against one of the grand jurors who'd indicted Franzese. One Ornge Tutt had violated the jurors' oath of secrecy by telling his girlfriend when they'd indict, and the girlfriend then got a few dollars for the information. There didn't appear to be any harm done; Franzese, tipped off about the date, didn't become a fugitive, or try to tamper with witnesses, or, as far as we knew, hide assets that he thought might be forfeited. But still it was a violation of the law to leak grand jury secrets for money.

As the new chief of Organized Crime and as heir to the Franzese agreement, I was determined to get something from the deal, so I assigned the Tutt prosecution to JoAnn Navickas and helped her try the case. Thankfully, it was assigned to a judge who sat in the Long Island Courthouse. In the relative obscurity of Uniondale out in Nassau County, we called a Colombo captain to testify against Tutt, an unemployed janitor who couldn't even afford to retain counsel. Poor Tutt got convicted, but the entire affair was embarrassing. Franzese had taken my predecessor to the cleaners.

There was no way Gravano was going to do the same to me. I wasn't about to explain all this to Debbie Gravano, so I just gave her the bottom line: "Debbie, Sammy is a murderer. He can't get immunity. It's impossible. A twenty-year cap is the absolute best he can hope for, and even that is not guaranteed. I have to meet with him first. He'll have to proffer. Also, forget about any one-year limit on his cooperation. It's not going to happen."

When I said the word "murderer," Debbie flinched. So did Matty and Frank. I could tell immediately they were angry at me, although I had no idea why, so I pressed on. "And what do you mean he won't testify against his friends? Who are you talking about?"

"Huck, Louie, Eddie," she said. These weren't just Gravano's friends, they were the made members in his crew. In fact, Lou Vallario had become captain of that crew when Gravano was elevated to consigliere. Huck Carbonara and Eddie Garafola were soldiers. Still, to Debbie they were her husband's buddies. I was struck by her apparent sincerity and sensed a connection between that sincerity and her reaction when I called her husband a murderer.

"Tell him to forget about that too. He either cooperates completely or not at all. No picking and choosing. It's not easy testifying against friends, but it's not unusual. People commit crimes with their friends. If they want to cooperate, they've got to cooperate against their friends."

"But Eddie's not just a friend. He's family. He's Sammy's brother-in-law, he's married to Sammy's sister Frances." This was Debbie speaking now, not Debbie passing along what she'd been told to pass along. She was clearly taken aback by the fact that her husband would have to give up his own brother-in-law.

"I know that," I said, "but it's too bad. We're not going to give your husband immunity, period. There will be no time limit on his cooperation. And no one gets a pass, not even Eddie. If any of those things are really deal-breakers, we don't need to set up a meeting."

I thought about explaining to Debbie how the process with Gravano would work, what steps had to be taken before I could decide whether to sign him up. The fact that he wanted to be a witness was great, but it didn't mean he'd be one. For lots of reasons, many people who want to be witnesses never make it because they can't bring themselves to give up their friends. When Patsy Conte, a Gambino captain, asked to meet with me secretly, Mouw was even more excited than he was when Gravano called. Conte, a Sicilian, had been a notorious heroin trafficker for decades. Nearing seventy, he'd been untouchable his entire life. The Southern District had come close in the mid-1980s, but their witness did a sudden about-face and the indictment was dropped. The prospect of signing up Conte, who could open the door to all the New York Families' Sicilian heroin trade, was huge.

I took Andrew Weissmann, a young and talented AUSA in my section, with me to a Manhattan hotel room to meet Conte and his lawyer. I let Andrew do the talking, and he got straight to the point.

"Tell me all the crimes you know anything about," he demanded.

"When?" Conte asked in a raspy, old man's voice.

"In your whole life," Andrew answered.

A long pause, then Conte said, "I don't know about crimes. I don't know anybody who committed crimes."

Andrew tried a different approach.

"Why don't you just tell us about your own crimes, then. Have you ever been involved in drug trafficking?"

Another pause. Behind his tinted glasses, Conte's eyes were fixed on the floor.

"I never committed any crimes," he finally whispered.

Andrew turned to the lawyer.

"I thought you told us he wanted to cooperate. How can he cooperate if he doesn't know about any crimes?"

The lawyer was upset. "I think we're having a definitional problem here," he said.

Conte's problem wasn't definitional; it was constitutional. After a lifetime of committing crimes and upholding an oath never to talk about them, there's no easy switch to flip to become a witness. Some people can't do it even if they want to, and Conte wanted to. It didn't make him a worse criminal than the ones who could. On the contrary, we all grow up believing that there's honor in refusing to tattle on others, so there was no shame in failures like Conte's. But it did mean that cooperation was not an option. We explained that there were no hard feelings, but his case was going to have to get resolved another way.

If Gravano was going to cooperate, I needed to know what he was going to say about the crimes we had under indictment. Would he try to minimize his own involvement? Would his version of the facts conflict with facts I believed were true, based on the rest of our investigation? I would have no interest in him if I doubted any part of what he had to say.

In addition to my need to know what Gravano had to tell us, I wanted to see *how* he'd say it. Trials are, in the end, personal encounters between witnesses and jurors, and also between lawyers and jurors. Witnesses have to be able to express themselves in a way that will convince a jury. It's not required that they speak the Queen's English or even be articulate, but they have to look and sound believable. Some people look as if they're lying when all they're saying is their name. Also, there'd be enormous pressure on Gravano if he took the witness stand against Gotti, and to be effective he'd have to be able to withstand it. A clever cross-examiner can make a wholly truthful witness look like a liar.

Finally, I had to hear about all the skeletons in Gravano's closet, which is always the most difficult part of a proffer session. It doesn't come naturally to criminals to tell a prosecutor about crimes the prosecutor knows nothing about, especially when it could result in a worse deal for the witness, but it has to happen if the witness is going to be effective. It's usually the case that those who'll be incriminated by the witness's testimony know of those prior crimes. If the prosecutor hears about them for the first time on cross-examination, that can harm both the witness, who can lose his deal, and the government's case.

Debbie was far too nervous to absorb a long pitch about the process, and I didn't want to run the risk that she'd report what I had to say incorrectly to her husband. Besides, I was annoyed that the immunity issue was still alive, and that I'd had to deal with the Franzese agreement and Gravano's request for a pass for his crew. If he was adamant about those issues, this whole interview was a waste of valuable time.

Debbie said she'd be seeing her husband the following day.

"Tell him what I've told you about the immunity and the twenty-year cap," I impressed on her. "Tell him the Franzese deal is not a possibility. We can't put a time limit on his cooperation. And he'll have to testify against everyone, including his friends and Eddie Garafola. Let Matty and Frank know if he still wants to meet me."

"You have to make sure no one knows about the meeting. If there's no deal, no one can know you met," she said.

"I know. I'll figure out some reason to have him brought over to the courthouse. Whatever it is, after it's done with, he and I'll meet. It will take some figuring out, but we'll do it."

I'd already given this some thought. There were ruses I could use to bring Gravano over from the MCC. He was the only defendant who filed tax returns, and we were planning to use them as evidence in the labor racketeering part of the case. I could subpoena him for handwriting exemplars.

We said our goodbyes, and my crew and I all left. Frank told Debbie that the room was already paid for but that she should wait a little while before leaving.

In the car on the way back to Brooklyn, I could tell Matty and Frank were still annoyed. They weren't the type to fly off the handle, though, and were keeping it to themselves. "Why'd you guys react like that when I said Gravano is a murderer?" I finally asked.

"John," Matty said, "you can't say that to her."

"Why not? It's obviously true. You don't think she knows what her husband does for a living? That he's the underboss of the Gambino Family, and that you don't get that high in the mob without killing?"

"You don't understand." Now it was Frank. "She's just Gravano's wife. She knows he's an important guy. She knows he's a gangster, and she knows what everybody knows about that life. But Gravano don't come home and talk about it with her. He don't come in the house and say, 'We whacked D.B. today, what's for dinner?' Debbie don't ask about what he does, and Gravano don't tell."

"Well, maybe if somebody told her, she'd realize how ridiculous it is to be asking for immunity," I said. "Just because she's in denial, it doesn't mean we have to be."

Frank was shaking his head. "When you call Gravano a murderer, you're not telling her anything that, deep down, she don't already know. But it's still like a slap in the face." We rode in silence for a minute, then Frank continued.

"It's like Big Lou, Huck, and Eddie. To her, they're just Gravano's friends. And Eddie's his brother-in-law too. Does she know, deep down, they're all committing crimes together? Sure. She's not stupid. She knows that Gravano wouldn't ask for a pass for them unless they'd committed crimes with him. But that's not her business. She likes those people, especially Huck's wife. To her, they really are friends."

I felt glad I wasn't an FBI agent. If their rapport with Debbie required them to pussyfoot around when it came to who Gravano was and what he'd done and who his "friends" really were, I was not eager to share that rapport. Matty and Frank went on, explaining that all they wanted was to make sure we didn't scare Gravano away by alienating Debbie. Without saying it directly, they let me know that the whole point of the hotel encounter was to get Debbie to like and trust me, and I hadn't helped matters.

When we pulled up in front of the courthouse, we agreed to talk late the following day, after Debbie had been to see Gravano.

I apparently didn't blow it completely, because the next day Bruce Mouw called and reported that Gravano wanted to meet with me. There was one new condition: whatever ruse we used to get him into the building for our encounter, we had to put Gotti and Locascio through it as well. If only Gravano were brought over, suspicions would be aroused. The deal was still on a knife-edge.

CHAPTER 27

"YOU'RE STILL GOING TO NEED A BODY"

George Stamboulidis and Chris Favo walked into my office while I was on the telephone. Both had huge grins and Favo was carrying a cassette player. Because the walls of our dingy workspaces were made of tin, the only electrical outlets were in the floor under our desks, and while I was finishing my call Stamboulidis was on his knees, plugging in his prized trophy.

"Let me guess," I said, "you actually got an admission from Harry Bonfiglio."

"Boss," Stamboulidis said, "you were right. As long as Bonfiglio didn't start yelling, 'What are you talking about!' we would have every right to call it a success. Tell us what you think of this."

I was being needled. I could tell from the Cheshire Cat smiles on their faces that they'd come by something exceptional.

"I've got this queued up to the good part," Favo said, "but I'm only skipping about fifteen minutes. We told Maffatore he didn't have all day, so he got right to it. Listen."

He clicked play, and the tape rolled.

Maffatore: "That woulda been funny if the trunk woulda opened on you. Huh?"

Bonfiglio: "Ming! All the way from Long Island to here with a stiff in the back, a murder victim! A hundred fuckin' years I woulda got! They woulda melted the fuckin' key!"

By the time Chris flipped off the tape, we were all high-fiving each other. It couldn't have been more devastating.

"You're not all the way there yet," I said. "You're still going to need a body. Maffatore might be wrong about where it is. Even if he remembers it right, it wouldn't be the first corpse they moved, precisely to avoid this situation."

"Sure, go ahead," George said. "Rain on our parade. Don't worry about it, we're gonna take Maffatore to Forest Park the day after tomorrow to dig us up a murder victim. We'll keep you posted."

Getting Maffatore out of jail to help us find Tommy Ocera was much easier than borrowing him the first time. He'd be in our custody throughout this mission, so there was an almost nonexistent risk of escape. The outing would consist solely of a trip from the Nassau County Jail to Forest Park, where we hoped Maffatore would point out Ocera's shallow grave and we'd dig him up.

Maffatore had a clear recollection of where he and Bonfiglio had dug the hole, and he was right. The first place he pointed out was off by only a few feet, and within a couple of hours the grisly remains had been exhumed. The decomposed body had been in two feet of dirt. Maffatore had told us that Leale had murdered Ocera using a garrote, and sure enough, a garrote was still around the neck.

The best laid plans: all of a sudden the pretrial detention of Gotti, Gravano, and Locascio, which we'd fought so hard for, was my enemy. Had Gravano made bail, a secret meeting with him would have been easy. But defendants in pretrial detention had only one reason for leaving the MCC—for court appearances. All defendants with cases on the trial calendar were roused from their cells, sometimes as early as 5:00 a.m., and brought down to holding cells in the MCC garage. After a couple of hours there, they were taken across the Brooklyn Bridge in Marshals Service buses. Once in the Brooklyn courthouse, they waited together in the holding pens—the "bullpen"—below ground level until it was time for them to be brought up to court. Then deputy marshals escorted them in special elevators to the pen next to the judge's courtroom, where they waited some more. At the conclusion of the court proceeding—which in many instances took only a matter of minutes—they reversed course, and waited in the bullpen for a return bus to the MCC. The whole experience was unpleasant, especially in the winter months, when the holding facilities were cold and all the prisoners wore were short-sleeved prison uniforms.

Codefendants were kept together every step of the way. Gravano might spend five or six hours in the courthouse for a ten-minute appearance, but there was no way to separate him from Gotti and Locascio without arousing suspicion. I needed a ruse that would get him in the courthouse by himself, but it had to be for a reason that applied to everyone in the case.

Gotti's take-no-prisoners trial strategy, which he felt had helped him win the first case, provided the answer. In September, we'd sent out a stack of stipulations to Krieger. Most long trials include a host of these—agreements that certain facts are true—which keep trials from being even longer. A stipulation that a stack of tapes had been recorded in the Ravenite apartment avoids the need to call witnesses to prove where the conversations occurred. A stipulation that the transcripts of the tapes correctly identified the speakers obviated the need to prove who was talking. These were audiotapes only. A careful prosecutor never wants to be in a position where the defense attorney can get up on summation and concede that the people on the tapes are guilty, but the government failed to prove beyond a reasonable doubt that the voices were the defendants'. So prosecutors ask for stipulations, and when the facts aren't really in dispute defense lawyers usually sign them. Sometimes they do it to build goodwill with the AUSA, to make a deposit in the favor bank. Maybe they'll need a withdrawal later—a stipulation in the defense case, or the prosecutor's agreement to a brief adjournment before summations. Saving the prosecutor the trouble of proving undisputed facts is a way to earn concessions elsewhere in a case.

But there was no favor bank when John Gotti was the defendant. He refused to let his lawyers make any deposits. He got mad if his lawyers even *talked* to prosecutors.

When we sent Krieger our stipulations, we knew they'd be rejected, but that didn't mean sending them was useless. If the trial got bogged down with voice identification testimony Judge Glasser was going to be unhappy. We weren't going to take the blame if he called the lawyers together to complain about hours of mind-numbing testimony about voice exemplars and the comparison of those exemplars with the voices on the tapes. "We agree, Judge," would be our answer, "but they rejected the stipulation." Most lawyers advise their clients not to get in that position, to avoid the risk that the judge will so resent the waste of time that, consciously or otherwise, he'll wind up punishing the defense. Unfortunately, the last thing Gotti cared about was avoiding pissing anyone off. He wanted to intimidate Judge Glasser, not appease him.

The letter from Krieger's office saying that there'd be no stipulation to voice identifications had arrived the week before. On the evening of October 18, 1991, I went to see Judge Glasser again with my tape recorder. I was letting him know that I'd be serving subpoenas on Gotti, Locascio, and Gravano for voice and handwriting exemplars. Because the procedure can be time-consuming, especially with an uncooperative defendant, we planned to bring the defendants in on successive days. Gravano would be last. After we'd finished taking handwriting and voice samples from him, we'd wait for Brafman to leave the building, then bring Gravano back up from the bullpen for a secret meeting.

By now, Judge Glasser was getting used to this. I'd bring the tape recorder into his chambers, turn it on, give him an update, turn it off, and leave. These were news bulletins; court permission wasn't being sought, so it couldn't be denied. We couldn't discuss the unfolding events, so our meetings were limited to my brief updates. Still, I could see that he was eager to hear about what was happening. I could also tell that he was hugely enjoying it all.

As soon as I served the subpoenas for the exemplars on the lawyers, they moved to quash them. The government would use the exemplars as evidence at trial, they wrote, so it would violate the Fifth Amendment to compel the defendants to give evidence against themselves. The motion asked for an oral argument.

Once again I began to wonder if I was being duped. I wasn't worried about the outcome. Whatever superficial appeal the argument may have to laypersons, all lawyers know the Fifth Amendment prohibits only compelled testimony. A person's handwriting and voice—like his or her fingerprints, blood type, or DNA—are physical characteristics. Gotti could not be compelled to say whether that was his voice on the Ravenite tapes—that would be testimonial—but he could be ordered to speak into a recorder so the jury could hear the sound of his voice and compare it to that on the tapes. Judge Glasser was almost certain to deny the motion, but not until I wrote a brief in reply and argued it in court. Those steps would cost me a couple of days. I couldn't shake the gnawing suspicion that a calculated scheme to derail our trial preparation was underway—and was working.

At the same time as our from-the-top-down Gambino Family investigation was about to enter a new phase, George Stamboulidis and Chris Favo were working their way up the Colombo Family ladder. Michael Maffatore had already delivered the recorded admission of Harry Bonfiglio that he'd helped bury Tommy Ocera in Forest Park. He'd also helped us dig up Ocera. Despite Bonfiglio's devastating statements that he had a murder victim in the trunk of the car and "they woulda melted the fuckin' key" if he'd been caught, he at first insisted on a trial, but eventually he flipped too.

With both men now aboard, Stamboulidis and Favo turned their attention to Jack Leale, the made guy who actually committed the murder. If we could charge, convict, and flip him, it would be up the line to captain Patty Amato and boss Vic Orena.

Leale had been given the murder contract directly from Orena. His work hadn't gone unrewarded. The day after the killing, he was given Ocera's two gambling clubs to operate as his own. But organized crime is a business, and a good business pays attention to risk. Leale had done away with Ocera to reduce the risk that Ocera's loan shark records would be used to prosecute Orena and Amato. Once the news spread that the FBI had dug up Ocera, Leale's world changed. Orena didn't even know the low-level criminals who'd given up Ocera's body, but he was well aware that they'd give up Leale as well. And Leale could give up both Orena and Patty Amato. Leale had gone from being the answer to Orena's troubles to being the actual problem.

Leale knew it, so he left his home and went into hiding, staying in the Plainview Plaza Hotel in Garden City on Long Island. On Halloween of 1991 he was on the pay phone in the lobby when he saw the risk reduction coming. He bolted toward his car, leaving the receiver dangling in the phone booth. But he wasn't fast enough, and was gunned down in the parking lot.

Stamboulidis and Favo were distraught. A man had been murdered, and as law enforcement officers they cared about that. Plus, this killing insulated two deadly gangsters from prosecution. Little did the two young investigators know that, at the very moment Leale was being gunned down, I was working on what would become the link they needed to convict the boss of the Colombo Family. Their from-the-bottom-up investigation was about to get a little help from the other direction.

On October 21, I argued against the motion in the Gotti case to quash the subpoenas for voice exemplars. Judge Glasser denied it from the bench. The following day we took Locascio's exemplars and set up a system for doing so with Gravano's secret meeting in mind. Reena Raggi, the Acting U.S. Attorney during the first trial, was now a judge. I'd heard she was out of town, so got permission from her chambers to use her jury room for the week. These rooms are only fifteen steps from the holding pens next to the courtrooms, but importantly, there are two doors in between—the door into the court-room from the holding pen and the door from the court to the jury room. Starting with Locascio, the plan was to have the deputy marshals hand off the prisoner to Matty and Frank at the door from the holding pen to the courtroom, and the agents would then bring the prisoner through the other door to the jury room. After the exemplars were taken, we'd call downstairs for the deputies to come back, and the FBI would return the prisoner to their custody at the door to the holding pen. Since case agents are typically present to take exemplars, there was nothing about the procedure that would arouse suspicion. Not even the deputy marshals would know about our meeting.

An old-school gangster well versed in the ways of prosecutors, Frank Locascio was not about to help us prove our case. Asked to read from the newspaper into a tape recorder, he halted between words, sometimes even between syllables. He grunted, and pronounced even simple words incorrectly. I wouldn't have been surprised had he broken into a falsetto to help disguise his voice.

Locascio's handwriting was obviously feigned as well, a herky-jerky chicken scratch that made me wonder whether he was using the wrong hand. As he wrote, I was thinking how unlikely it was that we'd ever use either exemplar. In all likelihood, the defense lawyers would admit in their opening statements that the defendants were on the tapes, but claim the recordings didn't prove the charges. In that event, we'd have no need for the voice exemplars. And we hardly had any written documents at all, let alone ones we thought Locascio had authored or signed. Still, his efforts at conceal-ment were so over-the-top that I wondered whether we should present the exemplars to the jury on the theory that anyone who'd go to such ridiculous lengths to disguise his voice and handwriting must be guilty.

The next day it was Gotti's turn. The contrast with Locascio was striking. The acting consigliere had been sullen and uncommunicative. He didn't once make eye contact with anyone, even his lawyer. And, like most older mobsters, he looked broken down—unshaven and in rumpled old clothes. But Gotti seemed to burst into the jury room. He'd arranged to change into an impeccably tailored suit, just as he had whenever he appeared in court. As he and one of Krieger's associates walked past me to sit at the table in the jury room, Gotti stopped and looked down. I'd made a mistake by remain-ing seated when he entered the room. With a huge smile, he said, "I don't know about youse, but my money's on me in this trial." He possessed an aura of supreme confidence.

Once seated, he asked what we wanted him to write. The truth was that we didn't care what he wrote or even whether he wrote anything at all. The only handwritten document related to him that we'd offer at trial was the family address book that we'd seized on the night of the arrests, but we knew the handwriting wasn't Gotti's. We gave him a sheet of typed sentences and words to copy, and he complied quickly. He wrote in an easy, fairly neat cursive.

The voice exemplars were almost as unnecessary as the handwriting. It was inconceivable that Gotti would deny that it was his voice on the Ravenite tapes. He was too enamored of himself and his position to allow his lawyers to suggest that someone else was talking like the Gambino Family boss. Besides, the tapes were loaded with identification clues. Gotti, Locascio, and Gravano frequently used each other's names in conversation—and Gotti even gave us self-identification. What were the chances that someone other than Gotti was yelling that someone needed to be told that "I, me, John Gotti, will sever your motherfucking head off"?

We may not have needed a good sample of Gotti's voice, but we sure got one. He acted as though he wanted to prove to us that his limited education had not held him back. We had all of that day's daily newspapers on the table. Offered the *New York Post*, Gotti took the *New York Times* instead. He carefully removed a pair of half-frame reading glasses from his breast pocket and read a few columns. He didn't stop until we told him to.

When we were finished, he rose from the table with the same beaming smile as when he walked in. There's your evidence, his smile said, we'll see what good it does you. "I'll see youse in court," he said as he made his way out.

Matty and Frank turned him over to the deputies in the holding pen and came back to the jury room. The four of us sat quietly for a few moments.

"He sure is confident," Matty said.

"I don't know why," I said. "Our tapes are devastating and he knows it. Even without Gravano on our side, he has no chance at trial." I was straining, and it was obvious. Gotti's performance had been impressive and it unnerved us all.

Gravano's visit was the following day. Mouw and I were determined to have at least an hour with him alone without anybody even suspecting the meeting was taking place. The dry runs with Locascio and Gotti had helped enormously, because the deputy marshals had become so used to our routine that it seemed like normal procedure.

Brafman arrived early and waited with us in the jury room while Gravano was brought up from the bullpen. There was no conversation, which was unusual for Ben, who normally can't stop talking. It made me wonder whether Gotti had prohibited him from having any communication with us, even the idle banter that typically fills downtime in the courthouse.

Through the two doors we could hear the distinctive rattle as the marshals unshackled Gravano's chains. A few seconds later, the jury room door opened and he walked in, followed by Matty and Frank. Brafman was facing away from the entrance, and I was able to make eye contact with Gravano before the lawyer turned to shake his hand. There was nothing in Gravano's look; it was the same steely expression he'd been wearing in court for the ten months since the indictment.

The voice exemplars were a little rocky. Gravano acted as if he could barely read. I thought it was an act, a feigned disguise for Brafman's benefit, but I'd soon learn that he was dyslexic, a condition that had caused him embarrassment throughout his life and led to his dropping out of school at a young age. The handwriting exemplars were provided quickly, and Gravano rose to leave. Brafman told him that he wanted to speak to him briefly, and would see him in the basement bullpen in a few minutes. This surprised us all, and Gravano shot me and Gabriel a quick look as Matty and Frank escorted him out of the room.

Matty and Frank reentered just as Brafman finished packing his briefcase. The original plan had been for them both to leave the courthouse along with Brafman. Whereas the agents would have parked their car blocks away, Brafman would have a Lincoln Town Car waiting for him at the courthouse door. As soon as the limousine turned onto the Brooklyn Bridge toward Manhattan, the coast would be clear. Matty and Frank would then beep Bruce Mouw, who was waiting nearby, and come back up. With Brafman heading down to the bullpen instead, we agreed that Matty and Frank would set up a surveillance of the courthouse door and return to the jury room once he'd gone.

Gabriel and I waited for a half hour until Matty and Frank returned with Mouw. I immediately called the bullpen and asked if Gravano was still there. I knew the answer would be yes. We deliberately scheduled the exemplars early in the day so there'd be no risk that the first return bus to the MCC would whisk him away before we were ready for him.

"Could you guys do us a favor?" I asked the deputy in the cellblock. "The recorder screwed up while we were obtaining Gravano's voice exemplars, so we got nothing. I have to redo them. Could you bring him back to Judge Raggi's jury room?"

"No problem," came the answer, and within five minutes the chains were clanking again in the holding cell. Matty and Frank took Gravano at the bullpen door and suddenly there we were, face-to-face with Sammy the Bull in a secret meeting right in the courthouse.

CHAPTER 28

THE FLIP

My heart was pounding. I reached out and offered my hand. Gravano shook it firmly. I'd decided beforehand that if I ever had to justify my meeting with Gravano behind Brafman's back, I needed to establish certain facts right away.

"Hi. I'm glad you asked to meet. But I have a duty to speak to you only through your lawyer. I know you wanted to meet with me alone, but I need to know why."

Certain answers would have ended the meeting. If Gravano answered that Brafman had advised him against meeting with me because I couldn't be trusted, or that Brafman said he was too busy to attend the meeting, I'd have no justification for bypassing counsel and I'd have to send Gravano back to the MCC.

"I can't trust Brafman. If I told him I wanted to meet with you, John would know immediately. I'd be killed."

So far, so good. I couldn't have scripted it better.

"Let me tell you the rules," I said. "Debbie has made it clear to us that you want secrecy in this meeting. We understand that. You have it. Nobody knows we're here except the people in this room and Debbie. I haven't even told the U.S. Attorney. Anything you say here stays here. If we don't reach a deal, I promise you no one except the people in this room will know we met, and we will tell no one. There's only one exception to that: if you testify at trial, I can use your statements here today to cross-examine you. To give you an example, if you tell me today that you killed Louie Milito, that admission will never be mentioned again, unless you actually take the stand at trial and deny it. Understand?"

"Yes. No problem." He did understand, and he was right that it posed no problem.

Made guys cannot take the stand at trial anyway, so the right to use his statements in cross-examination meant nothing to Gravano.

"Why did you want to meet?" I asked.

"I want to jump from our government to your government." That's an interesting way of looking at it, I thought.

Gravano was short, about five foot six or seven, and well built. He had been an active boxer at Gleason's Gym near the courthouse, and looked the part. My image of him based on almost a year of court appearances was him with his elbows on the table, head tilted forward, eyes darting around the room, looking as if he were ready to bolt for the door. But in the jury room he sat up straight, made eye contact, and seemed relaxed. He had a broad face with a large forehead, and I could tell already he had an easy laugh.

"Why do you want to switch to our side?"

"I think if we manage to beat the case, John will try to kill me when we hit the street. So if we do win, I'd have to kill him or be killed by him. If I kill him, I'll have to kill his brothers Gene and Pete. And his kid, probably some others too. It would get complicated."

"Why do you think John will kill you?" George asked.

"I haven't heard all of that December 12 tape. He won't let us listen to it. But the parts youse played in court sound like he's trying to get Frankie to go along with whacking me. I can't tell for sure. I'd like to hear the rest of that tape."

"You will soon enough," I told him. "Why do you think you're better off with us than with him?"

"Because I trust these guys," Gravano said, pointing with his chin at Matty and Frank. "I don't think they'll double-bang me. I like what youse did for me at the bail hearing about that time outside my office. It meant a lot to me."

I had no idea what Gravano was talking about, and was obviously the only one in the room suffering from that disability. But I figured I'd remedy that after the meeting; we had a lot of ground to cover and I had only an hour.

"Do you mind if I call you Sammy?"

"Sam. What do I call you?"

"John, for now." That would have to change later, but I was trying to connect with him. "Debbie told you the best you can get from us is a twenty-year cap? You understand that?"

"Yeah, that's okay." I knew from the way he said it that I'd been too lenient. As ridiculous as it was, his opening demand for immunity had worked. By offering a twenty-year cap, I'd left at least five years on the table.

"Sam, did we get anything wrong in the indictment?"

Silence. Gravano looked at Matty and Frank, then at Bruce and George. Deciding to become a rat was one thing; actually telling a prosecutor about crimes is another.

I understood the hesitation, but we had no time to waste. "Sam, did you kill DiB?"

"I liked DiB. I didn't want him to die."

I started sweating. Gotti and Gravano were both charged with murdering DiB. Gotti had said on tape that Gravano had reported DiB as a subversive, and that he took Gravano's word for it. According to Gotti in the December 12 conversation with Locascio, DiB was one of the people Gravano had asked permission to kill. Gotti actually said that they "whacked" him. It was the strongest charge in our case. Now Gravano was going to deny it?

In that instant it occurred to me that I'd made a promise I might not be able to keep. If Gravano were to say that neither he nor Gotti had been involved in DiB's murder, I'd have a constitutional obligation to disclose that evidence to Gotti, despite my promise of secrecy to Gravano. I'd have to tell Gotti that there was a witness— Gravano—who might be useful to his defense.

My mind was racing. Why would Gravano think we'd be receptive to this? If he were going to deny committing the crimes we'd indicted him for, he had to go to trial. We weren't going to drop the case just because he said he wasn't guilty.

"Sam, are you telling me that you're not guilty of DiB's murder?"

"No, I'm not saying I'm not guilty. I'm saying I liked him. I didn't want him to die, and he shouldn't have been killed. I never told John he was subversive. Angelo did. But the word came out of the MCC that John wanted him whacked, and I'm responsible for the murder."

I felt like hugging him. "What do you mean? Did you kill him?"

"No, but I'm responsible. I'll tell you the details some other time."

"Sam, are you guilty of that murder, like we charged you? You can't put that off till later."

"Yes, I'm guilty. I had him hit in my office on Stillwell Avenue."

"Were you there?" I asked.

"Yes."

"And John ordered it?"

"Yes, while he was in jail on your first case against him."

We were off to the races. Milito was killed because, as Gravano would put it, "he fucked with me; I had to get John's permission and I got it." DiBono was killed because he refused to come in when John called. Our solicitation count was wrong. It was true that Gravano had asked for permission to kill DiBono, but he'd asked Castellano, not Gotti. Still, the important point was that Gravano was guilty, if not exactly as charged.

"What about Castellano and Bilotti?" George asked.

"I was on the scene. So was John. The two of us were in a car across Third Avenue on 46th Street. Your eyewitness is wrong. We never got out of the car. We couldn't. If Paul or Tommy saw either one of us, they'd never have stopped. They'd have known something was up and would've driven right by the place. All the shooters were people they didn't know by sight."

"John was never on the sidewalk across 46th Street from Sparks?" I asked.

"We never got out of the car."

"You sure he never got out?" George asked.

"Positive. I was with him the whole time." So much for the Southern District's eyewitness.

Gravano next went on to describe the machinations of the Vastola murder conspiracy precisely the way we understood them. Barry Nichilo, the associate in Sally Dogs's crew in the Genovese Family, and the only person Vastola would meet with, had agreed, as a favor to Gravano, to kill Corky on a farm that Nichilo was going to buy in Jersey.

"What happened?" George asked. "Corky's still alive."

"We needed Chin's permission. You have us on tape talking about how we'd get it. Well, Chin said no."

"That killed it?" George asked.

"That killed it."

I was ready to jump for joy. Gravano was direct, plainspoken, matter-of-fact. He came across as very sure of himself but not the least bit cocky. He confirmed that Gotti had an NYPD detective on the payroll, which we knew was Bill Peist; that Gravano himself had controlled Bobby Sasso and Teamsters Local 282 ever since DiB was killed; and that the Family had numerous gambling and loan-sharking operations. They were guilty of everything, and he seemed ready to say so from the witness stand. As he spoke, I could barely contain my excitement. Gotti was soon going to have a very bad day.

While I was eager to hear about the crimes in the indictment, I first had to raise an equally important issue: Gravano's baggage. We had to know what else he'd done besides the three murders and the other crimes we'd charged him with.

"Sam, I'm gonna ask you a question, but before you answer it I need to tell you something. The question is how many other murders you did. Before you answer, understand that John and Frankie will pressure every single person you ever knew for impeachment information. Your entire life will be turned upside down. They'll know everything you ever did and come up with dozens of things you didn't do. That's fine, we expect it, and we'll help you prepare for it. The one thing we absolutely will not put up with is learning for the first time on your cross-examination about a serious crime, like a murder, that you actually did. If you put us in that position, you'll regret for the rest of your life the decision to cooperate."

Gravano responded in a measured voice. "Listen, I've been sitting in the MCC for ten months. I know I have to tell youse everything, and I will. I understand what you're telling me. I will not hold back, and I'm trusting you not to double-bang me."

"I won't." I still didn't know what that meant. "How many murders?"

"About eighteen."

"What does 'about' mean?" George asked.

"It means I think it's eighteen. Could it be one more or one less? Yes. I need to write them down, and you know I can't do that in the MCC." We all paused to reflect about the fact that he'd committed so many murders he needed a pencil and paper to do an exact tally.

"Frankie DeCicco?" asked George.

"No. I loved Frankie. That one's a mystery to me. To John too."

"Willie Boy?" I asked.

"We gave that one to Eddie Lino. The other Families were complaining that it took us so long."

Our investigation of Vic Orena for the murder of Tommy Ocera was fresh on my mind, so I asked Gravano if he knew anything about Ocera.

"Yes, John wanted Ocera killed. He was steaming about him because we thought Ocera had killed Mark Reiter's son." Mark Reiter was a heroin dealer close to Gotti. "Little Vic came down to the Ravenite to meet with John. John asked him to kill Ocera, and not long after that he told me they whacked him."

"Who else? Anyone special on that list?" I asked. "Anyone I should know about now? Jimmy Hoffa? Someone like that?"

"Debbie's brother is on it," Gravano said matter-of-factly.

Everyone was quiet. The number of murders did not surprise us, and we'd suspected Gravano in four or five specific hits other than the three we'd charged him with. There were several others we were less sure about, and we were eager to find out if we were right. But we didn't even know Debbie had a brother, let alone that Gravano had killed him. I tried to process the information, to evaluate its impact on the testimony of my new witness.

"When?" I asked.

"About fifteen years ago."

"What was his name?"

"Nick Scibetta."

"Does Debbie know you were involved?" George asked.

"No, and I will never testify about it and it can't ever come out."

I figured I could block cross-examination into the *details* of his prior, uncharged murders, including the murder of Scibetta, but keeping secret the fact that Gravano had murdered him bordered on impossible.

"What's going to happen if Debbie finds out?" I asked.

"She can't find out. We have no deal if she does."

This was a problem, but I was determined not to let it be a deal-breaker. "Sam, all I can tell you is we'll try. The decision on that will be up to the judge. We'll argue that there's plenty to cross-examine you about, they don't need this, and all it will do is drive a wedge between you and your wife. We'll take a shot at it, but I can't guarantee what the judge will do, and to be honest with you it's unlikely we'll win this."

He looked at Matty and Frank. "Sam, all we can do is try," Frank said. "We're not gonna bullshit you and promise you nobody will ever know. But we'll try our best."

Gravano shrugged. "Well, youse've won everything else so far in this case. You disqualified our lawyers. You're killing us in court. So maybe youse'll win that one too."

"What else?" I asked, relieved.

"I want a time limit on my testimony, like Michael Franzese got. Debbie told me what youse said, but listen to me. It's important. I'm the underboss. If I get the same deal anybody else would get, everybody's gonna think youse're double-banging me already, right from the beginning. I need to be able to show people that I got something in recognition of my position." He went on to explain that if he could show others that the government dealt with him fairly, and recognized that he was a special witness, it would help him recruit others to flip with him. I was immediately leery of the suggestion that Gravano might become our recruiter of accomplice witnesses in the Gambino Family. His techniques might not be what we were looking for.

Gravano wasn't the only one who'd been thinking about the Franzese issue. I had too. I had no problem assuring him that we'd move quickly on the cases we could make right away with his cooperation. I had every intention of indicting as many captains and made members of the Gambino Family as I could as soon as the Gotti trial was over. I knew from the Ravenite tapes that Gravano had dealings with the administrations of the Genovese, Lucchese, Colombo, and DeCavalcante Families as well, and I would push those cases as fast as I could. We'd had two lean years in the Organized Crime Section, and I intended to make up for that by getting all our AUSAs busy presenting evidence to the grand jury as soon as possible.

"Sam, I'll give you something in your agreement on timing, but it won't be what Franzese got. I won't agree to a time limit on your testimony. If I can make a case with your help in three years that I can't make now, I have to be able to use you as a witness. But the cases I can make now, I'll make now. We've got to try Gotti and Locascio first, but then we'll indict all the cases we can make with your help within a year. They'll take another year to get to trial. I'll agree to a promise in your agreement that we'll use our best efforts to complete your testifying within two years of the agreement, but as long as we've done our best, you've still got to testify for us even after the two years are up. If we indict a case in a year and some judge takes two years to get the case to trial, you have to testify. If Frankie flips in three years, and between the two of you we can make a case I couldn't make with you alone, you'll have to testify. But I promise you we'll do everything on our end to try to finish up your testimony within two years of our agreement."

"You'll put that in writing?"

"Yes," I said.

He lit up. What I'd agreed to was largely symbolic, but a symbol was all he was asking for. I'd surprised him, and he couldn't conceal his delight that he'd gotten a concession.

He wasn't finished. "I don't want to testify against my crew. I'll tell youse all about them, but I want an agreement that I won't have to testify against them in court."

"Sam, that's impossible," I said. "And it's not negotiable."

"Lou and Huck and my brother-in-law Eddie will be watching out for Debbie. She's gonna pretend she hates me when I cooperate with youse, so hopefully no one will bother her too much. But you know she's gonna get a lot of pressure from Gotti's people. If Lou, Huck, and Eddie are off the street, she'll be out there by herself."

"Look, I understand what you're saying. And that may affect *when* we indict those guys. The last thing I want is a witness who's so upset he can't focus on the work. But those will be *our* decisions, not yours. You will have to promise to testify against whomever we ask you to testify against. Even your crew. I can't budge on that."

I was glad I'd just given him the two-year "best efforts" clause, because it made this issue easier for him.

"All right," he said.

One issue we hadn't discussed with Debbie was timing. It was October 24. Jury selection was less than three months away. Gravano would have to get a new lawyer, and we'd need a more detailed proffer and time to negotiate the written plea agreement. The FBI had to find a suitable place that would serve both as a prison to continue Gravano's detention and as somewhere Gabriel and I could spend the hundreds of hours we'd need to debrief him and get him ready for trial. We were in for a protracted process and time was short. My impulse right then was to keep him.

Still, we knew he wouldn't agree to stay with us that day. He claimed that he needed more time to prepare Debbie. That could have been true. She was going to pretend to disavow him, so they needed to get straight how she was going to deal with family, friends, and the media—not to mention the wiseguys—once it became public that he'd flipped. We figured Gravano had another concern that would remain unexpressed: he was one of the biggest loan sharks in Brooklyn. Once he flipped, those loans would become the property of the Gambino Family. We suspected he wanted whatever leeway he could get from us to try to collect as much principal and outstanding vig—the interest on the loans—as he could. When I asked him how much time it would take to get Debbie set up, he said two weeks. That would mean that, when we finally got him, trial would be ten weeks away. We'd still have to negotiate a written plea bargain with a lawyer and do all the debriefing and trial prep.

Gabriel and I had discussed this problem beforehand, and decided that if we had to agree to send Gravano back to the MCC we'd get him to cross the Rubicon first.

I said, "Sam, I think we'll have a deal, and your handshake will be good enough for us right now. But if you want us to wait another two weeks for you, I need you to do what you can to make sure we'll have no wasted time when we take you out."

"What do you mean?"

"We're going to have to negotiate a written plea agreement when you get out, but I can't even start that process until you have a lawyer representing you. It's one thing to meet with you behind Brafman's back to see if we have enough common ground to go forward. But I can't negotiate and sign a plea agreement with an unrepresented defendant. I can't take the next step until you have a lawyer. I'm not going to wait two weeks to pull you out of the MCC only to have to wait two more weeks while you find a lawyer. Our backs are already against the wall. We have a January 21 trial date."

"So what do you want me to do?"

"Get the ball rolling with a new lawyer now. Do you know one you can trust?" We knew the answer to this already.

"No," he responded. "Can you give me a list or something?"

"Sam, the last thing I'm going to do is recommend a lawyer for you. No matter who it is, Gotti's lawyers will say I got you someone who'd do anything I said, who'd just roll over for us."

"So what do I do?"

"Ask the judge to recommend an attorney for you. Tell him your situation, and ask him if he can help you find a lawyer whom you can trust. That way there'll be a lawyer waiting for you when we pull you out."

"How do I ask the judge?" He was intent, determined. This was a man who'd done deals before, and he was doing a deal with us. An absence of knowledge of how the system works turns many would-be cooperators into putty in the hands of prosecutors, but Gravano gave no impression that he'd do whatever we suggested.

"He's upstairs. I'll ask him if he'll come down right now. All right?"

A pause. He knew what this meant. "All right."

I'd told Judge Glasser that we'd be meeting Gravano and that, depending on how it went, I might ask him to join us. I'd also told him that Gravano might ask him to recommend a lawyer to replace Brafman. The judge had not told me whether he'd get involved. Judges have an obligation to appoint an attorney for defendants who can't afford to retain one, but paying for a lawyer wasn't Gravano's problem. He had plenty of money, just no idea whom to retain because none of the lawyers he knew would represent a rat.

Our most important reason for getting the judge involved was there was no way he'd meet with a defendant off the record. Gravano, who turned out to be far more intelligent than we expected, may have understood this already. If he didn't, he found it out the moment Judge Glasser entered the jury room, because I pulled my tape recorder out of a Redweld folder, put it on the table, and turned it on. It took only a minute or two to get Gravano to confirm on the record that he didn't trust Brafman, which justified our meeting with him behind Brafman's back, and to ask the judge to recommend a replacement. The judge said he'd give it some thought and left.

As the jury room door closed behind him, I turned off the recorder. It was a small machine, shaped like a shoebox but only a third as tall. Still, when I shut it off it made a sound like a rifle shot in the enclosed jury room. Gabriel, Gravano, and I all looked at each other and the machine. At that moment, we all knew there'd be no turning back for Gravano. In truth, if he'd changed his mind, that tape would have remained sealed, possibly forever. But given who he was, how he thought, and how little time he'd spent with us, there was no way he could trust us with it. Until that moment, he could deny reaching out to me and that I'd ever met with his wife. He could deny that he'd made a proffer in the jury room, and that we'd talked about his flipping. He could claim I'd violated his right to counsel by setting up a meeting with him behind Brafman's back and trying without success to flip him. But now we had a tape recording of Sammy the Bull Gravano asking the judge for a lawyer to help him cooperate. Gravano could never return to his former life knowing that the government had such a tape. He was ours.

CHAPTER 29

THE REVEAL

After turning Gravano back over to the deputy marshals, the group of us stayed in the jury room for another hour, talking over what we had. When it came to presentation, Gravano seemed to have the makings of a good witness, maybe even a great one. He was exceptionally poised and confident and, the others agreed, much smarter than we'd expected. Most likely he wouldn't get rattled on cross-examination, which is how many witnesses make mistakes.

He was what he was, but he seemed a truth-teller. The agents were initially dejected that he'd contradicted the one eyewitness's testimony about the Castellano murder, but I saw an unexpected upside that could prove far more valuable than what we'd lost. Gravano had known we had a witness who would testify that Gotti was standing near the northeast corner of 46th Street and Third Avenue minutes before the murder. We had to disclose that to the lawyers so they could challenge the extremely shaky identification procedure used by the agents. This detail had now taken on a new significance.

"We're going to have to sell Gravano's testimony to the jury," I told the agents. "The defense lawyers are going to tell the jury that he's saying whatever we want him to say so he can get a break in his sentence. We're going to argue the opposite: that he's telling the jury what happened. To say that persuasively, we've got to believe it. We'll see what happens when we get a more complete proffer on November 8, but I'm starting to believe it already."

"Why?" asked Matty.

"Matty, if all Gravano wants to do is tell us what we want to hear, if he's going to tailor his testimony to fit our case, look how easy it would have been for him to do that. He knows we've got a witness who has Gotti standing on that northeast corner. Gravano says they were sitting in the car at the same intersection but across Third Avenue at the exact same time. How easy would it have been for him to say Gotti got out for a minute to be sure everyone was in place? His testimony on the Castellano hit might be more valuable to us if it dovetailed with the testimony of the eyewitness, but the fact that it doesn't tells me he's giving us the truth."

"What about the witness?" Bruce asked.

"Unless something happens and this deal with Gravano falls through," I said, "we won't call him."

"But won't *they* call him if we don't?" asked Bruce. "He was our witness. We believed him. He proves Gravano wrong. Why won't he be a defense witness?"

"Think about it," I said. "Put yourself in Krieger's shoes. You're going to call a witness to prove that Gotti was not in the car across the intersection, like Gravano says, but on the sidewalk across the street? It only helps them if the witness is believed. But if he's believed, Gotti's on the scene of the Castellano murder, and we have a ton of evidence that he hated Castellano. Besides, if they call the eyewitness, then I get to tell the jury what I just told you—Gravano's telling the truth precisely because what he told us contradicts what he knew to be our case. I like that argument."

Frank wasn't worried about either the witness or the Castellano murder. "Jesus Christ," he said. "He killed Debbie's *brother*? John, can we really keep that out?"

"The fact that he did it? I don't think so. It'll be part of our deal with him, so it has to get disclosed. We'll try, but we'll lose. Do I think we can preclude cross into the details of it? Yes. If there's a silver lining in the large number of murders, it's that the judge probably won't let defense counsel dwell on any one in particular very long."

"It's a killer fact," said Gabriel. "If he's a good enough liar to hide from Debbie for years that he killed her brother, how easy will it be for him to lie to the jury?"

"You got it," I said. "If you hear that theme one time at trial, you'll hear it a thousand times. That and 'one year per murder,' which is how they'll attack the twenty-year cap. But there's a silver lining there too. How do we know for sure that he's telling us about all his murders? How do we know he's not suppressing some? Well, it seems to me that if he was going to hold back, the last murder he'd tell us about would be Debbie's brother. We had no idea about it, it was a long time ago, and it could tear apart a marriage that he apparently wants to keep intact. If he told us about that, he must really have decided to come clean."

I asked Matty and Frank what Gravano was talking about when he mentioned the bail hearing. They told me that when we were trying to make the tax case on Gravano, they'd served a subpoena on Debbie. Gravano had filed joint returns with her and had made her and their children part owners of his company. Because she, unlike Gravano, didn't have a lawyer who'd accept service for her, Matty and Frank had delivered it to Debbie personally at the family's home on Staten Island.

Gravano had gone through the roof. "This is it. They've stepped over the line," he fumed to a number of made guys and associates, as we learned from informants. His reaction to the subpoena breached the unwritten rule that gangsters must not retaliate against agents, or even threaten to do so. His raging comments suggested just such a threat, so Matty and Frank immediately went to Gravano's Stillwell Avenue office to confront him. They told him it was his fault that they'd had to subpoena Debbie. By putting her name on the company and by having her mixed up in both the business and his personal income taxes, he put Debbie in play. They told him that it was he who was out of line, not they, by making comments to his crew that could be taken as a threat to FBI agents, and he'd better learn to hold his temper.

Gravano, who by then had cooled down, knew they were right and apologized. They shook hands, and Matty and Frank turned to leave. As they did so, Gravano said, "I guess I'll be hearing about this in a bail hearing someday." He was right. Had I known of that little episode, I'd have used it to prove his dangerousness.

"Why didn't you tell me?" I asked them. "We could have discussed whether or not to use it."

Frank answered for them. "Look, John, we know you. You use *everything*. But we just thought it might be a good idea to keep this to ourselves—that maybe something good would come from it. We never thought it'd be this good, but you never know."

"What do you mean?"

"We spend all our time dealing with gangsters. Sometimes we just talk to them, sometimes it's a formal interview, sometimes we serve a subpoena, like we did with Debbie, sometimes we arrest them. But we always treat them respectfully. Not because they always deserve it, but because it helps us do our job better."

"No, I mean what do you mean you never thought it'd be this good?"

"We mean that even when we treat them with respect, sometimes we get nothing. Sometimes we get a piece of valuable information. Once in a blue moon we even sign someone up as a confidential informant. But it never occurred to us that Sammy would flip and agree to testify in court. It looks like cutting him a little bit of slack at the detention hearing had something to do with his becoming the highest-ranking Mafia figure ever to cooperate."

When the agents left the room, I was beyond excited. In about three weeks we'd restructure organized crime not just in New York but in America generally. The underboss of the Gambino Family, who had criminal dealings, including homicides, with all the Cosa Nostras, would be our witness. The effect would be seismic. Gotti's prospects of beating yet another case would diminish significantly, and much of the rest of the mob would follow in his wake. George Gabriel and I knew we were on the verge of something historic. We didn't say it out loud, but we knew this could be the beginning of the end for organized crime.

At the same time, I felt sick about the fact that I'd hidden this development from my trial team and my bosses. I had no doubt that Laura Ward, Pat Cotter, and Jamie Orenstein, whom I'd added to the team six months earlier to be the designated brief-writer, would understand and exult along with me when they found out. They'd get the need for absolute secrecy, even from them. The fact that we were all close socially as well as professionally would help. But I didn't like one bit keeping them in the dark.

Andy and Mary Jo presented a problem. They were Southern District alums and would no doubt believe they were not only entitled to know about my dealings with Gravano in real time but also entitled to be in charge of the negotiations. Of the two, I was less concerned about Andy. He'd been our U.S. Attorney for several years, and his approach to the job had been to defer to the section chiefs he'd installed. And it had worked; in organized crime, business frauds, and narcotics, we were way outperforming the Southern District. I figured as long as I delivered Gravano and the conviction of Gotti, he'd feel that the trust had been well placed.

Mary Jo had been in the Eastern District as chief assistant barely a year. I didn't know her well personally. In addition to her Southern District experience, she'd been a partner in an elite law firm, where junior lawyers never fail to keep the partners in the loop. I had little doubt she'd be upset that I hadn't told her I'd been negotiating with Gravano. But I knew that if I had told her, she'd have told Andy. And even though I liked and admired Andy, he still gabbed with his buddies in the evenings, and I couldn't justify taking a monthlong risk that this information would slip. Besides, I had the benefit of Judge Glasser's admonition to me not to tell anyone. So with a lot of trepidation I decided I would continue to sit on the information a little longer.

On the morning of October 28, I called over to Andy's office to see if he was in and could see me. The answer to both questions was yes, so I took two sealed legal-sized envelopes with me. One was for Andy and the other for Mary Jo.

Their offices were in a single suite, separated by a large open area where their assistants sat, which also had a couple of old leather couches in it. As usual, both their doors were open. I walked in and gave Andy his envelope.

"This is important," I told him. "I'll wait outside till you're ready to see me, if you still want to after you read it." I walked out, closed his door, and went across to Mary Jo's office.

"I just gave a copy of this to Andy. It's about Gotti. I hope you'll understand. I'll be outside." I closed her door too, and sat down on one of the couches.

The memo began as follows:

> I have negotiated a plea/cooperation agreement with Salvatore Gravano. Subject to your approval, he will plead guilty to a racketeering count with an exposure of twenty years. He will testify against John Gotti, of course, and will be the centerpiece of numerous additional cases. The present plan is to pull Gravano out of the MCC on Friday, November 8, to take a final proffer, sign an agreement, and begin debriefing him.
>
> In my judgment, this is a tremendous positive development, which will have a profound impact not only on the Gotti prosecution but on all LCN organized crime in New York. Although my pride in delivering this deal to you is considerable, so is the trepidation I feel at having reached it without consulting you. For the reasons set forth below, I believe that I have acted prudently and within the bounds of the trust you've placed in me. I hope very much that you agree.

The memorandum then described in detail how the deal had come about, the meetings with Debbie and Gravano, and the preliminary proffer he gave us in Judge Raggi's jury room. In a section captioned "The Wisdom of the Deal," I wrote as follows:

> Gravano will obviously enhance our prospects of convicting John Gotti. The one weakness our case has always had is its lack of depth in the sense that we have no Gambino Family witness. To put it mildly, Gravano would be a Gambino Family witness. He will help us win a case that the Justice Department

and this office cannot afford to lose. Put another way, if Gravano had insisted on testifying *only* against John Gotti, it probably would have been worth it. Apart from its evidentiary significance, Gravano's breaking of the ranks will inflict serious damage to Gotti's aura of invincibility. It will legitimize our indictment before the trial begins, and I believe it will make more convincing our implicit message to the jurors that they need not be afraid because we have finally caught them and it's over.

Moreover, we know from our tapes (and Gravano has confirmed it) that Gravano is the liaison between the Gambino Family and the other Families. For example, meetings with "Little Vic" Orena and Anthony Spero, the bosses of the Colombo and Bonanno Families, respectively, are referred to repeatedly on our tapes. In short, Gravano can make many important cases, and we already have significant corroboration of him because of our tapes.

The most important part came last:

I am deeply troubled by the fact that I have kept everyone, particularly you and Mary Jo, in the dark until now. The secrecy stemmed principally from the fact that I gave my word to the FBI and, more importantly, Judge Glasser, that as long as there was a possibility that Gravano would turn away from us, no one would know of his contact. Since a principal reason for his initial contact was the ability of two FBI agents to keep an important fact quiet over a long period of time, I was particularly concerned not so much about a short-term breach of security, but maintaining long-term security so that if Gravano walked away now, he would feel secure in trying again in a year or two.

My secrecy was principally motivated by Judge Glasser, who expressly admonished me to tell no one. While the decision to proceed in secret was mine, that admonition heavily influenced me.

Mary Jo's office door opened. She crossed over and entered Andy's office without looking at me. She did not look pleased. An eternity passed before they summoned me in. I sat down on the couch just inside the door. Andy was seated across from me. Mary Jo was standing behind him, her elbows propped on the back of his big leather armchair. Because she's not tall, it was hard even to see her, but I could glimpse enough to know she was very upset. There was an identical armchair next to the one Andy was in, and her decision to stand behind his instead, together with her demeanor, was ominous. It was as though she were avoiding being splattered with blood.

Andy was looking down grimly, collecting his thoughts for what he was about to say. "Well, this is quite a development," he began. "You had no business not telling us." It occurred to me in that moment that I was about to be fired. I'd expected blowback for keeping the news close to the vest, but it never occurred to me that it would be job-threatening. I'd never come anywhere close to being fired before, and it didn't feel good. I immediately began strategizing how I could change their minds.

Andy was still looking down at the floor, but he tilted his head upward enough so I could see why: he was trying unsuccessfully to suppress a smile. I was going to be okay.

"I've always hated that Castellano predicate," he continued, "and it looks like Gravano makes it a lot stronger."

"Absolutely," I said. "He's on the scene with Gotti. And now it's not just us saying that all Gotti's denials on the tapes were bullshit. Gravano says it too. They *had* to keep denying it, even among themselves, because they never got permission from the Commission." We kept going, talking about the whacking of Debbie's brother, the eighteen murders, the twenty-year cap, everything. Andy didn't like the twenty years and thought we could have done better, but he still approved the deal. In fact, he loved it. No further criticism of how it came about ever passed from his lips.

We called over Laura, Pat, and Jamie, who couldn't have been more thrilled, which made me excited as well. The temptation to tell the world was powerful, but we were still in a delicate stage.

The last paragraphs of the memorandum I'd given Andy and Mary Jo said as follows:

> I would like your approval of this deal. I would like to go ahead and have the FBI find a suitable place of confinement, where Gravano can be debriefed and prepared for trial. I would also like to discuss the timing of informing our colleagues on the Gotti team. For different reasons, I feel almost as bad about keeping secrets from them as I do about keeping them from you.
>
> I also want to prepare Gravano's new counsel for the final proffer we will need before we are willing to sign the deal with him.
>
> Obviously, the need for secrecy now is just as great (if not greater) than it has been all along. Thus, once the trial team knows, I believe a team

meeting would be appropriate, at which you could impress upon them the need to keep this development to ourselves, because a witness's life hangs in the balance.

These were the points that I now reiterated for my trial partners, and we prepared to head back to the Organized Crime offices to start our revamping of the trial outline. Mary Jo had said hardly anything the entire time. As we were leaving, she asked if she could see me alone in her office. I followed her across the open area between the two offices. As she closed the door behind us, I said, "I'm sorry about the secrecy. I love and respect Andy, and I kept this to myself because he sees those guys for drinks almost every night. And I figured if I told you, you'd have to tell him."

"Of course I would have told him!" she snapped. "There'd have been no reason not to." She was even angrier than she'd shown during the meeting. I was ready to defend my view that there was a good reason not to tell Andy, but this wasn't an argument I was going to win.

"Anyway," I told her "if you were the United States Attorney, I obviously wouldn't have left you in the dark."

"If I were the United States Attorney," she said, "you'd be fired."

CHAPTER 30

BOSKO'S JUROR

I had been determined to keep our January 21, 1992, trial date even if we successfully flipped Gravano. Shortly after his first overture, I decided that if he switched to our side the theme of my summation was going to be that his testimony was a bonus for the jury but entirely unnecessary for them to convict Gotti and Locascio. The message would be that we'd indicted all three based on the Ravenite recordings. Gravano had seen the guilty verdicts coming and decided to jump ship at the last minute.

This argument became more difficult once we had to add the Castellano and Bilotti homicides onto our case, as the Ravenite conversations didn't prove those crimes; indeed, Gotti denied involvement in them. Still, our basic pitch would be that we never needed Gravano. I remained optimistic he'd be a great witness, but I wanted to be sure that, if he bombed, he wouldn't drag the case down with him. So there'd be no new charges based on his testimony, and not even a short delay of the trial if I could help it.

There was a lot of work to be done with Gravano before he could be signed up as a witness. George Gabriel and I pressured him through his wife to stick to our plan to pull him out of the MCC on November 8. Their world would change dramatically and permanently once that happened, so we expected some foot-dragging, but there was none.

At a couple of minutes past midnight on the chosen day, Gabriel walked into the ground floor of the MCC with an order signed by Judge Glasser. An FBI SWAT team waited outside. All orders have the case caption on them, and this one bore the heading "United States versus John Gotti." The one-paragraph order directed the MCC to transfer custody of Salvatore Gravano to the FBI.

Gabriel showed his credentials to the guard and said, "Hi. I'm here to take custody of one of your guests." Inmates are never whisked out of federal prisons in the wee hours of the morning, at least not by the good guys, so the guard knew immediately this was something big. Gabriel explained that the transfer needed to be done quickly and quietly.

The guard picked up his phone to call upstairs. Reading the caption of the order rather than the order itself, he said quietly into the phone, "Wake up John Gotti and bring him downstairs as quick as you can." The ever-alert Gabriel corrected him, averting what would have been a truly awkward situation.

Bruce Mouw had ordered the SWAT team to move Gravano to a safe place for the rest of the night. He'd be flown to Northern Virginia at daybreak. Mouw had chosen a motel in Floral Park, just across the border between Queens and Nassau County, close to the airport.

In the two weeks since our meeting in Judge Raggi's jury room, Judge Glasser had lined up a lawyer for Gravano. Bill Cunningham had been the chief of narcotics when I started in the office back in 1985. He left soon after and was now a partner in the respected Meyer Suozzi law firm in Mineola, part of Nassau County. The last kind of work that his firm undertook, and the last it wanted to do, was represent wiseguys, but when Judge Glasser calls and asks for a favor, lawyers don't say no.

Mouw had told both Cunningham and me that we'd be taken to meet Gravano at 6:00 a.m. We weren't told where that would be. I got to the motel first. It was crowded. In addition to Mouw, Gabriel, Frank Spero, and Matty Tricorico, the entire SWAT team was milling about the two rooms the FBI had reserved. The moment I arrived, Mouw took me aside. After a brief run-down of how the operation had gone so far, he told me that on the way out from the prison to the motel he'd chatted with Gravano.

"One of the things we talked about was your case in front of Judge Nickerson. We asked him about the party at the Ravenite after the acquittal and why people were congratulating him. He said, 'Simple; I fixed that case.'"

"Just like that?"

"Just like that."

I was stunned. Diane and I had given two years of our lives to that prosecution, and the high-profile acquittal of all seven defendants was the worst experience of my professional life by far. I'd done a good job of blocking it out, but this news brought it rushing back.

My mind returned immediately to an event the summer after the trial ended.

Detective John Gurnee, one of our witnesses, had gotten a call from one of the jurors. He wanted to meet Gurnee, who asked me if it was a good idea.

"Which one?" I'd asked.

"Number Eleven. The one Mike Pizzi said is a drunk. He said he wants to tell me something." This was the one we'd called Oil Terminal Operator, as that was his job. Gurnee met the juror out in Nassau County for dinner. He was already wasted when Gurnee arrived, and told him nothing. I'd put the subject out of my mind—until now.

I turned my attention back to Bruce Mouw.

"How?" I finally asked.

"Through Bosko."

Bosko Radonjich was one of those people who proved that the truth can be so much more bizarre than anything you can make up. He was a Serbian terrorist whom Gotti had put in charge of the Westies—the Irish gang in the Hell's Kitchen section of Manhattan—after Jimmy Coonan went to prison. He now had a hand in the construction racket, and his name came up several times in the Ravenite apartment conversations. Bosko could never get made because he wasn't Italian, but he was a key player in the Family.

"Sammy handed Bosko sixty grand to give to the juror," Mouw said.

"How did Bosko get to him?"

"He didn't. The juror already knew Bosko and went to him."

Gravano himself gave me the details, and there weren't many. Shortly after we picked the jury in Judge Nickerson's courtroom, Bosko came to Gravano and told him he had a juror who'd vote not guilty and try to convince the others to do the same. Since John Gotti was in detention, Gravano met with Gene Gotti, who spoke to his brother in court the next day. They were delighted and approved the plan. Gravano gave Bosko $20,000 in cash on three separate occasions during the trial.

In time I'd learn that it was no surprise to the FBI that Gravano had fixed the jury. In fact, one of their informants had told them as much while the trial was still underway. When information like that comes from an FBI confidential informant, it receives as much investigative effort as the FBI chooses to give it. Having been the AUSA who worked with the FBI in the investigation into the tampering of Gene Gotti's jury just a year earlier, I knew how thorough such inquiries can be. But Gene Gotti's trial was an FBI case. The FBI had dropped out of our case before Judge Nickerson when we indicted Willie Boy Johnson and Billy Battista, and it had little interest in investigating the tip. It had covered itself by reporting the information to others in the office at the time, and for some reason it was decided Diane and I should be kept in the dark. I would find out in the coming months that almost nothing was done during the course of our trial to root out Sammy's corrupt juror.

While I waited for Cunningham, my mind raced. There was a statute of limitations problem. If I were going to prosecute Bosko and his juror, I'd have to indict them before March 13, 1992, the fifth anniversary of the acquittals, so I had only four months. In the meantime we'd be debriefing the biggest mob turncoat in history and trying the most important case in the country. The Gotti trial was sure to take us past the date when the statute of limitations would expire, so if I waited until it was over Bosko and his juror could breathe easy. We were just going to have to find the time to make that case.

When Cunningham arrived, we let him meet alone with Gravano. It had to be tough for both of them. Neither would ever have picked the other if they had a real choice. Gravano had freely admitted that he didn't know a single lawyer he could trust to negotiate a cooperation agreement, so he was stuck with whomever the judge picked. For his part, Cunningham, a member of Long Island's most politically powerful firm—his partners included Clinton confidant Harold Ickes and the New York power broker Basil Paterson—had been conscripted into representing a high-profile mobster who would admit to committing nineteen murders. His colleagues wouldn't be enjoying the publicity.

The FBI wanted Gravano out of New York, so our meeting was brief. Mouw told me that I'd have a couple of days with him in a Northern Virginia office to work out a cooperation agreement. The Bureau had made reservations for Cunningham and me at a hotel near the building, and we'd be picked up the following morning and taken to the witness. After we reached agreement, Gravano would be moved to the FBI Academy in Quantico, Virginia. Underscoring his value to the government was that the director of the FBI had agreed Sammy could reside in his spacious suite at the Academy until the Gotti trial.

I went back to my office with a one-line letter in my hand. Cunningham had prepared it and Gravano had signed it in my presence. It was addressed to Ben Brafman and informed him that he was no longer Gravano's lawyer. I had it hand-delivered that morning to Brafman's office.

When Gotti and Locascio woke up in the MCC on the morning of November 8, Gravano was gone. They knew in an instant what had happened. I was left to imagine the looks on their faces when they became aware that Sammy Gravano, the underboss and consummate Family man, had turned on them. It was the ultimate power move, coming just ten weeks before trial.

Brafman was sure to call to give me a piece of his mind. I was dreading his call. He arguably had a lot to complain about. I'd gone behind his back in an indicted case and struck a deal with his client—one that would soon be reported on the front pages of every newspaper in New York. I was ready to defend my actions, but there were rules and constitutional protections that on the face of it prohibited what I'd done. Defense lawyers protect their clients from prosecutors, and I had both flipped Gravano and got Brafman fired without him even knowing I was having meetings with his client. I expected at least outrage from Brafman, and figured that eventually, if not right away, he might even file a grievance with the disciplinary committee of the New York bar asking that I be sanctioned.

Brafman called late morning. There was no outrage, no threat—exactly the opposite, in fact; he spoke softly and had fear in his voice.

"John, I understand from the letter the agent delivered this morning that I am not Sammy's lawyer anymore," he said. "I have only one request. I would very much appreciate it if you would make it clear that I had nothing whatsoever to do with his decision to cooperate."

That was it. I had overestimated him. He left me with the impression that the last thing on his mind was what was in the best interests of his former client. I'd naïvely failed to appreciate his predicament. Unless it was made clear to the wiseguys that I'd circumvented Brafman to strike the deal, he would be considered a rat lawyer. At best, that would be the kiss of death for his practice representing gangsters. At worst, it could land him in the trunk of a car.

"Don't worry, Ben. I'll make it clear to everyone that you had nothing to do with implementing your client's decision to do what was in his best interests." He ignored my sarcasm; he was being promised the way out he craved.

The following day Cunningham and I joined Gravano in a Tysons Corner, Virginia, office building to work out a cooperation agreement. The meeting got off to an awkward start. Gravano turned what was supposed to be an effort to translate our previous understandings into a binding agreement into a series of wish-list demands, delivered as though we were getting together for the first time.

"I will never cooperate against my crew," he insisted at the outset. "Big Lou. Huck, my brother-in-law Eddie. I will never testify against them."

It went downhill from there. We'd reached an understanding just a few weeks earlier that I couldn't put a hard-and-fast time limit on his cooperation, but Gravano acted as if we'd never discussed the topic. "There's no way I'm cooperating for more than a year," he declared.

He was on a roll, and his demands weren't over yet. "I don't want to do my time in a prison," he said. "I know I have to be in custody, but youse can keep me in custody anywhere."

Here he had a point. We were about to begin a three-month period in which his jail cell would be the FBI director's comfortable suite at the Academy in Quantico. Gravano, though, had even better accommodations in mind. He demanded to be stashed in the Pocono Mountains in eastern Pennsylvania. Agents would live with him in a chalet to minimize the risk he'd be killed, but he'd be able to enjoy the solitude and beauty of the mountains.

As he gazed out of the high-rise building we were in, Gravano got wistful. "I could sit by the picture window," he said. "I could watch the leaves falling from the trees." As he said this, he had his arms outstretched in front of him, palms down, and he wiggled his fingers to mimic the falling leaves. Then he paused. I couldn't have guessed what would come next.

"I could have a cat."

I glanced at Cunningham, and it was all we could do to keep from laughing. We both knew what the deal was, and I'd tell Gravano the facts of life as soon as his little reverie was over. All his demands were out of the question. If he were really insisting on them, the only option would be to return him to the MCC, and there was no way he could agree to that. He'd go back to bunking with Gotti after trying to cooperate with me against him?

So I let him go on, and the truth was I felt bad for him even though here was a man who had time after time murdered without compunction and was now wasting our time. For a thirty-year period that had ended thirty-six hours earlier, Gravano had been a successful career criminal. He'd reached the highest echelons as a gangster. It had to be humiliating for him to be removed from an environment in which he was feared and in which he bossed so many people around into one in which he was a prisoner, being told what to do by agents.

After Gravano's harangue I told him abruptly that every single demand he'd just made contradicted the understanding we'd reached in our previous meetings. I wasn't going back to square one with him. If he was insisting on those conditions, all I could do was call it all off and return him to the MCC. I told him to think it over and that his lawyer and I would see him the following morning.

At breakfast the next day, Cunningham and I hammered out the terms of a plea agreement. Before we left to see Gravano again, we joked about finding an animal shelter and getting a cat. I'd bring it and tell Gravano I'd reconsidered all his demands and had decided there was one I could grant.

Gravano was in a room with the agents when we arrived, and he acted as though our conversation the afternoon before had never happened. He was ready to get to work. We signed the cooperation agreement, shook hands, and then the FBI whisked him down to Quantico.

That evening George Gabriel and I flew back to New York. George drove east from LaGuardia to his home on Long Island. I was planning to go home, but all I could think about was Gravano's admission that he'd bribed a juror in the case I'd tried with Diane Giacalone. So I asked the cabdriver to drop me at the courthouse.

I got to my office around 9:30 p.m. I had four months to investigate and indict the case.

I imagined Bosko's juror out there somewhere, counting down the days, wishing the next four months of his life away so he could stop worrying about being arrested for having fixed a trial for John Gotti. I was determined to bring that protracted search for peace of mind to a very unpleasant end just before the juror reached his longed-for finish line.

The identities of the jurors from the first case were still locked in the office of the clerk of the court. I'd never known them, and without a court order I never would. Gravano's information gave me the grounds I needed for one, but that would have to wait until morning.

I also didn't have copies of the lengthy questionnaires the twelve jurors in the case had filled out during the selection process. Like the list of their names, neither the questionnaires nor copies of them had been provided to us or to defense counsel. Only Judge Nickerson had them. During the five weeks it had taken to pick jurors, he'd brought the candidates into the courtroom one at a time. While they were being ushered to the courtroom, he'd read us the basic information from the questionnaire the juror had filled out: whether they lived in the city or the suburbs, the type of job they held, their educational background, their marital status. Then, if the juror had checked "yes" in response to any of a long list of questions, the judge would follow up orally.

During selection, I had a box of blank questionnaires at our table. As the judge read information out loud to us, I'd fill in a blank copy for that juror. As much as possible, I re-created each juror's questionnaire, then supplemented it by writing in their responses to the judge's questioning. After more than four hundred jurors, Diane and I had used my version of each juror's questionnaire to decide whom to challenge. I'd kept the copies I filled in for each of the twelve jurors who eventually heard the case.

I would find out the following morning that the original questionnaires had been destroyed at Judge Nickerson's direction shortly after the trial ended, to protect the jurors' privacy. All that remained were the replicated versions I'd prepared.

When I imagined Bosko's juror, I already had the face. The moment I learned from Bruce Mouw that Gravano had fixed the case, I suspected Oil Terminal Operator, the drunk who'd reached out to John Gurnee after the trial. Gurnee had great instincts, and he had a bad feeling about Oil Terminal Operator. The man's posttrial invitation to meet Gurnee for dinner, inexplicable at the time, was now starting to make sense. He'd agreed to fix the biggest mob trial in a generation. Obviously, he had plenty to fear from us if we ever got wind of it, but he had much more to worry about with the wiseguys. Once the verdict was announced, he immediately stopped being an asset to them, and instead became a huge liability. At the least, he could put Bosko in jail, and possibly Gravano and Gotti as well. That would be a valuable bargaining chip if the juror ever got in trouble himself. From the wiseguys' point of view, Bosko's juror was particularly expendable. Fearful of both the good guys and the bad guys, Oil Terminal Operator had to have been feeling acutely lonely in the trial's aftermath. He might have intended to confide in Gurnee and lost his nerve amid all the alcohol.

Oil Terminal Operator was originally Juror 449. My questionnaire for him said he was forty-eight years old, married, and the father of two young children. It also showed that he'd checked "yes" to question thirteen, which asked whether he'd ever been questioned by law enforcement authorities. My notes of the judge's oral examination said "business acquaintance" and "FBI asked if I had ever seen dynamite in his possession." Now I was sure. Bosko was a Serb and had a long history of political terrorism. In the late 1970s he'd been convicted in Chicago of conspiring to blow up the Yugoslavian missions in New York and Chicago. Judge Nickerson's follow-up questioning about the FBI interview included his asking about what happened to the "business acquaintance." According to my notes, Oil Terminal Operator responded, "I believe he was convicted or something like that."

The next morning I asked Bruce Mouw to assign an agent to help me with the case. I also went to Judge Nickerson and told him we had solid information that the jury was fixed. Since Gravano's defection to our side had been front-page news, he knew where the information had come from and issued an order directing the clerk of the court to give me the jury list. Oil Terminal Operator turned out to be George Pape from East Norwich in Nassau County. Mouw assigned agent Scott Behar to me that same day, and I asked him to collect whatever he could about Bosko's Chicago case and any connection he might have to Pape.

It turned out to be the quickest case I'd ever built. Within a week, Behar and I had documents proving that Bosko and Pape had been far more than just business acquaintances. Pape had been the best man at Bosko's wedding, and when his friend had applied for citizenship it was Pape who'd signed the petition for naturalization. They even owned a business together. And unless Pape had a terrible memory, he was being way too cute when he said he "believed" his "business acquaintance" had been convicted. He knew it because the Bureau of Prisons records for Bosko showed that Pape had visited him *forty times* in prison. And even though Pape had said on his questionnaire that he'd never testified as a witness, he'd actually done exactly that for Bosko when he moved to suppress evidence in the Chicago case.

Pape had lied his way onto our jury, then he and Bosko had sold his vote to Gotti. I was enraged, of course. I kept thinking of all the time Diane and I had devoted to that case. I also couldn't help wondering whether we'd made a mistake asking for an anonymous jury. The goal was obviously to prevent the wiseguys from finding jurors and tampering with them; but even though only the defendants pose a risk of tampering, when a case is tried before an anonymous jury neither side knows who the jurors are. Pape showed us that all the measures taken to protect honest jurors from bad guys can *enable* a corrupt juror to work with those same criminals. Pape had dissembled to get on our jury. He never would have been able to do that had Diane and I known his identity. Emboldened by his anonymity, he turned the entire concept of anonymous juries on its head. If Gravano hadn't flipped, a measure designed to ensure an untainted jury would have ensured forever the success of a scheme to taint one.

In 1991 there were almost a thousand made guys in New York. For each there were many associates like Bosko. They all had their network of friends, just as Bosko had Pape. It was geometric, and also so obvious. Why contact someone you have no connection with—who might report the contact to the judge—when someone you already know can talk his way onto the jury and come to you without fear of being caught? It was a profoundly disturbing revelation, and not just because the jury process had allowed Gotti to fix the jury in Judge Nickerson's courtroom. We were about to use the identical process in the upcoming trial.

CHAPTER 31

ANGELO'S LIE

It was almost two years since I'd first met George Gabriel and agreed to be the lead prosecutor in his investigation of John Gotti. We'd worked together well, and become close, but our dozen or so trips to the director's suite at Quantico during the ten weeks between pulling Gravano out of the MCC and the beginning of the trial took our friendship to another level.

Because of all the other pretrial work, we had to visit Gravano on weekends. We'd take the Delta Shuttle from LaGuardia to National Airport, rent a car, and make our way down to Quantico. Most of the time it took less than three hours. We'd meet Matty and Frank there, because they'd drive down from Staten Island. The fact that they drove was key, because it allowed them to bring the big pots of Italian food that we'd eat on our breaks. Matty's mother-in-law's pasta e lenticchie was about the best meal I'd ever eaten.

One of our first jobs was to debrief Gravano about his thirty-year life of crime. We also had to go over the tapes with him, and those from the apartment alone were about six hours' running time. There was so much information packed in them that we'd have to stop the machine every few seconds to get his take on what we were hearing. Those conversations often led to others that had nothing to do with the tape itself. A recorded allusion to a sit-down with another Family on one issue would lead Gravano to tell us about other beefs that were addressed at that sit-down and other sit-downs with the same Family. It could take three hours to get through just twenty minutes of an apartment conversation.

I slowed us down by the way I worked. Gabriel had a running, lighthearted beef with me over my penchant for being absolutely sure of what was being said and all the things they could possibly be referring to. When we worked in my office, he'd roll his eyes and call his wife to say he'd be late getting home because I was stopping the tape every three seconds.

We were especially eager to go through the December 12 tape, in which Gotti had complained bitterly about Gravano getting rich in the construction business while the rest of the *borgata* was starving. It was also the one in which Gotti admitted ordering the murders of Robert DiBernardo and Louie Milito and said that Louie DiBono, who'd be murdered ten months later, would be killed for refusing to come in when Gotti called him. Gravano had heard a couple of snippets at the detention hearing shortly after the arrests, but Gotti refused to let him or Locascio listen to the tape during the ten months they were in the MCC together. Gravano knew he'd been bad-mouthed by Gotti in the conversation, and was as eager to listen to the harangue as we were to talk to him about it.

The three of us put on headphones and Gabriel started the recording. True to form, about one minute into Gotti's diatribe about Gravano I indicated to Gabriel to stop the tape. He chuckled, shook his head, and hit pause. Gravano took off his head-phones and put them down on the table.

"Don't gloat, guys," he said, obviously upset. "I know youse've got me. I'm here. But don't gloat. This isn't easy for me, you know."

We both explained that Gabriel's laugh wasn't his gloating but rather reflected his desire to cut to the chase instead of stopping the recording every time I had a question, no matter how inconsequential. Gravano accepted the explanation, and we got down to the substantial business of the recording.

"He was definitely laying the groundwork to kill me," Gravano told us. "Frankie was the acting underboss at the time. I was the consigliere. Youse don't know how un-usual it is for a boss to talk that bad about another member of the administration." He told us he'd grown up at a time when young wannabe gangsters thought made men really were Men of Honor, and that *The Godfather* accurately portrayed La Cosa Nostra. His statement in Judge Raggi's jury room that he wanted to jump from his "govern-ment" to ours was making more sense to me.

Based on the excerpts he'd heard at the detention hearing and the fact that Gotti forbade him from listening to anything more, Gravano expected that the recording would be bad. He also knew that if Gotti had been gearing up to kill him, he'd cer-tainly sell him out at trial. As long as Shargel was representing him in court, Gravano believed he'd be all right. They'd known each other a long time and together had beaten a tax prosecution in Judge Glasser's courtroom a few years earlier. But after we had Shargel disqualified, Gravano felt exposed. He didn't know Brafman, and didn't trust him not to sell him out. Fed up with a life that failed to imitate art, and worried that only he would end up doing life without parole, he had reached out to me. We hadn't previously realized that having Shargel disqualified was such an important factor in getting Gravano to flip.

He was straightforward about all the murders. When he got the order to kill Robert DiBernardo, he was disappointed. He liked DiB, who was more of a businessman than a gangster and ran the construction racket well. But Gravano did the job he was directed to do. He invited DiB to come to his office on Stillwell Avenue in Brooklyn, offered his guest coffee, and they went downstairs to talk construction. Gravano sat across the table from DiB and engaged him in conversation. Behind DiB was "Old Man" Joe Paruta, a loyal Gravano associate who could always be found at the Stillwell Avenue office. Paruta took a gun from a nearby cabinet and shot DiB in the back of the head.

Louie Milito had met the same fate but was a different story altogether. Milito was an experienced hit man. Gravano had killed with him. After the murder of Tommy Bilotti, the Gambino Family took over his business interests, and to Gravano's surprise they found that Bilotti shared a loan-sharking business with Milito. It was a surprise because Louie had previously had one with Gravano and ended it. "He went behind our back and went partners with Paul and Tommy," Gravano would later testify. Still, he assured Milito that he wouldn't be killed so long as he "stayed on the shelf," meaning limited his activities to Staten Island, minded his own loansharking business, and generally stayed low-key.

Milito didn't believe he was really safe and started asking others around Gravano what he was thinking. This checking up rattled Gravano. As he put it at trial, "Louie was relatively dangerous. He would be somebody I'd pay attention to." So he went to Gotti to ask permission to take Milito out, and Gotti gave it. Gravano asked Milito to come to Stillwell Avenue, and when he arrived Gravano offered him coffee. They went downstairs, and as they talked Old Man Paruta took the gun from the cabinet and shot Milito in the back of the head: the DiB killing reenacted to the letter.

There were so many murders we became numb hearing about them. Gravano insisted they were all part of "the life," and that the people who got whacked deserved it because they broke the rules of the organization they'd chosen to join. He told us about "Johnny Keys" Simone, whom Gravano was told by Paul Castellano to whack. Gravano found Keys on a golf course in New Jersey, and he knew why Gravano had come. Still, he didn't resist or run, just got in the car as he was told to do. When they reached the place where the hit would happen, Keys asked Gravano for permission to take off his shoes. Gravano asked why, and Keys said he'd promised his wife that he'd die with his shoes off. Gravano consented and Keys was soon in his stocking feet. He got on his knees, and when he bent forward Gravano shot him in the back of the head.

Even more murders were planned but called off. The Colombo Family had asked John Gotti to kill Colombo captain Greg Scarpa. Gotti gave Gravano the job and his crew planned it. They cased Scarpa's movements and decided where it would happen. Then the Colombos withdrew the ask.

"How close did you come to killing him?" Gabriel asked.

"Close. We had the kiddie pool and everything."

I was supposed to know what this meant but didn't.

"Kiddie pool?"

"You know, to cut him up."

After each debriefing we'd get in our rental car and head back to the airport. We'd time it perfectly, barely making the last shuttle back to LaGuardia, and as soon as we got on the plane we'd order two Sam Adams each for the forty-five-minute flight.

Back in Brooklyn, I'd sit with my trial team and tell them what we'd learned. Most of the information we'd obtained from Gravano wouldn't be part of the testimony at trial, but Pat Cotter, Laura Ward, and Jamie Orenstein were just as keen to hear what he'd had to say as Gabriel and I had been.

After the first of the many debriefings, Cotter offered some advice. "Hey, boss," he said, "do us a favor. If Sammy offers you a cup of coffee, say no."

Whenever an investigation produces a revelation, it's critical to reprocess all the previously gathered evidence in light of the new discovery. From December 12, 1989, when Gotti said that he'd "whacked DiB," until I met with Gravano in Judge Raggi's jury room almost two years later, our theory was that Gravano wanted DiB dead so he could take over the construction racket. We hadn't made that up. In the same conversation, Gotti said that he'd taken Gravano's word that DiB had talked about him behind his back. DiB was talking "subversive," Gotti told Locascio, but the only person who reported that was Gravano:

Gotti: "DiB, did he ever talk subversive to you?"

Locascio: "Never."

Gotti: "Never talked to Angelo, and he never talked to Joe Piney. I took Sammy's word that he'd talked about me behind my back."

Gotti even provided Gravano's motive to kill DiB. He told Locascio that Gravano said, "DiB cried behind my back," and now Gravano "got Bobby Sasso," the corrupt president of Teamsters Local 282 whom DiB had controlled. So Gravano had falsely reported that DiB was being subversive in order to get Gotti to kill him, all so Gravano could take over the lucrative construction racket.

Just a few minutes into our first conversation in Quantico, Gravano had said that he liked DiB and didn't want him dead. He freely admitted to the killing, but insisted that he disagreed with Gotti's order when it was given to him by Ruggiero. He told us that Ruggiero, who'd always wanted to be underboss and considered DiB his main competition, was the one who wanted him murdered. What was the truth?

The disparities between our evidence and Gravano's version of events made me believe him even more. He knew about the recorded conversation before he became our witness: we'd played that snippet at the detention hearing. Had he wanted, he could easily have tailored his testimony to fit what we had. He could simply have said that he told Gotti that DiB had been disloyal and should be killed, and Gotti ordered the hit. That testimony would dovetail perfectly with our evidence and be very powerful. But according to Gravano that wasn't what happened. The truth was someone else with an entirely different motive was responsible for persuading Gotti to have DiB whacked.

If Gravano were to be believed, we had a new narrative, and it went like this: in April 1986 underboss Frankie DeCicco, Castellano's Judas, was killed. The next month Diane Giacalone and I got Gotti remanded to the MCC for intimidating Romual Piecyk. Ruggiero wanted to succeed DeCicco as underboss but recognized that DiB, a consummate businessman, was better qualified for the job. To get him out of the way, he told Gotti that, according to Gravano, DiB was "talking subversive" behind his back and deserved to be killed. Gotti believed Ruggiero and ordered the hit, which a disappointed Gravano reluctantly but dutifully carried out. More than three years later, up in the Ravenite apartment, Gotti suspected that Gravano had been motivated by greed, not by loyalty, hence his diatribe about him to Locascio.

To test this new narrative, we reviewed all the evidence again. The MCC visitors log revealed that the only person who came to see Gotti in prison during May and June of 1986, apart from his blood family and lawyers, was Ruggiero. Gravano never made the trip, so he didn't speak to Gotti. All the messages in the seventeen days between when Gotti went into pretrial detention in our first case and the day DiB was killed were delivered to him by Ruggiero.

Even more significant was a series of statements that DiB's girlfriend, Nancy Drake, had made to an FBI agent shortly after he disappeared. Drake often stayed at DiB's home, and would answer his phone for him. A man named Angelo rang a lot, but would never tell Drake why he was calling. Then, on June 4, the day before DiB disappeared, Angelo called once more and DiB wasn't home. Angelo told Drake to let DiB know that it was very important that he meet with Sammy the following day. She duly passed on the message. After DiB left the house the following morning, she never saw him again.

Drake's evidence was consistent with the new narrative. At that time "Angelo"— Angelo Ruggiero, of course—had Gotti's ear all to himself. He could hardly tell his boss the real reason he wanted DiB dead, so he made up another—that Gravano had said DiB was disloyal. Gotti ordered the hit and thereafter Ruggiero showed his intense interest in how it played out through his calls to Drake. The reason no one else had ever told Gotti that DiB was disloyal was simple—he hadn't been.

We did everything we could to find other evidence that proved Gravano was being truthful. He told us that after he'd killed DiB he'd driven to Sheepshead Bay, part of Lower New York Harbor. There was a huge Toys "R" Us store right on the water, which could be seen from the Verrazzano-Narrows Bridge. Next to the store was a chain-link fence. Gravano had driven to the store parking lot, gone up to the fence, and tossed the murder weapon into the water.

George Gabriel and I wanted to find the gun, so the FBI got the NYPD's scuba team to look for it. The bay is deep and murky there, with strong tidal currents, so it was no easy task. But the opening to the water provided by the fence was narrow enough that there wouldn't be too much area to explore.

The afternoon of the search I waited by my telephone for a report. When it came, it was a good news, bad news thing.

"The good news is we hit the right place. We found a gun. In fact, we found twenty-two guns," Gabriel told me. "The bad news is none of them is the one we were looking for."

"You're kidding me."

"No, I'm not," Gabriel went on. "Brooklyn South Homicide should put a camera on that fence, but we're not coming back with anything that helps us."

So that didn't affect Gravano's version either way. On the other hand, we found a great piece of evidence to support his testimony about the murder of Louie Milito. Gravano had told us that he deliberately planned the murder for a Tuesday evening. Everyone in Gravano's crew met with him on Tuesdays at Tali's, a club on 18th Avenue in Brooklyn. And everyone knew that Kenny McCabe, an investigator with the Rackets Squad of the Brooklyn District Attorney's Office, was outside, noting who came and went. McCabe was one of the most respected organized crime investigators in the city. He covered those weddings, funerals, social clubs, and other special occasions where gangsters gathered. He knew everyone's face and recorded each person's name in a logbook. He was at Tali's every Tuesday night for almost a decade. Gravano wanted an alibi if he were ever charged with killing Milito. As he'd later testify at trial, "We knew there was surveillance by Tali's watching us every Tuesday night, so when we walked in about eight o'clock, eight-thirty, we looked normal and would have the government as our witness." McCabe would be his cover.

When Gravano got permission to kill Milito, Gotti told him to use his brother Gene's crew to get rid of the body. Gravano complied, and Gene himself, together with John Carneglia and Arnold Squitieri, disposed of the corpse. Squitieri drove home to New Jersey, but Carneglia and Gene went on to Tali's.

Milito disappeared forever on Tuesday, March 8, 1988, so we asked McCabe to bring in his surveillance logs from Tali's—all of them. He had boxes and boxes. We asked him to review them to see whether he'd ever seen Gene Gotti and John Carneglia there, individually or together. His immediate response was probably not; both men were Queens guys: they hung out at the Bergin, not Tali's. But we left him alone to search through almost ten years of surveillance logs. Eventually he emerged from the office we'd given him.

"They were there once," Kenny said.

"Both at the same time?" I asked.

"Yup."

"When?"

"March 8, 1988." One visit in ten years, the exact night that Gravano said they helped him kill Louie Milito. McCabe would be a witness all right, but his testimony wouldn't be helping the defendants.

One of the best pieces of corroborating evidence the squad came up with related to the conspiracy to kill Corky Vastola. The recorded conversations were clear when it came to the motive and the inter-Family machinations needed to get it done. However, they contained one anomaly: Gravano had said that the shooting would be done by Barry Nichilo on a farm. New York City and its suburbs don't have many of those, and wiseguys tend not to be regular visitors at the few there are. It was as if we'd recorded some Iowa farmers conspiring to whack a farmhand in a skyscraper.

Enter Joanne Conlon, a real estate agent from Monmouth County, New Jersey, about an hour south of the city. I had no idea how the Gambino Squad found her, and I knew enough about their relationships with informants not to ask, but for a six-month period in late 1989 Conlon had shown Barry Nichilo farms in Colts Neck, and they went to contract on one. It was a textbook example of how to corroborate evidence. At precisely the time when Gravano, up in the Ravenite apartment, was explaining that Nichilo had offered to kill Vastola on a farm, we had independent, unimpeachable evidence that Nichilo was agreeing to buy just such a property in Vastola's hometown.

Coincidentally, one of the farms Nichilo was interested in was on Route 34, only a few hundred yards from my in-laws, also in Colts Neck. If the Gambinos had gotten Chin Gigante's approval to use Nichilo to kill Vastola, my mother-in-law might have heard the shots.

Above: John Gotti and his famously loose-lipped lifelong friend Angelo Ruggiero (*far right*), outside the Ravenite Social Club in 1979. The 1982 bug in Ruggiero's kitchen helped us convict dozens and eventually brought down the entire Gambino Family.

Right: Gambino underboss Neil Dellacroce in the doorway to his "office"—the Ravenite—in 1979. Our lead defendant in the first case before he died on December 2, 1985, Dellacroce kept Boss Castellano and Captain Gotti from murdering each other. Two weeks after his death, Gotti struck first.

Left: Outside of Sparks Steak House on December 16, 1985, Gambino boss Paul Castellano (shown here sprawled on the street) and his driver were gunned down in front of dozens of witnesses during rush hour. John Gotti orchestrated the hits, was on the scene, and immediately took over as boss.

4

Above: Anthony "Tony Roach" Rampino, in a light-colored suit, stands in the doorway of the Ravenite on Christmas Eve, 1985, nine days after the murders at Sparks. One of the original members of Gotti's crew in the 1970s, Tony Roach had been part of the hit team.

Courtesy of the FBI

5

Left: Frankie DeCicco betrayed Paul Castellano by disclosing to Gotti the meeting at Sparks. DeCicco was named underboss as a reward. Seen here with the new boss on Christmas Eve, 1985, DeCicco lasted less than four months in the position before being blown up.

Courtesy of the FBI

6

Right: The hit on DeCicco, which generated this headline, was ordered by Genovese boss Vincenzo "Chin" Gigante and Lucchese boss Vic Amuso, who both thought Gotti—their primary target—would be accompanying him.

Anthony Pescatore/*New York Daily News*/Getty Images

7   **Left**: Gambino captain Robert DiBernardo ran the Gambino construction rackets when Castellano was the boss. DiBernardo disappeared in June 1986, and his body was never found. Fours years later we learned from the Ravenite bug recordings that Angelo Ruggiero had duped Gotti into ordering DiBernardo's murder.

Courtesy of the FBI

8   **Left**: Diane Giacalone, the gifted prosecutor who led our first RICO prosecution of Gotti, is shown here in the red suit she wore for opening statements in September 1986. There turned out to be nothing Gotti and his lawyers wouldn't stoop to in their efforts to avoid conviction.

Yvonne Hemsey/Getty Images

9

Right: One of Andy Warhol's final works was his portrait of John Gotti, which appeared on the cover of *Time* magazine's September 29, 1986, issue. The publication hit newsstands shortly before the first trial's opening statements. Gangsters typically tried to stay below the radar, but Gotti wanted to be a celebrity. If there was any doubt that he'd achieved that status, this erased it.

© 2021 The Andy Warhol Foundation for the Visual Arts, Inc./ Licensed by Artists Rights Society (ARS), New York; from *Time*. © 1986 TIME USA LLC

DAILY ◉ NEWS

NEW YORK'S PICTURE NEWSPAPER   Saturday, March 14, 1987

Gotti and pals acquitted

HE'S HOME FREE!

JOHN GOTTI, reputed Mafioso, arrives home in Howard Beach, Queens, after seven-month trial in Brooklyn Federal Court on a member of charges like racketeering and murder. He wasn't found guilty of anything.

PAGES 2 and 3

Left: That first trial lasted seven hostile months. Gotti called a defense witness who accused Diane Giacalone and me of serious crimes. The prosecution ended badly on Friday the 13th, March 1987, with across-the-board acquittals. Years later, we learned why.

New York Daily News/Getty Images

11

Right: Hours after the acquittals, Gotti; his principal enforcer, Sammy "the Bull" Gravano (to Gotti's right); and others gathered at the Ravenite for celebratory fireworks. Five years later, the front row (Frank Locascio is to Gravano's right) would make up the top administration of the Gambino Family—and be on trial as our defendants.

Mike Norcia/NYP/Globe Photos/Zuma Press

12

Left: Bosko Radonjich. Living proof that the truth is much more bizarre than fiction, this Serbian terrorist was tapped by Gotti to be in charge of the Westies, an Irish gang under Gambino Family control. Bosko played a critical behind-the-scenes role in the 1987 acquittals.

Courtesy of the FBI

13

Above: Arnold Squitieri (*right*) and Alphonse "Funzi" Sisca attending the wake for Gambino soldier (and close Gotti friend) Bobby Boriello in my old Brooklyn neighborhood, Carroll Gardens. We suspected Squitieri and Sisca of involvement in the Castellano murder. I prosecuted them in the summer of 1988 for heroin trafficking in the hopes of flipping them. Though they were convicted and sentenced to seventeen years, they "stood up" instead.

Courtesy of the FBI

14

Right: A rare photo of high-ranking gangsters after a 1989 "sitdown" to resolve inter-Family disputes. Boss John Gotti is in the red shirt; acting Gambino underboss Frank Locascio is to his left; Colombo underboss Benny Aloi is in the blue tie; acting Colombo boss Vic Orena is to Aloi's left, in front. Orena and Gotti both wanted Colombo soldier Tommy Ocera whacked.

Courtesy of the FBI

15

Left: When the bosses of two Cosa Nostras each want the same person killed, it tends to happen. Killed in November 1989, Tommy Ocera was exhumed from a shallow grave in Forest Park, Queens, almost two years later. His murder was ordered by Vic Orena to keep Ocera from cooperating against him. Gotti, meanwhile, had asked Orena to kill Ocera to avenge the murder of a friend's son.

Courtesy of the FBI

16

Left: The original "house counsel" to the Gambino Family, attorney Mike Coiro (*foreground*) had a corrupt "hook" in law enforcement. I tried and convicted Coiro of racketeering in November 1989 in the hope he would cooperate against Gotti. Instead, he testified for Gotti, so we convicted him again—for perjury.

Newsday R.M./Getty Images

Below: Gotti and his trusted lawyers, Jerry Shargel (*left*) and Bruce Cutler (*right*), heading into state court in January 1990. Charged by District Attorney Robert Morgenthau with ordering the shooting of a union official, Gotti was acquitted, burnishing his reputation as "the Teflon Don."

Robert Rosamillio/*New York Daily News*/Getty Images

17

18

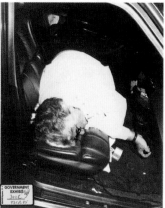

Left: In a recorded conversation in the apartment above the Ravenite Social Club on December 12, 1989, Gotti said Gambino soldier Louie DiBono was "gonna die because he refused to come in when I called. He didn't do nothing else wrong." Ten months later, DiBono was murdered in the basement garage of the World Trade Center.

Courtesy of the FBI

Right: In August 1991, Gotti, at the first court appearance after Shargel and Cutler were disqualified from appearing at the second trial, put on a show for the media. His target: me. Somehow, I was both a "bum" and a "Little Lord Fauntleroy."

NYP Holdings, Inc.

Right: On the morning after the April 2, 1992, conviction, the *Daily News* cover said it all.

New York Daily News/Getty Images

Left: My boss Andy Maloney and I can't resist smiling at the postconviction press conference, April 2, 1992. We'd waited five long years since the acquittals in the first trial to enjoy this moment.

Rick Maiman/Sygma/Getty Images

Left: The trial team posed for this photo shortly after the conviction. From left, Pat Cotter, Jamie Orenstein, Laura Ward, paralegal Karyn Kenny, FBI special agent George Gabriel, and me. Missing was our boss Andy Maloney, who'd tried the case with us.

Courtesy of John Gleeson

23

Above: When Gotti was sentenced, a mob of wannabe wiseguys rioted outside the courthouse.

Richard Perry/Sygma/Getty Images

24

Left: After Sammy "the Bull" Gravano—Gambino underboss and killer of nineteen men—flipped and became my star witness against Gotti, he was in great demand. Summoned to the U.S. Senate in April 1993 to testify about organized crime in professional boxing, he received a celebrity's welcome.

Courtesy of John Gleeson

CHAPTER 32

THE PRESSURE BUILDS

If Bruce Cutler thought being booted out of Judge Glasser's courtroom freed him up to bash the judge and us in the media, he learned how mistaken he was. On November 4, 1991, four days before we pulled Gravano out of the MCC, Glasser appointed a special prosecutor to investigate and, if appropriate, prosecute Cutler for contempt of court based on his repeated violations of the rule governing public statements about pending cases. Like his predecessor house counsel, Mike Coiro, Cutler had completed his transition from defense counsel to defendant, and would soon be experiencing a trial of his own in *United States v. Bruce Cutler.*

As the holiday season approached we were full of excitement. Our case had undergone a metamorphosis. We'd started out with a powerful RICO case based squarely on the Ravenite recordings. Every charge in it was proven by the defendants' own words.

Then the Southern District tried to steal it. To fend them off, we'd had to take on the Castellano and Bilotti murders as RICO predicates. That diluted the strength of our overall indictment because their evidence was so flimsy.

Then Gravano flipped. Our one-dimensional, recording-based trial now had depth and a dramatic centerpiece: the most prominent organized crime witness in history testifying against the most famous mob boss in history about one of the most spectacular mob murders in history. Gravano put all our tapes in context and rounded out our case perfectly, and yet inevitably the murders of Castellano and his bodyguard would be the main focus once we reached court.

Lawyers spend a good deal of time thinking about all that can go wrong at trial. I wanted a crisp, efficient presentation of all the recordings, having learned in the first case that few things make a trial drag like playing too many tapes. Mary Jo White accepted my invitation to both review the recordings we'd prepared and do a mock cross of the FBI supervisor, Lou Schiliro, through whose testimony we'd present them. Her advice was great, and I was surprised by the effectiveness of the mock cross, which we did in Judge Glasser's courtroom one weekend. She hadn't struck any of us on the team as a courtroom lawyer, but she knew how to cross a witness. The exercise also helped repair the damage done by my not telling her about my negotiations with Gravano.

As I imagined the moment I'd call Gravano's name as our next witness, my mind's eye saw a gallery packed with press and gangsters. To Gravano's right, in the well of the court, twenty feet away, would be Gotti and Locascio, the friends with whom he'd engaged in a lifetime of crime and with whom he'd spent almost a year in the MCC before betraying them. To his immediate left would be eighteen randomly chosen citizens—the selected jurors and alternates—staring at him. He'd be expected to tell those complete strangers about the crimes committed by his sometime friends, in direct conflict with the wiseguy oath of omertà so ingrained it was part of his DNA.

What if he couldn't do it? People choke in far less stressful situations. What if, once he looked Gotti in the eye, Gravano reverted to his old self, refusing to answer questions? Since that would be a disaster, I wanted to do everything in my power to make certain he had what it took to testify. We couldn't replicate everything from my disaster fantasy, but we could summon up a roomful of new faces for him to testify before. I decided we'd audition Gravano by having him testify before the Gambino Family grand jury.

Slipping him out of the director's suite in Quantico and into the grand jury room without anyone knowing would be tricky, so I picked the quietest non-holiday day of the year for Gravano's debut as a witness: New Year's Eve 1991.

The exercise would be useful to me as well. After about a hundred hours of debriefing Gravano, it was time to organize our dialogue into a direct examination. I chose one of our charged murder cases as our topic. We'd use Gravano's testimony to indict the other participants, whom we'd prosecute after the Gotti trial.

Unsurprisingly, come New Year's Eve, the courthouse was almost empty. The marshals whisked Gravano into the building and up the judges' elevator to the fourth floor, where the grand jury room was located.

We'd kept Gravano's appearance a secret and hadn't alerted the grand jurors to our plan either, and I was worried that because it was New Year's Eve we might not get the sixteen we needed for a quorum. But enough finally arrived, and they were shocked and delighted when we told them Sammy "the Bull" Gravano was about to be brought in to testify. By then they knew all about him, and had heard hours of his conversations up in the Ravenite apartment.

Gravano showed no nervousness at all when the foreman asked him to raise his right hand for the oath. Once he'd been sworn in, I walked him through the murder case, and his answers were crisp and confident. He showed that he could give evidence to strangers about the crimes other people, including his friends, had committed.

Laura Ward and Pat Cotter were sitting next to me, and we were ecstatic. We decided that Gravano should be our crowning piece of evidence, and be put on the stand toward the trial's end.

In the run-up to the trial, there was another development in our parallel investigation of Colombo boss Vic Orena. Stamboulidis and Favo had built a decent murder case. They had the body, and as witnesses the two low-level associates who'd buried it in the shallow grave in Forest Park. Michael Maffatore and Harry Bonfiglio were just a few feet away when Orena ordered Colombo soldier Jack Leale to kill Ocera. Orena had made our work more difficult by killing Leale before we could get to him, but Gravano would testify that Gotti had asked Orena to whack Ocera. The evidence as to his motive was muddled. The Colombo associates would testify that Ocera was dispatched because his loan shark records put Orena at risk; Gravano said he was killed in retaliation for murdering a Gambino drug dealer's son. The difference would help Orena's defense, but we weren't deterred. We'd argue that this wasn't the first time a wiseguy was whacked for multiple reasons.

In September 1991 the case got another boost because Little Al D'Arco, the acting boss of the Lucchese Family, flipped. D'Arco thought he was about to be whacked by Gaspipe Casso, the notoriously murderous underboss of the family, so he walked into the Southern District and asked to be placed in the Witness Protection Program. It was another striking defection, further evidence that the Mafia was unraveling. When we debriefed D'Arco, he told us that in late 1989, shortly after Ocera disappeared, the Lucchese and Colombo administrations met in Stella Ristorante in Floral Park to discuss some joint business. There Orena told D'Arco that Orena had ordered the hit on Ocera and had given him the "*lupara bianca*"—a mob expression, literally the "white shotgun," meaning his body would not be found.

On January 6, 1992, fifteen days before the Gotti trial jury selection, George Santangelo entered the case to join Frank Locascio's defense team. Unlikeable in the extreme, Santangelo had also been a last-minute addition to the defense team in our trial before Judge Nickerson. After moving unsuccessfully to disqualify both the judge and Diane Giacalone, he was constantly in our faces—and the judge's as well. Santangelo wasn't the most impressive lawyer in that case, but he was definitely the nastiest. He also made it clear that even though he nominally represented Nicky Corozzo, he was actually defending Gotti. On multiple occasions he'd ask the judge's permission to leave a conference up at the bench to confer with his client, and instead of speaking to Corozzo he would talk only to Gotti. One time Judge Nickerson asked wryly when he returned, "Mr. Santangelo, didn't you want to confer with your client?"

Three days after Santangelo entered the case, we had a court appearance. I told Judge Glasser that Santangelo was almost as enmeshed in our trial evidence as Shargel and Cutler, and if he'd paid any attention to the ethical rules he would never have come into the case. I offered to show Santangelo the evidence I was referring to, and if he declined to withdraw voluntarily I'd move to disqualify him.

After we left the court, we went back to our offices to walk Santangelo through the recorded conversations about him. These would establish at trial that even though Santangelo had never once represented Gotti, Gotti controlled him. As Cutler put it in discussing the matter with Gotti, Santangelo could be counted on to follow Gotti's self-described "credo"—no matter what the evidence showed, a lawyer being paid by Gotti must never admit the existence of the Mafia. He was not one of these "erudite, egghead types afraid to tell the government, 'Go fuck yourself.'" We would argue that it did not matter whom he formally represented—and that group included DiMaria, John Carneglia, and Gambino captain Sonny Ciccone—Santangelo could be counted on to protect the interests of John Gotti.

Santangelo was scornful and sarcastic as I laid the evidence out before him, and within minutes I'd had enough. He had no interest in the recorded conversations and kept saying there was no way he'd withdraw from the case no matter what the tapes had on them. My temper and voice rising rapidly, I told him we were finished and it was time for him to get the hell out of our offices. He left with a smirk on his face that evoked my worst memories of the first trial.

"What the fuck are you doing?" George Gabriel said to me when Santangelo was gone. "He's in the case three days and you've already lost your cool? This is the first time I've ever seen you angry. Don't you get it? That's exactly why Gotti brought him in, to get under your skin. If we can't get him disqualified, you're going to have to figure out how to handle him better than that." This was blunt stuff for an AUSA to hear from an agent, and it was a measure of how close Gabriel and I had become that he felt comfortable delivering it. He was obviously right. If I couldn't get Santangelo removed from the case, I couldn't let him do that to me again.

Six days later we moved to disqualify Santangelo. The next day—and just five days before jury selection would begin—the defendants cross-moved to disqualify me. The basis of their motion was, once again, Matt Traynor. I was embarrassed, the motion claimed, because Gotti had presented evidence five years earlier that my wife and I had tried to bribe Traynor with drugs. That gave me a personal interest in the case that was disqualifying. "Gravano's decision to cooperate," they argued, "was motivated in substantial part because of his concern that Mr. Gleeson would go to any ends to ensure his conviction." Finally, the motion argued that I should be disqualified on the eve of trial, after spending more than two years leading the investigation, because Gotti had called me a "rat motherfucker" up in the Ravenite apartment. My knowledge of the lead defendant's hatred of me, the argument went, entitled him to an order preventing me from prosecuting him.

The motion seemed to delight in exhuming the scandalous accusations made in the first trial. It of course made no mention of the fact that Traynor had admitted under oath that those accusations were lies, and had sworn that his perjury in that trial had been scripted by Bruce Cutler. In a way, the willingness of Santangelo to file such a motion was exactly why Gotti and Cutler liked him. The only real surprise the motion served up was that it wasn't *just* Santangelo on the papers. When he made his equally frivolous motion to disqualify Judge Nickerson and Diane five years earlier, none of the other seven defense lawyers would allow their names to be included, but Al Krieger's name was on this motion. That surprised me, as he was a real criminal defense lawyer, not a hack like Santangelo. Gotti had obviously made him do it, and that didn't bode well for how Krieger would act during trial. It was another warning shot.

On January 21, about five hundred citizens of the Eastern District were summoned to the courthouse to begin jury selection. The first step of the process, as in the first trial, would be a questionnaire. Since Judge Glasser's courtroom could not handle that many people, they'd all be brought from the central jury room to the huge ceremonial courtroom on the second floor of the courthouse.

The judge and all the lawyers began the day in his chambers to go over the logistics: what he would say to the prospective jurors, who would make the copies of the completed questionnaires, how many would be needed, and other matters.

When we arrived, the judge was behind a closed door, so both teams of lawyers waited together in the reception area of his chambers. It was crowded and awkward. The cross-motions to disqualify were still pending, so I found myself standing shoulder to shoulder with Santangelo. We found nothing to say to each other. After fifteen minutes went by, the door opened and Judge Nickerson came out. He walked past the crowd of lawyers and through the reception area without saying a word.

That's interesting, I thought. Judge Nickerson was the most respected judge in the district, and it looked as if he might have just been imparting to his fellow judge a few lessons based on experience.

We filed into Judge Glasser's office, where there wasn't enough room for us all to sit. He told us what he was planning to do when we entered the courtroom. At one point he asked Krieger how many copies of the completed questionnaires the defense team would need. Krieger responded by counting the lawyers who were standing in a line against the windows. He had two associates with him representing Gotti, and Locascio had George Santangelo and two others.

"Six, Judge," Krieger said as he got to Santangelo at the end of the line.

"Oh, you'll only need five," the judge said, "because you, Mr. Santangelo, are disqualified. And your motion to disqualify Mr. Gleeson is denied." It was an unusual way of conveying such important information, but I loved it. Santangelo looked shaken, but there was nothing he could do about it.

When we got to the courtroom, Gotti and Locascio were already there. The marshals had brought them in from the adjacent cellblock before the jurors entered, so no one would know the two men had been detained pending trial. Locascio saw that Santangelo was missing, and one of the other lawyers representing him whispered to him what had just happened.

Locascio blew up. "That's the American flag there!" he yelled, pointing up to where the judges sit for ceremonial proceedings. "That's not a swastika!" The connection between the Nazis and the disqualification of Santangelo wasn't obvious, but combined with Cutler's attack on Glasser a few months earlier it was becoming clear that the defendants were trying to rattle the judge, an observant Jew, by accusing him of being a Nazi sympathizer. I recalled the Nuremberg comparison from the first trial.

The specter of jury tampering arose the next day. Many of the jurors had returned home the evening before to find crude handbills on the cars they'd parked at the commuter railroad stations in Nassau and Suffolk Counties. Some had seen them taped to the walls of subway stations in the city. They consisted of a photo of Gravano's face superimposed on a drawing of a rat, and a caption: "Sammy 'The Bull' Gravano: The Epitome of a Rat Who Lies."

FBI informants reported that the handbills had been placed on hundreds of windshields by people from the Bronx neighborhood where Locascio's club was located, but we had no way of telling whether the people who did it were closely connected to our defendants.

Judge Glasser was visibly upset when we reported these events to him in his chambers and showed him one of the handbills. He instructed the marshals to bring in Gotti and Locascio. It's an unwritten rule that only lawyers come to a judge's chambers, never defendants. The judge's unusual request was intended to convey the significance of what he was about to tell both men.

When they arrived, the judge began by saying, "I am not suggesting that you have done anything wrong. Nor am I suggesting that you are responsible for anything that I am about to talk about." He went on to describe the handbills, then, addressing Gotti, made what sounded like a personal request of a mob boss: "I think maybe you ought to know about what is going on. If you know anything about this, can do anything about it, it might be a very good idea *if you have any influence at all* to put a stop to it."

It was brilliant. It didn't accuse Gotti of wrongdoing, and it ever so slightly questioned whether he was really as powerful as he claimed to be. Gotti's reaction showed how he was living in another world. The court reporter's transcript reads:

> I don't do them things with this flier baloney. This guy (indicating Mr. Gleeson) gets all my mail monitored every day. I get mail from Suffolk County, Nassau County every day, and I get all good mail. I never get one bad letter, your Honor, so the people out there like me. I don't have to do these kind of things.

The comments brought to mind Gravano's statements at Quantico: Gotti actually believed he had a "public" and that it supported him. He was the boss of the Gambino *Crime* Family, but over the years he'd come to believe that he was a different kind of celebrity, a *popular* one. I was of course not monitoring any of his mail—the Bureau of Prisons did that, and I was no more in contact with the BOP than I was with the New York State Department of Motor Vehicles. I did have my own flow of Gotti-related mail. As his prosecutor, I received letters praising him every day, most from federal or state inmates. The rest were obviously from fringe characters who saw Gotti as an American hero. Some from both categories confessed to having murdered Paul Castellano, and I happily sent those along to Gotti's counsel to assist in their defense.

In any event, Judge Glasser's approach worked perfectly. He'd suggested that Gotti might lack the power to halt the distribution of the handbills, and nothing could have pushed Gotti's buttons more effectively. They stopped immediately.

CHAPTER 33

"CHRIST-KILLER"

Jury selection was an ordeal. As in the first trial, a large number of prospective jurors were dismissed based solely on their questionnaires. Judge Glasser decided that the follow-up examination of the others would occur in less imposing surroundings than a large courtroom, so he arranged for us to use an empty set of judge's chambers. Groups of a dozen or so prospective jurors would be brought to a nearby room, then each one would be escorted in to be questioned by the judge.

Although a more intimate setting was a great idea, our experience with the first few jurors caused the judge to tinker with the protocol. The problem was the tight physical space. Judge Glasser would begin by welcoming the juror, introducing himself, then introducing the parties and their lawyers. When he got to "and this is one of the defendants, John Gotti," each prospective juror was only about eight feet away. They freaked, and a couple even burst into tears the moment they looked at him.

Judge Glasser decided that a little warning might help, so after some discussion it was decided that when the room down the hall was filled with a fresh batch of prospective jurors he'd go there and tell them what was coming. To avoid the judge talking to jurors without counsel present, we agreed that Andy Maloney and Al Krieger would accompany him. That too was a good idea. Armed ahead of time with the knowledge that they'd soon be sitting just a few feet away from New York's leading crime boss, the jurors handled it much better.

This wrinkle in the process left the rest of us, including the defendants, bunched together back in the otherwise empty chambers. With no adult supervision around, Gotti saw an opportunity to intimidate. He loved calling me an "Irish faggot," a holdover insult from the first trial, and he repeated it whenever the judge was not in the room. Cotter, who was not only Irish but looked like a leprechaun, got the same treatment.

During one of those breaks, Gotti turned his attention to Jamie Orenstein, the young AUSA who'd become our designated "law man," the team member who'd write briefs on a moment's notice as the trial progressed. Jamie could think and write well and fast, and had proven himself to be so valuable in the run-up to the trial that I wanted him in court for the trial itself. He wouldn't sit at the table or examine witnesses, but I wanted him in the first row of the courtroom at all times. As we waited for the judge, Maloney, and Krieger to return, I stood with Cotter on my left and Orenstein on my right. When I made eye contact with Gotti he smiled, pointed at us in order, and said, "Irish faggot, Irish faggot," then pointed a finger directly at Orenstein and snarled, "*morta Cristo*"—Christ-killer.

The ensuing silence was eerie. We were all speechless. All three insults were obviously awful things to say, but there really wasn't much to say in response. I couldn't say what I was thinking, which was just how contemptible he was in every way. I was instantly worried about Orenstein. He was still in his twenties, and out of the blue one of the most feared men in the country had looked him in the eye and called him a Christ-killer. Had he reacted by telling me he'd rather stay away from the trial I wouldn't have blamed him.

Soon after, the judge returned and our business got underway. At the lunch break I walked back to our offices with Orenstein, Cotter, and Ward. I wasn't sure how to handle the Christ-killer comment, but before I could say anything, Orenstein asked, "Am I wrong about this, or did the boss of the Gambino Family just try to intimidate me?"

"No, you're not wrong," I said. "He's definitely trying to intimidate you."

We continued walking in silence for another thirty seconds. Orenstein seemed deeply affected, and I was beginning to think I'd lose him, which was no doubt what Gotti wanted.

"Cool," he finally said, a smile spreading across his face. The rest of us smiled too, and all of a sudden the situation took on a different cast. I like this kid, I thought to myself; he's a keeper.

The jurors who made it through the initial questioning were in for a big surprise: they wouldn't be going home. This jury wouldn't only be anonymous, it would also be fully sequestered, the first federal jury ever to be housed in a hotel throughout both the trial and deliberations. A deputy marshal would drive them to their homes so they could pack a bag, then it was off to the hotel.

We might have done a better job preparing the prospective jurors for the sequestration. Many were shocked, and I couldn't help thinking that their answers on the questionnaire and to the judge's questions might have been different had they known what was in store.

The last stage of selection is when each side gets to exercise peremptory challenges. The defense could strike ten jurors; we could strike six. The twelve left after we did that would be our jury. Most of our decisions were straightforward, but there was one extremely difficult judgment call to make. One of the jurors, a woman in her twenties, had disclosed on her questionnaire that she'd previously been married to a man who was once in business with Paul Castellano's nephew. I was impressed by her. When Judge Glasser followed up on that topic, she insisted she could be fair, and she seemed both earnest and honest.

On the other hand, the defense seemed to like her too. When other jurors provided information from which they could be identified, the defense had sought to excuse them because the jury was supposed to be anonymous. But this one, whom we immediately dubbed "Castellano's niece," elicited no objections.

Peremptory challenges are made in six rounds, and with each passing round Castellano's niece remained on the jury panel. When we got down to the last one, we still thought it was possible the defense might strike her but they might have waited, wanting us to use up one of our challenges on her. Prosecutors go first in the last round, and there were some on our team who didn't want to take a chance on a juror Gotti could so easily identify. But so much of jury selection is intuitive, and I felt good about her. I struck a different juror with our final challenge. Then the defense made its last strike, and they used it on another juror as well.

So we had our jury, and each side had chosen to gamble. We couldn't both be right about Castellano's niece, and we'd all be watching her closely as the trial progressed.

George Santangelo had been disqualified on the first day of jury selection so, a few days later, a new lawyer was added to Locascio's defense team: Anthony Cardinale. At the same time, David Greenfield, who'd known Locascio for years and had been in the case from day one, asked to be relieved. We didn't know why both things were happening at once. We also didn't know Cardinale. He was a mob lawyer, but he practiced in Boston, not New York. Coming into a case with the complexity of ours at such a late stage is unheard of, and our immediate reaction was concern that later on, after conviction, Locascio would claim he'd received ineffective assistance of counsel. So we opposed Greenfield's application, telling the judge to keep him in the case to assist Cardinale. Judge Glasser, perhaps weary of our telling him which lawyers needed to be kicked off the case and which couldn't leave, let Greenfield out. It was too bad for us, as he wasn't only a good lawyer but also a calming influence, and easy to get along with.

On the morning of opening statements I noticed something new in my office. Way back in one corner, on the far side of my conference table, was a refrigerator. When I opened it there was a case of Foster's beer inside. George Gabriel arrived half an hour later and confirmed what I'd suspected, which was that the FBI had placed it there. The refrigerator became a symbol, saying to me every day for the next ten weeks that my trial team and I were with the FBI now, and the FBI takes care of everything.

Andy Maloney gave our opening statement. For a prosecutor, this is the only part of a trial that can be scripted way in advance. It's the first argument the jury hears, so there's never a need to use it to react to anything. Andy didn't share with us what he'd say, and since he was our boss we couldn't insist that he should. He was excellent. Without notes, he spent twenty minutes telling the jury that we'd prove that Gotti ran the Gambino Family, and that he'd committed or caused to be committed the various crimes with which he was charged.

Krieger stood up to make his opening statement, and I saw that under his arm he had a poster board exhibit on which was an excerpt from the first of the Ravenite apartment tapes. It was the conversation in which Gotti called me a "rat motherfucker," and Gotti, Gravano, and Locascio could be heard agreeing that the Department of Justice wouldn't entrust the next prosecution to me. They'd get someone "with more brains," someone from the Southern District. Krieger was going to begin his opening statement by playing a recording of that conversation while holding up the poster board. The lead tactic of the defense was going to be to attack me.

I asked for a sidebar conference, and on the way up to the bench I passed within two feet of Gotti. He was gloating, as if he'd just gotten away with shooting a spitball at the clock.

I told the judge that he'd recognize the conversation Krieger wanted to play from the motion to disqualify me from the case. The defense was determined to distract the jury by personalizing the prosecution. Their intent was to make the case *Gotti v. Gleeson* instead of *U.S. v. Gotti*. Plus it was harassment, an attempt to embarrass.

The judge agreed completely, and since only the lawyers were at the sidebar he also called out Krieger on his inability to manage his client. "I don't see that any of this is appropriate. As a matter of fact, I think it is inappropriate. You probably believe it is as well."

"That's beside the point," Krieger responded. "You've ruled on it." Soon enough, that would become a defining characteristic of his defense: unable to manage his client, he dutifully did what he was told, but from the outset his heart wasn't in the work.

Krieger then repeated the theme from the first case. Gesturing toward his client, he bellowed, "He wishes he went to college! He wishes he was a member of the Union League Club!" It was hard to believe Gotti wished either actually, but since I had no idea what the Union League Club was I couldn't be certain. We were prosecuting Gotti because he swore a lot, Krieger insisted, although he hastened to assure the jury that such profanities "never intruded on his conversations with women and children." He attacked Gravano as "cunning, conniving, selfish, and greedy." The problem he failed to address was that, even if Gravano was all of those things, Gotti, not us, had made him the underboss. We didn't pick Gravano to become an insider who could tell the jury all about the inner workings of the New York Mafia; Gotti did. Gravano wasn't like James Cardinali, our key witness from the first case. He couldn't be dismissed as a coffee boy to whom no made guy, let alone a captain, consigliere, underboss, or boss, would disclose serious criminal activity. Gravano was indisputably Gotti's right-hand man, all over the tapes and seen on hundreds of videos circling the block talking with him. If Krieger wanted the jury to believe that it couldn't rely on Gravano to provide evidence of Gotti's crimes, he needed a narrative explaining why, and calling him selfish and greedy wasn't a convincing story line.

The first four weeks of our evidence was essentially the case we'd planned before our star witness came on board. It was 90 percent tapes, presented methodically through FBI agent Lou Schiliro. In the pretrial motions, we'd gotten Judge Glasser's permission to divide the recordings into seven categories. Each had a book of transcripts, ranging from eighty to over two hundred pages. Schiliro would come back and forth to the witness stand each time we turned to a new book. In between his stints, we'd present evidence that fleshed out the tapes: surveillances, prison records, seizures of gambling materials, and witnesses like the real estate agent who sold Barry Nichilo his farm. Ward, Cotter, and I took turns at the podium presenting the various recordings through Schiliro and the other witnesses. They were both able trial lawyers, ready for all objections, able to formulate good questions on the fly when necessary, and unflappable.

We started with Book One—the enterprise recordings, 144 pages of excerpts from conversations about the Family structure, all from the Ravenite bugs. It was powerful stuff—clear, crisp excerpts about made guys, making guys, handling corrupt union officials, general beefs and sit-downs with other Families, and even the contingency plan for running the Family if Gotti was arrested and detained.

As we presented the enterprise evidence we also created what became known as the "captains chart." Gravano's testimony would be loaded with references to the captains of the various crews, and I wanted the jury to visualize each one. So the first time a Gambino captain's name came up in our presentation of Book One, we'd offer a large photo of him with a nameplate and add it to a huge chart entitled "The Gambino Family Hierarchy." At the top were the photos and names of the administration—Gotti, underboss Gravano, and acting consigliere Locascio. Below them we kept adding the captains until all eighteen were up there, affixed by Velcro strips to a poster board almost eight feet high and four feet wide. That chart stayed on an easel in full view of the jury for the rest of the trial. It got an inordinate amount of tabloid coverage because the courtroom artists couldn't resist sketching it. After the trial was over it became the cover of one of the several books about Gotti.

Book Two was a collection of state wiretaps that proved the Queens gambling operation run by Ralph Mosca and his son Pete. Gambling is such a minor crime that wiseguys actually use telephones to discuss it, so we intercepted daily reports from an associate in Mosca's crew to Pete Mosca about the previous night's income from a chemin de fer game (a version of baccarat) in Astoria:

"Had a nice night last night. Four-thirty they ended."

"And the score?"

"Two thousand seven hundred and forty."

"Ming! What a night! Now that's what I call a night!"

"Not bad for the middle of the week."

This was the territory on which Spiros Velentzas, the boss of Greek organized crime in New York, intruded with his barbut game—a close cousin to chemin de fer. That in turn resulted in Gotti's rant in the hallway that he'd "sever his motherfuckin' head off!"

Book Three was about the murders of Robert DiBernardo, Louie Milito, and Louie DiBono. The centerpiece of those conversations was Gotti's admission that he'd ordered the first two at Gravano's request and his simultaneous statement that DiBono was condemned to death because he'd refused to come in when called.

There were numerous recorded conversations over the years about the importance of "coming in." For instance, Gotti explained that one reason Tommy Bilotti "got sick" was because he, Bilotti, had once told a made guy in Connecticut that he didn't need to report to his captain, Tommy Gambino. Gotti used the "got sick" euphemism often, and whenever he did the illness consisted of a bullet in the head. We also had a recording of DiBono trying to buy his way out of getting killed. There was a ten-month gap between Gotti telling Locascio in December 1989 that DiBono was "gonna die" and the murder itself. DiBono showed up at the Ravenite in March of 1990. It was an unannounced visit, and it took everyone by surprise. DiBono spoke to Gotti in the hallway and assured him he'd paid all his drywall company's taxes, the issue at the heart of the beef DiBono had had with Gravano. We could hear the papers being shuffled as DiBono made his case to a boss who couldn't understand any paperwork, much less tax forms. Then he assured Gotti he was "back in the seat," and in a blubbering voice insisted that he was determined to bring in cash for the boss:

> "I wanna make money. I lost a lot of money. I gotta make, I gotta make
> money, and I gotta make money. I make money, we're making money."

That's how a gangster begs for his life. It didn't work. Gravano whispered to Gotti in the club that he should leave, taking the FBI surveillance with him, and Gravano would kill DiBono right there in the Ravenite. They opted against that in the end, and DiBono was finally killed in October.

Book Four was devoted exclusively to Gotti's motive for killing Castellano. It contained recordings from Ruggiero's home way back in 1982 and proved that Gotti's crew dealt in heroin. The jury listened to Ruggiero and Gene Gotti complaining that Castellano and Chin Gigante had "made a pact: any friend of ours that gets pinched for junk, or that they hear of anything about junk, they kill 'em. No administration meetings, no nothing, just gonna kill him. They're not warning nobody, not telling nobody because they feel the guy's gonna rat."

Book Five presented the Ravenite recordings about Castellano, including the three denials by Gotti that he was involved in the murders. The denials remained bad for us, but they could have been worse. Gotti's contempt for Castellano was clear. He stated explicitly that his rival deserved to be murdered, and he couldn't stop repeating all the reasons he hated him: he robbed his own men by sharing the earnings from construction with Chin; he disrespected Neil Dellacroce, both by staying away from his wake and by announcing a plan to break up the Ravenite after he died; he turned captains into rats by making them kill members of their crews who got arrested for drugs. Also, after one of Gotti's denials, Gravano laughed, and said to Locascio, "I love it when he does that, Frankie." We'd still need an explanation for the denials, but Gravano would provide it.

Book Six was a potpourri. It included recordings about the Connecticut gambling operation and the various obstruction of justice charges. The gambling case was easy. Tony Megale, the made guy in charge of Connecticut, had already pled guilty to running the operation. However, since he hadn't gotten Gotti's permission to do that, it almost got him killed. We'd recorded conversations in which Megale's captain, Tommy Gambino, briefed Gotti about Megale's case. They made Megale try to take his plea back because he admitted the existence of the Gambino Family as a criminal enterprise, and that admission could be used against Gotti. Our video surveillance also showed that Megale regularly reported to Gotti at the Ravenite.

The obstruction charges were even easier, and the defense didn't seriously contest them. Gotti's penchant for cultivating corrupt law enforcement hooks and for directing his subordinates to commit perjury or contempt resulted in dozens of criminal conversations. In recorded conversations, he said he'd directed Jerry Shargel to tell Joe Butch Corrao and George Remini to commit contempt at Tommy Gambino's trial. The jury listened to Gotti tasking Bruce Cutler with getting Tony Roach Rampino to commit either perjury or contempt in our grand jury. It heard Mike Coiro being sent to get information from his source, and Detective Bill Peist's leaks were repeatedly discussed, revealing him as an active hook of Gotti's. There was no defense to all this. If

Gotti could have gotten away with convictions on those charges alone he would have been ecstatic.

Book Seven contained the transcripts of the Vastola murder conspiracy recordings. It was our best predicate act, which would be held back until after Gravano testified. He'd passed his New Year's Eve audition in the grand jury with flying colors, but he could still stumble when it came to the trial itself. If he did, I wanted to present some good, solid evidence in between his leaving the witness stand and our resting our case.

CHAPTER 34

A DIFFERENT SHOW
OF FORCE

Krieger had come in late, replacing the disqualified Bruce Cutler, and as a result had some disadvantages. One was he didn't have the time to listen to all the Ravenite tapes. Shortly after indictment we'd produced copies of everything we'd recorded on all three bugs. At the same time we identified the small fraction of those recordings (far less than 5 percent) that we'd actually offer at trial. Krieger had sensibly focused his efforts on the seven or eight hours of tapes we'd play for the jury.

This was a disadvantage because by turning all the tapes over, we reserved the right to use any of the conversations to respond to Gotti's defense as it developed at trial. Because he was not familiar with those recordings, Krieger would have to be careful not to do or say anything that might be undermined by one of the conversations he *hadn't* listened to. When George Gabriel was on the stand putting into evidence some surveillance videos, Krieger proved how treacherous trial lawyering can be when you fly blind in this way.

The making ceremony that Gotti, Gravano, and Locascio talked about on January 4 and 17 up in the apartment took place on January 19. The video outside the club showed each new made guy arriving with his sponsor. When Gabriel identified them on my direct examination, Krieger misunderstood the testimony. All Gabriel had done was name the new members and their captains, but Krieger thought he was testifying that a making ceremony had occurred in the club itself, so he leapt up to cross and immediately moved into evidence all the video and audio for that entire day. Then he challenged Gabriel to find on the tapes a ceremony initiating new made guys. Gabriel responded that the new members and their sponsors were *returning* from the ceremony, which had taken place away from the club. This surprised Krieger, and his reaction got him in trouble. Reeking of condescension, he bellowed, "Then if the ceremony occurred someplace else, we do not have, have we, on the tape, at the Ravenite that night the persons who were initiated being congratulated?"

The smile was spreading across Gabriel's face even as the question was being asked. "As a matter of fact," he answered, "I have a tape of a person being congratulated by John Gotti." This was the Fat Dom Borghese recording I'd taped to the tin wall of my office six months earlier on the grounds that we'd never get it into evidence. We would *now*. I wrote a note that Jamie Orenstein passed to an FBI agent in the first row of the spectator section, asking him to run to my office, look for a cassette stuck on the wall over my conference table, and bring it to court. The agent looked at me as if I were crazy, but he had the cassette in the courtroom in five minutes, before Krieger completed his cross. When I offered it into evidence on redirect, the defense squealed, more from embarrassment than anything else. As soon as the judge learned that we'd given them a copy of that recording more than a year earlier, he told them to sit down; minutes later the jury was listening to Gotti congratulating Borghese and kissing him in the Ravenite hallway. Considering all our other evidence, the damage was minor, but it crystallized how Krieger had been forced to go to trial underprepared.

Cardinale then made it worse by choosing to recross Gabriel. How, he asked, did the agent know *why* John Gotti was congratulating Borghese? It was lame and ineffective, and as it was happening I looked over at Krieger. He was trying to keep a poker face, but we made eye contact and I could see he was sick—not just over this gaffe but with the whole case.

The biggest joke in the trial was the setting aside by the judge of one row in the gallery for the defendants' families. Real wiseguys don't let their wives and kids come to their trials, so it turned out indeed to be the Family row, but as in Gambino. Jackie Nose D'Amico, Gotti's driver, was there the entire time, and Tony Moscatiello, Joey DeCicco, and Carlo Vaccarezza came almost every day. Older brother Peter Gotti, whom Gotti referred to up in the apartment as "that moron I have downstairs for a brother," was there almost as often.

The row featured other cameos. One day Anthony Quinn made an appearance. He looked old and beaten up, and Jackie Nose walked him around the hallway during the break. Quinn left the tabloid reporters scratching their heads by saying why he *wasn't* there: "I'm not here to judge John Gotti." Mickey Rourke joined us one morning. He wore a long white fur coat and spent the break kibbitzing with the wiseguys. Rounding out the washed-up actor contingent was Al Lewis, who'd played Grandpa on *The Munsters*. Nobody recognized him until one of the wiseguys told the reporters who he was.

The other "celebrity" who visited the Family row was Renaldo Snipes, a professional boxer who Gravano testified was on the Mafia payroll and could be counted on to throw a fight. Subtlety wasn't among Snipes's talents. He sat down, immediately began glaring at the jury, then leaned forward on the bench, elbows locked straight, with his hands on his knees. Between the intensity of his face and the way he positioned himself it looked as if he were about to leap over the rail and rip the jurors' limbs off.

This freaked them out. At the morning break, just twenty minutes or so after Snipes had arrived, they sent a note to the judge complaining that he was intimidating them. The judge promptly kicked him out. I looked over at Gotti as Snipes was leaving, and he gave me a smile and a sheepish shrug. I got the impression that he'd expected Snipes to understand that he was supposed to help by being a celebrity in Gotti's corner, not by scaring everyone. Anyway, Snipes was gone and we never saw him again.

Throughout the trial I kept thinking back to the first one. Both were RICO prosecutions of John Gotti by me, but they had little else in common. The most noticeable difference between the two trials was Gotti. He was surly throughout the second one, and was just as hard on his own lawyers as on us. On breaks we could hear him screaming at Krieger and Cardinale back in the Marshals' pens. More often than not, those tirades were followed by ridiculous requests or arguments to Judge Glasser. When the lawyers made them, it was obvious their hearts weren't in it, and that they'd tried to convince Gotti not to make them. They had none of the control that good defense lawyers usually have over their clients.

There was one moment when I connected with Gotti in a positive way. It happened on February 26, the day Tommy Gambino finally resolved the criminal case Bob Morgenthau had brought against him. I'd promised Morgenthau I'd delay our prosecution of Gambino so ADA Eliot Spitzer could prosecute him for illegally controlling trucking in New York's garment district. Gambino and his brother Joe had been on trial in state court in Manhattan for a few months when they reached a deal with Spitzer and Morgenthau. During the afternoon break in our trial, people on both sides brought into court copies of the press release announcing the deal. Gotti was handed a sheet at his table at the same time I got one at mine.

The statement was brief. There'd be no prison term for Tommy or his brother. Instead, they'd pay a $12 million fine—for them no real hardship. Despite all the tough talk from Morgenthau when the case was originally brought about the need to loosen the Gambinos' grip on the garment center, Tommy Gambino was allowed to buy his way out of prison.

When I finished reading the release, I glanced at Gotti, who was looking up at me. He had a huge grin on his face. He pointed at himself and silently mouthed the words "How much would it cost me?" I chuckled—it was funny—and also pointed at him, mouthing back the words "You're not Tommy Gambino." He had a good laugh. It was a rare moment of shared understanding. And he genuinely enjoyed not being Tommy Gambino.

In early March, with almost a month of trial still to go, I got summoned to the marshal's office. "We have information from a reliable informant that John Gotti has put a contract on you," I was told. They let that sink in for a minute, then we talked about what to do.

If the information weren't reliable, they wouldn't have burdened me with it. But it didn't make sense that anyone in the street would kill a prosecutor for Gotti. He was in prison already, and it looked as if he'd be there for good. He was also despised by his fellow gangsters. His insistence on being a celebrity had brought greater heat on all the Families, not just his own. Besides, the Italian mob, at least in the United States, is way too businesslike to whack a member of federal law enforcement. Just three years earlier a DEA undercover, Everett Hatcher, had been killed in a drug deal in Staten Island. The suspect was Gus Farace, a Bonanno associate in Jerry Chilli's crew. It was the first murder of a federal agent in almost twenty years. All the agencies, joined by the NYPD, dropped everything to hunt down Farace. Within months they found him: the wiseguys had killed him, left him in a car in the Bensonhurst section of Brooklyn, and called 911 to alert the police where to find him.

The marshals wanted me to have round-the-clock protection. That would mean a deputy literally sharing our apartment with Susan and me, and that wasn't going to happen. We lived in a neighborhood loaded with gangsters, but I hadn't been spending any time in it for months. I was in the courthouse from six-thirty almost every morning till midnight, seven days a week. On Saturdays and Sundays I was coming in a little later, around eight. I was safe in the courthouse. And when I wasn't there, I was either at home sleeping or walking back and forth from Carroll Gardens. I was safe in my apartment building. The only real opportunities to harm me were on my trips to and from the courthouse. Was even that feasible?

Susan and I discussed the threat. It sickened her, of course, and brought back all the bad feelings Traynor had generated years earlier. We agreed there was no way they'd hurt her physically. Traynor's scripted perjury in the first case had defamed her, but only because it needed to do so to explain my access to the drugs with which I supposedly plied him. In Sicily the mob seemingly had no constraints at all, as would be proven in a matter of months by the assassinations of prosecuting magistrates Giovanni Falcone and Paolo Borsellino. But in America there are few acts more counterproductive to the way the Mafia does business than harming a family member of an agent or prosecutor. As for the risk to me, if indeed there was one, it would be short-lived, as it would do no good to retaliate after a conviction. Even so, I decided not to be cavalier.

"I'll make you a deal," I told the marshals after talking it over with Susan. I explained my daily routine. "How about if I get an FBI agent to bring me in every morning and take me home every night?"

When they asked whom it would be, I suggested George Hanna, and of course they agreed. Like everyone else in law enforcement, federal or state, in the city, they knew Hanna and respected him. He'd be my bodyguard—so long as he agreed.

"Hanna," I said, when I got back to my office and called him, "I committed us to something a few minutes ago." Even though he lived out in Nassau County and I'd just committed him to nineteen-hour working days for the rest of the trial, Hanna was his usual upbeat, generous self.

"No problem," he said. "Just beep me every evening thirty minutes before you want to leave."

That compromise with the marshal cemented a relationship with Hanna that would last a lifetime. After the trial ended, the morning rides continued—but they were to Prospect Park, where we'd go for a run, then on to the YMCA in downtown Brooklyn to shower before work.

Late one night when the trial was still underway, we were stopped at a light.

"Hanna," I said, "what if someone stepped out of the shadows with a gun right here? How long will it take you to shoot him? Go ahead, let's see." He wore his gun on his ankle, under jeans that were a snug fit. Hanna was big, carrying 240 pounds on his football-player frame, almost all of it across the chest and shoulders. Add to that the bulky winter coats we were wearing, and there was considerable fumbling around before he got his weapon out of its holster and up above the steering wheel.

We both laughed. "We better hope that contract never made it out to the street," I said. "Because if it did, first they'll shoot me, then they'll have a cup of coffee and shoot you."

CHAPTER 35

"BY GOSH, TOMMY BILOTTI IS DEAD"

We sailed through the first six books in three weeks. On February 28, 1992, I told the judge and the defense that the next day we'd be calling Sammy Gravano.

The following afternoon, not long after the lunch break, I repeated to the judge in open court, "Our next witness is Salvatore Gravano." The jurors, who'd gotten to know Gravano by listening to the Ravenite recordings and looking at surveillance videos, reacted visibly, sitting up straight and whispering to each other. It took a few minutes for the marshals to get Gravano from his safe place in the courthouse, and we all sat silently in the packed room while we waited. I could feel the anticipation.

As Gravano, having been sworn in, sat down in the witness chair, the chamber was completely still. Even empty courtrooms aren't as quiet. I began with a direct examination that consisted of simple, short questions to which he gave even shorter answers. Nothing to object to, no opportunity to interrupt the narrative or throw the witness off. Gravano's eyes were locked on mine, and I'd arranged for familiar FBI faces to be behind me in the gallery, in his sightline. After a few minutes I asked him whether he was on his own when we arrested him. He said no, he was with John Gotti and Frank Locascio.

"Do you see them here in the courtroom?"

"Yes."

"Would you point them out?"

He gestured toward the defense table, which was crowded with five lawyers in addition to the two defendants.

"John is sitting over there next to Krieger, and Frankie is sitting in the back with a blue suit."

When he indicated them, Locascio tried to rattle him by baring his front teeth and tilting his head back. He looked deranged, and I decided to draw attention to it.

"Frankie is the one who is smiling at you right now?"

The jurors laughed. "Yes." Locascio wiped the wolverine look off his face and we never saw it again.

Gravano grew increasingly confident. I'd structured his testimony so we'd get through the decision to kill Castellano and the preparations for the Sparks murders before the end of the day. Efforts to shape a witness's testimony don't always work, but this one did. Just as I reached the moment where Gravano and Gotti were parked across Third Avenue and Castellano was driving by, the judge asked if it was a convenient point to break.

The trial was unique in countless ways, one of which was the care of the star witness. In time, other gangsters would begin to flip in large numbers, including underbosses and even bosses. Gravano, though, broke a mold, and a horde of dangerous men wanted him dead. The FBI and the marshals saw that risk and they took sizeable precautions.

During the days that a witness is on direct, a prosecutor is free to speak with him in the evenings to prepare the next day's testimony. When the witness is incarcerated, that meeting usually happens in the prosecutor's office and the agents return the prisoner to the detention center when it's over. However, there was no way Sammy Gravano would be brought to my office. It was too dangerous, and we needed to find another strategy.

At the end of Gravano's first day on the stand, George Gabriel drove me to a heliport on the Hudson River in Manhattan, where an FBI helicopter was waiting. As we walked toward it, the rotating rotors on its roof and tail were deafening. It was dark, and there was a man with headphones and a long light in each hand motioning us toward the passenger door. As I went to climb the steps, the man leaned over and shouted into my ear, "When you get out, make sure you turn right! If you turn left, you will be chopped to bits!" Good to know.

Gravano himself had been whisked out of court and taken to a military base in central New Jersey. My helicopter took us down the Hudson and over New York Harbor. We were given helmets wired for sound. As we passed the Statue of Liberty, the pilot turned and hovered. We were level with and about a hundred feet from Lady

Liberty's face, paying some kind of homage to her. This was apparently a long-standing tradition for helicopters, and the pilot's voice came through my helmet in an effort to explain its origins. It was all wasted on me. "Right, not left; right, not left," I kept repeating to myself.

The next morning Gravano's testimony was riveting. Castellano, he explained, was headed to Sparks to meet with a group of captains and soldiers. One, Frank DeCicco, was in on the plot to kill him, and he told Gotti and Gravano in advance that the meeting would happen. There were four shooters: Eddie Lino, Fat Sally Scala, John Carneglia, and Vinnie Artuso. They waited on the sidewalk not far from the front door to Sparks, ready to close in from different angles as soon as their prey arrived.

Tony Roach Rampino was directly across 46th Street. Joe Watts, Angelo Ruggiero, and Iggy Alogna, a longtime member of the crew at the Bergin, were up the block toward Second Avenue. The four of them, along with Gravano, in the car with Gotti across Third Avenue, would be backup shooters should anyone try to interfere. As Gravano put it to the jury, "We had Sparks Steak House sandwiched in."

Each of the men had a walkie-talkie, so when Bilotti stopped his car at the red light, just a few feet to the right of Gotti and Gravano, Gravano told the shooters and backups to get ready.

The murders happened quickly. Castellano was dead within seconds of the car pulling up. He was in the process of getting out of the car when the shooters descended on him. By the time the shooting began, Bilotti had already gotten out on the driver's side and "squatted down to look through the window," Gravano testified. "And then somebody came up behind him and shot him. He was actually watching Paul get shot."

From across the street, Gravano was watching the dozens of other people on the scene. The murders took place at the busiest time of day at one of the busiest spots in the city. If any of the many commuters or tourists or neighborhood residents had tried to help Castellano or Bilotti, Gravano would have raced from his car and killed that person if Rampino or one of the other backups hadn't done so already. The same would have been true if there'd been a cop on the scene who attempted to intervene.

Castellano was dead, but in the crucial hours after the killings Gotti still had to seize control of the Family. Two nights later, all the captains were summoned to a restaurant on the Upper East Side. They sat around a table in the basement. Gravano and Ruggiero, who both had guns, stood on opposite sides of the room for intimidation purposes. Gotti had Joe N. Gallo, the Gambino consigliere at the time, do the talking. The captains were assured they were safe. Castellano had been killed, Gallo said, although nobody knew who'd killed him. Not a single person believed this, but everyone knew why it was being said.

"There's a Commission rule about killing a boss," Gravano testified. "And we weren't ever going to admit it. We could never tell the truth as far as killing Paul." Official messages were sent to the other Families that the Gambino Family weren't at odds, that there'd be no war within it, and that the other Families shouldn't get involved.

Two weeks later the captains met again. Once more, Gallo presided. "They talked about electing a new boss," Gravano testified. "I believe Frankie DeCicco got up and nominated John. They went right around the table. Everybody nominated John."

The witness was clear, matter-of-fact, confident. The silence that had descended on the courtroom the moment Gravano took the witness stand the day before endured. As we reached the end of his testimony about the Castellano murder, however, an older, modestly dressed woman burst though the rear doors of the room and ran up the center aisle of the spectator section. She screamed, "He killed my sons! I want to spit in his face!" FBI agents and deputy marshals intercepted her before she could get into the well of the courtroom.

The woman was Anna Carini. She had two sons who'd been associated with the Colombo Family and been murdered. They weren't among Gravano's victims, but she thought they were, hence the dramatic scene. I immediately looked at the jurors, who were startled and frightened. The sudden noise alone was unsettling, and the sight of the poor woman screaming bloody murder made it far worse. To a person, they were looking at me, not the judge, for what to do next. I began to ask the judge to send them back to the jury room, which he did even before I could finish my request. They looked fine as they filed out, and I felt good about their reaction.

Gravano was an almost unimaginably good witness. He made no effort to minimize his crimes, and was aided in his attitude by a deep-seated belief that they were all justified by "the life." Even the murders; "they broke our rules," he testified, and by breaking the rules of the life they'd chosen they had it coming.

His testimony made it seem as if he were still part of that life. Anyone who dropped in on the trial without knowing how Gravano had ended up on the witness stand would think he was still the underboss, and that once his testimony was over he'd go back to his daily routine.

Krieger's cross made Gravano an even more devastating witness. The lawyer spent an eternity on the DiBono murder, trying to establish a convoluted tax-related reason why Gravano wanted to postpone the killing of DiBono for almost a year, only then to whack him entirely on his own. The strategy was ill-advised to begin with, because it made almost no sense, but what made it fail spectacularly was that Gravano knew more about taxes than Krieger. Having tried for months without success to make a tax case against Gravano, I'd already gone through what was now happening to Krieger, but at least my confusion about the tax laws occurred in the privacy of the grand jury room. Krieger was being embarrassed in public and in front of the jury. Gravano corrected his misunderstandings about the personal liability of business owners for company taxes, about subchapter S corporations, about the tax liability that would flow to DiBono's estate if he died, and about how taxes were levied on a successful construction project. More than anything else, he confounded the defense by being respectful throughout. For more than an hour, Gravano patiently showed the jury that he was actually trying to help Krieger understand how corporate tax liability worked.

Another ill-advised defense strategy related to the murders of Castellano and Bilotti. The Ravenite recordings handed Krieger a defense on a silver platter: Gotti had repeatedly denied involvement in those murders in conversations he had no idea were being recorded. It rarely gets better than that for a defense lawyer, but instead of focusing on those statements Krieger grilled Gravano about whether they checked parking restrictions on 46th Street in advance, or thought about the risk that the getaway route might be blocked by another motorist, and about the oddity of the shooters wearing identical clothing. When a theme finally began to emerge, it seemed as if Krieger were suggesting that no one would ever try to commit murders where Castellano and Bilotti were killed, or when, or in that way.

"I don't get it," Gabriel whispered to me. "There were two dead guys outside Sparks, and there were an awful lot of shots fired for it to be a double suicide."

Krieger also had odd ways of expressing himself that made him seem out of touch, and Gravano handled it perfectly. Krieger thought it implausible that Gotti and Gravano would take the time to check the bodies to be sure they were dead, and suggested that real murderers would have raced away from the scene as fast as possible. Mocking Gravano's testimony that they drove steadily across Third Avenue and slowed down even more to eyeball Bilotti, Krieger asked sarcastically, "You looked out the car and said, 'By gosh! Tommy Bilotti is dead'?"

"Without the 'by gosh,'" Gravano answered, deadpan.

The cross lasted nine days. Less than halfway through it was clear to everyone in the courtroom that here was a devastating witness and that no amount of questioning would change that.

I could see—and hear—that the Gotti supporters were distressed by Gravano's performance. It was mid-March and the weather was warming up outside, but the courthouse heating system was still in full winter mode. During breaks in the trial and at lunchtime, the usual contingent of wiseguys—including Tony Moscatiello from the famous Buddy My Balls recording, Jackie Nose, Carlo Vaccarezza, and Peter Gotti—made camp in the stairwell landing, down the hall from Judge Glasser's courtroom. They propped open the steel doors to the hallway then went down to the lower floors and propped open those doors too, creating a breezeway out in the stairwell. Somehow they managed to find chairs too, most likely by smooth-talking the clerk's office employees whose rooms were near the stairwell. I'd pass them on the way to the restroom or elevator and admire their resourcefulness. They'd turned the stairwell landing into an impromptu social club, with its own air-conditioning, and no one was about to tell them to move along.

Moscatiello was gregarious and friendly by nature, so he'd talk to me as I got near. "John, he's killing us!" he said on one of my passes. "We're not even touching him." He had his arms crossed behind his head, and his entire body was stretched out across two chairs as if to catch as much of the breeze as possible.

The others with him had never spoken to me before and I could tell that wouldn't change, but they were muttering their agreement. There was a strong feeling of collective disappointment, as if they'd backed the wrong man in a prizefight. They acted as though someone had guaranteed that Krieger and Cardinale would destroy Gravano, and were now realizing that wouldn't happen.

Midway through Krieger's cross-examination I decided we should wind things up as soon as we could. Although I'd saved the Vastola murder conspiracy as a fallback, I no longer wanted any distance between Gravano's testimony and resting our case.

The defense lawyers helped out by crossing him extensively on his testimony that their clients had agreed to kill Vastola. That enabled me on redirect to play almost all of Book Seven, the last of the Ravenite recordings. Instead of employing the tapes as a buffer between Gravano and resting, I seized the opportunity to keep him on the stand even longer. He didn't disappoint. He remained patient and straightforward and followed my instruction that he treat the defense lawyers courteously even when they tried to paint him as a maniacal, lying serial murderer.

Building the Vastola predicate into Gravano's redirect left only a bunch of miscellaneous recordings, a couple of days of surveillance testimony, and our tax case. We rested on March 23. The defense lawyers announced a witness roster that bordered on a joke. Corky Vastola would testify that as far as he knew nobody schemed to kill him. Before the parallels to Romual Piecyk could sink in, the judge precluded the testimony as irrelevant, and he did the same with regard to a different witness who'd allegedly hypnotized Gravano. Next was an "expert" who, they argued, would testify to what Gotti really said on the recordings, as opposed to what we'd set forth in our transcripts. But the tapes were there for the jury to listen to, and there's no such thing as an expert listener. The defense was free to propose its own transcripts, and it did just that, but which side's versions more accurately captured the spoken words was obviously not the proper subject of expert testimony. "What, does this guy have really big ears or something?" Cotter said.

The judge refused to allow this as well, and Cardinale responded by jumping out of his chair and yelling at him. Gotti of course loved this, but the judge didn't and ruled Cardinale in contempt of court on the spot, although he delayed sentencing him until the trial concluded.

Only one of the proposed defense witnesses was permitted to testify, and he was called to rebut our tax evidence. We'd charged Gotti and Locascio with agreeing to help Gotti defraud the IRS. The defense called a tax "expert," Murray Appelbaum, an obscure tax preparer who testified that any person who thought they might be under investigation had a constitutional right to refuse to file tax returns. That was laughably contrary to law, so Cotter had fun with him on cross. I wanted to get the case to the jury and didn't care much about the tax count, so I kept handing Cotter notes telling him to wrap it up. But Appelbaum was such a bad witness Cotter couldn't help himself and kept boxing him around. My notes got increasingly impatient until I walked up to the podium and handed him a yellow Post-it saying, "END THIS FUCKING CROSS!" That finally did the trick.

All the while Gotti's hostility to me was relentless and palpable. He loved the needle-to-the-arm gesture and used it whenever I made eye contact with him in front of the jury. "Your mother's a whore," I'd hear when I passed his table on the way to sidebars. He'd disparage me to his sycophants in the Family row while we argued up at the sidebar, his voice just loud enough for the jury to hear. Jamie Orenstein remained in his seat and so heard it all, and from time to time we complained to the judge.

At one point Judge Glasser warned Gotti that if he kept up his nonsense he'd watch the rest of the trial from the bullpen in the basement. The next morning a small but conspicuous camera appeared on the witness stand, aimed at the witness. A wire out of the back of it went down to the floor and disappeared beneath the carpet. I had little doubt that wire went nowhere, but it had a significant placebo effect—another excellent move by the judge, who to our team seemed to be in total control.

We lost one of our jurors just before we rested. Midway through the trial, the judge had begun to permit conjugal visits from spouses and significant others. After one such visit, the marshals found a note in a bag the juror had given her husband. It bore the names and telephone numbers of the other jurors. The attempt to compromise their anonymity got her excused.

CHAPTER 36

SUMMATIONS

It was time for my summation. There'd been enough distraction over the six weeks of the trial that I felt the need to orient the jury to its task. My introductory lines were spontaneous, but they had traction at least with the media, because they were quoted in a *Sunday Times* editorial three days later:

> This is not a media event. This is not a movie. It's not about movie stars. This is not a stage for oratory. This is a trial in an American courtroom.

I warned them that what I was about to say would at times be boring, because trials are about evidence and sometimes walking through the evidence gets detailed and tedious. I then had the most enjoyable seven hours in my professional life. I walked the jury through the evidence that the Gambino Family existed, how it worked, and how it bore no resemblance to the popular conception of the Mafia as some sort of quasi-governmental force run by men of honor. They were backstabbing, treacherous thieves, and worse. They killed people. I discussed in detail our proof of every one of the predicates, and gave what amounted to thirteen separate summations, piecing together our evidence on each racketeering act, with timelines, exhibits, and recorded conversations.

Interspersed between those mini-summations were collections of miscellaneous pieces of evidence that helped place in context the crimes charged. Jamie Orenstein had pulled together all the statements recorded over the years about the money flowing up to John Gotti. Many were innocuous standing alone, but the compilation of the tribute from labor racketeering, the birthday gifts of tens of thousands of dollars in cash, the even larger Christmas present payments, and income from sources like gambling businesses was astounding—multiple millions in cash per year to Gotti alone. But whereas the jurors paid taxes on all their income, Gotti told the IRS he earned only modest amounts as a zipper salesman and by spotting potential job locations for a plumbing company. Orenstein prepared a similar collection of offhand comments about murders: Gotti reminiscing about "pieces of work" he was given in the past; why certain dead gangsters "got sick"; who could be trusted to be sent at night to split someone's head with an axe. We had powerful evidence of the racketeering acts, but these presentations were a kind of connective tissue. They allowed us to show holistically what a dangerous and demented enterprise these men ran.

I finished by telling the jury that the FBI's bug up in the Ravenite apartment opened a window into organized crime in New York. And even with that window opened for just the six hours during which we overheard conversation, the jury was able to see how pervasive and varied the criminal activity of these Families had become.

"If you listen to the tapes again," I told the jury, "based on that evidence alone you can and should convict on all the charges. If you have Gravano's testimony read back to you, based on that evidence alone you can and should convict."

It was now the defense's turn. Tony Cardinale summed up first, and it was one big attack—not on the evidence and not on our case, but on me. Some lawyers work themselves into a frenzy during summations. Cardinale started out full throttle, so much so that he had to apologize to the jury for his obvious state of agitation.

"What you see, ladies and gentlemen, is outrage, outrage at what the government is trying to do. And when I say the government," he snarled, pointing at me, "I refer to him." He quoted President Kennedy's admonition that the government must not abandon integrity and fairness just to achieve a desired result, then said, "His name, Mr. Gleeson's name, is John Get-John-Gotti-at-any-cost Gleeson!"

The rest of the summation was constructed around the theme that I'd "framed" the defendants. "When the stakes are this high, ladies and gentlemen, when careers, when ambition are at stake, you can't expect that everything is going to be absolutely by the letter, that everything is going to be totally fair. Use your own common sense. If you think of the blind ambition of Watergate or of the incredible arrogance of Iran-Contra."

He was on a roll. "This prosecutor," Cardinale bellowed, pointing his finger in my face, "will do anything it takes to win this case." My name was mentioned every few seconds. "This entire production is wrapped up and put together by this man, Mr. Gleeson. He wants to put his credibility on the line like that? Good, it's on the line."

The approach couldn't have been more improper, but I intended to deal with it in rebuttal, so I sat poker-faced. However, the judge had no interest in waiting, and even though there was no objection he summoned Cardinale to approach.

"I don't think it's professional," he told Cardinale, "and I think you ought to reconsider what it is that you're doing—attacking Mr. Gleeson personally. I think it's wrong. I think it violates the fundamental canons of professional responsibility, as well as every protocol that I'm aware of in connection with summations."

Cardinale said nothing in response and returned to the podium, where he just continued his rant. He said I'd told Gravano to make up a reason why Gotti would deny the Castellano murder. I prosecuted Mike Coiro and then, after he got fifteen years, immunized him and called him at trial. "It's just astounding!" Cardinale railed.

It all fell flat.

In the only part of his summation that wasn't a personal attack, he focused on one snippet of the Vastola recordings. Instead of telling Gravano, "We whack this kid," Cardinale argued at considerable length that what Gotti actually said was "We *ain't* whacking this kid." It was absurd. For a start, the argument implicitly conceded that one of Gotti's routine tasks was deciding whom to kill, a dangerous item to focus the jury on in a murder case. Also, Cardinale acted as though if he kept saying his version of Gotti's words over and over, it would become true. But the recording remained stubbornly the recording, and Gotti did *not* say those words. Finally, the argument did not even try to reconcile Cardinale's version of Gotti's words with the entire conversation. He did not deny that Gotti hated Vastola, thought he might be a rat, wanted him dead, thought it necessary to kill him "before he died of old age," and spoke to the boss and underboss of the DeCavalcante Family about killing him. Against that undisputed backdrop, it wouldn't make any sense for Gotti to say, "We ain't whacking this kid." But this performance wasn't about making sense.

Krieger followed, and he tried a different tack. Attacks on Gleeson were over; I was now a "skilled, professional" advocate. Krieger's focus was exclusively on Krieger. He started with his role as defender of the accused: "I walk through that door ten feet tall, three axe handles wide across the chest, my eyes shooting lightning, my voice is thunder."

They were obviously opening lines he'd delivered many times before, and they might have been an effective way to get the jury to snap to attention if he hadn't seemed so beaten down by the trial. Delivered without much feeling, they invited scrutiny instead. Krieger was actually not even six feet tall; he was much wider in the belly than in the chest; he had tired eyes; and his heart was not in it. The jurors looked at him not with awe but with a mix of commiseration and bemusement.

Krieger said he was the best there was, "liberty's last champion." The best, he told the jury, "is not measured in terms of IQ. The best is measured in heart and soul and dedication and principle and integrity."

What followed was a summation that continued Krieger's insistence on stilted, formal language. There are no doubt juries somewhere that find his kind of erudition impressive, but not in Brooklyn. His argument that the jury should disregard the murder admissions in the Ravenite apartment went as follows: those admissions "show John Gotti speaking in terms that are so confused as to pronouns that it may be more than passingly difficult on analysis to understand exactly what he's saying." The jurors' faces conveyed that they found it more than passingly difficult to understand what *Krieger* was saying. When I got up for rebuttal, I put the enlarged transcript of the conversation before the jury. "Let's see," I argued, "let's take a look at the pronouns. 'I whacked him' equals 'I whacked him.' 'I was in jail when I done it' equals 'I was in jail when I done it.'" The jurors were polite, but they were holding back laughs.

Many of Krieger's mistakes remained the result of coming into the case late. One pillar of his summation was the bargain we'd struck with Gravano. Krieger said we'd forced the twenty-year cap down the *judge's* throat. "All the court can do, maybe gagging at nineteen murders, is impose twenty years." But the transcript of Gravano's guilty plea made it clear that rather than wait until his sentencing to obtain the judge's approval—the typical practice—we'd specifically asked for it then, and received it. When I pointed that out in rebuttal, Krieger objected, but he couldn't conceal his embarrassment. He was a much better lawyer than this trial made him appear.

His awkward diction blunted the argument he might have made based on Gotti's repeated denials that he'd murdered Castellano. He returned to an obscure image he'd used in his opening statement: "Sometimes in very expressive and harsh terms they make reference to Castellano, and there are also, as you know, statements of denial of any participation or knowledge or aiding and abetting in the homicides of Mr. Castellano and Mr. Bilotti, on the tape coming from the apartment, coming from that sanctum sanctorum—I'll use my phrase again. Yes, I did refer to it in that fashion in my opening." The jurors cocked their heads sideways, none the wiser.

My rebuttal, which occupied more than two hours, consisted mostly of hitting the softballs the two lawyers had served up. When the defense summations weren't attacking me or the deal with Gravano, I said, they were full of misrepresentations, and I called each one out. In response to Cardinale's claim that we gave Gravano access to our surveillance evidence, I said: "Not true. Mr. Cardinale made that up." And then I told them why he'd lied—because our surveillance evidence, like Kenny McCabe's observations at Tali's the night of the Milito homicide, made it so clear that Gravano was telling the truth.

Cardinale became almost a stooge for me. Each time I called him out he popped out of his chair to complain. About an hour in, the judge held another sidebar to try to protect Cardinale from himself: "Let me just say this, Mr. Cardinale. I don't think I ever presided at a case where I've heard as many objections during the course of summation as I have in this one. It's just bad form. I really had no notion of the extent to which you just ignore ordinary protocol of professional behavior in a courtroom. For you to have jumped up and made the speech you did during the course of the government's summation is something that I never heard of in eighteen years on the bench."

I wondered what the jurors thought the judge was telling Cardinale. They must have guessed he was being reprimanded. When I started up again, I brought them back to our main theme. As recently as ten weeks before the trial began, we'd been ready to convict Gotti and Locascio of every charge based solely on their recorded statements. Gravano's testimony amounted to icing on the cake, an extremely useful addition to our evidence but in fact unnecessary.

The real significance of Gravano flipping, I told the jury, would be felt not by the defendants on trial but by the numerous other criminals we'd convict because of his cooperation. "Mr. Krieger says Gravano's plea agreement gives him a sick feeling. This is fine; it gives a sick feeling to all of the people on that chart too," I said, pointing at the eight-foot-high poster, which had the photographs of the eighteen captains. "And all of the people in the Gambino Family and all of the people in the administrations of the other four crime Families in New York, about whom Gravano has provided information and testimony and who will be convicted based on his testimony. It gives them all a sick feeling. They are next."

And then I sat down.

There wasn't much time between the completion of summations and the verdict, but our team spent it well. George Stamboulidis was ready with the Vic Orena case, and on April 1 Orena and Patty Amato were arrested for the murder of Tommy Ocera and other crimes. The case was assigned to Chief Judge Jack Weinstein. After Judge Glasser instructed the Gotti jury and it began deliberating, we went up to Judge Weinstein's courtroom for the arraignment.

As Cotter, Ward, and I sat in the spectator section, I reflected on how far our Organized Crime Section had come. We were about to convict John Gotti. We now had in custody Orena, the acting boss of the Colombo Family. In a couple of months we would be trying Vic Amuso, the Lucchese boss, in the Windows Case we'd inherited from the disbanded Strike Force, an extortion scam where the mobsters charged a $1–2 "tax" for every window replacement in New York City's public housing projects. All the cases were strong, well investigated, and staffed with first-rate attorneys. I had twenty lawyers in the section, and we were all in our twenties or thirties. We were already riding high, and we had at least a dozen Gotti spin-off cases ahead of us. We were engaged together in something hugely worthwhile, and it would bind us together for the rest of our lives.

The next morning Cotter and Orenstein asked me if they could go out to lunch across the park with Neil Ross. It wasn't as if the lawyers in my section typically had to ask my permission for such things. They asked because when juries reach a decision judges usually take the verdicts right away, and the entire trial team should be there. They wanted my take on whether we might get a verdict before they returned.

The jury had been deliberating for about five hours. The conventional wisdom is one day of deliberations for each week of evidence, and we'd had six weeks. I thought there was no chance we'd get a decision that day, let alone before early afternoon, so I granted the request. We'd been cooped up in the courthouse all day every day since jury selection in January, so it was good for them to get out. Besides, Ross had a beeper, so I could alert him if necessary.

A half hour later Ethel Cohen called to tell me there was a verdict, and the judge wanted to take it right away. I was alone in my office, and my mind raced. Conventional wisdom says a lightning-quick verdict is not good for prosecutors. Before jurors consign a defendant to life behind bars they tend to go over all the evidence carefully. I knew our case had gone in as well as I could possibly have hoped, but the speed of the verdict still rattled me. I immediately thought of the gamble I'd made by leaving Castellano's niece on the jury. She seemed impressive and strong, but reading jurors during a trial is like reading tea leaves. When the foreperson stood up in Judge Nickerson's courtroom Diane and I were sure we'd hear guilty verdicts. Instead we were crushed.

Castellano's niece, our foreperson, would be standing up in a couple of minutes in Judge Glasser's courtroom. If we were crushed again, how would I respond to criticism that I'd made a mistake keeping her on the jury?

I thought about what it would mean for law enforcement if John Gotti walked out the front door of our courthouse again, as he had five years earlier. We had such strong evidence, and it was hard to believe anyone else could build a better case. This would be the fourth failed prosecution of him in five years. If he beat this one, there was good reason to believe the Teflon Don would never be convicted. We'd have inoculated him for good. He was only fifty-one years old.

I also thought about what an acquittal would mean for me personally. I'd be forever known as the guy John Gotti beat *twice*, the lawyer who on two occasions had failed to prove that the most flamboyant and public mob boss in history had committed even a single crime. The rest of my career wasn't going to be pretty if an acquittal awaited me.

At the same time, I knew I could be headed in a few minutes to an event that would alter my career just as dramatically in the other direction. This was the most important case in the country, again. If the verdict was guilty, that would redeem me for the 1987 acquittal. Plus, I had a juror from that case under a sealed indictment. We'd already convicted Matt Traynor of perjury. If we could convict Gotti and that juror, all my loose ends from that first trial would be tied up.

I called Andy Maloney to tell him we had a verdict and that I'd meet him in the courtroom. Then I rang Laura Ward and asked her to walk over with me. I got no answer from Cotter, and then it hit me that I'd let him go to lunch with Orenstein and Ross. This put me into a panic. Cotter and Orenstein had worked nonstop for months and deserved to see the result. I'd obviously made a mistake letting them go out. As long as Andy and I were there, the judge would take the verdict. He wouldn't care if other members of our team weren't.

Ross's beeper allowed me to enter a phone number for him to call me back. I wasn't going to be there when he did, and wanted to convey the urgency of the situation. I plugged in my extension—"7038"—which he certainly knew by heart. I followed that with "911" to communicate the emergency.

Across the park, Cotter, Orenstein, and Ross were enjoying their first leisurely lunch in months. They were in a diner, but it seemed like a fancy restaurant to them after the ordeal of the trial. Ross felt the beep and looked at the readout.

"703-8911," he said. "I have no idea who that is."

They discussed whether 703 was even a New York exchange. It was a Virginia area code, Neil Ross observed, but the beep showed only seven numbers. Finally, it hit Cotter.

"Holy shit! It's Gleeson! He's 7038, and the '911' means it's an emergency. We must have a verdict!"

The press had obviously been notified because there were far too many reporters for the courtroom to hold, and the corridor outside was jammed. They stepped aside for Laura Ward and me to get in. Andy was already there, as were the FBI agents and defense counsel. The judge directed the deputy marshals to bring in Gotti and Locascio. It looked as if Cotter and Orenstein were going to miss the great moment, but just as the judge's case manager was bringing in the jury they and Neil Ross came rushing in.

Judge Glasser asked Castellano's niece to stand. Because the RICO count was the first one on the verdict sheet and the murder of Paul Castellano was the first racketeering act within the RICO, the first words out of her mouth would tell us if we'd convicted Gotti of killing Castellano. That was both our weakest and most important charge, and everyone knew that if he were pronounced guilty of that we'd likely convict him of all fourteen of the crimes with which we'd indicted him.

The case manager asked the obligatory question. "Has the jury reached its verdicts?"

"Yes," Castellano's niece replied.

"On Count One, Racketeering Act One, the murders of Paul Castellano and Tommy Bilotti, how does the jury find as to John Gotti, proven or not proven?"

If Castellano's niece was nervous, she did an excellent job of hiding it. She paused a moment, and though she held the verdict sheet in her hand she didn't look at it. She focused directly on the judge. The packed courtroom was taut with anticipation but perfectly silent.

"Proven," she said, in a strong, clear voice. Most of the reporters bolted for the half dozen phone booths in the corridor, but the verdicts kept coming: all thirteen racketeering acts proven, guilty on the RICO counts, guilty on all the other counts as well. A clean sweep. As each verdict was read I thought of all the not guilty verdicts I'd had to sit through just five years earlier. A wave of vindication and redemption washed over me.

Once the jury filed out, Judge Glasser turned to Cardinale and asked him whether he was ready to be sentenced for his contempt. We'd actually forgotten about that. "It doesn't get any better than this," I whispered to Andy Maloney. Krieger convinced the judge, without any objection from me, to delay any punishment of Cardinale, and the judge eventually rescinded the contempt citation.

Andy convened a press conference down in the large conference room in the basement offices of our General Crimes Section. The whole trial team joined him at the podium, as did George Gabriel, Bruce Mouw, and Jim Fox, the head of the New York office of the FBI. It was a lovefest. The moment the verdict was announced the press pivoted. During the trial the journalists had ignored us and shamelessly sucked up to Gotti. Now he was history, and all of a sudden we were media darlings. Jim Fox had some good lines that someone had obviously thought up ahead of time. "The Teflon is gone," he said, "the Don is covered with Velcro." Andy spoke briefly, thanking the FBI for its assistance. I didn't fully appreciate until I watched him at the podium how much of his own time and reputation he'd invested. The acquittals five years earlier happened at the beginning of his tenure as U.S. Attorney. He'd devoted himself to redeeming the office, and now he'd succeeded. True to form, he was low-key, but it was obvious that a great weight had been lifted off him.

I followed Andy, and as I approached the microphone I saw the General Crimes AUSAs jammed into the room, way in the back. They were all new to the office since the acquittals. My first thought when I saw them was of the party Andy had thrown in his office on the day of those acquittals to comfort Diane and me after such a humiliating ordeal. I felt we'd lost that first case as an office, and so I said we'd just won the second one the same way, as a single team that had pulled together. My trial team was ecstatic. Together with George Gabriel and the other agents, we all felt the exhilaration that came with knowing we'd accomplished something momentous. I got a bunch of "how does it feel?" questions, and someone asked who I thought would play me in the movie.

The trial team, minus Andy, left the courthouse to celebrate in an Irish bar on Montague Street, the commercial strip in Brooklyn Heights. Quite a few AUSAs, the entire Gambino Squad, and my wife, Susan, joined us. One of the agents, who'd joined the squad well after the first case but had heard much about it and the schism it produced with our office, asked me to explain. I told him about Willie Boy and the bizarre pretrial hearing in which someone in the FBI helped the defense by secretly providing confidential information from an FBI personnel file to Jerry Shargel. The agent couldn't comprehend how the relationship with the office had gotten so bad that something like that would happen.

We talked about the jury selection in that first case, and how we'd had to scrap the panel after a month and start all over. It occurred to me for the first time that if I counted up all the days I'd spent either on trial or in pretrial hearings against John Gotti, they totaled well more than a full year.

When I arrived at my office the next morning I bumped into a guy on his way out with a handtruck. He had the refrigerator on it. "Well, that didn't take long," I said, but he looked at me as if he had no idea what I was talking about. A couple of hours later my phone rang; it was Diane Giacalone. She'd disappeared from my life after the first case, leaving the profession and the country as well, cutting off all ties with her former colleagues. She'd had close friends in the office before the acquittals, but had abruptly stopped communicating with all of them. She'd met a man from the Netherlands, married him, and was living in a suburb of Amsterdam, where she was raising their son.

No one appreciated more than she how satisfying the conviction must have been, and she warmly congratulated me. We had a long conversation about the Ravenite bugs and the flipping of Gravano. I told her about George Pape, the juror we knew as Oil Terminal Operator who'd taken a bribe to throw our case. There was no bitterness, no carping about the fact the FBI had information at the time that Gravano had a juror but was not about to help us out. She just wished me good luck.

Shortly after the trial ended, George Gabriel knocked on the front door of George Pape's home in East Norwich, New York. After a few seconds, a tired-looking man answered.

"Are you George Pape?" Gabriel asked.

"Yes," the man replied. "Who are you?"

"I'm George Gabriel. I'm with the FBI. I have a warrant for your arrest for obstructing justice when you were a juror in the trial of John Gotti."

Pape asked permission to go to the bathroom before being taken to the FBI offices in Queens for processing, then to court for arraignment. Gabriel checked out the room for weapons and escape routes before letting him in. Pape closed the door behind him.

A few seconds later Gabriel heard a long, primal scream from inside. Then Pape came out and said he was ready to go.

CHAPTER 37

LITTLE VIC; GEORGE PAPE

The sentencing of John Gotti that June was a fiasco. First, the famous civil rights lawyer William Kunstler showed up with his sidekick Ron Kuby. They promptly accused me of a crime. According to Kunstler, I was responsible for the dismissal of the sequestered juror who'd tried to smuggle identifying information about the other jurors out of the hotel during the trial. He accused me of sneaking into the jury room and planting the note so we could get rid of her. When I responded by saying he was making up facts— weird ones at that—he said: "The government doesn't come into any courtroom with clean hands." He likened me to an AUSA in another district who sent death threats to a magistrate judge, and also to an FBI agent who supposedly forged a letter to a juror in the Chicago Seven trial in the 1960s. It was way too absurd to get worked up about, and Judge Glasser gave him the back of his hand.

What happened next was a riot, literally. The courtroom proceeding was brief and unremarkable. Gotti and Locascio had to get life without parole, so I didn't make any sentencing pitch at all, and neither did the defense lawyers or their two clients, so in a matter of minutes the proceeding was over.

Outside the courthouse was a different story. Kunstler had organized a dem-onstration by several hundred junior wiseguys, many of them friends of John A. Gotti, our defendant's son. They convened in the park across the street and whipped themselves into a Free John Gotti frenzy. When they heard of the life sentence, they stormed the courthouse. They shouted at the deputy marshals in front of the doors, then turned over cars and continued their shouting from on top of the upside-down vehicles.

My office looked out over the entrance to the courthouse, so when I got back from the sentencing we all watched it. The building was closed for two full hours while the marshals and the NYPD quelled the riot and made arrests.

As if to demonstrate just how hilarious they can be even when they're trying hard to be tough and fearsome, the baby wiseguys had brought signs with them. There were "Free John" signs and "Justice for All" ones. The placard that stood out for me was held by a screaming young man on top of one of the overturned cars. It read, "Equanimity Under the Law!"

The moment Gravano stepped down from giving his testimony in Judge Glasser's courtroom, he was the most sought-after witness in the country. It seemed as if every federal law enforcement agency were calling me to ask to meet with him, and quite a few state ones as well. I should have anticipated it. Gravano had committed thousands of crimes with a wide array of people over a period of almost thirty years. He was smart, had a great memory, and presented himself well. Under the harsh glare of the Gotti case spotlight he'd proven himself an overwhelmingly effective witness. Agents, police, and prosecutors wanted to talk to him to see if maybe he could provide them with information about crimes within their jurisdictions.

Gravano himself was a good sport about all the attention. He even brought his sense of humor to the task. While in the Witness Protection prison facility in Phoenix he'd seen television ads for a local car dealer named Gambino. When we let Arizona law enforcement debrief him, Gravano casually told them, "We're into cars out here," which got them very excited. Before they rushed off to put the poor car dealer under a spotlight he told them he was just kidding.

In addition to having to answer legitimate requests to debrief Gravano, I had to deal with large numbers of people who simply wanted to meet him. Organized crime buffs are everywhere, including in state and local police departments and federal law enforcement agencies. Gotti's underboss had famously flipped and buried the Teflon Don with testimony that was universally regarded as devastating. Law enforcement officers, especially the experienced ones who appreciated what a phenomenon Gravano was, were naturally attracted to him. Even if there was no chance he had information that could be of assistance to them, they wanted to talk to Sammy the Bull.

And it wasn't just law enforcement. Members of Congress rightly saw Gravano as a klieg light opportunity for themselves. In the spring of 1992 I got a call from a staffer to the Senate Permanent Subcommittee on Investigations. Sam Nunn, the chair of the committee, and William Roth, the ranking minority member, wanted Gravano to testify about whether organized crime was involved in professional boxing.

"You're kidding me," I told the staffer. "Of course it is. You don't need Gravano for that. Besides, he's a critical law enforcement asset who will testify in at least ten more trials. There's no way I'm providing him so you can have a media circus on Capitol Hill."

Within a week I got a call from a lawyer I'd never heard of at Main Justice. He was in some kind of legislative affairs office, and he gently pleaded with me to reconsider my decision. "This is Sam Nunn," he said. "He can influence a lot of things. We're afraid that the appropriation for the DOJ in next year's budget might suffer if you tell them to pound sand when all they want is half an hour of Gravano."

"Listen to what you're suggesting," I told him. "The entire Department of Justice might suffer if Sam Nunn, William Roth, and the other senators on that committee don't get Gravano in their hearing room? They might retaliate by cutting the budget for all federal law enforcement if I don't cooperate with their effort to attract media attention to themselves? You know that's all this is about, right?"

"I know. You're right. But this is Washington. All I can say is this could be really important to the department. I'm sorry to put you in such a position, but they honestly couldn't care less about your other cases. They should, but they don't. They just want the witness and they're in a position to hurt us all if you refuse. Please."

It was the perfect approach. I was prepared to fight anyone who told me I had to produce Gravano, but I wasn't prepared for a guilt trip. Whoever this legislative affairs person was, he was a good lawyer, because somehow he was making *me* feel like the selfish one, even though it was all about some senators' desire for publicity. So I agreed to produce Gravano. The staffers and I would script the senators' questions. I would sit next to Gravano at the table in the hearing room to make sure the interrogation didn't stray too far afield.

Most of the requests to meet Gravano came from law enforcement, not the legislature, and I found myself spending way too much time managing my witness. It felt as if I were managing a top musician—except that one of the general rules I was stuck with was that members of federal law enforcement had to be given access to him for at least a short debriefing on demand. Actually calling him as a trial witness was something else again, and I had some leeway to push back on that, but for the most part George Gabriel and I had to produce Gravano for interviews by feds. State and local law enforcement didn't get the same treatment. With them, it was all case by case, and my general approach was that they had to have really convincing grounds unless we needed their goodwill for some other reason.

These debriefings were a litigation headache. If an FBI agent from Chicago debriefed our witness about something and created a report of the interview—an "FBI 302"—that became part of Gravano's file. Any errors in it could be used to cross-examine him in future trials. A mistake in the report could damage his credibility, even if it were solely the fault of the agent who wrote it. The last task we had time for was the policing of those interviews and making sure the reports were accurate. But because Gravano would testify in so many future trials we never stopped worrying about the land mines these debriefings would create.

That autumn we prepared the Orena case for trial. We had an impressive array of witnesses lined up, including Gravano and Al D'Arco, the former acting boss of the Lucchese Family. In addition, Stamboulidis and Andrew Weissmann, whom I'd assigned to the case, had flipped a handful of Colombo associates we would use.

A case so top-heavy with accomplice testimony is especially hard on defense lawyers. They can't cross-examine tape recordings but they can cross an accomplice. The preparation is extraordinarily time-consuming and the cross itself grueling. Orena was represented by Gus Newman, while Ben Brafman represented Patty Amato, his codefendant. (Evidently, Brafman had managed to retain the Mafia's good favor.) Brafman's pretrial motions included all the typical requests for relief, including a severance. There was no basis whatsoever to try them separately, but I saw an opportunity. Gus was sixty-five years old, Brafman twenty years younger. In a joint trial, the two lawyers would split up the work of crossing accomplices. I saw a tactical advantage in requiring Gus to do it all by himself, so we agreed to the severance.

"You're *joining* in the severance motion?" Brafman asked on the phone when he got our brief. "You guys never do that."

"Well, now we have," I said.

We picked the jury right after Thanksgiving. Judge Weinstein was determined to get the verdict on Orena before the holidays, so he pushed us hard. We were grateful we'd eliminated the time-consuming second cross-examinations by agreeing to sever the trial of Amato. Gus Newman was a legendary defense attorney and also a pleasure to deal with. He helped prove that I could try a mob boss for murder without the rancor and vitriol that characterized my two trials of John Gotti. I'd never thought the problem was me, but Gus put any such ideas to rest for everyone else.

Vic Orena was the same way. We shook hands every morning and evening, and exchanged pleasantries. When the jurors were in the room it was all business and the crosses were tough, but otherwise everything was cordial, even enjoyable.

Judge Weinstein was obviously impressed by Gravano. At one of the breaks he told the marshal not to remove the witness, and he spent the entire fifteen minutes talking to him privately up there at the bench. Gravano didn't mind. On the contrary, Judge Weinstein was a legend, so Gravano regarded the attention as evidence that he was no ordinary witness. He was proud of what he was doing.

Stamboulidis and Weissmann handled most of the prosecution and were excellent. We shared the three jury addresses and I handled the rebuttal summation. Judge Weinstein felt strongly that it gave an unfair advantage to prosecutors to allow them to work overnight on a rebuttal, so when Newman sat down at 9:00 p.m. on December 20, 1992, the judge turned to me and said, "Any rebuttal?" I pleaded with him to adjourn for the day because several of the jurors were nodding off after more than twelve hours in the box.

"No, go ahead," he said. Then he did something I'd never seen before. He went down into the jury box and sat in one of the empty alternate chairs. The jurors immediately perked up and paid close attention to a rebuttal that lasted an hour.

The next morning Vic Orena was convicted of the murder of Tommy Ocera and multiple other crimes.

During the Orena trial my team went to Washington to receive recognition for our work in the Gotti case. I knew Judge Weinstein wouldn't consider an award ceremony a good reason to take a break, so I didn't bother to ask, and Susan went with them instead.

We'd been nominated for the John Marshall Award on the theory that it was as important a case as the DOJ had ever won. However, Attorney General Bill Barr informed us that only I would get it; the rest of the team would receive the Distinguished Service Award instead. I said no way. We investigated and tried the case as a team and we all deserved the highest honor federal prosecutors can receive. For some unexplained reason the AG held firm, so I told them they could keep their John Marshall Award, and we all got the Distinguished Service Award instead, which is nothing to sneeze at.

Vic Orena acted like a gentleman toward me, but his son John, who was in the mob with him, was another story. It wasn't the best idea for him to sit in the back of the courtroom, allowing us to point to him as his name came up in testimony, and he was visibly fuming by the time George Stamboulidis and I pointed him out again during our summations. He didn't leave his anger in the courtroom. Just after Christmas I got a visit from an agent on the Colombo Squad. They had an ongoing investigation of John Orena, and on December 23 he was recorded speaking to Frank Lastorino, the Lucchese family consigliere. Fresh from his father's conviction on charges that would get him life in prison without the chance of ever being paroled, the younger Orena was defiant.

"We're going to keep fighting," he told Lastorino, "what the fuck. We can't stop fighting."

Lastorino agreed: "We can't give up like fucking lambs."

Then Orena expressed his rage at my summation. "You know, they fucking call you—they pointed at us, my brothers." If his father weren't on trial, Orena explained, "I would have jumped over, I would have looked to get locked up punching that mother-fucker in the face, pointing at us and saying things, this and that."

"Who's that," Lastorino asked, "that Gleeson?"

"Yeah."

"Cocksucker," Lastorino said.

"You know, this motherfucker couldn't shine my father's shoes, this fucking hard-on."

After playing the tape for me, the agent asked if I wanted protection again, but we both concluded that John Orena was no real threat. He was a fairly smart kid as wiseguys go, not the type to make the life-altering decision to retaliate against a federal prosecutor. He just needed to cool off. Besides, I was still beginning every day by being picked up at home by George Hanna. "If I see John Orena on the sidewalk in the next few weeks," I promised, "I'll cross the street."

The most interesting part of the Pape case was speaking to the other jurors from the first Gotti trial. Acquittals require unanimous votes—all twelve must vote not guilty—but only Pape was bribed. So why an acquittal, as opposed to a hung jury?

Almost all the other eleven jurors agreed to speak with me and Geoff Mearns, whom I assigned to try the case. It had been more than five years since the trial, and each of them knew from newspaper reports of the recent trial that we had claimed their jury was tainted by the bribe. But Mearns and I didn't know what to expect.

It was odd meeting them again. I'd spent seven months together with them in court without exchanging a word, and now we could talk about it all. To a person, they described their experience as one of the most significant events in their lives. Their week-long deliberations had been tense but always civil. No one thought at the time that Pape had been corrupted. Sequestered together in their hotel, a couple of them recalled him vehemently objecting to the two-drink maximum at dinner. That fit in with what we knew of him.

Pape had argued for acquittal throughout. He was focused like a laser on one element of our RICO charges that he felt strongly hadn't been proved: the so-called enterprise element. We hadn't charged our defendants with participating in the affairs of the Gambino Family. We'd charged them instead with engaging in the affairs of an enterprise consisting of two crews of the Family that answered to Dellacroce, the underboss. In other words, the indictment alleged, and therefore had to prove, a separate venture within the Gambino Family enterprise.

Pape, the other jurors told us, insisted during deliberations that even if the evidence showed that the defendants had participated in the affairs of the Gambino Family, they couldn't find beyond a reasonable doubt that there was this sub-enterprise consisting solely of two crews and the underboss. The other jurors were troubled by this argument. As it turned out, our weak proof of that element, combined with the fact that it seemed unlikely to the jurors that our defendants had admitted committing murders to a coffee boy like James Cardinali, resulted in the unanimous vote of not guilty. Pape was a corrupt juror but an educated one and we'd helped make his case.

Pape was tried alone. His friend Bosko, who'd delivered the bribe, was back in Serbia, assisting war criminal Radovan Karadzic in the Bosnian War. I testified at the trial. Because the original juror questionnaires had been destroyed, the one I'd created for Pape when he was questioned during jury selection became important. I enjoyed being a witness, especially against him. Gravano testified as well, and Geoff Mearns gave a terrific summation. The jury made short work of it and Judge Glasser sentenced Pape to three years in prison.

CHAPTER 38

THE SUPERSTAR

It's different traveling with someone so many people want to kill. For a start, you get your own plane. Gravano, George Gabriel, Alfie McNeil, and I were the only passengers on the FBI flight to Washington for the media event billed as a hearing on corruption in professional boxing before the Senate's Permanent Subcommittee on Investigations. Alfie was with the marshals and in charge of moving Witness Protection Program witnesses in New York. There was no waiting around, no line of people to stand behind, and no sitting on the tarmac waiting for clearance to take off. I thought this must be what it's like to be President. We even flew into Washington's Andrews Air Force Base.

Snarled in rush-hour traffic in the tunnel beneath the Capitol, the deputy marshal driving our too-wide security van used the shoulder, scraping off the side-view mirrors of a long line of cars. We were whisked through a back door into the Dirksen Senate Building and into a waiting area adjacent to a hearing room. While we waited, I could hear Sam Nunn outlining the strict security rules mandated by the Capitol Police. Everyone there had to remain seated during the entire time Gravano was in the room. There'd be no photographers allowed on the floor in front of the witness table. Anyone who tried to enter or leave the room once the meeting had started would be arrested.

They finally ushered in Gravano and me and we sat at the witness table. There were cameras everywhere and we were looking into blazing bright lights. Senator Nunn had Gravano take the oath and asked me if I was his lawyer. I made it clear that Gravano had a lawyer but it wasn't me; I was his prosecutor and the person who'd worked with the committee's staff to get Gravano to the hearing. I didn't want to look like his protector, but I wanted to get all the credit I could for our team.

Gravano told the senators that the Gambino Family had taken itself out of boxing by 1960, after the Rocky Marciano era. The purses were small, and as Gravano explained, "organized crime became more sophisticated. We got into unions, construction, shipping, garment, garbage, and they became more lucrative than the boxing industry." But he himself had been a boxer and had become friendly with Renaldo Snipes, the heavyweight good enough to have had a title fight with Larry Holmes, the WBC champion from 1978 to 1983. (I hadn't forgotten Snipes trying to intimidate jurors at the Gotti trial.) By the 1980s, purses for high-profile boxing matches had grown dramatically, so Gravano hatched a scheme involving Snipes.

The plot also involved Francesco Damiani, a heavyweight who was with an organized crime Family in Italy. Damiani was undefeated in Europe and the WBO heavyweight champ. The Gambinos were close to his Italian crew, and Gravano's plan was to arrange a big-money bout between Damiani and Mike Tyson. The setup would be a Damiani-Snipes fight. Damiani would earn a date with Tyson by beating Snipes in Donald Trump's Atlantic City hotel. For all this to work, two things had to happen: Snipes would have to be highly ranked; and once the fight with Damiani was arranged, Snipes would have to lose it.

To accomplish the first part, Gravano flew to Las Vegas to meet with Joey Curtis, a boxing referee who'd once visited the Ravenite. Gravano testified that Curtis said he'd get Snipes moved up the WBC rankings for $5,000—a 50 percent discount since it was a favor for John Gotti.

The second part was even easier. Gravano said he would tell Snipes to make it look good, but to lose the fight.

Senator Nunn's colleagues on the committee were William Roth of Delaware, John McCain of Arizona, and William Cohen of Maine. McCain and Cohen wondered how Gravano could be so sure Snipes would lose just because Gravano told him to. Gravano explained that he knew his man, and that there'd be some money in it for Snipes as well. Cohen, still perplexed, wondered why the boxer, whose career showed he was far from a whipping boy, wouldn't double-cross the wiseguys if he "smelled victory" in the middle of the fight. Then he asked, as though he were speaking to a lawyer, "What deterrent exists, either expressly or implicitly, to make sure someone lives up to an agreement?"

Gravano understood the legalese and was amused. He was smiling, but not disrespectfully. The deterrent, he responded, was "our whole background, John Gotti's and mine. I believe if he would have knocked him out by accident he would have picked him up."

The room broke out in laughter, including Cohen. The deadpan delivery brought to mind the Jacoby & Meyers line in Judge Glasser's courtroom. Gravano then took control of the hearing. He explained that the popular conception that mobsters threaten people to get their money was mostly wrong. "Organized crime, from what I have seen, has a history of sharing," he said. He wouldn't have had to bully Snipes any more than he'd have had to bully contractors who made him and Gotti millions in the construction industry. "It's a two-sided greed," he explained. The contractors who hired Gravano's companies got favors with the unions as a result, so everybody made money. Similarly, Snipes, by then in the twilight of his career, would get a good payday and a last hurrah. Gravano finished his account by saying how much respect he had for Snipes as a friend and a fighter.

The senators were eating it up, and Gravano was getting more and more confident. Cohen asked if there was anything the federal government could do to keep organized crime out of boxing.

"Make the purses very small," Gravano said, which got another round of laughter. Then Senator Roth said Joey Curtis, who'd already testified before the committee, had admitted visiting the Ravenite but claimed that there was nothing sinister about the club. It was an innocent call to a completely public place, Curtis had urged. Gravano, again amused, set the senators straight about the Ravenite: "It's the Gambino headquarters. If you want me to explain it slightly, there is a brick wall with almost no windows, a steel door with, at any given time, ten, fifteen guys standing outside, smoking cigars and stuff. I don't really think that's a sign that we're open to the public."

By then he owned the room. He was confident, engaging, and respectful, but he had no qualms about correcting the misimpressions of some of the most powerful people in America. The senators went far beyond the questions I'd helped their staffers script, but Gravano was so completely in charge I never even opened my mouth.

The AUSAs in my Organized Crime Section watched the testimony on television and were giddy about how impressive our witness had been. Apparently I had been in the camera shot with Gravano the entire time and my silence hadn't gone unnoticed. Above my office door was a newly printed sign that read "Chief, Potted Plants."

In late September of 1994, not quite three years after he first reached out to me, Gravano was sentenced. He'd testified in ten separate cases, and but for some defendants' decisions to plead guilty there would have been half a dozen more.

Since I was his prosecutor, I represented the government at the sentencing. Gravano had asked me about a hundred times over the years what I thought he'd get. I told him I had no idea, which was true. He couldn't receive more than twenty years, thanks to the cap I'd agreed to, but whether he'd get a sentence below that number, and if so how far below, was up to Judge Glasser. And since Gravano had admitted killing nineteen men, the judge would be fully justified in giving him all twenty.

Part of my job was to explain his accomplishments as a witness. The list was impressive. Three bosses, an underboss, and two consiglieres had already been convicted. The trial of Chin Gigante, boss of the Genovese Family, was still to take place, and he too would be convicted based on Gravano's testimony. Eleven captains had been convicted; another was forced from his union position. Fourteen made guys and some two dozen associates and corrupt union officials also went to prison. There was Bill Peist, Gotti's corrupt hook in the NYPD, and of course George Pape, the juror from the first trial. Even Bruce Cutler was convicted of contempt, though Gravano had no direct role in that one.

His contributions couldn't be measured solely in terms of convictions, I argued. His cooperation had led to a flood of additional cooperating witnesses. For example, Carmine Sessa, the consigliere of the Colombo Family, came to us and said he wanted Gravano's prosecutor, Gravano's lawyer, and Gravano's deal. Captains and made guys lined up to cooperate.

Normally, when someone flips, the word in the street is there was something wrong with him. "What we heard from the people who followed Gravano to become cooperating witnesses," I told the judge, "was that when he cooperated it did not indicate there was something wrong with Salvatore Gravano; it showed that there was something wrong with the mob. It was very much sort of an attitude adjustment, very much a turning point."

Though we were still churning out prosecutions, the mob was already on the road to obliteration. I'd brought to the hearing the same captains chart we'd used at trial, and this time I'd put red banners saying "convicted" over the photos of the men who'd gone to prison based on Gravano's cooperation. It was just another way of expressing what I was telling the court, but it was effective.

My presentation lasted an hour. I told the judge I felt an enormous responsibility because I was charged with representing the dozens of prosecutors and law enforcement officers who'd filled the courtroom, each one of whom had brought significant criminals to justice with Gravano's help. But I felt no nervousness, just pride, as I walked the judge through the extraordinary results we'd achieved.

Our sentencing submission attached various letters attesting to Gravano's usefulness. One came from Congress, applauding his "extremely valuable" testimony about organized crime's involvement in professional boxing. The letter was initially signed by a staffer but I called the committee and said since the request for Gravano's appearance had come directly from Sam Nunn and William Roth, they should sign the letter. To their credit, they sent another copy signed by the two of them. So Gravano had in his corner the chair and ranking member of the Senate Permanent Subcommittee on Investigations, attesting to his assistance of the Senate and the steps he'd taken "to make amends for his past criminal conduct."

The judge took it all in, and after I finished he described Gravano's cooperation as one of the bravest acts he'd ever seen. He went on at length about all the results Gravano's testimony had produced, many in his own courtroom. He described the need to encourage others to follow in Gravano's footsteps, and in large part to incentivize them he imposed a sentence of just five years in prison.

Gravano was blown away. With good time, he'd be released in a matter of months. His extraordinary cooperation had earned him unparalleled leniency. The sentence would spread through the prison system like wildfire. The flood of cooperation we'd already seen since Gravano flipped would soon become a tsunami. There were editorials both praising and excoriating the sentence. For years, judges who rewarded cooperation less leniently would hear complaints about how much better Sammy Gravano did.

As Gravano was being removed by the marshals, we both realized we might never see each other again. He was grateful, and thanked both me and Larry Krantz, who'd taken over his defense. We shook hands and I wished him good luck. That was it.

When I returned to my desk, there was a message from the White House. I knew what it was about. Less than a month earlier, Senator Pat Moynihan had introduced me at my confirmation hearing for a district judgeship. President Clinton had nominated me a few months before that. If confirmed, I'd become Judge Nickerson's and Judge Glasser's colleague. There was no doubt I'd be confirmed, and that had nothing to do with me. A grand total of one senator, Herb Kohl from Wisconsin, showed up for my confirmation hearing. He asked a few questions, and after it was over came down from the dais to shake my hand. "Pat Moynihan has put you forward. He's the chair of the Finance Committee," he told me. "There's no way you won't become a judge. Congratulations."

I returned the call and was informed that my nomination had been confirmed. As a direct result of John Gotti, I was a district judge at the age of forty-one. My life in crime had paid off.

EPILOGUE

I served as a United States District Judge in the Eastern District of New York for twenty-two years. In 2016 I left the bench to practice law at Debevoise & Plimpton, where I represent clients in civil and criminal matters, mediate and arbitrate disputes, and provide expert testimony all over the world regarding United States law. I teach Sentencing at New York University School of Law and Yale Law School and Complex Federal Investigations at Harvard Law School.

Andy Maloney stepped down as United States Attorney in December 1992, eight months after Gotti's conviction and one month after Bill Clinton was elected president. He practiced criminal defense in a small firm for many years and is now retired.

As mentioned earlier, Diane Giacalone left the law entirely not long after our trial together. She married and moved to the Netherlands, where she works at raising a son, Neils.

Mary Jo White left our office a year after John Gotti's conviction to become the first woman United States Attorney for the Southern District of New York. After her tenure in that position and a subsequent stint as chair of the Securities and Exchange Commission, she returned to Debevoise & Plimpton, where she and I are law partners.

George Gabriel left the FBI in 2006 after twenty-seven years with the Bureau, finishing his career as the agent in charge of the Long Island office. He joined the Virginia Beach office of the consulting firm WBB, where today he is a program director.

Laura Ward left the United States Attorney's Office in 1997, when she was appointed to the New York state bench. Judge Ward continues to serve as an Acting Supreme Court Justice in Manhattan.

Pat Cotter left the Eastern District in 1993 to teach at law schools in Cork, Ireland; Missoula, Montana; and Chicago, his hometown. He currently practices white-collar criminal defense in Chicago.

Jamie Orenstein became a member of the trial team that convicted Timothy McVeigh of the bombing of the Alfred P. Murrah Federal Building in Oklahoma City in 1995. After that he served as a magistrate judge in the Eastern District of New York until 2020, when he and his family moved to Maine, where he practices law.

George Hanna left the FBI in 2005 after thirty years of service. For ten years he was senior director of investigations for Major League Baseball, and then he worked as a director at the First Data Corporation. He is now retired.

Bob Morgenthau remained the Manhattan District Attorney until he stepped down in 2009. He joined the law firm Wachtell, Lipton, Rosen & Katz, where he remained until he died ten days shy of his one hundredth birthday in 2019.

Albert Krieger returned to his Miami law practice. We became good friends, and remained that way until his death in 2020 at age ninety-six.

Mike Coiro added to his prison time by testifying falsely at John Gotti's 1992 trial and subsequently pleading guilty to perjury. He was released from prison in 1998 and moved to Las Vegas, where he died in 2003.

Bruce Cutler was convicted of contempt of court based on his public statements in defiance of Judge Glasser's order. Sentenced to three months of house arrest, he bounced back and defended clients in other high-profile criminal cases. He remains a lawyer in New York.

Sammy Gravano was released in 1995 from the five-year term imposed by Judge Glasser and moved to Arizona. In 2000, he was arrested on charges of trafficking in ecstasy. He served a twenty-year sentence on those charges and now lives out west. I think of him every time I see a plastic kiddie pool.

John Gotti, despite his incarceration, remained the boss of the Gambino Family until he died of cancer in federal prison in 2002 at the age of sixty-one.

ACKNOWLEDGMENTS

I was given the opportunity to lead the successful trial of John Gotti by Andy Maloney, the United States Attorney in Brooklyn and my boss. The nastiness and personal attacks on me in the first trial would have provided a sound justification for keeping me away from the second one, and I'll go to my grave grateful to Andy for placing his trust in me instead.

I owe so much to the rest of the trial team—Assistant U.S. Attorneys Laura Ward, Pat Cotter, and Jamie Orenstein and FBI Special Agent George Gabriel. A trial that high-profile is a crucible, and we got through ours without even a single disagreement, which was a testament to their abilities and personalities. We're all close to this day.

The larger groups of which we were part were the Organized Crime Section in the Brooklyn U.S. Attorney's Office and the FBI's Gambino Squad. The other men and women in both played an essential role in dismantling organized crime in New York, and were a pleasure to work with as well.

In the first case, Diane Giacalone empowered me by giving me so much responsibility, and then taught me how to try a case. When a defense that started out as criminally misogynistic and then became just plain criminal resulted in across-the-board acquittals, she showed me and everyone what grace under pressure looks like.

Dean John C. Jeffries, Jr., has been my guardian angel in the legal profession since we first met at the University of Virginia School of Law in January 1978. All the good things that have happened to me as a lawyer and judge can be traced to him. At a critical juncture in the odyssey that led to the completion of the book, he and Dean Paul Maloney gave me space in the law school to work on the manuscript, for which I will always be grateful.

ACKNOWLEDGMENTS

I tried John Gotti first before Judge Eugene H. Nickerson and then before Judge I. Leo Glasser. All told, I was on trial against that one defendant in their courtrooms for more than a year. Great judges both, they first taught me how to be a trial lawyer, and then they taught me how to be a judge.

Susan Gleeson was my wife during the period covered by this book and for more than two decades afterward. There's no overstating how grateful I am to her. She was dragged through the mud in the first trial. Falsely accused of crimes by Gotti's defense witness and lawyers during that debacle, she might have objected to my getting back in the ring for round two. But, instead, she supported me throughout, all while excelling in her own profession. She then watched me labor over this book for way too long. It gives me special pleasure to thank her here.

I will never be able to determine whether my wife, Robin Wilcox, is my boss or my consigliere. But that's the way it should be, and she has performed her roles with great distinction. In the face of demands that have included mothering adolescent boys and being general counsel of a major New York law firm, she found the time to help me understand and describe the remarkable events that caused me to write this book, and to provide crucial editing of the final manuscript.

For literally their entire lives, my daughters, Molly and Nora, now in their mid-twenties, have heard their dad talk about working on "the Gotti book." But they never once rolled their eyes, and never once doubted that I'd finish it. Most of the book was written on weekend mornings when they were growing up, while I waited for them to finish classes they were taking or orchestra practices. I love them to pieces. They inspire me every day, and I hope they like the way the book turned out.

Shirley Turton, Catrina Beggins, Kayla Bensing, John Cusick, and Christopher Norton all helped me write this book in one way or another. Dr. Peter Halper kept me healthy for the quarter century it took to complete it. The U.S. Attorney's Office for the Eastern District of New York, and particularly Bill Muller and later Una Dean, graciously gave me access to the government's files for both of the cases against Gotti. The late Dick Todd provided valuable editorial wisdom. I owe special thank-yous to Kathy Robbins, my extremely patient agent, and to Richard Cohen, a superb editor. Finally, I owe so much to Rick Horgan, my editor at Scribner, whose help in shaping the manuscript and preparing it for publication was extraordinary. Rick is the real deal, and I was lucky to have him on my team.

INDEX